EXTRACURRICULAR ACTIVITIES

THE MACMILLAN COMPANY
NEW YORK · BOSTON · CHICAGO · DALLAS
ATLANTA · SAN FRANCISCO

MACMILLAN & CO., Limited
LONDON · BOMBAY · CALCUTTA
MELBOURNE

THE MACMILLAN CO. OF CANADA, Ltd.
TORONTO

EXTRACURRICULAR ACTIVITIES

BY

HARRY C. McKOWN

ASSISTANT PROFESSOR OF SECONDARY EDUCATION
UNIVERSITY OF PITTSBURGH

New York

THE MACMILLAN COMPANY

1928

COPYRIGHT, 1927,

BY THE MACMILLAN COMPANY.

Set up and electrotyped. Published June, 1927. Reprinted
October, 1927 ; May, September, 1928.

Norwood Press
J. S. Cushing Co. — Berwick & Smith Co.
Norwood, Mass., U.S.A.

TO A GOOD SCOUT
MY MOTHER

MY MOTHER.

PREFACE

THE increasing importance of extracurricular activities is evidenced by a number of very definite facts: the amount of space given to the discussion of them in educational journals and magazines; the number of studies and experiments that are being made; the appearance of books in this field; the inclusion of extracurricular activities in the regular schedule of the school; the allowance of teachers' time for directing them; the equipment that is provided for them; and the rapid development of honor, athletic, press, and other similar organizations. This means that they are increasingly being considered *curricular* instead of *extracurricular*, and that spending school funds in the form of schedule- and teacher-time for developing them can be justified on sound educational principles. This in turn means that the teacher or prospective teacher must be prepared to handle her assignment in this field as effectively as she handles her assignment of classes in the regular work of the school.

A great deal of material has been written on this subject but it is so scattered through educational journals and magazines that much of it is not available to the average teacher. Moreover, although a part of this material represents practice, a great deal of it is theoretical. The purpose of this book is to help the teacher or administrator to develop these activities by presenting concrete material. It will deal rather briefly with principles because these principles are now pretty well established. Its main purpose is to present programs of activities. Material representing all types and sizes of schools in all parts of the country has been gathered over a period of years and the most significant of this will be presented — material indicating a variety of practices and procedures, without too much stress upon the exceptional. This is the material which, in the author's estimation, will be of most value.

No school should take over bodily a program which some other school has developed, and the reader is warned against looking for ready-made schemes for his school. Many programs and much material are presented which have worked successfully and which will work again; but local conditions, traditions, and background must be considered in building wisely a program of activities. The program must be developed, and development does not mean mere adoption.

The references selected are those which the author believes will be the most helpful and available.

The author wishes to express his appreciation to many teachers and administrators for direct and indirect contributions; to the *School Review* for permission to use material, previously published, on Handbooks; to the National Society for the Study of Education for permission to reproduce data and tables on financial administration of extracurricular activities published in the twenty-fifth *Yearbook;* and to *School and Society*, the *Pennsylvania School Journal*, and the *Scholastic Editor* for quoted material.

Data, suggestions, and articles on the organization and work of the non-school activities were furnished as follows: Girl Reserves, by Gertrude Gogin, Executive, Girl Reserve Department, Young Women's Christian Association, National Board; Hi-Y, by Glenn E. Jackson, Secretary of Work with High School Boys, Young Men's Christian Association, National Council; Junior Red Cross, by Arthur W. Dunn, National Director, Junior Red Cross; Girl Scouts, by Elizabeth Kemper Adams, Educational

Secretary, and Eleanor Perry Wood, Research Secretary, Girl Scouts, National Headquarters; Camp Fire Girls, by C. Frances Loomis, Editor of the *Guardian;* School Banking, by W. Espey Albig, Deputy Manager, American Bankers Association, and L. W. Korona, Head of the Commercial Department, High School, New Kensington, Pennsylvania.

Special acknowledgment is made to the author's teachers, Professors Thomas H. Briggs and Elbert K. Fretwell, for programs, points of view, criticism, and inspiration.

CONTENTS

CONTENTS

encourage proper use of leisure time. (8) They narrow the sympathies and interests of the student. (9) They foster habits of extravagance. (10) They stir up strife and contention. (11) They dissipate the energies and ambition of the students. (12) They lower ethical standards. (13) They cause disciplinary troubles. How shall secret societies be dealt with? (1) Ignore them. (2) Control them. (3) Exterminate them. Summary. References.

Arguments for student supervised study halls: (1) It makes the student increasingly self-directive. (2) Student control is sound psychologically. (3) More effective use can be made of the study period. (4) Using teachers for study hall duty is uneconomical. Objections to student supervision. Plans for student participation in study hall control. Principles of student control: (1) Student participation must be desired by the students. (2) Participation must be under close supervision. (3) Monitors and student leaders must be carefully chosen. (4) The individual members must be made to feel honored in being under student monitorship. (5) The plan should be tried on a small scale. (6) Provision must be made for those who violate regulations. (7) The difference between monitoring a study hall and teaching the student to study must be recognized. (8) Wherever possible, competition should be utilized. (9) Student-teacher coöperation is essential. Student participation in control of the school library. Values of student participation in library control. Organization for student participation in control of library. Activities of student assistants. Relation of school library to other libraries. Danger of student librarians. Summary. References.

Methods of emphasizing training in citizenship: (1) morality codes; citizenship creeds and pledges; work of the Character Education Institution; (2) citizenship balloting; (3) self-rating scales; (4) records and reports; (5) citizenship awards; (6) citizenship contests; (7) Discussion and dramatization of citizenship; (8) organized courses in citizenship. School spirit. Basic elements of morale or spirit. Methods of developing school spirit. Summary. References.

Teaching courtesy: (1) The faculty must recognize and accept its responsibility. (2) Students should participate in planning and executing plans. Methods of teaching courtesy: (1) by association and observation; (2) in literature and history; (3) by campaigns and drives; (4) by formulation

LIST OF FIGURES

LIST OF TABLES

EXTRACURRICULAR ACTIVITIES

CHAPTER I

PRINCIPLES UNDERLYING EXTRACURRICULAR ACTIVITIES

The object of education. — " The first duty of education is to teach people to do better the desirable things that they are going to do anyway. Another duty is to reveal higher types of activities and to make them both desired and to an extent possible." This statement by Dr. Thomas H. Briggs clearly implies a sound philosophy of education. The main function of the school through the ages has been to create good citizens. " Good citizens " has meant different things at different times among different peoples. To some peoples it has meant brave and efficient soldiers; to others, individuals well versed in art, music, and the so-called cultural subjects; still to others, it has meant individuals who not only supported themselves vocationally, but who also took an interest in the welfare of their community and country, although such an interest did not benefit them financially. But no matter what the ideals of the particular peoples have been, the school has been looked upon as the maker of citizens who could take their places in the existing state of affairs and contribute to the further development of the ruling type of civilization.

All this is neatly summed up in the above quotation.

Two Theories of Education

1. Knowledge constitutes education. — According to this theory, knowledge is synonymous with education. For those who hold to it the memorizing of a mass of facts is the main process of education, and the most highly educated person is the one who has the greatest accumulation of facts.

Such a conception of education existed before printing became common. Few books were in existence. The master read from the book or the students read in it as it was chained to the racks of the early library. It was but natural that the material of such books should be looked upon as sacred. This idea developed also because much of the book material dealt with facts about which readers or listeners had little or no knowledge. Much of it came from the Greeks, Saracens, and Orientals, and it was new. The novel is always highly esteemed. It is something different and tends to command a respect and attention that the old and more familiar does not. So it was but natural that content should be looked upon as the important thing.

This emphasis was further developed by two facts: first, the appearance and development of the " formal-discipline " theory, which justified much material on the ground that it was " good for the soul " and developed qualities, capacities, and abilities; second, the fact that it is easy to test the proficiency of students in such material. Promotion machinery was necessary, and examinations were essential. The ability to think or to appreciate is exceedingly hard to estimate or to rate, but it is comparatively easy to test knowledge. Consequently, the idea that knowledge is education became more and more established as generation after generation passed through the school.

However, if we try to relate knowledge alone to the business of being a good citizen, we have to stop short and cudgel our brains for the real connections. For knowledge, alone, cannot compose a symphony, write a poem, paint a picture, or build a house. It takes something more than that. In like manner, all the knowledge in the world as to how a good citizen acts and behaves does not mean necessarily that the individual having such information will act in any certain way. Knowledge of law is no guarantee of its observance. It is only the basis upon which intelligent observance may and must be built.

2. Knowledge and practice must go together. — The second theory of education is based on the idea that what the individual does is at least as important as what he knows. The individual must act habitually in certain established ways, and merely knowing a body of facts does not mean that he will act in these ways. He must be taught to act properly. Habits are made only through practice; so practice in making proper actions is necessary.

There are persons who talk about " being good." Evidently they imagine that there is a general quality of " goodness." The same attitude is often expressed in " being a good citizen." Such persons do not seem to consider that it is impossible to be good apart from doing good acts. The same holds true in citizenship. It is possible to be a good citizen only through doing the acts which the good citizen does. The being comes then as a by-product of the doing.

An analysis of the good citizen should be the first step in making one. If we want to know what a good watch is, we analyze the elements that go to make up a good watch, for example, accurate time-keeping, reasonable cost, and good appearance. Then these elements are analyzed into smaller elements. For instance, the watch looks well because it is made of proper materials, it is properly assembled, engraved, and polished. If we are to make a good citizen, we should analyze the good citizen into his elements or characteristics and then deliberately try to produce these elements.

It is trite to say that intelligence is the basis of good citizenship. If the individual has no intelligence he cannot become a good citizen. But other elements are also important — ideals and habits. He may have either without the other. If he has ideals

without the habits that make them function, he is as incomplete
as an automobile without an engine. On the other hand, if he
has the habits and not the ideals, he is merely an automaton,
acting always in a predetermined way, and incapable of choosing a course intelligently. He cannot be said to be moral, even,
because morality implies on the part of the individual a choice
between right and wrong, or between the good and the better.
If the individual is merely a machine, he acts without exercising
choice.

It seems, therefore, that it would be reasonable to help the
student to become conscious of his ideals, then provide situations
in which the ideals would be forced to function. " Practice
makes perfect."   But practice may make perfect in the thing we
do not wish the youngster to do, as well as in the thing we wish
him to do.   Therefore, the functioning of the ideals must be
watched, criticized, and corrected in exactly the same way that
practice in playing baseball, acting in a play, or driving an
automobile must be watched, criticized, and corrected.   Only
by such careful watching and correcting can practice really
make perfect in the desired direction.   Extracurricular activities
have a very important function in developing the citizen because
they offer so many opportunities for this practice of desired ideals.

The Objectives of Extracurricular Activities

The main objectives of extracurricular activities may be
briefly stated as follows :

1. **To prepare the student for life in a democracy.** — If he is
to live in a democracy, it is but reasonable that he should be prepared for it, not only by learning about it, but also by having
actual contact with it.   The early life of a child is not democratic ;
of necessity it is largely autocratic.   He is restricted in many
ways by his parents and his teachers.   He must be restricted

because he is not born an adequate social being. Training in habits is necessary, too, because he has not arrived at the point where he can reason about ideals and practice them. Consequently, he must be made to do certain things in certain ways. Now, as he nears the time when he will take his place as a free man he must be taught the obligations and responsibilities of his coming membership in a democratic state. If he is not taught to assume these duties gradually and thoroughly, he will not be able to perform them successfully when they are thrust upon him. Training in a democracy is the best preparation for membership in it. If the school is so organized and administered that the student has opportunities and responsibilities somewhat similar in a small way to those he will have later as a grown-up citizen, he will be the better able to meet and discharge these responsibilities.

2. To make him increasingly self-directive. — The child must be brought gradually from the place where he is unable to control himself to the point where he is master. Here again it is a matter of a few ideals and much proper practice. It is interesting to note that many boys and girls who fail in conduct during their first year at college or away from home are those whose parents watched them most anxiously at home. There they had little or no practice in controlling themselves and in directing their affairs, and consequently, they had not developed these abilities. They were lost, and the things they did were usually not the wisest. Here again, extracurricular activities provide numerous opportunities in which the student may gradually assume increasing responsibility for his own direction.

3. To teach coöperation. — Coöperation is recognized as one of the most important demands of citizenship, and yet little is done in the traditional work of the school to teach it. It is not taught in the usual subjects of algebra, history, or languages. True, it is taught about, but this is not sufficient. There must be practice in it. Membership in a student council, athletic team, or club, teaches coöperation because the student has to exercise it in order to retain his position and standing.

4. To increase the interest of the student in the school. — This is done by giving him a small part in the management of its activities. " Student self-government " does not exist and probably never will. Students have ideals and good intentions, but they may lack the judgment necessary to rule themselves. This comes from actual practice and experience of maturity. However, while students may not be able to rule themselves, they are able to manage many of the smaller affairs about the school. He who said, " It is more blessed to give than to receive," was right. The student who gives of his time to his school cares for it the more because of his contribution of effort.

If we can multiply these opportunities around the school so that more students can participate in " running " it, the more contacts we have made with the students and the more friends we have made because more are working for the school. In addition to benefiting the school, this also develops the abilities and widens the interests of the students.

5. To foster sentiments of law and order. — The poorest discipline in the world is that which is effected through fear. It is not even intelligent discipline. The best discipline is that which comes from within and comes because the group itself takes pride in holding up its own standard. The more students there are interested in the welfare of the school, the less discipline there will be necessary, because there will be more lovers of the school to stand up for it. Rules always are a challenge. We like to take chances, and many a high school principal has found to his grief that making threats, publicly from the assembly platform, for instance, has only increased his trouble.

6. To develop special abilities. — Such qualities as initiative and leadership are little developed in classes in Latin or English or

Chemistry. With the changing emphasis from subject to student, it is but natural that we should look for ways of developing these personal characteristics, which after all may be the most important assets to the school and to the community. The opportunities for such development in extracurricular activities are not only numerous, but very suitable, as the student is working with other students of his own age, ideals, and understanding. Assuming and faithfully discharging responsibility develops character.

BASIC PRINCIPLES OF EXTRACURRICULAR ACTIVITIES

There are certain principles underlying extracurricular activities that must be given careful consideration if these activities are to function at their best. The most important of these principles are the following:

The student is a citizen of the school. — The citizen has rights and privileges as well as duties and obligations. If this point is not admitted, all the framework of our school system must topple, for if the school does not prepare the child for efficient citizenship, it cannot be justified. Preparing a student for membership in a democracy by training him in an autocracy or an oligarchy is an incongruity.

The school must have a constructive program. — A score of states in America have legislated against high school fraternities, but they still exist. Merely outlawing them will not abolish them. Something must be developed to take their place, something that will capitalize the strong tendencies existing in young people which are responsible for the existence of these organizations.

Extracurricular activities should help motivate the regular work of the school. — The school does not exist for extracurricular activities, however important they may be. It was established originally for curricular work, and that must still be its primary purpose. But much that is uninteresting though valuable could be made more interesting and more valuable by proper connection with student interests and instinctive tendencies. Extracurricular activities cannot be used to " sugar-coat " curricular work, but they can be used legitimately to increase interest and improve work. Extracurricular and curricular work need not be separated; they should be mutually complementary.

These activities should be given school time. — Many schools, and the number is increasing, are giving a certain amount of time in the regular schedule each week for these activities. The good old days when the Literary Society met after school, and the Dramatic Club at night, are fast passing, and the day when activities will be recognized and dignified by being given time in the regular schedule is fast approaching.

The entire school should participate. — If these activities are good for one student, they are probably good for all students. This is theoretically true, but may not always be administratively expedient. If we force a student to participate in any extracurricular activity, we tend to destroy immediately some of the fine things about that activity. The principal who would force a student to join a club when he wanted that period to study would be " played up " about the town as a man who would not let the students study when they wanted to. Not all of the students will succeed in all of their work; neither will all of them graduate; and in like manner not all of them will be interested enough to participate in the extracurricular activities. However, the ideal should be to interest as many as possible.

These activities should be considered in the regular program of the teachers. — That this attitude is increasingly developing is found in the fact that, of the questions asked about prospective teachers, the one which is asked as frequently as any other is, " What can she do outside of the classroom? " The day of the fine teachers who stayed after school or gave of their time in the evening to help with these activities is nearly past. They are legitimately a part of the regular load of each teacher.

The teacher-sponsor must be an adviser and not a dominator. — It is extremely hard for a teacher to be anything but a dominator; all of her training and all of her practice is in a superior-inferior relationship. The students are in her classes because they do not know as much as she does about the subjects. Exercising this attitude of superiority in her teaching, she naturally tends to carry it over to other affairs in which students are engaged. If the teacher dominates the organization or club, she has marked it for early disintegration. She is older than the students, has better judgment, and has had more experience, and this should be capitalized for the good of the organization. The function of the teacher is that of a counselor and adviser.

Summary

The main purpose of education is to make good citizens. The good citizen is an individual who not only has knowledge, ideals, and attitudes, but who also has worthy habits. Habits are developed only by practice. The regular work of the school offers comparatively few opportunities for the development of desirable social ideals and habits. It is concerned mostly with knowledge. The extracurricular activities offer many such opportunities. The main purpose of these activities is to give the student opportunities for practice in social relationships. Extracurricular activities must be built upon the broad principle that the school is a laboratory for citizenship and wherever possible the situations in the school should resemble the situations which the future citizen will face. These activities are important and should be recognized as a legitimate part of the school life and work. Care must be used however that they do not become formalized.

REFERENCES

ALLEN, C. F. *Outlines of Extracurricular Activities*, Little Rock High School Print Shop, Little Rock, Arkansas.

ARCHER, C. P. "School Government as an Educative Agency," *School Review* 31 : 430–438, June, 1923.

BAHER, M. P. "Motivating the Outside Activities of a Junior High School," *Journal of Educational Method* 1 : 112–116, November, 1921.

BELTING, P. E. *The Community and Its High School*, Chapter XI. D. C. Heath and Company.

BENNETT, H. S. and JONES, B. R. "Leadership in Relation to Intelligence," *School Review* 31 : 125–128, February, 1923.

BOYD, P. P. "Extracurricular Activities and Scholarship," *School and Society* 13 : 158–166, February 5, 1921.

BRIGGS, T. H. *The Junior High School*, Chapter X. Houghton Mifflin Company.

—— "Extracurricular Activities in the Junior High School," *Educational Administration and Supervision* 8 : 1–9, January, 1922.

CALDWELL, O. W. "Some Factors in Training for Leadership," *Fourth Yearbook*, National Association of Secondary School Principals, 2–13, 1920.

CLEVELAND TEACHER'S FEDERATION, *Special Guidance in the Cleveland High Schools*, Cleveland, Ohio.

COX, P. W. L. "The Ben Blewett Junior High School," *School Review* 27 : 345–359, May, 1919.

—— *Creative School Control*, J. B. Lippincott Company.

CUBBERLEY, E. P. *The Principal and His School*, Chapter XVI. Houghton Mifflin Company.

DAVIS, J. B. "The Administration of the Social Activities of High School Students," in JOHNSTON, C. H., *The Modern High School*, Chapter XVI. Charles Scribner's Sons.

DEMENT, A. L. "Values in Extracurricular Organization in High Schools," *School Review* 32 : 40–48, January, 1924.

FOSTER, C. R. *Extracurricular Activities in the High School*, Chapters I–II. The Johnson Publishing Company.

FOWLER, B. P. "Social Organization of a High School," *School and Society* 12 : 396–399, October 30, 1920.

FRETWELL, E. K. "Education for Leadership," *Teachers College Record* 20 : 324–352, September, 1919.

FRETWELL, E. K. "Bibliographies on Extracurricular Activities of Secondary School," *Teachers College Record*, January and March, 1923, January, 1924, and June, 1926.

HATCH, R. W. *Training in Citizenship.* Charles Scribner's Sons.

HORST, H. M. "Student Participation in High School Responsibilities," *School Review* 32 : 342–355, May, 1924.

INGLIS, A. "Socialization of the High School," *Teachers College Record* 16 : 201–216, May, 1915.

JOHNSON, F. W. *Administration and Supervision of the High School,* Chapter IX. Ginn and Company.

JONES, G. "Three Principles Underlying the Administration of Extracurricular Activities," *School Review* 33 : 510–533, September, 1925.

KOOS, L. V. "Evaluating Extracurricular Activities," *Twenty-Fifth Yearbook,* National Society for the Study of Education, Part II.

LUCEY, M. H. "The Application of Democracy to the Organization and Administration of the High School," *Educational Administration and Supervision* 10 : 205–211, April, 1924.

LYMAN, R. L. "Guidance Program of the Holmes Junior High School," *School Review* 32 : 93–104, February, 1924.

MEYER, H. D. *Handbook of Extracurricular Activities.* A. S. Barnes and Company.

NATIONAL SOCIETY FOR THE STUDY OF EDUCATION, "Extracurricular Activities," *Twenty-Fifth Yearbook,* Part II, The Public-School Publishing Company.

ODELL, C. W. and BLOUGH, J. H. "An Annotated Bibliography Dealing with Extracurricular Activities in Elementary and High Schools," University of Illinois, *Bulletin 29,* February 15, 1925.

PICKELL, F. G. "Training for Citizenship through Practice," *School Review* 28 : 518–528, September, 1920.

POUND, O. "Need of a Constructive Social Program for the High School," *School Review* 26 : 153–167, March, 1918.

PRINGLE, R. W. *Adolescence and High School Problems,* Chapter XI. D. C. Heath and Company.

ROHRBACH, Q. A. W. *Non-Athletic Student Activities in the Secondary School,* Westbrook Publishing Company.

SLEEZER, M. M. "Student Citizenship at the Senn High School," *School Review* 32 : 508–521, September, 1924.

SMITH, W. A. *The Junior High School,* Chapter VII. The Macmillan Company.

STEEPER, H. T. "Extracurricular Activities in the High School," *Education* 39 : 376–373, February, 1919.

SWANSON, A. M. "Effect on High School Scholarship of Pupil Participation in Extracurricular Activities," *School Review* 32 : 613–626, October, 1924.

TERRY, P. W. *Extracurricular Activities in the Junior High School*, Warwick and York.

THORNDIKE, E. L. "Education for Initiative and Originality," *Teachers College Record* 17 : 405–416, November, 1916.

WILDS, E. H. *Extracurricular Activities*, Chapters II–IV. The Century Company.

WILEY, W. E. "Organization of Extracurricular Activities as a Device for Training in Citizenship," *School Review* 33 : 62–67, January, 1925.

WINNER, H. E. "Place and Value of the Extracurricular Activities in the High School," *Proceedings*, National Education Association, 1923, 1021–1023.

WISE, J. H. and ROEMER, J. "A Study of Extracurricular Activities in the Public Schools of Florida," *Bulletin* of the University of Florida.

CHAPTER II

THE STUDENT

The student as the basis of education. — In planning the construction of anything, it is essential to consider the material to be used. . This is as important as the contemplation of the finished product, for it is upon the basis of material that the plans must rest. Similarly in our school work, in order to educate intelligently and effectively, we must consider the material with which we work — that is, the student.

We must build upon what the student has, or is. It is the business of education to discover and develop the desirable characteristics of the youngster. Our capitalizing of the characteristics of the student becomes a process of investing our time and attention in the cultivation of those characteristics which promise the most in good citizenship. Extracurricular activities offer many opportunities for the development of these characteristics.

We shall discuss briefly only a few of the more important in order to suggest just how the program of extracurricular activities can help to develop the student by capitalizing the better factors of his personality.

The student of high school age is an adolescent. When he arrives at adolescence he enters a new world, new at least in many respects. He sees, hears, and feels things he never before experienced. At high school he has many teachers instead of one; he goes to several rooms located in different parts of the building; he has more freedom of choice in his activities; he must exercise more self-direction than ever before. He frequently leaves home to go across the town to the high school. In short, this age is the beginning of the end of childhood for him.

Growth and development, which have been moving slowly, now hasten to a climax. Consequently, it is important that we consider him from a sympathetic point of view, and that we help him to find himself in this maze as easily and as soon as possible.

The physical characteristics of adolescence. — Many of the most outstanding characteristics of the adolescent boy can be laid to his rapid physical changes. He increases rapidly in height and weight. His mother complains that she cannot keep him in his clothes. His arms dangle out of his sleeves and his trousers always seem too short. His voice changes and frequently " gives way," much to his embarrassment. He is awkward, clumsy, and unlovable. He knows it. He is terribly self-conscious. He is restless and does not know why. The girl develops less rapidly than the boy and is less awkward and clumsy, but what she lacks in this respect she more than makes up for in her silliness.

The mental and social characteristics of adolescence. — *Curiosity.* — Curiosity is at the root of all education. If we were not curious, we would never be educated. Curiosity forces us to search for and acquire the thing about which we are curious. Sustained, well-guided curiosity is one of the richest veins which the teacher can discover or develop. Curiosity is, in a way, the vestibule of interest. Every one is interested in something. Even at an early age the student has his interests, however few in number and narrow of range. Some are good, others probably are not so good. The function of the teacher is to find out student interests, to encourage the good ones, to develop them, and to increase their range by bringing the student into contact with new situations. Extracurricular activities offer many opportunities for the student to try himself out, and to develop his powers by employing them in real situations.

The migratory instinct. — Nearly all boys, and girls too, have thought of " running away." Thousands of them do run away each year. This is due to the expression of a migratory feeling coupled with typical adolescent restlessness. No matter how good the home or how loving the parents, few children there are who have not conceived of the possibility and desirability of "running off." Since this characteristic is so strong and so common, why not capitalize it instead of repressing it, thinking we have thereby crushed it? The school trip or excursion offers a valuable means of doing this. Travel clubs, geography, science and history clubs, wherein the student is imaginatively carried to other countries and localities, help to give expression to this instinct. So likewise do trips with athletic teams, even the ordinary going about school and town in arranging for dramatics, issuing a publication, staging a concert, or boosting some similar activity.

Imitation. — The youngster is an imitator. He is also a hero-worshiper. He imitates his heroes, whether they be teacher, policeman, baseball idol, or movie star. Frequently this imitation is carried to an absurd degree, which shows how important and how strong this tendency is. The high school student imitates the college student, or what he thinks the college student is and does. He imitates him in clothes, in manner, in organizations, and frequently in general attitude towards his school work. Consider the many college activities which have found their way into the high school, athletics, assemblies, fraternities, musical clubs, dramatics, and honor organizations. It appears that the chief responsibility of the teacher is the proper guidance of the student in the selection of the thing or things to be imitated, and in regulating that imitation. Frequently a student imitates an act not because it is good or bad, but because his idol does it. Consequently, the function of the teacher is to draw attention from the idol and focus it upon the trait imitated.

The importance of imitation may be seen when it is considered that approximately three fourths of all the inmates of penal institutions of the country are under twenty-one years of age.

On the other hand, more people affiliate with churches under twenty-one than at any other time. This does not mean that the child is either immoral or moral by nature, and whether he goes to jail or goes to church depends in a large measure upon the opportunities he has for imitation. The more intelligence exercised in this imitation, the more intelligent will be the citizen. To act right habitually without the ideal and the idea of the act is to be merely an automaton, not a thinking individual. Thinking the idea without following it with the act is of little practical value. Both the ideal and the resulting action should be present to make the intelligent citizen in the true meaning of the word.

Gregariousness. — Persons like to be together. A large part of the fun at a world-series baseball game is to be found in watching the crowd and acting as it acts, groaning, booing, and yelling. We stand in line for hours and go to considerable expense and inconvenience to attend a game when we know many people will be there. We probably would not spend a cent to see the same teams play if we were the only spectator present. It is natural for us to want to be with other people. There is no punishment like solitary confinement. The student very early becomes a member of some society or gang. The high school age has been called the age of secret societies. And we find many of these small organizations with their mysterious signs, looks, handclasps, and passwords.

This desire of the student to be with his group brought the high school fraternity with its attendant evils. Nearly half of the states have legislated against these secret organizations, but in many states they still exist in open violation of the law. Fraternities have no place in high school affairs. But merely banning them by official decree will not eliminate them. If they are to be eliminated, they must be displaced by something else, something which will satisfy the craving of the youngster for " joining."

The youngster wants to join and he will join. Let us therefore see that he has the opportunities to join the right kind of group, and that these groups be educational and valuable to him and to the school in general. A variety of interesting clubs should help to reduce to a minimum the clique and gang danger. Of course, these clubs must not be fraternities by other names. They must be democratic in membership requirements and open in their practices and programs. No secret clubs should be allowed. Secrecy is what many students want, and consequently, the school club falls short of their estimation of what a real club should be. The school cannot afford, however, officially to sanction undemocratic or secret clubs. Formal installation services and perhaps some little formality at meetings might give the student in a harmless way the secret work he desires. In brief, the school just must utilize this strong urge to belong. If it does not, it will find within itself selfish and undemocratic cliques which hinder rather than help.

Loyalty. — This is closely related to the preceding characteristic, gregariousness. If the individual joins an organization he usually does it because he wishes to do so, and consequently brings with him an interest and pride in it. If he does, he will naturally stand up for it when it is attacked. He is loyal to it. Loyalty is another strong urge which the school must recognize and appropriate. All of us respect loyalty, even in our bitterest enemies. The little freckle-faced youngster who, when caught in some mischievous prank, refuses to " peach " on his gang because it is his own, and who prefers to be thrown out of school rather than to give his crowd away, has a fine something that we should recognize and honor. He is loyal. If we can only detach that sense of loyalty from his little gang and attach it to the school and its life, we will have to make fewer exhortations in assembly and at meetings calculated to call out the school spirit. We can get this loyalty only by making the student feel that the school is his; naturally, he has no interest in being loyal to something which belongs to some one else.

We can make the school his own by giving him small jobs around it and causing him to feel that in doing these he is helping the school itself. Then he is giving to the school, and then only will he become interested enough to " fight " for it. The person who talks about school loyalty more than any one else is the athlete, and the reason is clear. He goes out for practice each day and stands abuse and hard knocks, loses much time, and in other ways gives to the cause. Of course, he gives to a great extent because of the personal glory he will receive, but it is still true that he is giving to the school and naturally is interested enough to talk about school spirit and loyalty.

By increasing the number of opportunities so that more students may be used, and their variety in order that more interests may be touched, we can increase the number of givers to the school and the number of loyal and altruistic supporters. Students will inevitably be loyal to something; if we do not offer them opportunities to be loyal to the school, they will find smaller and less worthy causes about the school upon which to expend their loyalty. In that case we have failed by not capitalizing one of the strongest characteristics of youth.

Love of approbation. — Every one likes to be complimented. The movie actor and radio performer complain that it is hard to put forth their best efforts, because they are not heard, seen, and applauded by a visible and immediate audience. Large crowds spur athletes, racers, and actors to extra efforts. The student too loves approbation. He loves to be seen and heard. Such approbation is a very strong incentive towards improving his work or activities. Consequently, a wise program of school work should seek to make capital out of this tendency in the student. Not too much praise should be given, it is true, for many a fine youngster has been spoiled by having his name streamered across the top of the sporting page, and many a fine student made unduly " cocky " and " conceited " by the praise of principal and friends. But within reason, such praise is good. The good administrator knows the value of a pat on the back and the wise teacher knows the value of a few words of encouragement. Here again the program of extracurricular activities may offer many opportunities for recognition. Student offices, parts in dramatic performances, musical productions or organizations, and other duties around the school offer chances for the student to win reasonable approbation by worthy conduct and action.

Sympathy. — The young child appears to have little sympathy in comparison with the older person. But as he becomes older he begins to develop a sense of sympathy for other people as well as for animals. By proper guidance this can be made a fine solid type of emotion or feeling quite different from silly sentimentality. Such extracurricular interests as charity work, Christmas baskets, loan funds, clothing and shoes, care for the books and belongings of absentees, and visits to sick classmates all add to the development of a sensible type of sympathy — one of the qualities of the good citizen.

Love of mastery. — The baby likes to see the blocks tumble when some one knocks them over. But he takes more pleasure in knocking them down himself. So with the student. He likes to see things happen, but he likes better to make them happen. There are, of course, chronic rooters who would rather sit on the sidelines than play, but most normal students would rather play themselves. This characteristic of the student can be put to good use by means of a program of activities in which there are many opportunities to " do." Naturally, an extended program offers larger and more varied opportunities than a small one.

Not all of the characteristics of the adolescent have been mentioned. There are many more that can be capitalized in this program to the good of the youngster and his school. But enough have been discussed to show what such a program may do in the building up of the student. And strangely enough, many of these characteristics are not built upon in the regular classroom work of the school. Any program of outside activities which puts them to work, and makes profit of them, should be valuable enough to be utilized and carried out.

Individual differences. — No discussion of the student would be complete without a consideration of individual differences. We have always known that men differ physically in height, weight, size of chest, color of hair, and other physical characteristics; but it is only within the last decade or two that we have begun to consider differences in mental ability, aptitude, and interests as related to school work. Studies in retardation focused attention upon this problem more than any other single thing. The study of twins by Thorndike and others has added much to our knowledge of the subject. When it is considered that there are hundreds of distinct characteristics — mental, social, physical — and that each of us is a combination of these, and further that in any one individual these characteristics vary from zero to excess, it will be seen that no two people would ever be alike save by rarest coincidence.

The study of individual differences has been directly responsible for a number of progressive movements in education, among which might be mentioned Supervised Study, The Junior High School, Vocational Education, Guidance, Expanded Curriculum, and Try-Out Courses. This study has also centered new attention on the field of extracurricular activities.

Not all students have the same interests or the same intensity of interests, and consequently, if the program is to be valuable to all the students, it must be large enough and of sufficient variety to offer opportunities to all of the students of the school. Recognizing these differences and meeting the problem intelligently, instead of trying to herd all students into the same activities, irrespective of their interests, will do much towards making for success in the activities of this field.

Summary

Before constructing anything, consideration must be given to the material. The business of the school is to make good citizens. The material out of which the school must make these citizens is children. Children in the secondary school are adolescents; that is, they are in the period of growing up from childhood to adulthood. Many of the physical, mental, and social characteristics of the child develop with rather startling rapidity. It should be the business of the school deliberately to attempt to utilize as many of these characteristics as possible and divert them into wise and intelligent expression. They cannot be ignored successfully. No two students are alike in physical, mental, or social characteristics, and hence any school program should provide for the education of individuals of different interests, aptitudes, and capabilities. This will mean that the program must have considerable variety.

References

Boas, J. "Growth," *Cyclopedia of Education*. The Macmillan Company.

Counts, G. S. *Selective Character of American Secondary Education*. University of Chicago Press.

Gruenberg, B. C. *Outlines of Child Study*. The Macmillan Company.

Hall, G. S. *Youth*. D. Appleton and Company.

Inglis, A. *Principles of Secondary Education*, Chapters I–III. Houghton Mifflin Company.

Johnson, J. W. *Administration and Supervision of the High School*, Chapter VII. Ginn and Company.

King, I. *High School Age*. The Bobbs-Merrill Company.

Norseworthy, N. and Whitley, M. T. *Psychology of Childhood*. The Macmillan Company.

Pechstein, L. A. and McGregor, A. L. *Psychology of the Junior High School Pupil*. Houghton Mifflin Company.

PRINGLE, R. W. *Adolescence and High School Problems.* D. C. Heath and Company.

SANDIFORD, P. *Mental and Physical Life of School Children.* Longmans, Green and Company.

SLAUGHTER, J. W. *The Adolescent.* Allen, London.

STARR, L. *The Adolescent Period.* P. Blakiston's Son and Company.

SWIFT, E. J. *Mind in the Making.* Charles Scribner's Sons.

TRACY, F. *Psychology of Childhood.* D. C. Heath and Company.

WHIPPLE, G. M. "The Psychology and Hygiene of Adolescence," in MONROE'S *Principles of Secondary Education*, Chapter VII. The Macmillan Company.

CHAPTER III

HOME–ROOM ORGANIZATION AND ACTIVITIES

Home-room or report-room organization is a movement which has but recently appeared in the large American high schools. By it is meant that the student reports to a certain teacher in a specified room at designated times during the day, usually the first period in the morning and afternoon, and frequently the last period in the morning and afternoon. Details of checking attendance are usually cared for at these times. The student leaves his wraps, books, lunch in the home room. In other words, the room is a school headquarters or home for him.

Values of Home-Room Organization

It enables the teacher and student to become better acquainted. — One of the weaknesses of American education is that the average student does not know his teacher as an individual. He knows him only as a formal instructor in the classroom and all too frequently as a taskmaster. Many school principals desire just this. They do not want the student and teacher to get acquainted. These principals seem to think that such fraternizing cheapens the teacher and lessens his authority. We have even heard principals order their faculties to leave the building immediately after school is dismissed and not to loiter about with the students or give the latter opportunities to see them in their rooms. It is perhaps safe to say that if all the student learns in school is what he learns out of books in the way of formal lessons, he is probably wasting his time. Lessons are important; but the great lessons of life learned from a wise and sympathetic teacher are also valuable.

The teacher who has a home room has an opportunity to become acquainted with his students, and because of this can assist them and direct them more intelligently; they, in turn, can encourage this mutual understanding by learning to come to him for advice. This relationship of teacher-student friendship is particularly important for the new student. He comes into a type of school to which he is a stranger. He now has several teachers, many new duties and responsibilities, goes to several rooms, and is frequently lost in the maze. Little wonder that so many students drop out after the freshman year at high school! Probably the fear of what may happen is responsible for many more students not entering high school at all. Intelligent guidance of the student must in all cases rest upon a familiar knowledge of him. A wholesome, pleasant, and congenial atmosphere is a prerequisite to good school work. The home room helps to engender this. " Home-room " is a better term than " report-room."

It provides opportunities for developing the personal qualities of the student. — The adult must coöperate, be loyal and responsible, have pleasing social characteristics, initiative, and right ideals and habits. These can be developed better in a small group than in a large group. In the small group the students soon learn to know each other and hesitate less to share in its activities. Further, the smaller the group the larger the number of opportunities for each pupil, the larger the amount of practice he will receive, and the more educated he will become.

Other values. — Other lesser values of the home-room organization include education of the student in the rules, regulations, and common or integrating knowledge. Again, it is the most natural unit for the development of some form of student participation in school control. Attendance, enrolment, excuses, discipline, and other routine matters can be easily and intelligently handled in it, as also the sale of tickets, student drives, and campaigns. To the teacher *coöperation* all too frequently means that the student must coöperate with him, and too infrequently that he must coöperate with the student. In such cases he too can find educative value in this form of school organization.

HOME-ROOM ORGANIZATION

Preparation for organization. — The home room and its organization cannot be forced upon either the teacher or student, and calling a fifteen minute report period a *home-room period* does not make it one. The home room must originate with the faculty. It takes a sympathetic faculty to develop the idea and ideal successfully. Consequently faculty study of objectives and procedures through appointed committees, with thorough discussion of plans and materials from other schools, should precede any attempt to organize. Student committees should also make a study of materials, opportunities, objectives, and the possibilities for organizing the school. The interest of student and faculty both is essential to the creation of the proper sentiment for the initiation of such an organization. Essential also are carefully selected sponsors and student leaders who meet frequently in order to consider further developments and adjustments. An organization built on any other basis than that of careful study will be inadequate, inefficient, and unsuccessful.

Membership. — The membership of the home room may be selected in a variety of ways. The students may be classified according to mental age or attainments; according to sex; by class if the classes are small; on the basis of their course of study; on the basis of special interests; or according to geographical distribution. Probably the best way to group them in the average school is according to classes if the classes are large enough. This method provides congenial groups.

Officers. — Pleasing social characteristics and other elements of good citizenship are established in habit only by definite desirable responses. In other words, we must provide opportunities which require the acts we want the student to perform habitually. An organization offers many of these educative opportunities. The home room should have a simple organization, if for no other reason than to take it, to some extent at least, out of the teacher's hands. For as long as he is responsible, the students are not becoming educated. A relatively small organization is preferable to a large complex one.

The usual officers — chairman or president, vice-president, secretary and treasurer, or financial secretary — may be chosen. The chairman assumes control of the formal meetings and acts as an assistant to the teacher. The secretary records the minutes of the meetings; reports them to the council, principal, or publication; and finds out what other rooms are doing. He schedules, with the help of the chairman and the program committee, desirable programs or program elements from other rooms. The treasurer acts as the financial agent in such matters as the sale of tickets, papers, or the collection of contributions.

Committees. — The selection of a few committees by the officers and teacher not only adds to the number of educative opportunities offered but provides a distribution of labor which should result in a greater interest and success.

Program Committee. — The duty of this committee is to arrange the programs for the meetings. The committee surveys the group and discovers the interests and abilities of each member. These interests and abilities are catalogued and serve as a basis for the programs. All students have interests even though they are frequently hard to discover. If these interests are tapped for program material, and the students made to feel that the group really wants to have their contributions and that no formal or extensive contributions are expected or desired, they will be encouraged to participate in the programs. For instance, one girl likes pictures; another plays the saxophone; another likes to read ; one boy likes chickens ; another likes football ; and another is interested in cabinet-making. It is easy to see how each one of these interests could be developed into an element of a program.

Scholarship Committee. — This committee has as its object the raising of the scholarship of the group. The high school has taken many things from the college. One of the latest of these imitations is that of looking upon the average mark as the " gentleman's mark." The scholarship committee may do a number of things to encourage better marks. It may keep an up-to-date list on the blackboard or bulletin board of the marks made by the members of the group. Or if this is thought to be discouraging to those whose marks are low, the committee may list on an " Honor Roll " the names of the students whose work is good. This committee may also help the students who are low in their work. It may have a staff of helpers who either aid or obtain aid for the students who need it. It may also carry the assignments to students who are absent. It can help the absentee in making up his work when he returns. By thus constantly working with students it also extends the desire to do good work.

Attendance Committee. — This committee takes charge of the routine of attendance, tardiness, and absence. If excuses are required, they can be checked by the proper members of this committee. It might be supposed that these duties will offer temptations to the student to slight the excuses and tardinesses of his friends. Such may be the case ; but an occasional check by the teacher will help to show him that he is charged with a serious and important task. The committee can keep an attendance chart on the board, urge students to avoid absences and tardinesses, and in other ways keep the ideal of perfect attendance before the group. *Numquam Tardum, Numquam Flunkum,* and other catchy slogans may be adopted by the group to help in this work.

Welfare Committee. — This committee looks after students who need help. This help may be in the form of visits to sick classmates, of flowers, magazines, and fruit sent to them, or caring for their belongings while they are absent. Some schools have loan funds and also furnish shoes, clothes, books, and carfare to students who really need them. The contact with such a central fund or organization should be made through the Welfare Committee. Needless to say all such work should be kept confidential in order to avoid embarrassing those helped.

Housekeeping Committee. — The job of the housekeeping committee is to care for the classroom. This task must not be looked upon as the acquirement of the duties of the janitorial force. It is not. The committee encourages respect for the room; discourages the useless and needless cluttering up of the floor with papers; discourages writing and carving upon the desks and walls; provides for care of curtains; acquires flowers and flower boxes, pictures, and flags or other decorations which add to the appearance and atmosphere of the room. Care of lockers and cloakrooms might also be a part of its activities.

Other committees. — Additional committees may be added as needed. There might, for instance, be committees on publicity, devotionals, socials, supplies, and information. Good organization demands that the group be not over-officered or over-committeed. It is better to have few officers and few committees with actual jobs than many offices and committees for which jobs have to be made. Temporary committees may of course be appointed and discharged as required.

Meetings. — Two general types of home-room period are common. In the first type a short period of about fifteen or twenty minutes is given three or four days and a longer period of thirty or forty minutes once or twice a week. The shorter periods are set aside for routine work, devotionals, banking, and study. The longer ones may be used for a home-room program or other special activities. The second general type of organization provides a full period each day. The use of this period as an " activities period " is becoming more and more common. For instance, the schedule for a week might appear as follows : —

> Monday — General School Assembly
> Tuesday — Banking Day and other special duties
> Wednesday — Club Day
> Thursday — Home-Room Program
> Friday — Guidance, Counseling

One good substantial home-room program a week is enough. Many schools have tried to have these programs every day and the result has been failure. Of course, parts of these periods may be used for special campaigns, Thrift, Courtesy, and Better English, and for other activities; but one student program a week is enough. Setting aside a full period each week for the activities simplifies the work of the schedule makers and prevents losing time from regular classes. This arrangement also dignifies the activities to be carried on in these periods.

Programs. — Programs and program material may come from a variety of sources. Materials on such topics as Good Speech, Courtesy, and Thrift might well come from a central body or from the principal's office. If the drive or campaign extends throughout the school, it must occur simultaneously in all rooms to have the best results. Suggestions for such programs should come from the persons who know most about these activities. For instance, material on Thrift might be provided by the Commercial Department, and that on Good Speech by the English Department. All programs should be instructive and interesting, and most of them should be socialized.

The following schedule is part of one developed by Principal Fickinger and the faculty of the Langley High School of Pittsburgh.

Suggested Home-Room Schedule

September   8 — Social and get-acquainted period
September 15 — Values of home-room period
                     Election of class officers; Duties of officers
September 22 — Parliamentary procedure
September 29 — American ideals: Sympathy and Courtesy
October   6 — Fire prevention Week (Oct. 5–11)
October   13 — Discovery Day, Report cards
October   20 — American ideals: Honesty and Truthfulness
October   27 — Birthday of Theodore Roosevelt, Good Health Week
November   3 — Life stories of leading presidential candidates
                     Straw ballot on candidates
November   10 — Children's Book Week
November   17 — Education Week emphasizing art
November   24 — Thanksgiving program or party
December   1 — American ideals: Reverence
December   8 — Safety Week, Report cards
December   15 — American ideals: Regard for civic beauty
December   22 — Christmas program
January   5 — American ideals: Courage to overcome difficulties
January   12 — Biographies of great Americans, Courses of study, schedules
January   19 — American ideals: Thrift and Industry
January   26 — American ideals: Working members of society
March   17 — How can we improve our school?
March   24 — How to study
March   31 — Report card period, Individual conferences with pupils
April   7 — Student participation in school activities
April   14 — Loyalty
April   21 — Manners and courtesy
April   28 — Health
May   5 — Leadership
May   12 — Report period, Individual conferences
May   19 — Protection of property
May   26 — Safety Week
June   2 — Facts about occupations
June   9 — Courses of study, Schedules
June   16 — Flag Day program
June   23 — What I am getting out of High School

The topics were worked out in considerable detail and the outlines mimeographed and sent to each room to serve as a basis for the particular discussion. Below are a few samples of these mimeographed suggestions. Note the care used in making applications and also in choice of illustrations.

SUGGESTED HOME-ROOM PROGRAM

November 17–23

ART AND THE COMMUNITY

I. The need and value of Art in enriching our lives by teaching love and appreciation of all beauty

II. The need and value of Art in relation to matters of personal attire to produce greater refinement in dress

III. The need and value of Art in manufacture and salesmanship to produce articles of real beauty

1. Decoration of objects used by all peoples, even the most primitive

2. Love of beauty indicated by general admiration of well-decorated products

3. Great demand of workers in Art products, those who excel being able to command worthy salaries

4. Excess of demand over supply of skilled designers at present

5. Application by local manufacturers of the principles of Art in their products

IV. The need for, and value of, Art in the beautifying of our homes; benefit of such exhibitions as Better Homes in the Motor Square Garden, Electrical Homes

V. The need for, and value of, Art in the beautifying of our towns and cities

1. Local architecture

2. Local public monuments

3. Local parks, art galleries, museums

4. Private homes

VI.   Art as a vocation

VII.   Art as an avocation

VIII.   Study of pictures in our school
(See exhibits in Library, Halls, and Classrooms)

SUGGESTED TOPIC FOR HOME-ROOM PERIOD

December 1, 1924

AMERICAN IDEALS: REVERENCE

1   We should show reverence to our parents; old people; heroes; our rulers; our flag; our country.

2.   By obedience and loyalty we show reverence to our parents.
Read *King Lear* to illustrate obedience to parents.

3.   By respectful words and manners, and prompt and cheerful services, we show reverence to age.
Read Whittier's "Barbara Frietchie." Three kinds of reverence are shown in this poem. These are: Barbara Frietchie's reverence for the flag; Stonewall Jackson's reverence for age; Stonewall Jackson's reverence for heroism.

4.   By grateful acknowledgments of their services we show reverence to heroes.

5.   By refraining from needless criticism and by prompt obedience to law we show reverence to our rulers.
Read the story of King David and the water from the well of Bethlehem. (Chronicles xi. 15–20.) Discover three kinds of reverence in the story.

6.   By removing their hats in the presence of the flag, and by standing when our national anthem is sung men show reverence to the flag of their country.
Read "The Flag Goes By" by Henry H. Bennett.

7.   By obedience to law, by living worthy lives, and by cherishing in ourselves and in others the best ideals for the United States, we show reverence to country.
Read "The Man Without a Country" by Edward Everett Hale, to illustrate reverence for country.

SUGGESTED PROGRAM FOR HOME-ROOM PERIOD

March 17, 1924

HOW CAN WE IMPROVE OUR SCHOOL?

1. Duties to teacher:

   a. Obedience: in all things
   b. Respect: in address; in attention; in speech
   c. Courtesy: in refraining from interruptions in speech; in raising hats; in opening doors; in handing dropped articles
   d. Honesty: in speech; in manner; in actions; in recitations
   e. Industry

2. Duties to comrades (Golden Rule):

   a. In classroom: quietness; attention; self-control
   b. In the playground: kindness in speech and manner; honesty in play; unselfishness; thoughtfulness
   c. Cleanliness: in person; in dress; in speech; in books; in papers
   d. Courtesy toward girls: to be shown them and to be expected from them

3. Duties to self:

   a. Accuracy
   b. Cleanliness
   c. Honesty
   d. Industry
   e. Punctuality
   f. Self-control
   g. Self-respect
   h. Trustworthiness

4. Duties to the school at large:

   a. Care of building, of books, and of other property belonging to school
   b. Cleanliness of building: coöperation with janitor
   c. Conduct in Assembly: politeness to speaker; courtesy to listeners
   d. Fire drills: order and quiet during drills
   e. Passage from class to class

Drives for ticket selling or for other boosting purposes should be organized by a central body, preferably the council, and definite material placed in the hands of the proper students from each home room. This insures uniformity and thoroughness, both of which are essential to any " drive."

Student programs are probably the best because the student develops by participating in them. He learns from any program, but he is really educated only by what he does himself. Consequently the home room should provide for most of its programs, and for student participation in these programs. It is not always expedient for the program committee to have a rehearsal of the program, but it is always important that it know what is to be presented. Variety makes for interest in any program.

At the Langley High School each home-room secretary must make a report to the principal following each meeting. The reports are then filed for reference and for data on future programs. Such a device is good administratively, for it requires the room to have a good meeting. The things we are held accountable for in written reports or examinations are the things we do best. Such a report makes for a worthy discharge of the responsibility and in addition gives the principal, who cannot visit all of the rooms at once, a view of what the various rooms (and teachers) are doing. The following is a sample, chosen at random, of such a report.

HOME-ROOM MEETING, ROOM 23

After the reading of the minutes, J—— S——, with the assistance of two boys, showed us a rope trick in which two boys were tied together, then freed themselves without untieing any of the knots. E—— S—— gave a talk on the "Season of Rejoicing, Spring!" S—— W—— and C—— W—— sang a duet. W—— T—— gave a review of a speech on the subject "Be Kind to Animals." G—— W—— read an article on domestic animals entitled, "Man's Best Friends." D—— S—— gave a review of Booker T. Washington's book, *Up from Slavery*. H—— Y—— gave a short article on

"Our duties to our Families." This concluded the program; the meeting was adjourned. R—— T—— Reporter.

Programs or elements of programs which have exceptional merit should be passed along to other home rooms. For instance, a whole program might be taken to another room. In this way, the best of these programs will reach other rooms and more pupils of the school. If the program is very good or if elements of it are particularly excellent, it or those elements should be further developed for the general assembly program. The place to develop pupil material for the assembly is in the home room.

Activities. — The following list of activities is suggestive of what may be done through the home-room.[1]

1. Discussion of ideals and purposes of home-room organization
2. Election of officers and representatives
3. Discussion of proposed programs
4. Daily routine, bulletin notices, and attendance
5. Collection of contributions of school funds; sale of tickets
6. Selling subscriptions to school publication and distributing the same
7. Discussion of attendance and punctuality requirements
8. Discussion of courses offered by school
9. Discussion of scholarship requirements
10. Presentation of brief history of the school
11. Relation of this school to college
12. Informal talks about what is needed to better school life and work
13. Talks on guidance — vocational, educational, social, and recreational
14. School songs and yells
15. Reports from visitors to other rooms
16. Getting-acquainted games (for first few days of school)
    Students name themselves
    Students given cards to get names of members of the class
    Students grouped according to residence
    Progressive introductions — change seats each one minute or so
17. Debates on current, local, national, and international topics
18. Life stories of leading presidential candidates

[1] The *Winfield Manual* suggested in the bibliography contains a wealth of excellent material for home-room programs.

19. Straw ballots on candidates
20. Elections and demonstrations of election procedure
21. Discussion of political questions — recall, primaries, initiative
22. Location of local registration and voting places
23. Discussion of local civic problems, water, police, and fire-protection
24. History and etiquette of the American flag
25. Biographies of great Americans
26. Discussion of great American documents
27. Current events, local, state, national, and international
28. Naming favorite book or author and reasons for preference
29. Program of two-minute speeches on resources of the state
30. Investigation of, and reports on, city's resources
31. Charity work, Christmas baskets
32. Mock trials, civil and criminal
33. Imaginary banquet scene and toasts
34. Conversations and interviews between imaginary individuals
35. Invitations and introductions enacted by the students
36. Introduction of, and talk by, imaginary explorer, inventor, statesman, athlete, army officer
37. Presentation of imaginary automobile, watch, medal to member of the class
38. Debates on school affairs, athletics, examinations, and the honor system
39. Story telling — adventure and heroism
40. Talks and demonstrations by outside speakers
41. Presentation of programs from other rooms
42. Inter- and intra-room contests of various sorts
43. Good form in dancing
44. Industries, history of the community
45. Aiding absentees in making up work
46. Boosting school enterprises
47. Use of ornamentation in dress, architecture
48. Talks and discussions of ethics, honor, honesty, and loyalty
49. Dramatization of proverbs
50. How to study
51. How to use the library
52. Automobile accidents and their prevention
53. Visiting day of other home rooms
54. Contests between two sides of room on tardiness, scholarship, ticket selling

55. Discussion of clubs and other extracurricular activities of the school
56. Model business meeting
57. Reports of visits to other schools, cities, and countries
58. How vacation was spent by various students
59. Orphanage Day. Making and bringing of toys
60. Interesting things about the school
61. Geographical program. One student represents a different country or city
62. Stories of the great operas
63. Duties to others and self
64. Plans for vacations
65. Musical appreciation. Use of the victrola for demonstration
66. Contests — spelling, geography, and rhymes

Summary

Home-room organization is an arrangement by which the student is assigned a school home or headquarters. It offers an opportunity for the student and teacher to become better acquainted and consequently makes for more intelligent guidance. It also affords the student many opportunities to prepare for membership in a democracy by participating in the life of a small democracy. A simple organization with officers and committees is desirable. Regular meetings with student programs and activities not only develop participants but add to interest in the school.

References

COWING, H. H. "The Four-Year Home-Room Period," *School and Society* 15 : 627–629, June 10, 1922.

COX, P. W. L. *Creative School Control*, Chapter V. J. B. Lippincott Company.

EMERSON, T. C. "The Home-Room Period," *Junior High School Clearing House*, Sioux City, Iowa, 2 : 11–15, October, 1923.

FOSTER, C. R. *Extracurricular Activities in High School*. Johnson Publishing Company.

Foster, C. R. and FICKINGER, F. "Langley Junior-Senior High School, Pittsburgh." *Twenty-Fifth Yearbook*, National Society for the Study of Education, Part II, 213–215, 1926.

FRETWELL, E. K. "A Survey of the Extracurricular Activities of Philadelphia High Schools." *Report of the Survey of the Public Schools of
Philadelphia*, Book IV, 117–121.

PECHSTEIN, L. A. and McGREGOR, A. L. *Psychology of the Junior High
School Pupil*. Houghton Mifflin Company.

PRUNTY, M. "Tulsa High School," *Twenty-Fifth Yearbook*, National
Society for the Study of Education, Part II, 188–190, 1926.

SMITH, R. R. "Democratizing a High School of Eighteen Hundred,"
Education 38 : 374–379, January, 1918.

TERRY, P. W. "Administration of Extracurricular Activities in the High
School," *School Review* 33 : 734–743, December, 1925; 34 : 15–25, January,
1926.

—— "General Survey of Practices, Junior High Schools." *Twenty-Fifth
Year-book*, National Society for the Study of Education, Part II, 34–35.

—— *Extracurricular Activities in the Junior High School*, Chapter V. Warwick and York.

THOMAS-TINDAL, E. V. and MYERS, J. D. *Junior High School Life*. The
Macmillan Company.

*Winfield Manual of Activities and Administration and Outline of Home-Room
Study and Activity*. Published by Winfield High School, Winfield,
Kansas.

CHAPTER IV

THE STUDENT COUNCIL

Training for membership in a democracy. — Training the student for living in a democracy can be best accomplished by having him live in an organization which most nearly represents that democracy; it will never be accomplished by living in an autocracy or a bureaucracy. If the school is an autocracy " run " by the principal, or a bureaucracy governed by the faculty, and the student a subject, then we need not expect to see him exhibit many of the qualities of good citizenship when he emerges from this training. It has not been such as to fit him for self-direction. Everything he has had to do has been chosen for him and outlined. Training for life by having to meet situations which resemble, to some extent at least, the real situations of life is fast becoming the theory and practice of good schools. This means that they are making some provision for student participation in control, adopting some form of representative government. This conception of education for democracy is the basis of the widespread interest in student councils.

The Student Council is only one of a variety of terms used to designate this organization. Any plan which enables the student body to coöperate with the principal and the faculty in meeting the problems of the school falls within the term Student Council. Whether known as the Student Senate, Civic Association, Cabinet, General Organization Committee, Welfare Committee, City Council, School Congress, or some other name, if it facilitates student participation in the general control of the activities of the school community, the organization is what we shall refer to as the Student Council.

There is, in reality, no such thing as " student self-govern-ment," and there never will be. Students lack the good judg-ment which must go along with executive, legislative, or judicial power. They may possess the desires, ambitions, intentions, and perhaps knowledge with which to legislate and execute wisely, but they lack the judgment. Judgment comes only with experience and the students lack that experience.

This does not mean however that they cannot participate in the handling of the many affairs of the school. With wise and sympathetic guidance from those who are more experienced, they will be able to serve many useful ends. In the end, the values of the council rest in a large measure on the teacher-sponsors, and great care should therefore be used in the selection and appointment of these.

Values of Student Participation in Control

There are two main groups of values of the student council organization : benefits for the student and benefits for the school. The latter is really a part of the former, for if the school in its work benefits, the student also benefits.

Development of the student. — The first group of values con-sists of those found in the direct education of the student. The entire list of values of the extracurricular program as discussed in Chapter I could be attached to the council. Teaching coöper-ation ; making the student more self-directive ; giving him oppor-tunities for developing leadership and initiative, and introducing him to democracy — these are the main values mentioned in that chapter. The student profits by actual participation. He learns by doing. He might learn about it by hearing moralizing ser-monettes, but he really profits only to the extent of his formation of definite habits of action. Listening to sermonettes does not furnish the opportunities for the formation of these habits. The student as a member of a council or of an organization which elects this body has responsibilities and obligations. The educative opportunities do not all belong to the few numbers who compose the council. If they did, the council could not be justified. The voter must be educated. Responsibility of the voter for a good city or state administration can be talked about, or it can be taught by giving the student the right to elect his own representatives and letting him suffer or benefit by the acts of these representatives.

The organization of the extracurricular program. — The second main group of values is to be found in the effect of the council on the school and its life. Frequently the extracurricular activities of the school are chaotic, unrelated, and unarticulated, each one striving for its own ends by any method it chooses. Internal dissension, petty politics, and unsound financial and business organization are all too common in high-school extracurricular affairs. The council can and should administer and supervise all of these activities. It should be an elected body representing all the interests of the school, and as such should see that each worthy interest is properly recognized, organized, and financed. The school patrons have as much right to expect efficient organization and administration in these activities as in the regular curricular work of the school. The council can help to make them successful.

ORGANIZATION

Principles. — A number of different kinds of organization have been used successfully. There is no one and only successful type of organization. There are, however, general principles upon which the council must be built. Briefly these principles are as follows :

The council must be demanded by the school. — No principal, faculty, or group of students can force a council upon a school. The consent of the governed is important. The plan must have the support of the individuals who compose the society for which it stands. This support may never be unanimous; but it should be a solid majority. A study of the ends to be accomplished must precede any attempt at organization. To form an organization and then try to find work for it to do is not good practice.

The council must represent the school as a whole. — Special activities — athletics, for instance — are frequently over-emphasized in school work. The council may be made up of representatives from the various clubs and activities, or it may represent the school as a whole. If it represents the former, petty politics, " pork," and all the " log rolling " common in legislatures will develop. A club which elects a member to the council has a certain hold on that member. He owes his allegiance to it and will naturally try to get concessions for it. If the council has the good of the school at heart and represents no particular interest alone, then the school as a whole will be benefited.

The average student must feel that he is represented. — The smaller the group represented the more the student feels his representation. A student in a group of two hundred will not feel as much responsibility in the matter as the member of a group of thirty.

Both student body and faculty should be fairly represented. — Neither the faculty nor the student body should feel suspicious of the other. Such a feeling may very easily arise through unequal representation.

The council should not be too large. — A large committee is unwieldy and ineffective. There are too many members to educate and win over to the various propositions and too many chances for bickering and petty politics. If the council is a large body, it should elect an executive committee to act for it and should provide committees to do specialized work.

The organization should have definite powers and duties. — A body which meets only to talk is of no interest or value. To be able to accomplish useful ends it must have powers and privileges. These are delegated to the council by the faculty and principal. In order that they be defined, a constitution is desirable. Limitations and checks will be defined as clearly as powers and privileges.

The council must not be considered a disciplinary body either by teachers or students. — An attitude commonly taken by faculties is that the council is the dumping place for the many little disagreeable items about the school. Such an attitude is wrong and will only hinder the growth of the council. The establishment and development of the council will not mean less work for the faculty, but rather mean more; for responsibility for the success of the project probably lies more with the faculty than with the students.

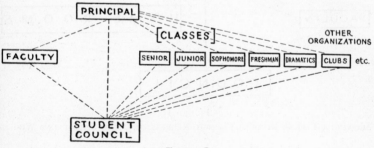

FIGURE I

SHOWING A TYPE OF STUDENT COUNCIL REPRESENTING THE MAJOR INTERESTS OF THE SCHOOL

Types of student council organization. — In general there are three main types of council, as determined by the method of representation.

Representation of specialized interests. — In this type of council organization the members represent specialized organizations, clubs, or activities of the school. One of the main objections to this type is that each representative will feel more allegiance to the club which elects him than he will to the school as a whole. Another weakness is that the small electorate is one established for a narrow specialized purpose and not for the training in democracy such as is given to a much greater degree by the home-room plan. A third danger is that the individual club may demand financial help or other consideration from the council, while resenting other attention.

Representation by home room or at large. — This type of council is composed usually of representatives from the various home rooms or report rooms, or, in small schools, elected from the school at large. The following diagram illustrates this type of organization.

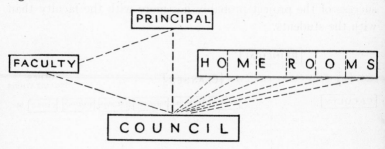

FIGURE II

SHOWING A TYPE OF STUDENT COUNCIL REPRESENTING THE SCHOOL AS A WHOLE

These representatives may be either girls or boys or both, depending upon the number of rooms. They are elected once or twice a year, in accordance with the membership of the home room. Where the home room is organized with the usual officers, the president may be its representative. A better practice perhaps is to elect a special representative. Probably there will be as many freshmen in this type of council as representatives of all other classes combined. This need not be harmful, however. The officers will be upper classmen, and no committee would be entirely composed of freshmen. The effectiveness of freshmen will be checked by their natural shyness. Other checks are faculty sponsorship and the principal's veto. The council will be interested in the welfare of the school as a whole and not in particular interests only.

Representation of school, alumni, and board of education. — The third type of student council organization is illustrated below. Members from the schools are elected by their classmates; faculty members are elected by the faculty; an alumnus is elected by the alumni; and the member from the board of education is selected by the board.

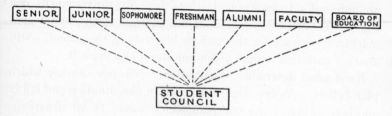

FIGURE III

SHOWING A TYPE OF COUNCIL REPRESENTING THE SCHOOL, THE ALUMNI, AND THE BOARD OF EDUCATION

It will be noticed that thus organized, the council has a direct contact with the school board. Whether this is a hindrance or a help depends entirely upon the type of representative elected; and this will be determined in a large measure by the general attitude of the school board towards the organization. One hostile member can kill the council and its work. On the other hand, one who is favorable may help in a great many ways, chiefly financial, in encouraging and developing school enterprises.

The final test of any method of organization or procedure is to be found in the answer to the question, "How does it work?" or "Does it get results?" Even if it appears to be doing very fine work one cannot and could not say whether or not another organization would do better work. A board of the above general type is in operation at Kittanning, Pa., and has done good work for the school.

Other types of council organization. — There are many variations of these three general forms of council organization, but the same general principles of representation underlie all of them. In some schools the class officers form the school council or cabinet. In the larger schools grade congresses are frequently found. Each grade or class has a council of its own, which in turn elects members to the senate or general council. Other schools have a complicated system in which all three departments of the state are imitated. In such organizations there are three councils, one legislative, one executive, and one judicial, with complicated machinery to care for the various interests of the school. Still another variation is that which imitates a city council.

Need must determine organization. — No one can say which plan is best. A plan might work well in one situation and fail in another. There is no one plan which would fit all situations. No plan should be taken over and adopted bodily by any school. Local conditions, traditions, school organization and size must be considered, and the organization must be fitted to these conditions. Need, then, must determine the form of organization. One thing which must be remembered is that the council does not exist for itself and that attention to building up nicely articulated machinery should not blind one to the real purpose of the council. If the school is not too large, it is probably good practice to have one body, simply organized, which legislates, executes, and, in case of necessity, adjudicates.

Internal Organization of the Council

Officers. — The usual officers may be elected. The question frequently arises as to whether the council shall elect its own officers or whether they shall be elected by the general association. Both plans have been used and found successful. Both have advantages and disadvantages. The chief advantage of the former method is that the council knows best just what material is available and what is the nature of the work to be done. Consequently it is probably more competent to choose its officers than the student members of the association. Moreover, it seems right that it should do this. If left to popular vote there is a danger that popularity will determine an election, and popularity does not necessarily mean ability successfully to manage an organization.

The officers should be fittingly and suitably installed or inaugurated. This should be done at a general assembly, and it should be a dignified, more or less serious occasion. The officers should be seated on the platform with other school or local dignitaries. The president and the other officers are sworn in and charged with their duties in some formal manner. The president then accepts with an inaugural speech outlining policies and plans. The school song may well close such a program. Nothing should be done to detract from the seriousness of the event.

Committees. — The council should be responsible for the entire extracurricular program of the school. In the handling of this program a system of committees will be found helpful. A system of this sort is illustrated on the following page.

Various standing committees are named to look after particular interests in the school. The president of the council appoints one or two members from the council as the backbone of the particular committee. The council recommends, and the president appoints from the school at large, a sufficient number of students to do the work with which the committee is charged. The council recommends to the principal and he then appoints a teacher-adviser for the particular committee. The teacher is not a member of the council. The committee chairman must be one of the members of the council, for he is responsible to it. In order to illustrate the committee organization and function a few of the committees will be discussed briefly; a more complete discussion will be found in later chapters.

Assembly Committee. — The chairman of ·this committee is appointed by the president of the council because of his interest in such work and his ability to accomplish things. The student members-at-large are selected for similar reasons. The teacher-sponsor is the instructor in music or dramatics, or one who has an

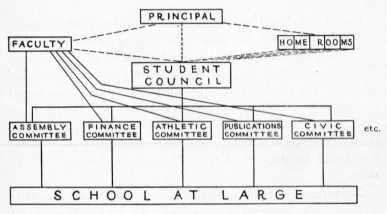

FIGURE IV

SHOWING A DESIRABLE TYPE OF INTERNAL ORGANIZATION OF THE STUDENT COUNCIL

The chairman and one or two members of each committee are appointed from the council. Additional members to complete each committee are appointed from the school at large. A member of the faculty acts as sponsor for each committee.

interest and ability in such work as well as a knowledge of it. The committee surveys the school and makes up a schedule of assembly programs for the year. It recommends this schedule to the council for consideration and adoption. In case changes have to be made hurriedly, the committee is empowered to make these changes. All the details of management as well as scheduling are in charge of this committee.

Athletic Committee. — The chairman is a student who knows and is interested in athletics. The members-at-large are students who are interested in the various phases of sports — football, basket ball, etc. — all sports being fairly represented. The faculty adviser of this committee might be the coach or physical director. The committee helps to stage the athletic contests. It does not assume any duties which rightfully belong to any one else, but helps wherever possible. It helps to advertise the games, sell, distribute and collect tickets, meets the teams, cares for equipment, holds pep meetings, and trains cheer-leaders.

Finance Committee. — This committee is formed in a similar manner, of students and teacher who have financial interests and who know financial methods. All of the money from all the activities of the school comes to this committee. The various activities operate on a budget adopted by the council upon recommendation of this committee. All expenditures are made through it. Auditing, bookkeeping, and banking are handled in a businesslike way. All recognized activities are supported by the budget, irrespective of whether or not they add to the income.

Organizations Committee. — This committee is charged with the chartering and regulating of all the organizations of the school. It accepts applications for charter and considers them in the light of such questions as, Does the contemplated organization duplicate the work of any other? Are its membership requirements democratic? Is it a desirable addition to the school? If the committee decides favorably, it then recommends to the council that the club be chartered. The council then grants a charter with the understanding that at any time the provisions are violated the charter will be declared void and the organization abolished.

Publications Committee. — This group assumes similar charge over the various publications of the school. It does not edit or manage them, but arranges the elections or appointments by which the editors and managers are chosen. It sets the standards for the publications, helps to develop them, prevents duplication, and helps to put the school publications on a high plane.

Social Committee. — This committee makes a study of the social needs of the school and methods of satisfying them properly and adequately. It arranges the social schedule for the year and recommends it to the council. It makes a study of games and other elements of social events, trains leaders, and in other ways helps to develop a proper social spirit in the school.

Other committees. — Other committees, both standing and temporary, might be named as the need arises. Such committees are specialized groups which study the various concerns from the point of view of their value and interest to the school as a whole. They then make the recommendations to the council, and the council accepts, adopts, adapts, or rejects as it sees fit. The final say in all cases is with the council and not with the committee.

In some schools these committees are called " squads," the squad being merely a large committee. In the Latimer Junior High School at Pittsburgh the following squads are maintained : Assembly, Patrol, Sanitation, Lunch Room, and Ushers. Other squads or committees might be Flower, Entertainment, Awards, Printing, Store, Banking, Publicity, Cafeteria, Traffic, Safety, Welfare, Inspection, Law and Order, Fire, School Property, House and Grounds, Teachers' Assistants, and Library.

Student Court. — The question continually arises concerning the advisability of establishing a student court. Such a court has been successful in many cases and can be found now in many schools. There have also been many failures of student courts. However, the same may be said of student councils. The chief value of such a court is that the students themselves will take more interest in the regulation of the school. They will build up among themselves a sentiment for law and order and will feel more personally offended when the general rules or traditions of the school are violated. The students get training incidental to the trials, prosecuting, and defending, but such training is necessarily small when it is spread out. On the other hand, the disadvantages are that the students lack the judgment necessary successfully to settle questions of discipline — it is well known that students usually deal too harshly with offenders; the danger of stirring up animosities, hatreds, and petty politics among the students, and the evils resulting from improper publicity through the community. The general trend seems to be away from the student court. There are many of them, but most supervisory officers hesitate to approve them.

Values of committee organization. — The main values of this committee type of internal council organization are evident. The council is elected on a school and not on an activity basis. It represents the various activities, but the final authority lies with the council as a whole and not with the committees. It utilizes expert interest and knowledge; and, by selecting student committee members from the school at large, makes more contacts with the school. These contacts are extremely valuable. In other words, instead of having a council of thirty members, this arrangement provides, counting members of sub-committees, for at least as many more. The sub-committeemen are in reality members of the council. Thus is the number of educative opportunities doubled. Further, each committee is carefully sponsored.

Constitution. — The powers, rights, and privileges of the council should be set forth definitely in a constitution formally adopted by the student body. This constitution will also state the general aims and method of organization. It should be the result of careful study on the part of students and teachers. Publishing it in a neat little booklet adds to its dignity.

The constitution may follow some such outline as this:

Article I	Name and purpose
Article II	Membership and how elected
Article III	Officers and how elected
Article IV	Duties of officers
Article V	Meetings
Article VI	Powers of body
Article VII	Activities and work
Article VIII	Amendments

Each school should develop its own constitution. The following very brief sketch will give an idea of a typical constitution.

SKELETON CONSTITUTION OF GENERAL ORGANIZATION

ARTICLE I

NAME AND PURPOSES

SECTION 1

NAME

The name of this organization shall be the Student Government Association of the.....................................High School.

SECTION 2

PURPOSES

The principal purposes of this organization shall be:

1. To unify all student organizations under one general control.
2. To aid in the internal administration of the school.
3. To foster sentiments of law and order.
4. To promote the general activities of the school.
5. To develop in the student a growing appreciation of membership in a democracy by providing the educative responsibilities of, and privileges of participating in, such a democracy in the school.
6. To promote in all ways the best interests of the school.

ARTICLE II

MEMBERSHIP

1. All students, teachers, and the principal of this school shall be considered members of the Association.

2. The council shall consist of one member elected from each home room.

3. The principal shall appoint two faculty members to the council.

4. Elections shall be held not later than the third week of each school year.

ARTICLE III

OFFICERS

1. The officers of the council shall be a President, Vice President, Secretary, and Treasurer.

2. All officers must be members of the council.

3. All officers shall be elected by the council.

4. Officers shall serve for one school year.

ARTICLE IV

DUTIES OF OFFICERS

1. The President

   a. Shall preside at all meetings of the council.

   b. Shall call extra meetings whenever necessary.

   c. Shall vote only in case of a tie.

   d. Shall appoint committees.

2. Vice President
3. Secretary
4. Treasurer

   The above officers shall perform the usual duties of their several offices.

ARTICLE V

MEETINGS

1. Regular meetings shall be held once each week during school hours. The day and time of these meetings shall be determined at the first meeting of the body.

2. Special meetings may be called at the discretion of the President.

Article VI

POWERS

The Council shall have the power:

1. To make and enforce any rules necessary for the betterment of the school, its life, or interests.

2. To grant charters to clubs and organizations.

3. To supervise and have final decision in all matters concerning the extracurricular activities of the school.

4. To recommend the appointment of necessary committees.

5. To investigate and report on matters especially referred to it by faculty or administrative officers of the school.

6. To have charge of all the financial matters pertaining to extracurricular activities.

The powers of the council being delegated to it by the Principal, he shall have the right of veto over any measure which the council passes.

Article VII

ACTIVITIES

1. Care of school and personal property:

Lost-and-found department.

Care of school trophies.

Promotion of proper respect for neighborhood property, etc.

Article VIII

AMENDMENTS

A petition for amendment must be signed by one third of the students of the school and presented to the council. The council shall hold a special election, and if three fourths of the students of the school vote for the amendment, the constitution shall be so amended.

In addition to a constitution, by-laws for the government of the council are usually drafted and adopted. Such by-laws may follow this outline:

Article I	Quorum
Article II	Committees
Article III	Elections
Article IV	Vacancies
Article V	Reports
Article VI	Amendments to By-Laws

Initiating the council. — Great care must be exercised in initiating a new student council. No organization can be established without the coöperation of the faculty and the student body. It must be built upon a need actually felt and not upon a shallow desire to have an organization. The teachers and students must want and demand it. By getting the help of important students about the school, sentiment favorable to the establishment of a council may be built up. But the principal and faculty must remember that they cannot actively control it; their function is to interest and suggest. The faculty must be brought to appreciate its responsibility in the matter. The citizens of the community must be enlightened about the organization, its plans, work, and activities. Such a program requires education in the real sense, not cheap propaganda.

The lot of the council in many cases is not an enviable one. Probably 85 or 90 per cent of the failure of student councils in secondary schools is due to the fact that they are not given anything definite and useful to do for the school; or are so hampered by faculty domination that they soon realize the anomaly of their position and despair of doing anything. The council is too often looked upon by the students as the pawn of the principal and faculty; and by the faculty, as a mischief-maker, especially if it has the effrontery to presume to offer of its own initiative suggestions for the betterment of the school. A council which is suspected from both sides will not carry on its work very effectively. All parties concerned must recognize and appreciate the limitations as well as the possibilities of council organization. Both the faculty and the student body must be kept in close touch with what the council is doing. Good honest publicity is desirable at all times.

First work of the council. — There is always danger that the new council will attempt to do too much. It is far more likely to err on this side than on the side of attempting to do too little.

" Begin small and grow large " is a much better motto than the reverse. It is natural that the council should attempt to do much because of its feeling that it must prove its worth immediately. The principal and faculty sponsors must see that it assumes responsibility gradually. The first few jobs should be small, very definite, and easily seen and appreciated by the student body.

Care of bulletin board. — Such a simple thing as the addition and care of a bulletin board is a task of this type. In many schools, the bulletin board is a disgrace. Frequently it is in a dark, unlighted, unattractive place. Many of the notices are old and out of date. Many of them have been hurriedly composed, scratched on scraps of paper, and hastily posted, as the bulletin board is used by everyone. The result is a collection of faded, torn, out-of-date announcements of all sizes, shapes, and forms fastened with an assortment of pins, tacks, nails, and paste. Here is an opportunity for the council to do something of value which can easily be seen and appreciated and which in itself is not particularly hard to do.

The council may appoint a " Bulletin Board Committee." This committee will make or procure a neat bulletin board. The size will be determined by the committee after a study of the number, frequency, and size of notices to be posted. Liberal allowance should be made for growth or miscalculations. The board should be too large rather than too small. It should be neatly constructed with hinged glass enclosure and provided with a lock. Billiard table cloth is a good background because it will not show tack holes. The board should then be placed in an appropriate place. If the light is poor, good light should be provided. The committee should then make rules regarding the size, shape, material, neatness, and dating of all notices. These rules will be typed or neatly printed and posted on the board together with the name of the person or persons to whom notices may be sent, or the place where they may be left. The committee should have a post-office box in the office. The committee keeps the board up to date, posts new notices, and refuses those which are not neat or which in other respects fail to meet the requirements set. The regulations which govern the notices of students or student organizations should also govern anything which the principal and faculty want posted. The members of the committee may take turns caring for the board. Notices may be regularly posted once or twice daily or more frequently as local conditions demand. If the school has no newspaper, a part of the space of the board may be given to this purpose. News of what this or other schools are doing would add to the interest in the board. A neat little card or plate bearing the date and the information that the student council is responsible for this board and its upkeep is desirable publicity.

Lost and Found Bureau. — Another simple matter which can be taken over by the council and made capital of in the development of confidence is the responsibility for a *Lost and Found Bureau.* The author recently was walking down the corridor of a high school with the principal. As we walked along, the principal took his knife out of his pocket and tossed it to the floor. We did not stop and he did not pick it up. A few moments later we were walking down the corridor on the second floor when the principal drew a silver dollar from his pocket and tossed it to the floor. Nothing was said about this strange procedure. Two periods later while we were seated in the office, the principal suddenly remarked, " Oh, yes, I want to show you something." We went out to the bulletin board — a neatly kept student affair near the front door. At one end of the board there was a " Lost and Found Department," and in this section both the knife and the dollar were advertised as having been found! Now it may be suspected that this was just a stunt for visitors, and that the first thing that every student learned when he entered school was what the particular dollar and knife looked like and what was to be done with them when they were found; or perhaps that students were assigned to follow the principal and visitors around the building for the purpose of retrieving the articles. It may have been so arranged; but the author does not believe that it was. It was the functioning of an efficient " lost and found " department initiated and supported by the council.

He was convinced of this when he learned of the work of this particular committee. It had two big drawers in the office, under lock and key, into which went all articles found about the school — pens, pencils, books, rubbers, and umbrellas. These were classified in a card index. A list of these articles was made up and each was advertised for a week. If according to the records the student lost it for the first time, he received it back by merely identifying it; if for a second time, he had to pay a small fine of five or ten cents to redeem it. What happened the third time or later was determined by the nature of the article, the circumstances of losing it, and the student himself. The drawers were cleaned once a semester, and all material remaining unclaimed was sold at auction and the money turned into the general treasury.

Articles lost were reported to the committee and similarly posted, if they were not to be found among those listed or turned in. The members of the committee took turns at handling the routine work of receiving, classifying, and returning articles. A post-office box was available at the office, and into this were placed articles which the students themselves picked up around the school. Of course when the activity was first started many of the students' things were " lost " by being taken and dropped into the box in the spirit of fun. But such fun soon ceased when the seriousness of the matter was realized.

The test of the value of a program is to be found in how it works. The first month in this school 211 articles were turned in; of these 187 were returned to their owners. The second month 124 were turned in, and 110 were returned to the owners. the third month the figures were 88 and 80, and the fourth month 62 and 58. Thus in four months the number of lost articles was reduced from 211 to 62, or about three fourths. And the real value to the students in being saved from inconvenience cannot be shown by figures. Nor can be estimated the training which they received through the continual educational campaign of caring for personal and school property carried on by this committee. Properly published reports of the activities of such a committee should help to make its work appreciated by the average student.

School Night. — A third activity by means of which the council can establish its right to consideration is the holding of a " School Night." Many schools have had " School Night," dismissing school the last two periods of the day, holding these classes at night, and inviting the parents and patrons in to see the school in operation. These affairs, however, are usually arranged by the principal or superintendent with some help from the faculty. At Latrobe (Pa.) such a " Night " was recently promoted very appropriately during Education Week by the student council of the high school. The council organized for the event three weeks ahead by appointing four main committees, Usher, Pupil and Parent Directions, Information, and Assembly. Each committee had, in addition to the student members, a faculty adviser.

The Usher Committee selected and trained fifty students to act as guides and ushers. The Directions Committee invited the parents and gave them suggestions concerning their children's schedules, rooms, and talks with teachers. To the students it gave suggestions concerning lessons and attention to visitors. The Information Committee, fortified behind the school files and records in the main hall near the door, answered all questions concerning classes, rooms, and location of various students and teachers. The Assembly Committee developed a typical student assembly program of short introductory remarks, welcome, explanation, music, and a short play.

The affair went off very smoothly and successfully. About five hundred parents and patrons of the school attended, as well as the entire student enrollment. Very favorable comment was heard on all sides concerning the event and the manner in which it was conducted.

It is a well-known fact that parents and patrons rarely visit schools unless called into consultation over a refractory child or to attend programs, plays, musicales, and games. An event such as that described demonstrates to the taxpayer the work which justifies, or should justify, the school's existence. This assures a better understanding and a closer coöperation between the school and the community.

Other activities. — Usher, traffic, and messenger service and various small tasks may be handled by properly appointed and trained committees of the council. The school must be careful, however, that the students do not do those things which should be done by paid help provided by the community. For instance, if the students can and do care for the library even fairly well, probably a trained librarian will never be employed. This of course represents a loss to the school. The council must distinguish between the things which the community should supply and those which it cannot or should not provide.

Such activities as these carried through successfully by a student council establishes the confidence and self-respect of that body and shows to the student body that it is capable of accomplishing things. This of course means the development of an attitude of respect and coöperation on the part of the faculty and student body which will be of inestimable value to the council as it attacks other important problems of the school.

Veto power. — The power of complete veto should be retained by the authorized head of the school. The principal is responsible for everything that goes on in his school. Consequently, he should have final authority on any matter which concerns the school. To use his power frequently would be to blast the very foundations upon which representative government is built. There would rightfully be no demand for participation. If the council recognizes that its powers are delegated to it by the principal and faculty and that it will be held responsible to these for its actions it will be more careful to do the job as it should be done. Then, too, if the principal does not save the council from all of its failures, but allows it to fail occasionally, such failings will be educative not only for representatives but for the general school as well. The electorate must be educated to the job of electing wisely. It may learn a good lesson from electing unwisely, and having to suffer the consequences. The principal will exercise his veto only in very exceptional cases.

On the other hand, if the council is to supervise the various organizations and activities of the school, it would not only be courtesy for the principal to work through it when he has something to be done, but would add to the general morale, and be sound business organization as well. This must be done very carefully. The principal will act through his council advisers. They represent him and his faculty and should at all times be thoroughly acquainted with the desires and policies of the principal and faculty.

SCOPE OF ACTIVITIES OF THE COUNCIL

There are many things about the school which the council can do or help to do. Of course it has no right to attempt to handle technical affairs for which the principal, faculty, or janitorial forces are responsible. It must confine its attention to student affairs, and most of these will fall under the general head of

extracurricular activities.   Suggestions of some of the things
which the council might handle may be found in the following
list.

CARE OF SCHOOL AND PERSONAL PROPERTY

1. Teach respect for all property
2. Conduct Lost and Found Department
3. Care for school trophies
4. Care for school equipment, desks, halls, walls, grounds
5. Promote proper respect for neighboring private property
6. Care for school books and supplies
7. Care for personal property, books, rubbers, and umbrellas
8. Promote safety first to and from school
9. Organize and conduct fire drills
10. Study student accidents and make plans for elimination

SERVICE

1. Establish employment bureau
2. Supervise service to new students
3. Administer student loan fund
4. Manage student assistance department (books, clothes, and carfare)
5. Provide student coaches and helpers for weaker pupils
6. Care for property of absentees
7. Provide make-up helpers for absentees
8. Help in community service, Christmas baskets
9. Assist Red Cross and other service bureau drives
10. Provide special help to teachers and librarians
11. Supervise sanitation work
12. Manage book exchange
13. Establish information bureau
14. Do flower and visitation work
15. Provide milk and food for needy students
16. Manage tutoring bureau

DISCIPLINE

1. Make and enforce general regulations and rules
2. Appoint study hall and library monitors
3. Encourage good behavior about the school

4. Supervise corridor, stairways, and traffic police
5. Be responsible for behavior in assembly and at public events
6. Eliminate cribbing, petty thieving, dishonesty in home work
7. Encourage good behavior before and after school
8. Recommend special measures to faculty and principal
9. Recommend action beyond own powers

SOCIAL TRAINING

1. Schedule, plan, and promote social functions
2. Teach party courtesy
3. Encourage courtesy to teachers and visitors
4. Teach lunchroom manners
5. Teach manners for the home, the street, the car, the theater
6. Teach proper manners for the assembly room
7. Welcome new students
8. Encourage good manners at athletic contests
9. Receive and entertain teams

CONDUCT OF CAMPAIGNS

1. Better speech week
2. Clean-up week
3. Safety first
4. No tardiness
5. How-other-schools-do-it week
6. Better health week
7. Better English
8. No unnecessary absence
9. Fire prevention
10. Inventory week
11. School beautiful week
12. "Look nice" campaign
13. Smile week
14. Stay in school
15. Know your neighbor week
16. Better book week

PUBLIC FUNCTIONS

1. Promote "Open House"
2. Schedule debates and speaking contests

3. Schedule inter- and intra-scholastic contests
4. Provide programs for assemblies, special days, and commencements
5. Promote dramatics, movies, pageants, lyceums
6. Promote musical productions, contests, and programs
7. Promote exhibitions of work in art, manual training, and home economics
8. Promote gymnastics and swimming exhibitions
9. Hold a "school night"
10. Train ushers and guides
11. Hold pep meetings, parades, and demonstrations
12. Award honors and insignia
13. Promote circus, fair, carnival, and bazaar
14. Arrange lecture courses and outside talent programs

FINANCE

1. Adopt financial and accounting system
2. Appoint treasurers and bankers
3. Provide for proper auditing, reporting, and publicity
4. Budget all activities
5. Raise revenue by various means
6. Care for and distribute funds
7. Assume responsibility for financing all extracurricular activities

MISCELLANEOUS FUNCTIONS

1. Collect songs and cheers for the school
2. Develop a "Point Scale" system to limit participation in extracurricular activities
3. Provide messenger service for the office
4. Provide publicity for various campaigns
5. Promote school publications
6. Issue school handbook
7. Make awards for scholarship, music, and citizenship
8. Charter and regulate all organizations of the school
9. Cultivate proper attitude towards questions confronting the school
10. Stimulate scholarship
11. Stimulate student participation in extracurricular activities
12. Introduce students to progressive movements in education

13. Determine eligibility
14. Hold academic contests
15. Develop constructive home-room programs
16. Show what other schools are doing, and how
17. Post calendar for the year
18. Develop ideals and desire for good citizenship
19. Make a study of tardiness, and absence
20. Conduct book and supply store
21. Organize excursions and trips
22. Assist in assimilation of new students
23. Promote "Come to High School" week for eighth graders
24. Adopt insignia and regulations
25. Provide publicity for all commendable work about the school
26. Promote good dress and neat appearance of students
27. Hold fashion shows
28. Care for bulletin board
29. Care for bicycle racks
30. Decorate school rooms
31. Provide and care for school flag
32. Collect material for museum

SUMMARY

Some form of student participation in control of school affairs is desirable because such organization approximates the democracy in which the student as an adult will live. It will consequently help to train him for this membership. Further, such participation will help to organize and systematize the extracurricular activities of the school. It must be based on sound principles of representation and organization with suitable checks and balances. It must be desired by the majority of teachers and students and should be developed very slowly. Its activities must be clearly defined, and these must not include technical duties of the school staff. Student council organization will develop only through successful accomplishments which the school and community can see and appreciate.

REFERENCES

AMOS, T. W. "Student Government," *Proceedings* of the National Education Association 63 : 440–449, 1925.

ARCHER, C. P. "School Government as an Educative Agency," *School Review* 31 : 430–438, June, 1923.

BARTON, J. W. "Possible Saving in High School Control," *School and Society* 9 : 626–628, May 29, 1919.

BELTING, P. E. *The Community and Its High School*, Chap. IX. D. C. Heath and Company.

BRIGGS, T. H. *The Junior High School*, Chap. X. Houghton Mifflin Company.

—— "Extracurricular Activities in the Junior High School." *Educational Administration and Supervision* 8 : 1–9, January, 1922.

CLAPP, H. L. "Pupil Self-Government in Education," *Education* 38 : 593–609, April, 1918.

CHEWNING, J. O. "Student Self-Government," *Proceedings* of the National Education Association 63 : 737–742, 1925.

CRADDOCK, E. A. *The Class Room Republic*. A. and C. Black, London.

COX, W. L. "The Ben Blewitt Junior High School," *School Review* 27 : 345–359, May, 1919.

—— *Creative School Control*, Chap. XI. J. B. Lippincott Company.

FOSTER, C. R. *Extracurricular Activities in the High School*, Chaps. IV–V. Johnson Publishing Company.

FOWLER, B. P. "Social Organization of the High School," *School and Society* 12 : 396–399, October, 1920.

FRETWELL, E. K. "Education for Leadership," *Teachers College Record* 20 : 324–352, September, 1919.

—— "Bibliography on Pupil Participation," *Teachers College Record* 24 : 60–72, January, 1923.

HARWOOD, H. M. "Extracurricular Activities in High Schools," *School Review* 26 : 273–281, April, 1918.

HAYDEN, F. S. "Democracy in High School Government," *School Review* 30 : 187–182, March, 1922.

HORST, H. M. "Student Participation in High School Responsibility," *School Review* 32 : 342–355, May, 1924.

JACKSON, N. A. "Pupil Government in Secondary Schools," *Education* 42 : 198–210, December, 1921.

Jones, H. W. "Student Coöperation in School Government," *School and Society* 13 : 251–257, February 26, 1921.

Kittrell, C. A. "An Important Factor in Teaching Citizenship," *School Review* 29 : 366–372, May, 1921.

Lewis, G. T. "Centralizing Student Activities in the High School," *School Review* 31 : 612–627, October, 1923.

Lewis, W. D. "Student Participation in School Organization and Government as a Training in Democracy." *Third Yearbook*, National Association of Secondary-School Principals, 1–9, 1919.

Lowe, B. E. "Student Government in our High Schools," *School and Society* 22 : 556–557, October 31, 1925.

Lyman, R. L. "Washington Junior High School, Rochester, New York," *School Review* 28 : 178–208, March, 1920.

Meyer, H. D. *Handbook of Extracurricular Activities*, Part III. A. S. Barnes and Co.

Miller, A. R. "Teamwork in the Management of a Large High School," *Sixth Yearbook*, National Association of Secondary School Principals.

Parmenter, E. M. "Student Government: A Project Method," *School Review* 33 : 115–125, February, 1925.

Pound, O. "School Reconstruction in the High School," *School and Society* 14 : 500–513, December 3, 1921.

Palmer, J. T. "Democratizing Influence of the Schools of To-day," *Elementary School Journal* 24 : 464–467, February, 1924.

Richardson, B. C. "Faculty Organization," *School Review* 28 : 628–287, November, 1920.

Ryan, H. H. "The Government of the School," *Seventh Yearbook* of the National Association of Secondary-School Principals, 44–48.

Sackett, S. F. "An Experiment in High School Democracy," *Educational Review* 67 : 262–265, May, 1924.

Sass, D. M. "Student Service in the High School," *School Review* 33 : 661–670, November, 1925.

Sleezer, M. M. "Student Citizenship in the Senn High School," *School Review* 32 : 508–520, September, 1924.

Smith, R. R. "Three Experiments in Pupil Self-Government," *Education* 37 : 230–234, December 3, 1916.

—— "Democratizing a High School of Eighteen Hundred," *Education* 28 : 374–379, January, 1918.

Thomas-Tindal, E. V. and Myers, J. D. *Junior High School Life*, Chap. IX. The Macmillan Company.

The Student Councils, Pamphlet from Lincoln School of Teachers College, 1922.

VAN DENBERG, J. K. *The Junior High School Idea,* Chap. XIX. Henry Holt and Company.

VOELKER, E. W. "The Organization and Functioning of Pupil Opinion in High School Control," *School Review* 34 : 654–667, November, 1926.

WILDS, E. H. *Extracurricular Activities,* Chap. IX. The Century Company.

WOELLNER, F. P. *Education for Citizenship in a Democracy.* Charles Scribner's Sons.

CHAPTER V

THE ASSEMBLY

Origin and development. — The predecessor of the high school assembly was the college chapel. The older colleges prepared for the ministry, and held a devotional service every day as a regular part of the work. Most colleges have ceased to prepare directly for the ministry, but many of them still retain a chapel service at which attendance is compulsory. The high school, imitating the college, established a chapel service. State laws requiring that the Bible be read in the school have encouraged a continuance of the chapel idea, and a pseudo-religious service is the result. Times are changing, however, and the chapel service is fast giving way to the assembly or auditorium period as teachers and administrators come 'to realize the fine educational opportunities of this kind of school activity.

Values of the Assembly. — *As an administrative device.* — The assembly is valuable as an administrative device or convenience. It makes, through announcements and otherwise, for a common knowledge of rules, customs, and traditions, which means the unification of school spirit. This administrative feature is important and essential; but it is probably over-emphasized in many schools. How many assemblies are largely recitals of announcements, long and confusing!

As an educational opportunity. — The main value of the assembly is educational. It should inspire a worthy use of leisure time by means of good demonstrations. It should instill the common ideals and virtues indirectly, by dramatization, rather than by sermonizing and moralizing about them. It should supplement classroom work; develop self-expression; widen the interests of both students and teachers; correlate the interests of the school and community; and be a place for the recognition of worthy achievement. Good organization and administration are necessary for the accomplishment of these ends.

Organization. — The school assembly should be as carefully planned as any other activity about the school. Frequently the assembly is unplanned until just about time for it, when the principal hustles around, finds a few extra announcements, hurriedly thinks up a sermon, or loads the responsibility upon some student or teacher who is always ready for just such an occasion, and thus the assembly program goes off in sorry fashion but on scheduled time. And little wonder that the students have to be patrolled.

Assembly Committee. — One good plan that is meeting with great success is that of having an Assembly Committee composed of several students and two or three teachers. The chairman of this committee is a teacher, director of activities, or other faculty member who gives time as part of her regular duties. If there is a student council in the school this Committee should be a Committee of the council. It is responsible for all assembly programs for the entire year (or semester). It canvasses the school, surveys material and abilities, and makes up its program from available material. It may assign one program or one day to each of the more important clubs or organizations about the school, classes, and home rooms, and thus start competition among groups. A suitable prize and "honorable mention" might be offered for the best programs of the year. Such competition with its demand for a rating or judgment on each program will be very beneficial in helping to set standards for assembly programs. Organizations are scheduled for dates suitable to them and are entirely responsible for the program. Such programs should be reviewed by this Committee before being staged. One good assembly program a week is enough. Good daily programs are impossible.

Outside attractions, speakers, musicians, actors, and companies are often available on short notice, and the principal may secure these if it is inexpedient for the Committee to make the arrangements. However, the principal will act through the Committee wherever possible. Postponement of a regularly scheduled program should be very infrequent, but it is justifiable occasionally if a fine outside number is available then, and then only. A serious study of the situation can do much to make the assembly so interesting and valuable that teacher-patrolmen will not be needed during it.

If the school does not have a suitable auditorium the work of the Committee will be increased considerably. Every school should have an auditorium, but lack of one need not prevent the school from holding assemblies. The ordinary study hall can be utilized for nearly everything that the auditorium can be used for except perhaps dramatics. It may be necessary to hold the assembly in two sections because of the size of the room : but even this is not a vital handicap. Anyway, it is better to have a handicapped program than none at all.

Material for assembly programs. — It is safe to say that there are far too many outside performers at school assemblies. There should always be a few of such ; they represent high development in art, music, law, education, and travel, and it is proper to have them. But the majority of programs should represent the school and its work. There is untold wealth around every school out of which good programs can be made. Having the students put on the programs is preferable, for they are interested, first, in what their friends do ; and secondly, in the things that happen about their own school.

Subjects and topics for use in the school assembly. — The following list of topics and subjects is merely suggestive of what can be done in this way. Note how many of these topics could be handled by the students themselves.

GENERAL WELFARE

Red Cross or Junior Red Cross
Accident prevention
Health habits
Fire prevention
Swat the fly
Kill the mosquito
Clean-up day
Sanitation
Physical exhibitions
Safety first
Posture
Foods and the school lunch

CURRENT INTERESTS

Community events of interest
New inventions and how they work
Elections
Conventions
World events

COMMUNITY INTERESTS

Outside speakers and singers
Chief of Police, on "Protecting you."
Fire Chief, Mayor, and other Officials of City
Postmaster, "What happens to your Letter."
Garage Manager, "How not to Treat your Car."
Travel Talks, preferably illustrated with pictures

SCHOOL INTERESTS

Student Council
Publications
Athletics
Booster and pep meetings
Cheer leader try-outs
Assembly Sings
Good sportsmanship
Traffic regulations
Clubs: purposes and membership requirements
Codes, slogans, and creeds

Recognition of achievement and letters
Installation of officers
Campaigns
  Punctuality and attendance
  Better English
  Courtesy Week
  Smile Week
  Health Week
  Thrift Week
  Safety Week
  Red Cross Week
  Scholarship Week
  Traffic Regulations
Explanation of school sports and activities
Explanation of school honors and awards

CLASS WORK

Nature's protection of animals
Liquid air
Structure of plants and flowers
Snakes
Dramatizations from Literature or History
Art : brief talk with pictures
Typewriting contest
How to use the library
Music memory contest
Spelling matches, Arithmetic matches
Tableaux of famous pictures
Burial of Bad English
Good scholarship
Trial of Poor Speech and Slang
Work in Domestic Science and Manual Training with demonstrations
Demonstration classes
Short book and play reviews
Poetry Day
Plays by the business club or department
Mock trial by the Civics class
Naturelogs on Birds, Fish, Flowers, and Butterflies
Industrial progress, illustrated

Athletic exhibitions
Mathematics programs
Foreign Language: plays, songs, and recitations

MUSIC

Vocal and choral
Assembly sings
Musical instruments, history, and development
Music memory contests
Explanation and interpretation, with use of Victrola
Music and instruments of other countries
Music in the Bible
Glee Club, orchestra, and band
Discussion and illustrations from opera

SPECIAL DAYS

Columbus Day
Hallowe'en
Armistice Day
Thanksgiving
Christmas
Lincoln's Birthday
Washington's Birthday
St. Patrick's Day
Arbor Day
Easter
May Day
Memorial Day
Flag Day

MISCELLANEOUS

Courtesy
Style show (both girls' and boys')
Americanization of foreigners
Debates and talks
Original poems, playlets, and music
Vocational guidance talks
Good form in dancing
Films, slides, and charts
Curricular exploration
Pageants, school, community, great events

Stunts
Program by parents
Alumni program
Know-your-city program
Mock trials
Demonstrations on good manners at party, table, and school
Teachers' travels and visits
Faculty take-offs
Pantomimes, *Alice in Wonderland*
Æsop's Fables applied to conditions in the school
  (Given each week by different students)
Shadow pictures to illustrate any poem or picture
Rendition of popular songs, translated into foreign languages
Reading of school "Paper"
Boy-Scout and Girl-Scout programs and demonstrations
Minstrel show with local hits
Parents' Day, Seniors entertain parents
Take-off of Seniors, Freshmen, by other classes
Circus
Stay in school

Moving pictures
College Day
Travelogue

It is usually much better to dramatize or demonstrate a topic than merely to talk about it. Even a few pieces of equipment or apparatus will add greatly to the effectiveness of a talk. Charts and other illustrative material can be used to good advantage if simple and large enough to be easily read anywhere in the room.

Typical assembly programs. — The following programs illustrate some of the things which may be presented in this activity.

School Activities Assembly

Song	School
School Activities — Explanation	President of Council
Short Debate	Literary Club
Radio Demonstration	Radio Club
Songs for All Occasions	Glee Club

1. Try this Song on Blue Monday
2. This for Candle Lightin' Time
3. When Baby won't go to Sleep
4. Family join in

Short Play
Where YOU come in
School Song

Dramatic Club
Principal or Student
School

RADIO PROGRAM

A regular program is broadcast by performers who are hidden from view. The station bears a significant name. The announcer conducts the program in the usual way.

PEP PROGRAM

The scene opens with the "players" seated on the platform. They are sleepy and drowsy and indicate a lack of energy. Dr. Pep enters carrying a huge bottle of "Parapep." He injects this into each player in turn. Each player after injection makes a snappy speech and then sinks to his former position. When the last speaker has finished, Dr. Pep throws Parapep over the entire group, which immediately jumps up and gives the school yell. The cheer leaders and the band can be employed in this program to good advantage.

UNITY PAGEANT PROGRAM

This pageant represents the crowning of....................(name of school) spirit. Each department is represented by a character properly costumed. Each character has a few lines to represent the work or spirit of the department. These characters, after speaking, form the school letter or other appropriate design. All join in the school song at the end. The use of colored lights adds to the attractiveness of this program.

ELECTION CAMPAIGN PROGRAM

A mock-political mass meeting is held with the usual campaign speeches. The speakers are introduced by the chairman of the meeting. A real program may be held where students are campaigning for election to various school offices.

THE POLICEMAN, YOUR BEST FRIEND

A most interesting program can be built around this general topic. The average boy looks upon the "cop" as a brawny, slow-witted fellow appointed to prevent him from having any fun. Movie comedy and other burlesquing have done great harm, probably, in ridiculing the policeman. The chief of police could make one of the most interesting and valuable programs of the year by explaining police methods, demonstrating or exhibiting equipment — handcuffs, revolvers, night stick, etc. — and relating experiences. Such a program would do much to make the student look upon the policeman as his friend and not as the stupid actor depicted in cheap movies.

AMERICAN POETS DAY

Ben Franklin Junior High School, Newcastle, Pa.

"Paul Revere's Ride"	Longfellow	Student
"The Skeleton in Armor"	Longfellow	Student
"The Duel"	Eugene Field	Student
"Boola Song"		School
"To a Waterfowl"	Bryant	Student
"O Captain, My Captain"	Whitman	Student
"A Little Dutch Garden" Song in costume		Student
"Old Ironsides"	Holmes	Student
"The Raggedy Man"	Riley	Student
Acts from Dramatic Club plays		

A TEA PARTY TO THE SHADES OF HISTORY

David B. Oliver High School, Pittsburgh, Pa.

This very interesting program was staged by the students of the 12 B History class. Mrs. Washington, Mrs. Lincoln, and Mrs. Wilson served the tea. Among the characters were the following: Father Time, Liberty, America, Uncle Sam, Pershing, Wilson, Columbus, John Smith, Winthrop, Standish, John Alden, Franklin, Penn, Minute Men, Washington, Spirit of '76, Jefferson, La Fayette, Betsy Ross, Washington, England, France, Democracy, and others. This more comprehensive pageant type of program requires an enormous amount of work, but it also represents something which the students never will forget.

SHADOW-PICTURE PROGRAM

Almost any story, fable, or poem can be pantomimed behind a screen while some one reads it. Little equipment and few costumes are required.

SHOT AT SUNRISE
A COMEDY IN ONE ACT
Better English Week

Characters:

Better Speech	A Doctor
Mother Tongue	Head Nurse
Good Diction	Ass't Nurse

Wounded Officers and Soldiers

Major Verb	Private Preposition
Capt. Noun	Bugler Interjection
Lieut. Adjective	Wounded Captives
Lieut. Adverb	Gen. Bad Grammar
Traitor Carelessness	Private Slang
Lieut. Pronoun	Private Poor Pronunciation
Corporal Conjunction	Red Cross Nurse, Misspelling

Time: Soon after a prolonged battle between the armies of Good English and Bad English.

Place: Base Hospital somewhere in the land of Language.

MODERN LANGUAGE PROGRAM

Song — "In Old Madrid" . . . . School

"Spanish Serenade" by Victor Herbert . . . . Orchestra

One-Act Play — "La Broma" (The Jest)

Songs — "La Paloma" (The Dove) ⎱ . . . . Student
       "La Perla"   (The Pearl) ⎰

Dialogue in Spanish . . . . Students

Playlet — "El Criado Astuto" (The Clever Servant)

Songs — "Flores a Maria" ⎱ . . . . Student
       "O Sole Mio" ⎰

"Spanish Dance" by Moskowski . . . . Orchestra

Food Program

Topics Discussed

1. Do you choose luncheons that will make you strong and fit?
2. What magic is there in a glass of milk?
3. Animal Nutrition

   a. What does the horticulturist do in feeding the plants?
   b. What care does the cattle-raiser take in feeding animals?
4. Human Nutrition

   a. What foods do for our body
   b. Regulation of food — time, amount, kind
5. What is meant by going into training?

In all these talks charts may be used for demonstration purposes. Students will attend visually when they will not otherwise. The Art Department may coöperate in making charts and posters. Health and weight cards may be handed out at the close of assembly.

Musical Program

The Seasons in Music

(Use of victrola and colored lantern slides.) [1]

Spring	"Spring Song" — Mendelssohn
Summer	"A Dream of Love" — Liszt
Autumn	"Serenade" — Drigo
Winter	"Largo" from *New World Symphony* — Dvořák

Emotions in Music

Sadness	"Ase's Tod"
	"Elegie" — Gluck and Zimbalist
to	"Sunshine Song" — Lucy Marsh
	"Tarantella" — Caruso
Joy	"Figaro's Song" (*Barber of Seville*) — Amato

[1] Secure pamphlets and other material from the Victor Talking Machine Company, Camden, N. J., or Columbia Graphaphone Company, New York.

FLOWER STUDIES IN MUSIC

(Use of colored slides with corresponding records.)

Many exquisite lyrical numbers are available, such as
"To a Wild Rose" and "To a Water Lily" — McDowell
"Waltz of the Flowers." (*Nutcracker Suite*) — Tschaikowsky

GOOD-SPORTSMANSHIP PROGRAM

Chairman	President of the Council
Group singing	School
Statement of purpose of the meeting	Chairman
"Unsportsmanlike Yells"	Cheer Leader
"The Old Fight *vs.* Unnecessary Roughness"	Student
"Recognizing Merit in Opponents"	Student
"Sportsmanship and the Ideals of the School"	Principal
Yell practice and School Song	School

VOCATIONAL PAGEANT PROGRAM

A procession of the chief occupations which boys and girls may enter is made across the stage. Each actor is dressed to represent the occupation. Each moves slowly, and as he comes to the center of the stage makes a short speech, in which he tells who he is; where he is from; his opportunities for promotion; compensations; preparation necessary. Another way of doing this is to arrange a "Vocational Pilgrim's Progress," and pattern it somewhat after the famous story. Not nearly all of the occupations which interest the students can be presented in one program, but the resulting interest in occupations which one such program will cause will make it profitable.

LATIN PROGRAM

A ROMAN SCHOOL

by

Susan Paxon

Program as given at Langley High School, Pittsburgh.

Time: 90 B.C.

Place: Rome. In the open except for the roof.

Characters:

Magister (Teacher)

Servi (Slaves)

Paedagogus (Attendant of Appius Claudius)

Judices (Judges) { Aulus Licinius Archias
{ Publius Licinius Crassus

Discipuli (Pupils)

Marcus Tullus Cicero — victor in oratorical contest

Quintus Tullius Cicero

Lucius Sergius Cataline — a bad actor

Marcus Antonius

Gaius Julius Caesar — Loser in oratorical contest

Appius Claudius Caecus — another bad character, tardy

Gnaeus Pompeius — a good but bashful student

Publius Coldius Pulcher

Marcus Junius Brutus

Quintus Hortensius Hortallus

Lucius Licinius Lucullus

Gaius Claudius Marcellus

Marcus Claudius Marcellus

Synopsis:

When the play opens, the students are noisily engaged in various sports. The teacher arrives and calls the roll. Two students are tardy — the notoriously bad characters, Cataline and Appius Claudius. As the grammar lesson proceeds, Cataline tries to sneak in, but is detected by the teacher and Paedagogus, who tries to excuse Appius by saying that he was ill. Appius, however, is compelled to pay the penalty by reciting a poem.

Toward the close of the day, two visitors arrive who prove to be judges for the oratorical contest. As they are unable to determine which boy is victor, they decide by lot. Cicero's name is drawn out and he is declared victor by the will of the gods. Archias crowns Cicero with the victor's wreath. Cicero consoles Caesar.

School is dismissed and the pupils depart rejoicing that it is time for play and bidding the teacher farewell.

Costumes: University of Pittsburgh

Notes: Watch the placards. Observe that Cataline and Appius Claudius started on their downward course by being tardy at school.

Special day celebrations. — There are a number of days which
are observed nationally as special days or holidays. In addition
to these there are several others, not officially holidays, which
are set aside for the honoring of individuals or groups, or the
celebration of events. By presenting special programs on these
days the school can lead students through their own expression
to a better understanding and appreciation of their country and
to a broader conception of patriotism. Local special days such
as Founders Day also have their values in teaching the student
to respect his community. Much material is now available for
the celebration of these days. Nearly every state issues a bulletin
on Special Day celebrations and many issue pamphlets for Bird
Day, Arbor Day, and other days. These can usually be obtained
free by writing the State Department of Public Instruction.
The following programs are illustrative of what may be done in
the school assembly in observing these days.

COLUMBUS DAY — OCTOBER 12TH

Columbus Day may be celebrated in a variety of ways. A program of
selections may be recited, a "Columbus Play" may be given or the program
may be made up of tableaux of famous paintings. The following is an
example of a program of the latter type.

Song	School
"Address to America" by Walt Whitman	Student
Tableaux: "Life of Columbus"	

1. "Columbus' Appearance before the Council of Salamanca."

A short exposition of the facts previous to this incident should
be given by one of the pupils. The Perry picture of this scene
may be used as a guide.

2. "On Shipboard"

   Joaquin Miller's poem "Columbus" may be used as the basis of conversation between Columbus and the sailor.

3. "In the New World"

   This scene shows Columbus and his sailors claiming the newly discovered land for Ferdinand and Isabella.

4. "The Reception of Columbus by the King and Queen"

   Recitation, "The Western Land" by Caroline Hazard, Student

ARMISTICE DAY — NOVEMBER 11TH

There are any number of possibilities for the celebration of this day. A simple pageant can be used effectively. Girls dressed in white robes against a dark background, may represent such qualities as Liberty, Justice, Peace, Love, and Goodwill. Suitable recitations can be found, or, better yet, made up in the English or other classes. An ensemble arranged at the end unifies the ideal portrayed. By the use of good lighting arrangements, electric fan playing on the American flag, and similar devices, this program can be made uplifting and effective.

A more formal program might be made up as follows:

Song — America the Beautiful	School
Flag Drill	Students
Patriotic Music	Glee Club
Address on Armistice Day	Speaker, student or outsider
Music	Orchestra
Playlet and tableaux	Dramatic Club
"In Flanders' Fields" by John McCrae	Student
"America's Answer" by R. W. Lillard	Student
Song — Star-Spangled Banner	School

THANKSGIVING PROGRAMS

One program might be arranged as follows:

MISCELLANEOUS PROGRAM

Overture	High School Orchestra
Short History of Thanksgiving	Student
"Let us Give Thanks" by Faringham	Student

Pilgrims Going to Church, students in costume march across stage; from a famous painting.

Indian Scene: The peace pipe; from Hiawatha, with the foreword from Miss Curtis' book.

"The Pumpkin" by Whittier . . . . Student
Indians Showing How to Plant Corn
Husking Bee
Quilting Party
Spirit of the Harvest Home
"Every Day Thanksgiving Day" by Spofford . . Student
"America" . . . . School

The altar is heaped high with harvest fruits and vegetables, with America seated. Representatives of North, South, East, and West bring offerings to America.

The hall should be decorated with corn, pumpkins, and vegetable festoons. Covering the lights with red crêpe paper is effective.

Another program might be based on the following outline:

THE HARVEST

Act I. Planting the Seed

      Scene 1. New England settlement

Act II. Old Fashioned Corn-Husking

      Scene 1. Husking the corn
      Scene 2. The frolic
      Scene 3. Going home

Songs: America, The Harvest Home

Reading: George Washington's Thanksgiving Proclamation of 1795. Material from early colonial times; stories of John Alden and Priscilla and of Hiawatha make interesting and suitable material.

CHRISTMAS PROGRAM

Music	High School Orchestra
"Keeping Christmas" by Henry Van Dyke	Student
"Hark! The Herald Angels Sing"	School
"Christmas Bells" by Longfellow	Student
"Holy Night, Silent Night"	Solo by Student
"Christmas Goose at the Cratchets"	Read by a Student

" Jingle Bells "	School
"The Real Christmas Spirit"	Teacher
"Ring Merrily, Bells"	School

Singing by the school will probably give a better Christmas feeling to the students than many speeches. Stories of Christmas in the different countries also make fine material for Christmas programs.

LINCOLN'S BIRTHDAY — FEBRUARY 12TH

Music	High School Orchestra
Salute flag draped over Lincoln's portrait	
High Spots in the Life of Lincoln	Student
"Battle Hymn of the Republic"	School
Talk by a Civil War Veteran	
"Marching Through Georgia"	School
"Gettysburg Speech"	Student
"Star-Spangled Banner"	School
Humorous Incidents from Lincoln's Life	Students
"Tramp, Tramp, Tramp"	School
"O Captain, My Captain," by Walt Whitman	Student
"Abraham Lincoln," by Cole	Student
America	School

Rail fences, axes, hatchets, wedges, mallets, and national colors make effective decorations.

WASHINGTON'S BIRTHDAY — FEBRUARY 22ND

"Washington's Birthday" by Holmes	Student
"Character of Washington" by Sparks	Student
"Red, White and Blue"	School
"The F ag of Washington" by Gillett	Student
"Hail Columbia"	School
"Star of the West" by Cook	Student
"Flag of the Free"	School
"Farewell Address" of Washington	Student
"America"	School

The hall should be decorated with all the patriotic emblems available, flags, banners, and flowers, including a portrait of Washington centrally and prominently located with the motto, — "First in war, etc.," and the dates of his birth and death, 1732, 1799. The former should be trimmed with flowers, the latter with crêpe. Nothing should be omitted to make the hall as bright and as attractive as possible.

Arbor Day — Second Friday in April

History of Arbor Day	Student
What Arbor Day Has Done	Student
What Arbor Day Can Still Be	Student
"A Plea," by Henry Van Dyke	Student
"Ten Commandments of Tree Planting" by Draper	Student
"The Year's at the Spring," by Browning	Student
The Principal Trees of Our Community and Their Uses	Student
Loss to the State by Forest Fires	Student
"Trees," by Joyce Kilmer	Student

Planting of the trees by the students.

Memorial Day — May 30th

A unique way of observing Memorial Day is to present a musical program. This program should include real American songs, those which were sung by the soldiers for whom the day is a memorial. These songs can be so grouped as to give the spirit of the Civil War, its cheer and pathos, and the spirit of the people and soldiers during the last war.

GROUP I.

"Battle Hymn of the Republic"	Howe
"Tenting on the Old Camp Ground"	Kittredge
"We are Coming, Father Abraham"	Hutchinson
"Wake, Nicodemus"	
"Marching Through Georgia"	C. H. Work

GROUP II.

"Tramp, Tramp, Tramp"	G. F. Root
"When This Cruel War Is Over"	C. C. Sawyer
"When Johnny Comes Marching Home"	P. S. Gilmore
"The Vacant Chair"	G. F. Root
"The Battle Cry of Freedom"	G. F. Root

GROUP III.

"When the Boys Come Home"	Oley Speaks
"In Flanders' Fields"	Tours
"A Khaki Lad"	F. Aylward
"God Be with Our Boys Tonight"	Sanderson
"When Pershing's Men Go Marching into Picardy"	J. H. Rogers

GROUP IV.

"Over There"	G. M. Cohan
"Rose of No Man's Land"	Brennan
"Smiles"	L. S. Roberts
"Dear Old Pal of Mine"	Gitz Rice
"Madelon"	C. Robertson

Another type of program suitable for Memorial Day is the following:

"Columbia the Gem of he Ocean"	School
"Battle Hymn of the Republic"	School
Origin of Memorial Day	Student
"The Blue and the Gray"	Student
"Keep the Home Fires Burning"	Solo
"In Flanders' Fields" by John McCrae	Student
Stories from the battlefields of 1861 and 1918	Veterans
"The Gettysburg Address"	Student
"America"	School

FLAG DAY — JUNE 14TH

Song, "The Star-Spangled Banner"	School
"The Name of Old Glory," by J. W. Riley	Student
Patriotic Music	Orchestra, Music Clubs
"Old Glory," by Hubbard Parker	Student
Song, "We'll Keep Old Glory Flying," Montayne	School
"Flag Day Address," by Woodrow Wilson	Student
Presentation of new flag	
Flag Raising	Color Guard
Flag Salute	School
Song, "America"	School

STATE DAY

Brief History of the State (This might be dramatized)
The Resources of the State

Agricultural   Industrial
Mineral   Power

Geological and Physiographical Features
Noted Sons and Daughters
Illustrations from authors, artists, and musicians
The State's Contribution to the World War
Singing of the State Song

BIRD DAY

THE TRIAL OF MR. T. CAT

An interesting program of the lighter type can be built around the theme of the damage that the ordinary house cat does to bird life. A formal criminal trial can be worked out, providing for judge, jury, prosecuting and defense attorneys, bailiffs, witnesses, and all other court officials. Material damaging to the cause of the cat can be found in state publications on Bird Day and also publications of the Audubon Society. Such a program should be thoroughly rehearsed and practiced before being staged publicly.

MUSIC WEEK

A MORNING WITH BEETHOVEN AND MENDELSSOHN

"Minuet in G, No. 2" . . . . Piano Solo by Student
"The Moonlight Sonata" . . . . Reading by Student
"The Moonlight Sonata" . . . . Solo by Student
"Hark, the Herald Angels Sing" . . . . School
"Spring Song" . . . . Piano Solo by Student
"Oh for the Wings of a Dove" . . . . Piano Solo by Student

Short biographies of the composers may be included.

INDIAN SONGS

The Story of the Indians . . . . Student
"Far Off I Hear a Lover's Lute" . . . . Student
"Navajo Indian Song" . . . . Piano
"By the Waters of Minnetonka" . . . . Solo by Student

"Medicine Song" . . . . Piano
" From the Land of the Sky-Blue Waters" . . . . . Solo by Student
Brief discussions of Indian music . . . . Teacher
"The Moon Drops Low" . . . . Solo by Student
"The White Dawn Is Stealing" . . . . Solo by Student

SCOTCH AND IRISH SONGS

"Wearin' of the Green" . . . . School
"Mother Machree" . . . . Solo by Student
"Come Back to Erin" . . . . School
"When Irish Eyes Are Smiling". . . . . Solo
"Annie Laurie" . . . . School
"Auld Lang Syne" . . . . : . . . . School
"The Blue Bells of Scotland" . . . . School

CLEAN-UP AND PAINT-UP WEEK

If the school has a motion-picture outfit, short films may be used to good advantage on these programs. A great many of these films have been made just for this purpose and can be obtained at small expense from such companies as Community Motion Picture Bureau. Examples of such films are:

> "An Investment in Boys" (Gardening)
> "The Deadly Fly"
> "The Vision Beautiful"
> "Hearts and Voices" (Musical)

Other "Weeks" which may be made the basis of special assembly programs are Better English, Courtesy, Smile, Vocational Guidance, and Education. It is always proper to begin and end such a "week" with a good assembly program.

SUGGESTED SCHEDULE OF ASSEMBLIES FOR THE YEAR

Sept. 9 Pep Assembly. Singing, yells. Students may participate and conduct the assembly; the principal may extend a word of welcome.

Sept. 16 Installation of officers

Sept. 23 Cheer leaders' contest. Use community singing

Sept. 30 Outside artist or speaker

Oct. 7 Unity meeting

Oct. 14 Columbus Day Program

Oct. 21 Radio Program

Oct. 28 Hallowe'en Program (Dramatic Department)

Nov. 4 Pep meeting. Dr. Pep will fit in here well at this time of the football season

Nov. 10 Armistice Day Program

Nov. 18 Combined Glee Clubs

Nov. 25 Thanksgiving Program. By the History Department or Club

Dec. 2 Better Food Program. Domestic Science, Chemistry, and Art Departments

Dec. 9 Hi-Y Program

Dec. 16 Awarding of football letters and certificates

Dec. 23 Christmas Program. Musical and Dramatic Clubs. Here is an opportunity to make your assembly religious, if you choose. Old chants and carols may well be used to make the occasion impressive.

Jan. 6 Poetry Assembly. Greek symposium idea

Jan. 13 Stephen C. Foster Memorial Program in charge of the Music Department. Old Fashioned Album by the Dramatic Club.

Jan. 20 Better Speech Assembly. Dramatize Better Speech

Jan. 27 Art Program. Contest in cartooning

Second Semester

Feb. 3 Pep Meeting

Feb. 10 Lincoln Program

Feb. 17 History Club. Emphasize Washington

Feb. 24 School Orchestra Program

Mar. 3 Health Program under the direction of the Physical Education Department

Mar. 10 Girl Scout Program. First Aid, illustrated and dramatized

Mar. 17 Program of Irish songs and dances. Music and Physical Education Departments

Mar. 24 Dramatic Club Playlet

Mar. 31 Science Club Program. Chemical Combinations

Apr. 7 Courtesy Week Program. Begin with talks in the home rooms, culminating in the assembly in the form of playlets and pantomimes.

Apr. 14 Style Show. Design Department

Apr. 21 Chief of Police. Our Protection

Apr. 28   Glee Club and Orchestra Combined
May   5   Safety First Week
May 12   Outside Speaker and Singer, or both
May 19   Botany Club
May 26   Memorial Day Program.   Under direction of the Boy Scouts
June 2   Alumni Program.   May be of the News Letter Type
June 9   Senior Stunt Day
June 16   Flag Day and last assembly.   Farewell to the Seniors

Singing. — One of the most important elements of the program is singing. Nearly every one likes to sing. But nearly every one, and especially the youngster, likes " snappy " music. There is something in a good fast march, for instance, which stirs us. In the average school assembly when a hymn is sung comparatively few students join in, but when a rollicking sea song, or a fine old southern melody is used, nearly all sing. One strictly religious hymn is enough for any secular program. The meeting is not a religious one and never will be, and a sure way to kill it is to try to make it such. The first song may be a hymn, preferably a good live one; the other songs may then be melodies, well-known airs from operas, choruses, semi-popular songs. An occasional verse from famous war songs will add to the interest.

Summary

The main purpose of the assembly period should be educational. Most of the programs should be given by the students themselves, and should represent the school and its work. An assembly committee responsible for the entire schedule of assemblies can help to improve this activity. Competition between groups of students can help set and raise the standards for the program. One good program a week is preferable to daily routine affairs consisting of formal devotionals and announcements.

REFERENCES

ASSEMBLY

BETTES, A. D. "A Project for Assembly," *Journal of Educational Method* 5 : 145–146, December, 1925.

CHADWICK, R. D. "Auditorium Studies," Bulletin 4, Vol. II, *Second Yearbook*, Department of Elementary School Principals, July, 1923.

COOK, F. J. and Others. "The Morning Exercise as a Socializing Influence," F. W. Parker School *Yearbook*, Chicago.

COX, P. W. L. *Creative School Control*, Chap. IX. J. B. Lippincott Company.

CUBBERLEY, E. P. *The Principal and His School*, Chap. XVII. Houghton Mifflin Company.

EVANS, E. E. "What to Do with the High School Assembly," *School Review* 31 : 282–286, April, 1923.

FOSTER, C. W. *Extracurricular Activities in the High School*, Chap. VI. The Johnson Publishing Company.

FRETWELL, E. K. "A Bibliography on High School Assemblies," *Teachers College Record* 25 : 61–69, January, 1924.

—— "The School Assembly," *Sixth Yearbook* of the National Association of Secondary-School Principals, 147–154, 1922.

HAYWARD, F. H. *A First Book of School Celebrations*. King and Company.

—— *A Second Book of School Celebrations*. King and Company.

HORN, E. "Typical Program for an Assembly Period at Speyer School," *Teachers College Record* 18 : 331–344, September, 1917.

MEYER, H. D. *Handbook of Extracurricular Activities*, Chap. III. A. S. Barnes and Company.

ROGERS, K. W. "Experiments with the School Assembly," *Journal of Education* 94 : 311–315, October 6, 1921.

SPAIN, C. L. *The Platoon School*, 80–89. The Macmillan Company.

WILSON, G. H. and WILSON, H. B. *Motivation of School Work*. Houghton Mifflin Company.

SPECIAL DAYS

All Special Days. Moffat, Yard and Company.

CHUBB, P., and others. *Festivals and Plays*. Harper and Brothers.

Four Great Americans. American Book Company.

MACKAY, C. D. *Plays of the Pioneers*. Harper and Brothers.

SCHAUFFLER, R. H. *Our American Holidays Series*. Moffat, Yard and Company.

CHAPTER VI

CLUBS

The adolescent is a " joiner." Proof of this is evidenced by the many secret societies, cliques, and organizations to be found among students of high school age. The school club offers a fine opportunity for the beneficial capitalization of one of the strongest urges in the adolescent student.

VALUES OF CLUBS

Enrichment of student interests. — Important in the education of the child is his use of leisure time. This is becoming more and more important as economic and social progress add to the amount of leisure time the individual has at his disposal. Wise use of leisure depends on interests — their number, variety, and value — and opportunity for expression. Many legitimate interests are represented in a group of a hundred students, and providing they are legal they must be recognized even though teachers and administrators themselves have no concern in them. It is, of course, the business of the school to improve these interests to the betterment of the student. School clubs, because of their variety and number, offer fine opportunities for exploring, developing, and widening the interests of the students. Naturally the greater the variety and number of the clubs, the more educative possibilities there will be.

Motivation of school work. — Clubs may help to motivate the regular work of the school. In fact, the club should whenever possible be linked up with some school subject. The Latin Club should be related to the work in Latin; the Shakespeare Club to the work in English Literature; the Radio Club or Science Club to the work in Science; and the Life-Saving Club to the work in Physical Education. Students attracted to any subject or phase of a subject may have, through clubs, opportunities for further work in it. Clubs should provide for a more informal type of activity than is usually found in regular classroom work. Thus the club and classroom may supplement each other.

ORGANIZATION

The club program should be based on student interests. — In some schools the club program is based on teacher interests and abilities. The principal finds the particular interests of each teacher and then makes up his schedule of clubs on this basis. In a way this may be right. Certainly a sponsor who has no interest in a club has no business to sponsor it. On the other hand, however, the club does not exist to satisfy the interest of a teacher but to help to develop the student. A better method of establishing a program of clubs is to allow each student to choose according to his interest.

Chartering the club. — The club should be formally chartered or licensed by the council or other central organization. Many clubs fail to function after a few days or weeks. This failure is frequently due to the fact that the club was not well organized and established in the beginning. The students may have acted hastily in choosing the club; the sponsor may have been hastily assigned without a survey of her interests or abilities; or the club itself may not have stood for any definite program of activities or policies.

No club should be formed hastily or allowed to die out without protest. If a group of students wants a Radio Club, for instance, it should think the matter through and make its plans very carefully. These plans should include the following elements:

1. Name of the club.
2. Purpose of the club. What is it for? What are its values?

3. Organization of the club. Time, place, and frequency of meeting. Officers, Constitution, Committees.

4. Activities, Programs and other work. What is it going to *do?* How? When? Where?

5. Membership Requirements. Who may belong? How initiated?

6. Miscellaneous. Fees, Insignia, Slogans, Colors, Flower. When these phases have been carefully studied, a formal application is made to the proper authorities for a charter. This application contains all of the data suggested by the above questions.

The authority then considers the application in the light of the following questions.

1. Is this club reasonable and legitimate?
2. Is there a place for it in this school?
3. Are its purposes and values worthy?
4. Are these purposes and values attainable?
5. Is its projected organization feasible?
6. Is its projected program workable and worthy?
7. Are its membership requirements democratic?
8. Will this club duplicate the work or activities of any other club?
9. Is there a suitable sponsor available?

If after thorough consideration the authority decides favorably, it issues a charter with the understanding that at any time the club ceases to function or violates any provisions of the charter, the latter will be declared null and void and the club abolished. If the authority decides unfavorably on the application, it will suggest the proper changes in the projected organization. Such a procedure not only dignifies the whole program of clubs, but it also safeguards and guarantees their success because of its demand that they be based on sound considerations rather than hasty judgment, and that their activities reach certain standards.

Constitution. — " All respectable organizations have constitutions " is frequently heard and often many hours of valuable time are used in making the club or organization "respectable" by developing a constitution. In many organizations developing and amending the constitution seems to be about the only reason for the existence of the organization ; at least, that appears to be its most frequent item of business. A club may have a simple constitution, defining its purposes, organization, activities, etc., but this is not necessary to the success of the club. It does add to the formality and dignity of the organization. However, the most important work of the club is not to be found in the useless wranglings over constitutional amendments. If the club is formally chartered, as was suggested before, probably the " application " is as good a constitution as any, because it lists and defines all of the elements necessary.

Officers and committees. — Many organizations are officered and committeed to death. No officer should be elected until a definite job has been found for him to do. The job first and then the election of the officer, should be the order of procedure. Special and suggestive names can be substituted for those commonly used. For instance, the president of the Chemistry Club might be called the " Chief Chemist " ; the president of the Travel Club, the " General Manager," " Conductor," or " Guide " ; the president of the Civics Club, the " Mayor " ; the president of the Military Club, the " General " ; and the president of the Home Nursing Club, the " Head Nurse."

Few standing committees are desirable. The policy of appointing committees as they are needed and discharging them after they have completed their tasks is sound organization, and it probably offers more opportunities for participation by the various members of the club. A committee which has as its function the finding out of what similar clubs in other schools are doing would be of value to the program committee. Such material might be gathered from the papers and magazines of other schools or through correspondence and visitation.

Membership requirements. — All clubs should be open to all students who have the necessary interest or skill. This means that there should be no balloting on candidates by members of the organization. Cliquishness and clannery come early enough in the life of the citizen without their being encouraged in school. In some clubs, however, such as music or dramatic, an interest alone may not be sufficient to justify membership. The applicant may be required to show suitable proficiency in the activity. This proficiency should be shown by try-outs, when a special committee, not the club as a whole, passes upon the candidates. This committee should probably be composed of the sponsor, perhaps another teacher or two, and one or two members of the club.

Should all students be required to belong to a club? The answer to this puzzling question is, theoretically, Yes; practically it may frequently be, No. A requirement that every student must belong to a club might be proper if there were an adequate number and variety of clubs. If the student does not find an interesting club or group and is forced into joining something, he looks around and finds the club which will be least exacting. Many schools require the student who does not join a club to go to the study hall for that period. This in itself is probably wise; but when the student is made to feel that he is being punished by his refusal to join a club, it is decidedly bad. Joining a club under pressure is anything but healthy for the club. Its members rightfully resent the incoming of this dead wood. A dilution of interest inevitably results.

If membership fees are charged, they should be small. It is probably good practice not to have such fees. If books, materials, or equipment are required, they should be paid for by the general school fund and not by student members of clubs. This does not apply to small assessments for parties or picnics, but to material actually needed to carry on the regular work of the club.

The membership of all clubs should be limited, because an overcrowded club defeats its own purpose. No one can say what this limit shall be, but if the club is just being established the limit should be too small rather than too large. If small, it can be increased; if large, it cannot be easily reduced. All clubs will not be of the same size.

When a student joins a club it should be with the understanding that he will remain a member until the end of the semester. Such a requirement will work hardship on some students, probably, but it will be for the general good and will insure that the student does not join because of some slight passing fancy. He will consider membership seriously. A member who habitually absents himself from the club or who refuses to take part in its activities should be dropped from the club. He should not be permitted to join another club until the regular time has elapsed.

The question of eligibility of students for membership will arise. Shall the student who is failing, or who has failed in a subject or two, be allowed to join a club? No general answer can be given to this question. On the one hand, it might be said that if the student cannot carry his school work he is not justified in joining a club, and that his time should be given to his school work. It might also be said that such a restriction will help to keep students up in their work because of their desire to belong. On the other hand, it may be that the club is the thing which motivates the failing student, and that except for it he would have dropped out long ago. If he is failing badly, he will probably drop out soon enough anyway, and any additional time he can be held in school through any means will be of value to him. No general answer, therefore, can be given to this question; it depends upon local circumstances, conditions, and individuals.

Representing the school publicly in competition should be limited to students who are carrying their work successfully.

Club pins or other insignia probably add to the interest and pride of the students in the club. They can be obtained at reasonable rates. Small modest types are preferable. No close approximation of any of the school honors, insignia, or emblems should be allowed. On the whole, because of the possibility of frequent changes of personnel, and because of the more or less cheapening effect club insignia have upon honor and merit insignia awarded by the school, good practice probably does not favor the use of the former. Slogans may be adopted to suggest the work or ideals of the club. Flowers and colors are also adopted by some clubs.

Time of meeting. — If these activities are worth carrying in school, they are worth carrying on school time. Clubs held at noon or after school are handicapped. Including them in the regular schedule not only makes them more convenient for the students and teachers, thus encouraging a good attitude toward them, but dignifies them as well. Another important reason why they should be in the regular schedule is that, as community money is being paid for their support, the community has a right to demand the same efficiency in their organization and work that is demanded in the classroom work.

Place of meeting. — All clubs should meet in the school building unless for special reasons they are permitted to meet elsewhere. The student council, or other central body, should draw up a schedule of rooms and places of meeting with due regard for the wishes and needs of the club. If a club desires to hold a meeting elsewhere or for special reasons desires to go outside, it must have the permission of the council or the sanction of the principal before it goes. This is only reasonable, for the school is responsible for these activities and consequently should have the final control of them.

Frequency of meetings. — One good club meeting every two weeks is worth more than twice as many routine and uninteresting affairs for which little special preparation has been made. However, it is entirely possible to have good meetings each week. Weekly meetings are more usual. Some schools have two different types of clubs, academic and social, and each student may belong to one of each. The meetings of these are held in alternate weeks. Game, athletic, dancing, and recreational clubs compose the social group, while academic clubs are closely related to the formal subjects of the school.

Sponsor. — No club should exist without a sponsor. Needless to say this sponsor should be interested and sympathetic and at least reasonably popular with the students. Popularity in itself is not a guarantee of successful sponsorship, nor is interest and ability. A combination is desirable. The sponsor may be chosen by the club, or appointed by the council or by the principal. The wishes of both students and teachers must be considered. The recommendation might well come from the council and the appointment from the principal. It occasionally happens that an outsider might be a good sponsor for a certain club. For instance, some outside amateur or professional radio enthusiast might make a good sponsor for the Radio Club, or the city librarian a fine sponsor for a Library Club. It is always more or less dangerous, however, to have a sponsor who is not under the immediate control of the school authorities.

Club sponsors should meet a few times each year for the purpose of furthering and developing adequate and intelligent sponsorship. It is difficult for a teacher who daily practices the " superior-inferior " relationship not to carry such an attitude into any group which is made up of students. The teacher must realize that he is a sponsor, and not a dominator of the activity. His experience and consequent riper judgment should be of benefit in counseling the group, but any attempt to dominate it will be met with signs of proper dissatisfaction on the part of the student members.

ACTIVITIES

Variety means interest, and the club which has a variety of types of meetings will probably be more interesting and valuable than the one which has only the regular formal traditional type of meeting. Social, recreational, humorous, and other types of meetings and programs may be interspersed with the regular type. Care should be taken, however, that the club and its activities do not deteriorate in quality.

In the next few pages will be found details of the purposes and activities of a few typical school clubs. These outlines are brief. They are not intended to be complete but merely suggestive.[1]

AIRPLANE CLUB

Purpose: To awaken and develop an interest in aviation; to give the members an understanding of aëronautical principles and to acquaint them with the history and development of aviation, including the present status of the airplane and its possible future.

Activities: Talks and reports on early attempts to fly dating back to the mythological Icarus; on Lillienthal, Chanute, Langley, the Wrights, Bleriot, Curtiss and many others. The contributions of these men.

Discussion of the principles of sustained flight, of nomenclature, fuselage, pontoons, airdromes, rudder, wings, and under-carriage, the construction of an airplane; operation and control of the airplane; maintenance of the airplane; airdromes, repairs, equipment, etc.; the airplane in war and peace; commercial and mail possibilities.

Records in aviation; stories of flying by local flyers or mechanics; study from photographs, illustrations, and silhouettes; use of magazines on aviation, air service, and popular mechanics; trips to aviation field, hangars or shops; making and flying of models; the building of a glider or small airplane.

[1] For a more complete analysis of individual clubs see the excellent discussion in *Junior High School Life*, by Thomas-Tindal and Myers. The Macmillan Company.

ART CLUB

Purpose: To discover and direct artistic ability; to study the principles of art; to give the student more opportunity for self-expressional work than is permissible in the regular class; and to help teach him to appreciate beauty and fineness.

Activities: Discussions of principles of form, mass, color, composition.

Poster Work. The group might be responsible for all posters used in the school during the year. Poster contests.

Drawing and sketching birds, animals, landscapes, marines. Exhibitions of birds and animals; the zoo and the parks could provide models.

The history of art. Illustrated by examples.

Interior decorating. Trips for observational purposes. The designing of interior decorations.

Scenery designing for plays.

Camera and kodak work. Might be the basis for the photographic work of the yearbook and magazines.

Portrait painting and photographing, posing, expression.

Cartooning and caricaturing.

Illustrative and commercial drawing and sketching.

Costume designing. Might be capitalized for fashion show or for dramatic club purposes.

Trips and visits to museums, art galleries, and exhibits.

Exhibitions of pictures loaned or rented for the occasion.

Designs, covers, and inserts for the annual or yearbook.

Talks by art collectors and artists.

General assembly program for the school.

Cut and torn paper designing.

Study of furniture for the home.

Decorative use of cretonne.

Art in sculpture. Uses of marble and stone.

Clay modeling.

Art in wood carving, cardboard, leather, metals, and beads.

Christmas and birthday cards.

Modeling and designing with plasteline and enamel.

Lamp shade designing and making.

Vocational discussions about the work of the following:

  Book, magazine or newspaper illustrator

  Commercial artist who illustrates catalogues, advertisements, posters, bulletins and pamphlets

Designer of textiles, wall paper, furniture, linoleum, jewelry
The political, philosophical and humorous cartoonist
Photographer
Architect and landscape architect
Letterer and sign painter
Art director in the magazine
Art director in the movies
Art teacher and supervisor

CAMERA CLUB

Purpose: To interest the student in making better pictures; to teach him accuracy in the art and the technique of taking, finishing, printing, and mounting pictures, and the care of the camera lenses and equipment; to acquaint him with engraving and the processes used by publishers.

Activities: The history of photography; contrast of early methods with those more modern.

Study of present day cameras; box, folding, portrait, view, panorama circuit, and motion picture.

The operation of various cameras and their work.

Study of lenses and their uses, anastigmatic, rapid rectilinear, portrait, wide-angle copying, telephoto, cinematograph.

Developing by tray and tank methods.

Instruction and experimentation with various formulas.

Printing with various kinds and grades of paper, toning processes.

Enlarging and freak printing.

Photo displays for art shows.

This club could be responsible for the photographic and snapshot work on the yearbook and magazine.

Picture contests.

Assembly programs on pictures, illustrated with the camera.

Demonstrations in posing, showing effects.

Making lantern slides.

Speed and still-animal portraits.

Study of lights and shadows, and backgrounds.

FRENCH CLUB

Purpose: To develop and increase interest in French life, language, customs, traditions, and history; to improve facility in speaking French; and to put to practical use in a French atmosphere the French learned in the classroom.

Activities: Choose name — Cercle Français, Club Français, Alliance Française, Amis de la France, Cénacle.

Discussion of influence of French on English Literature.

Study of French customs and traditions.

Singing of French or American songs in French.

Dramatizations.

Intensive study and reports on periods of French literature.

Travel talks in French.

Illustrated lectures on the beauties of France; on the Roman remains; on the battlefields; and on the buildings and parks of Paris.

Amusements, such as

Reading of an anecdote aloud to the group.

Playing of the game Prince of Paris has lost his hat.

Divided fable. Cards are issued which have parts of sentences in French. Completed story must be collected and connected.

What is it? Card pinned on individual's back with name of flower or animal. Person must guess what is on his tag.

Vocabulary. Each member must respond with a word for each letter of the alphabet.

Spelling matches, matching words, synonyms, and idiomatic expressions.

Bill of fare, naming the things that one would like to have for dinner.

Buying. Each makes up a list of things he would buy on a trip.

Fruit Basket. French names instead of English.

Proverbs. Member starts a proverb and another finishes it.

Authors, using French names.

What I see in the picture, naming all items in French.

Presenting French plays.

Progressive conversation or continued story.

French on the victrola.

French letters to French boys and girls.

French folk dances.

Fashion show.

"Promenade." All must speak French while on it.

Adoption of French orphan.

Visitation of French families in the vicinity.

Visits to museums.

Debates, essays, and readings.

Use of French newspapers and magazines.

Use of railroad, travel, and commercial house folders and advertisements.

Celebration of French national holidays and festivals.

Get-acquainted conversation, home, name, occupation of father.

Current events in French: school, community, and nation.

HEALTH CLUB

Purpose: To teach the student to appreciate the importance of good health and to take care of his physical machine; to interest himself in the general health of the community.

Activities: Discussion of physiological and hygienic principles of health.

Keeping health charts individually and for the family.

Discussion and practice of "First Aid."

Causes and prevention of automobile accidents.

Traffic laws, violations, penalties, enforcement.

Fire.

Safe milk, garbage, sewage, water, gasoline, and electrical devices.

The responsibility of the authorities for the health of the community.

Federal, state, and community agencies for health.

House planning and building.

High lights in the history of medicine.

Mental health and hygiene.

Study of examples of health habits — Roosevelt, Florence Nightingale, William Gorgas, Edward Trudeau, Pasteur, Koch, Jenner, Carrel, Lister, Grenfell, and other noted workers for health.

Care of sick and sick-room technique.

Care of parks, alleys, buildings, vacant lots, and streets.

Making campaign posters.

General health work.

Trips about the city to soda fountains, water supplies, sewage-disposal plants, dumps, and bakeries.

Assembly programs.

Health clippings, use bulletin board space and scrapbooks.

Dramatization of Safety First and Safety Last.

HISTORY CLUB

Purpose: To afford opportunity for the student to widen his historical interests; and to acquaint him with methods of research, sources, and scientific judgment.

Activities: Study of local history, documents, records, letters, maps, and relics.

Discussion of:

Famous citizens — American, British, French, and German.

Historical pictures, drama, music.

Historical trees, roads, spots, and houses of the vicinity.

Historical Pageant, preferably of local historical significance.

Life of the slaves.

Political conventions.

Travels through foreign countries by means of guide books and transportation folders.

Writing up the history of the high school or of the school system.

Dramatization of historical episodes, tableaux, reproduction of forms of government, Roman senate, and making the first flag.

Trace the origin of law; breaking down of social and racial barriers.

Debates on historical events, policies, personages.

Special-day programs for assembly and home-room periods.

Take-offs — Boston Tea Party; Sir Walter Raleigh and Queen Elizabeth.

Collection of old pictures and maps.

Making scrapbooks.

Visits to museums.

Keeping a bulletin board of interesting current history.

Modeling of plaster or clay — Roman tablets, old instruments of punishment, stone implements, weapons of warfare, costumes.

Playing Roman games and stunts.

Seeing historical movies.

Exhibition and discussion of historical relics, helmets, swords, rifles, grenades, medals, and honors.

Readings from magazines such as *Current History, News Outline, Outlook,* and *Independent.*

Stereopticon slides and postcards of war and historical events and personages.

Impersonations — Patrick Henry, Burke, and others.

Open Forum.

LATIN CLUB

Purpose: To vitalize the study of Latin by bringing the student into contacts which might be unsuited for classroom work; to broaden his knowledge of Latin and Roman history; and to cover innumerable points for which there is no time in class.

Activities: Dramatization of Roman wedding, Roman banquets, Roman Court, School, Senate-Meeting, Feasts, Family Quarrel, Courtship.

Discussion of:

Use of Latin in business to-day.

Roman mythological characters — Apollo, Jupiter, and others.

Manners, dress, customs, traditions, amusements of the Romans.

Great cities of ancient classical times.

Famous Roman buildings; use of models, pictures, postcards, and slides.

Famous Romans; biography.

Collection of Roman curios, pottery, coins, pictures, and jewelry.

Memorization of quotations, flag salute in Latin.

Translation of songs, Mother Goose rhymes, riddles, anecdotes.

Giving school songs and yells in Latin.

Making an imaginary trip to Rome.

Publication of a Latin paper.

Latin plays or pageants, dialogues, plays, movies.

Construction of charts showing practical uses of Latin phrases and words, mottoes.

Identification games; heads and bodies of famous Romans interchanged.

Visit to Pompeii.

The attainment of a Roman-club room with suitable mural decorations, furniture, and busts.

Charades, spelling matches, vocabulary contests, and derivative games.

Trips to museums.

Singing and studying Latin hymns.

MATHEMATICS CLUB

Purpose: To create and promote interest in mathematics; to furnish incentives for further study; and to supply material not possible to be given in regular classroom work.

Activities: Plays. "Adventures of X," a number play in three acts (*Mathematics Teacher*, March, 1924).

Minstrel Show, Mr. X Y Z and other performers; mathematical jokes, conundrums, fallacies, parodies, songs, and games.

Dance of the Angles.

Mock School Room.

Tricks, Magic Squares (See White, *Scrapbook of Mathematics;* Smith, *History of Mathematics*).

Tricks with nines (See Ball, *Mathematical Recreations and Essays;* White, *Scrapbook;* Smith, *Number Stories of Long Ago*).

Mathematical puzzles.

Various program topics (See Young, *The Teaching of Mathematics*).

Contests (See *School Science* and *Mathematics*, and *Mathematics Teacher*).

Applied mathematics.

Instruction in mathematical instruments, abacus, slide rule, transit, comptometer.

Visits to factories, demonstrations of applied mathematics and mathematical instruments.

Graphic records, making and using them, illustrations.

Short methods in mathematics.

Mathematical magic (See Clark, *Knots*, and Smith, *Complete Arithmetic*).

Curiosities in numbers.

Origin of the use of x for unknown.

Paper folding and cutting.

Fourth dimension.

Codes and ciphers.

Life and works of great mathematicians.

Mathematics in agriculture, industry, chemistry, and **art.**

Mathematics in war.

Pythagorean theorem.

Pascal's mystic hexagon.

Mathematics of Hindus, Arabs, Greeks, Egyptians.

Optical illusions.

Squaring the circle.

Mathematical symmetry in nature.

Mathematics with cards or chess.

TRAVEL CLUB

Purpose: To broaden the student's interests by giving him opportunity for contact with customs, peoples, traditions, institutions, buildings, and scenery of other countries as well as of his own; to teach appreciation of these countries; and to give him some practice in planning a trip of his own.

Activities: Planning of trips of short duration to near-by points.

Planning a two weeks' vacation to some American point or points.

Planning European trips of various durations and to various points.

Planning a round-the-world trip.

Study of countries represented by members of the Club.

See America First, what, when, where, how?

Use of folders and transportation booklets from railroad companies, hotels, chambers of commerce, steamship lines, travel bureaus.

Estimation of expenses.

Luggage needed on the trip.

A study of each country visited under some such outlines as this:

History of country	Form of government
Contributions	Relation to America
Standards of living	Strange customs
Costumes	Art treasures
Places to visit	Traditions and language
Famous men, past and present	

Making a library of travel books, novels, descriptions, and magazine articles.

Making a scrapbook.

Use of slides, films, and pictures.

Study of foreign games, dances, stories, and songs.

List of Clubs

Accounting	Bird	Chemistry
Advertising	Blue Print	Choral
Afternoon Helpers	Boating	Christmas
Agriculture	Book Lovers	City History
Airplane	Botany	Citizens
Antiquarian	Boxing	Civic
Applied Mechanics	Boys Cookery	Classical
Archery	Bulletin Board	Coins
Art	Business	Collecting
Astronomy	Cadet	College
Automobile Mechanics	Camera	Commercial
Baby Association	Camp Cookery	Community
Bacteriology	Campfire Girls	Contemporary
Banking	Camping	Cooking
Basketry	Candy	Corn
Bicycling	Cartooning	Correspondence
Big Sister or Brother	Checkers	Cosmopolitan
Biology	Chess	Craft

Cricket
Crochet
Cross-Country
Curios
Current Events
Custodian
Dancing
Debating
Decoration
Drafting
Dramatic
Dressmaking
Dot and Dash
Economics
Egg
Electricity
Embroidery
Employment
Engineering
English
Etiquette
Exploration
Farm
Fencing
Fiddlers
Financiers
First-Aid
Flower
Forestry
French
Gardening
Geography
Geology
Gift
Girl Reserves
Glee
Golf
Good English
Government

Gun
Gymnasium
Handball
Handicraft
Harp
Health
Helping-Hand
Hi-Y
Hiking
History
Hobby
Holiday
Home-Beautiful
Home Economics
Home-Environment
Home-Nursing
Hostess
Household-Chemistry
Junior Red Cross
Journalists
Kipling
Kitchen
Kite
Knitting
Know-Our-City
Illustrations
Inventions
Landscape
Language
Latin
Laundry
Law
Leaders
Library
Life-Saving
Literary
Little Mothers
Live-Stock
Live-Wire

Luncheon
Machinist
Mandolin
Manual-Training
Marine
Marketing
Masonry
Mathematics
Mechanics
Military
Milk and Dairy
Millinery
Minute Men
Model-Making
Movies
Music
Music Lovers
Museum
Mythology
Nature Study
Needle Craft
Office Practice
Opera
Oratory
Pageant
Paint Pot
Painters
Parliamentary
Pen and Ink
Pets
Philanthropic
Physics
Pigs
Pilgrimage
Poetry
Poster
Potato
Pottery
Poultry

Press
Prize Story
Public Speaking
Publicity
Radio
Readers
Religious
Renovation
Restoratory
Rooters
Repair
Reporters
Riding
Salesman's
Sanitary
Santa Claus
Saturday-Night
Scenario
Scholarship
School Gardens
School Improvement
Science
Scouts

Scrapbook
Scribes
Secretarial
Serving
Sewing
Shakespeare
Sheet-Metal
Sketching
Small-Animal
Soccer
Social Hour
Social-Service
Spanish
Stage
Stamp
Steam-Engine
Stenography
Stereopticon
Story-Telling
Style
Success
Sweets
Swimming

Tatting
Tennis
Textile
Thrift
Traffic
Travel
Tree
Typing
Ukelele
Valet
Vegetable
Violin
Vocational
Volley Ball
Welfare
Walking
Wild-Flower
Wild-Animal
Willing Workers
Wireless
Woodworkers
Wrestlers
Zoölogy

SUMMARY

The main purposes of the school club are to widen and deepen the interests of the students and to motivate the regular work of the school. Clubs fail most frequently because they have not been organized on a sound basis or carefully thought-out plans. The council should charter all clubs in the school, and no club should be chartered until it has met very definite requirements set by the council. Such formality will help to insure the success of the club. Club membership should be open to all who have the requisite interest or technical ability. No club should be allowed to elect its members. An interested and sympathetic sponsor is essential to the success of any club. Meetings should be held on school time, and should be varied in type so that interest may be maintained.

REFERENCES

BENSON, C. H. "Boys and Girls Club Work; Its Principles, Policies and Requirements," *Educational Journal* 33 : 11–12, January 6, 1916.

BERNHEIMER, C. S. and COHEN, J. M. *Boys Clubs.* Walter H. Baker Company.

COX, P. W. L. *Creative School Control*, Chap. VIII. J. B. Lippincott Company.

DAVIS, C. O. *Junior High School Education*, 358–362. World Book Company.

FERRIS, H. J. *Girl's Clubs; Their Organization and Management. A Manual for Workers.* E. P. Dutton and Company.

FRETWELL, E. K. "A Survey of the Extracurricular Activities of Philadelphia High Schools." *Report of the Survey of the Public Schools of Philadelphia*, Book 4, p. 144–152.

FOSTER, C. R. *Extracurricular Activities in the High School*, Chaps. II–III. The Johnson Publishing Company.

HARTSON, L. D. *Psychology of the Club.* Clark University Press.

JOHNSTON, C. H. *The Modern High School* 373–377. Charles Scribner's Sons.

KENDRIC, W. H. "Boys and Girls Four-H Clubs and the School," *Proceedings* of the National Education Association, 564–565, 1921.

LYMAN, R. L. "The Ben Blewett Junior High School of St. Louis," *School Review* 28 : 26–40, 97–111, January, February, 1920.

—— "Guidance and Some Club Work," *School Review* 32 : 93–104, February, 1924.

—— "Washington Junior High School, Rochester, New York." *School Review* 28 : 203–204, March, 1920.

MEISTER, M. *Educational Values of Certain After-School Activities and Materials in Science.* Columbia University Press, 1921.

MEYER, H. D. *Handbook of Extracurricular Activities*, Part II. A. S. Barnes and Company.

POUND, O. "Social Life of High School Girls; Problems and Opportunities," *School Review* 28 : 50–56, January, 1920.

POWERS, C. "Social Program for the Unsocial High School Girl," *School Review* 32 : 773–778, December, 1924.

Powers, C. "Regulation of High School Societies," *School Review* 28 : 167–169, March, 1920.

The Boys' Federation Publications, World's Tower Building, 110 W. 40th St., New York.

Thomas-Tindal, E. V. and Myers, J. D. *Junior High School Life*, Chaps. XIV–XV. The Macmillan Company.

Wilson, E. E. "Girl's League as an Agency in the Education of High School Girls," *School Review* 32 : 773–778, December, 1924.

CHAPTER VII

DRAMATICS

From earliest times the importance of drama as a teaching instrument has been recognized. The pagan priest and the Christian Church Father both utilized the dramatic instinct. By illustrating the history or embodying the spirit of their religions in services of action and pageantry, they interested and instructed the people. Children first appeared as actors in certain Greek plays. The Miracle and Mystery plays of the Middle Ages were partly didactic in intention. Companies of boy actors were found at an early day at some of the great public schools of England, and plays were occasionally written expressly for them. In 1776 Mme. de Genlis, a French noblewoman, founded the first " Theater of Education " (*Théâtre d'Éducation*) for young students. " Amateur " dramatics have been defined as productions whose main function is to please the audience, while " educational " dramatics serve primarily to educate the student. The plays of Mme. de Genlis were written and produced for the sole purpose of educating children.

Drama also had a place in the early American schools. We learn, for instance, that in 1798 Charles Stearns, Preceptor of the Liberal School at Lincoln, Massachusetts, published a book entitled *Dramatic Dialogues for Use in the Schools*. In the Introduction he says,

"The rudest nymphs and swains by practicing on rhetoric will soon acquire polite manners, for they will often personate the most polite character."

Each of the dialogues was intended to teach a particular virtue. They bore such titles as, " The Woman of Honour " (goodness and veracity) ; " The Mother of a Family " (patience) ; " The Male Coquette " (absurdity of lying and hypocrisy). Since this early date, pageantry, pantomime, musical productions, fairs, carnivals, circuses and other kinds of dramatic production have been added to school activities until now one finds a large and distinctive literature on the subject.

All students are interested in some form of dramatics. All of them like, if not to take part in plays, at least to attend them, especially if their friends and classmates participate. Acting, by its very nature, gives the student a means of getting away from himself and of being another personality. It serves to satisfy the natural desire for action. The student likes to express himself. Traditional school practice has tended toward conformity and the suppression of individuality. Plays, musical productions, carnivals, circuses, pageants, and similar types of " shows " can all be classed under the broad head of dramatics.

VALUES OF DRAMATICS

Values to the actors. — Dramatics afford the student a suitable opportunity for the expression of any histrionic talent he may have. They help to discover and develop this talent. The student learns to express himself clearly and vividly, adds many words to his vocabulary, enunciates more clearly, gains confidence and poise. For a training in team work, dramatics are at least the equal of athletics. And they give the student a fuller life by enabling him to understand other lives through acting them out. Mackaye says, "The development of the dramatic instinct does not tend to make actors, but imaginative human beings."

Educational dramatics are of value in setting standards of dramatic excellence. The cheap movie or vaudeville house advertises its thriller or melodrama with gaudy posters and draws many patrons, and most of these patrons attend because they have not been habituated to like anything better. The patrons of the cheap theater or the readers of the cheap novel are fairly satisfied with them because they have never experienced anything better of their kind, and consequently have no standards whereby to judge them. An important business of the school is to teach the student to use his leisure time wisely. This can be done through careful presentation of good plays and music. The student must be shown what is good and informed why it is good. Dramatic taste can be cultivated. Discrimination can be taught.

Many schools have as yet not seen their responsibility in this connection. This is evidenced by the large number of farces which are staged by high school dramatic organizations. Some of them are interesting and exciting, and probably send the parents, students, and patrons away well pleased; but they are in no sense really educative. The artistry of the average farce lies with the writer and not with the actor. More substantial plays might not provoke as much fun, but they represent deeper emotions, require more from the actor, and are more profitable. Of course this need not mean that the students should try productions too difficult for them. But in any case an abundance of farces in the club program means that the box office is being considered more important than anything else.

Values to the school. — The school should receive its share of the benefits from dramatic productions. An ever important problem in modern education is that of motivation. How can we get the students to become really interested in the work? The use of educational dramatics is at least a step in the direction of an answer to this perplexing question. Experience has shown that a dull and disinterested class may be transformed into an interested and busy one when a few lessons have been dramatized under the direction of a skillful instructor. Miss Finlay-Johnson found a class in a small English school actually studying grammar for the fun of it.[1]

One very interesting and suggestive use of dramatics was made recently at the Wilkes-Barre (Pennsylvania) High School. A "Tabard Inn," suggested by the famous Tabard Inn in which Chaucer assembled the Canterbury Pilgrims, was erected in the gymnasium of the school. Each class in English selected a classic to present. Contributions of from five to twenty-five cents a student were taken to meet expenses. The Departments of Mechanical Drawing, Manual Training, and Art coöperated in making and arranging the booths and costumes. In each booth were the principal characters of the classic properly dressed and grouped. Student guides showed visitors around and explained the significance of each booth. The Tabard was open for several afternoons and evenings.

Nearly every department may profitably employ dramatics or dramatic procedure. Play and scenario writing will give practice in English composition. Dramatizing stories and events in history makes them more vivid. In geography a quasi-dramatic method may be employed. Models may be constructed; games may be built up around the location of states and nations. The teacher of literature can probably employ dramatics with the greatest effectiveness. Four of the chief forms which may be used are as follows: [2]

1. Simple dramatic dialogue.

2. Dramatization of various situations chosen from the classics and combined in such a way as to form a dramatic unit. Scenes from *Treasure Island*, *Silas Marner*, *Ivanhoe*, etc.

3. Dramatization of the whole story, as the Robin Hood Ballads, *Gareth and Lynette*.

---

[1] Finlay-Johnson, Harriet. *The Dramatic Method of Teaching.* Ginn and Company.

[2] See Simons, S. E. and Orr, C. I. *Dramatization.* Scott, Foresman and Company.

FIGURE V. — A RECONSTRUCTED "TABARD INN" ERECTED IN THE GYMNASIUM OF THE WILKES-BARRE HIGH SCHOOL.

4. Dramatic reading accompanied by a tableau or living-picture representation of the text.

Another value to the school is to be found in the demand that the various interests and departments of the school coöperate in order to insure the success of the production. The manual training department may help to provide necessary equipment and fixtures; the home economics department can assist in the arrangements of the settings and the costuming. The art department can assist with scenery and posters; the commercial department can help with the advertising and sale of tickets; and other departments and individuals around the school can help in one way or another. This not only utilizes the more expert knowledge and technique, but makes the affair a " school " affair, and thus strengthens the morale.

Furthermore, the use of dramatics is effective in raising funds for the support of various school activities. Dramatic productions are the best revenue producers of the extracurricular program. But they could probably not be justified solely on that basis.

Values to the community. — Educational dramatics of the school are beneficial to the community. The parents become interested in better plays and better literature when such are shown to them. They thus become more critical of the legitimate stage and of the movie. Moving pictures, though better than formerly, can stand improvement, as can also the sex drama and musical comedy of the stage. But improvement either of the stage or of motion pictures must first be demanded by patrons. The school could do much to bring about a public demand for better pictures and a higher type of dramatic production. Certainly it should assume a measure of responsibility for the literary tastes and standards of the community. As its educational center, the school can become a force for better things in the community.

ORGANIZATION OF DRAMATIC CLUB

Dramatics may be controlled by a number of different types of organization. Perhaps the best, certainly the most common, is a Dramatic Club. Such a club is under the sponsorship of the dramatic department, if such a department exists, or under a coach or other teacher who has an interest in dramatics.

Membership. — The membership of the club is composed of those students who have the necessary qualifications and an interest in dramatics; proficiency in acting should not be a requirement. As staging a play requires stage hands, scene painters, electricians, and others who never appear to the audience, an interest in dramatic production is probably a sufficient qualification for membership. Proficiency in acting and suitability for the part should be considered in selecting the characters for the various plays. In any case election to the club or part should not be by ballot. A student who is failing in his regular school work should be allowed to be a member of the club, but should not be allowed to take part in any public performance.

Committees. — There are a great many details to be attended to in the staging of any production. These might be cared for by delegated individuals or by committees. Such committees might include the following:

Music Committee. — This committee arranges for the necessary music, music before the play begins, between the acts, and after it is over. Special music for certain scenes, or musical specialities are frequently desired. The business of the music committee is to see that this music is provided.

Costume Committee. — The costume committee is charged with the responsibility of properly dressing the actors. Its membership should be largely from the students of the home economics department. Making and borrowing costumes; research work in costuming, to find what is suitable; care of the costumes; listing and care of material which belongs to the school, compose the work of this group. It can make a business of collecting from the students discarded and unused clothing and effects. These frequently can be adapted. In pageantry and other large productions this committee will have much work to do. The success of a play depends in a large measure on costuming.

Properties and Scenery Committee. — This committee provides, makes, or borrows the necessary equipment for the production. Settings, furniture, hangings, curtains, pictures, and equipment of all kinds must be had. A member of this committee whose father is a furniture dealer will be a good asset.

Usher Committee. — On this committee should be both boys and girls who like to usher. They should be thoroughly trained in their work. Neat uniform dress is desirable. A head usher and an assistant are essential. Students should be selected on the basis of their manners, courtesy, and general attractiveness.

Ticket Committee. — The ticket committee attends to the printing, distribution, sale, and collection of tickets. Usually there is a great deal of money handled and there are many loopholes through which money may disappear. It is necessary to adopt a business-like method of distributing and selling the tickets. A representative of the faculty of the business department should be adviser of this group.

Publicity Committee. — The publicity for a play will include advertising in newspapers, by means of posters, show-cards, handbills, theater slides, and assembly or home-room notices. The campaign should be thorough and dignified. If there is a commercial department in the school, its knowledge and technique should be utilized by this committee.

Cast Committee. — Selecting students and assigning them to the various parts is no easy task, for charges of favoritism and partiality fly very easily if there happen to be several actors available for the various parts. The committee must not only thoroughly know the play and the parts but must also have a good idea of the available potential actors for them. Understudies should be provided for all of the parts. This not only makes provision for the part of any actor unable to participate, but gives so many more students educative opportunities and keeps the actors working hard to hold their parts.

Stage Management Committee. — This committee arranges the stage, assigns the various helpers to certain definite duties, provides " off-stage stuff," and in other ways helps to make the intervals between acts short.

Business Committee. — The business end of the production may be handled by a committee whose chairman is business manager. This committee receives receipts and pays bills. It makes a final formal report and turns over the cash to the central treasurer. Formally auditing its records and accounts adds to the dignity of the job, and checks against carelessness.

Other Committees. — Other committees might be appointed. These might include a rehearsal committee; a make-up committee, which studies make-up and helps the actors to make up; lighting, which provides lighting and special effects; a program committee which arranges the program, has it printed, and solicits the advertising necessary to pay for it. The machinery for staging productions should be complete and well articulated, but not cumbersome. It should never be more important than the end for which it is provided. Local conditions determine the number and size of committees required.

Choice of plays. — The play to be used should be chosen by a committee, preferably a committee of teachers with perhaps one or two student members, probably the main officers of the club; or by the sponsor. Miss Gertrude E. Johnson of the University of Wisconsin suggests the following:

Considerations in Choosing a Play

I. *Who is producing.* Age, training, and ability of the group.

II. *Nature of the audience.* General, selected, young or old, cultured or otherwise.

III. *Ends desired.* Dramatic or literary training, entertainment, money.

IV. *Producing considerations.* Place of production, its size, size and equipment of stage.

V. *The situations.* These should be free from undue emotional stress.

VI. *The royalty.* A large one cannot be paid ordinarily. Twenty-five dollars is about the best for manuscript plays.

VII. *Dramatic movement.* This is essential to the play. It must be capable of being acted and must not be too talky.

VIII. *Questionable situations.* They should be avoided.

IX. *Author.* It is desirable that he should be a person of some literary ability.

X. *Balance.* This should be considered in the acting values.[1]

The program for the year should include a variety of types of plays, farces, comedies, fantasies, and musical plays. Tragedies, bedroom comedies, and plays dealing with immorality and social problems should not be used. The committee should feel free to " cut " a play wherever it is necessary. Profanity, for instance, should be deleted. The use of three one-act plays on the program nearly triples the number of educational opportunities found in one three-act play. Moreover, increase in number of opportunities means increase in variety of opportunity.

[1] Johnson, Gertrude E. *Choosing a Play.* H. W. Wilson Company.

FIGURE VI. — A DETAIL OF THE "TABARD INN," SHOWING TWO OF THE CLASSICS PRESENTED

The coach or director. — Some schools employ an outside or professional coach to handle the dramatics. Some provide for athletic coaching in the same way. Such a procedure is wrong. This outsider all too frequently does not have the interest of the student or school at heart. He is employed to coach and is more interested in turning out a perfect team or perfect production than something which is really educative to many student participants. Excellence and success are to some extent necessary in any play or game, but over-emphasizing the affair for the audience or crowd usually means under-emphasizing it for the participants. Pleasing the parents is not as important as educating the students. The use of a regular member of the staff is preferable to the employment of an outsider for play coaching. Better still is the arrangement whereby a teacher gives his full time to the dramatic work.

ACTIVITIES OF THE DRAMATIC CLUB

The dramatic club is responsible for any dramatic production of the school. The senior class or other organization may of course stage a play. But the club can be of great service in helping to arrange and stage it. Other activities of the club might include the following :

Study of the drama, which may come under four headings :

Historical — developments of the drama and theater
Literary — study of the drama and dramatic style
Artistic — study of actors, managers, producers
Mechanical — study of stage equipment and mechanics

Study of such topics as the following :

The drama as a natural mode of expression
Dramatic terminology, stage phraseology, terms for stage settings, and lighting signals
Stage sets and terms of various periods
Lighting scenes

Ventilation and heating of theater

Contemporary drama, actors, producers, plays, playrights (including study of styles, methods, and current criticism)

Little-theater movement in America

New world-movements in the theater

Position of the motion pictures to-day

Motion picture production

Pageants and pageantry

Voice requirements in characterization

Unity of voice for individuals and groups

Bodily postures, movements, and actions

Make-up

Sculpture for action, paintings for postures, groupings, and facial expressions, folk dancing for body rhythms

Costumes and costuming

Analysis of construction of chosen plays

Dramatic criticism

What dramas to read.   How to read a drama.

Ideals in presentation of plays for public performance

Notebooks and scrapbook work:

Keep outlines of plays and important criticisms, etc.

Preserve notes on discussions, lectures, and visits

Collect pictures and critical comments for scrapbook

Acting:

Readings — poems, monologues, stories of various kinds

Dramatization of

Historical stories

Poems

Legends

Scenes from favorite fiction

Fairy stories and fables

Original scenes or scenarios

Miniature stage work:

Study of puppet shows

Construction of cardboard stages, scenery, and properties

Coöperation with Art Department in studying and making scenery

Make puppets of plasteline

Produce puppet show for assembly, Children's Hospital, or elementary school

Trips or parties to theaters, studios, or exhibitions:

Miscellaneous activities:

Voice development
Exercises in various groupings and movements on stage
Training in interpreting stage directions
Study of by-play
Presentation of scenes for illustrative purposes
Laboratory work
  Construction of model stages and buildings in miniature
  Designing of costumes
  Rehearsal of chosen plays for public presentation
  Writing plays and scenarios
Production of circus, fair, or bazaar
Development of a local pageant

PAGEANTS

The pageant is as old as history. It was the forerunner of the drama and was early employed by the priests and rulers. The ancient Hebrews with their feast and festival days had pageants of a religious nature. The Greeks had pageants of harvest and vintage. The Romans found pageants in the tribes they conquered and promptly adapted them to their own use. The modern pageant is a dramatic treatment of some historical, social, or allegorical theme. It usually deals with some important event in the life of the community and illustrates loyalty, civic truths, etc. Recently famous poems and stories have been made into successful pageants, such as " Evangeline," " The Pied Piper of Hamlin," and others. The term *pageant* is still rather loosely applied to large spectacular dramatics.

Types of pageants. — Three types of pageants may be mentioned. The first, a parade rather than a pageant, is made up of decorated and illustrative floats, companies, characters. Usually no attempt at unity is made. A typical parade on " Home-Coming " day in a Middle Western town is an example of this type. In a strict sense it is not a pageant. The second type is the indoor pageant. This may be either a continued story with a movement running entirely through it, or it may be a series of scenes held together by a thread of unity. Such a production is narrowed by the limitations of space, size of cast, and equipment. The third type, the usual outdoor production, often on a large scale, is what is usually known as the pageant. Provision for a fine natural setting and the number and variety of opportunities for participation make it the most attractive of the three types.

Presentation of the pageant. — Staging a pageant involves about the same general kind of work as staging a play. Of course the production is much larger in general scope and size of cast, and consequently takes a great deal more work. The pageant includes singing, dancing, and many mass movements as well as speaking. The choosing of suitable settings and costuming are also large problems which must be solved.

The general organization for production may be much the same as mentioned above for dramatics. A " pageant master " becomes a coach. He has his assistants, and the details of the work may be handled through many committees or individuals charged with certain very definite duties. Finances, publicity, cast, properties, costuming, and the many other matters may be attended to in the ways suggested for dramatics.

Source of pageant material. — The pageant itself may be bought or it may be written. Writing the pageant will give many an interesting motive to the students in the school. The English, Civics, History, Home Economics, Manual Training, Business, Music, and other departments must coöperate to make it a success. Writing the pageant means a great deal of work, but it has an added interest in that school people actually wrote as well as produced it. Moreover, it can be closely fitted to the local situation, people, events, and history. It requires that much time be spent in research as well as in writing and staging, but this offers many educational opportunities to students and teachers. The coöperation required of the various departments makes for unity and morale in the school.

The material of which pageants are made comes from four main sources. The first is history; outstanding events or personages may be made the central theme of the story. Nearly all pageants have some historical material in them. The second source of material is to be found in forms, rituals, and ceremonials. Past social practices with their ornamental, suggestive, symbolic costuming are rich fields for the pageant-maker. Folk lore, stories, dances, and songs also furnish good material. Imaginative, mythological characters, fairies, monsters, and supernatural exhibitions form the third great group of pageant material. The fourth source is to be found in the life and spirit of the community itself. Progress, the civic virtues, and developments are usually illustrated by means of definite local situations, events, or personages.

The following topics are suggested as typical of those which may be and have been used by schools:

> History of the community
> Evolution of the newspaper
> Christmas Day in 1805 (Oregon)
> Development of our school
> Ideals of our school
> The rise of woman
> Thanksgiving in 1620
> Evolution of Athletics, Dramatics, Music
> Progress in education
> Historical scenes, national, state or local
> Our first school

Origin of our national holidays
The celebration of special events and days
Plays of pioneers
Pageant of freedom
Pageants of literature
Victory and Peace
Makers of America
The four seasons
The Children's Crusade
Pageant of citizenship

OTHER FORMS OF DRAMATICS

It was suggested at the beginning of the chapter that, judging by the nature of the dramatic productions of many schools, the box office is frequently considered more important than the student. Of course, all dramatic productions have some educational merit, but some have much more than others. Because of the present lack of financial support of the extracurricular program by boards of education, however, some forms of dramatics must be used to support the various activities of the school. Dramatic productions of the lighter type, which probably have little educative value but which are good money makers, are the circus, carnival, fair, and bazaar. Each one of these activities takes its name from the real activity which it imitates. The puppet show and pantomime are other types of dramatics which are widely used in the schools. These two probably have more educational value than the four previously mentioned.

Circus. — Junior high schools especially have welcomed the circus and fair, and many of them hold one or both of these annually. The circus program is made up of numbers contributed by the various home rooms. If the school is large, the numbers must be kept within strict time limits in order to give all rooms opportunity. Even then the show may become tiresome because of its length and, frequently, its lack of variety.

Direction. — The director is the chairman of the main committee which plans the circus. His main task is to assign the various parts of the circus to the other members of the committee, each of whom heads a sub-committee for the development of that particular phase of the production, and so to coördinate and articulate these several phases that a well-rounded comprehensive event will be the result. One committee, for instance, may be responsible for the construction of animals, wagons, cages, chariots, calliope, and other equipment. Another committee selects, develops, drills, and makes up the clowns. Other committees are in charge of side-shows, refreshment stands, music, costumes, parade, advertising, and financing. The circus itself is usually conducted by a ring-master who introduces the numbers.

Animals.[1] — Wild animals are an important part of any circus. Animals for the school circus are of two general types which might be designated as "skin" and "framework." In the former type, use is made of skins to represent lions, tigers, monkeys, and dogs. These costumes may be made or rented. The "framework" type is used in the representation of the larger animals such as elephants, horses, giraffes, and ostriches. Less common animals, or imaginary animals like the gook, hootus, parasang, snark, wampus, and woofus may also be represented. These animals are constructed of a light framework of wood and poultry netting, stuffed at proper places with excelsior or paper, and covered with burlap or muslin. Raveled rope is commonly used for tails. Movement of tail, head, mouth, ears, and eyes may be easily produced by simple mechanisms. These frames must be light because they will be carried. Both types of animals can be "trained" for stunts and exhibitions.

Circus Activities. — The activities of the real circus are imi-

---

[1] *How to Put on an Amateur Circus*, by Hacker and Eames, contains complete directions for financing, developing, and staging this event, and constructing the animals and equipment.

tated by the school circus in such items as trained animals, clowns, rope walkers, performers, chariot races, Indians, music, side-shows, refreshment stands, and hawkers.   A parade usually precedes the show, and it can include circus exhibitions, band, clowns, animals, calliope, chariots, wagons, and banners.

In addition to these, more substantial numbers may be developed by the department of physical education.   If the circus is held in the gymnasium good use can be made of the flying rings, horizontal bar, buck, horse, rope, and ladder.   The mats may be used for wrestling, boxing, pyramid building, acrobatics, tumbling, and spring-board work.   If a swimming pool is available it too can be utilized not only for exhibition purposes in swimming, diving, demonstration of life-saving methods, water polo, and other games, but for freak races and stunts.

There is probably not a great deal of educational value in the average school circus.   Education, however, is not its main purpose.   The main purposes are to raise money and to offer amusement.   Not more than one of these events a year can be justified.   Probably a better plan than the circus is a program of exhibitions — gymnasium and swimming pool activities, music, and dramatics of a more dignified type, with a few comic numbers.   This program will undoubtedly be less profitable financially, but it will be more profitable educationally.

The fair. — The fair imitates the typical county fair with its exhibits, side shows, lunch and drink stands, amusements, and barkers.   The booths and stands are scattered around in the gymnasium, auditorium, and halls.   The home rooms are usually responsible for the various amusements and stands.   Prices charged are small.   Such activities have educative merit, but they lower the dignity of the school temporarily.   Consequently, they should be held at the end of school on Friday so that the general lowering of morale will not affect school work when the school opens again.   It is probably not good practice, however, to hold these affairs just before an important holiday or vacation. The bazaar and carnival are somewhat similar in organization and activities.

Puppet show. — Another form of dramatics especially interesting to younger folks is the puppet show. It has long been a favorite amusement in certain European countries where traveling companies carry it to the people. The companies are made up of men and women who spend their lives making dolls and settings, perfecting mechanism, and practicing the shows. Much work along this line can be done now in America in the elementary school. The students make the marionettes, compose the lines, and operate the stage, the show, settings, and puppets on the day of the exhibition. Such shows must be given to limited groups because of the small size of the stage and its settings. They are now used with the elementary students to emphasize the teaching of certain virtues or to present stories which the students have read or know.

Pantomime. — Pantomimes are being used more and more in school dramatic work. They are easily arranged, require little rehearsing, and are interesting because they are novel. The use on the stage of a frame modeled after a motion picture screen will help to give the impression of a " live " motion picture. The dramatic club could well afford to spend time on the study and staging of a few pantomimes.

SUMMARY

Dramatics is one of the oldest forms of teaching. The main values of dramatics are in the discipline of the actor, the benefits to the school from coöperation by the various departments, and the stimulating in the community of a desire for a higher quality of dramatics. A central club which makes a serious study of dramatics is a good general organization to take charge of a dramatic production. This organization through its committees can attend to all the requirements for staging a production.

Plays should be chosen with care, and with a proper consideration of available material and the end desired. Pageants built around local events are educative and valuable. Other types of dramatics which the school may make use of are the circus, fair, puppet show, and pantomime.

REFERENCES

PLAYS

General

ABBOTT, A. "Producing the Festival," *Teachers College Record* 17 : 156–166, March, 1916.

—— "The Shakespearian Exhibit," *Teachers College Record* 17 : 184–195, March, 1916.

BALCH, E. *Amateur Circus.* The Macmillan Company.

BARNES, W. "Dramatization of Literature; its Use and Abuse," *Journal of Education* 91 : 59–62, January 15, 1920.

BULLOWA, A. M. "Pantomime: its Uses in the High School," *Quarterly Journal of Speech Education* 7 : 213–220, June, 1921.

BURCHENAL, E. *Folk Dances and Singing Games.* G. Schirmer.

CHAPLIN, A. W. *Six Rehearsal-less Entertainments.* Walter H. Baker Company.

CLARK, B. H. *How to Produce Amateur Plays.* Little, Brown and Company.

CRAFTON, A., and ROYER, J. *The Process of Play Production.* F. S. Crofts and Company.

DOREY, J. N. "Dramatization of High School Classics," *English Journal* 1 : 476–481, October, 1912.

FERRIS, H. *Producing Amateur Plays.* E. P. Dutton and Company.

FINLAY-JOHNSON, H. *The Dramatic Method of Teaching.* Ginn and Company.

HACKER and EAMES. *How to Put on an Amateur Circus.* Denison and Company.

HEDGES, M. H. "Group Playwriting," *English Journal* 8 : 39–41, January, 1919.

JOHNSON, G. *Choosing a Play.* H. W. Wilson Company.

KIES, P. P. "Teaching Opera Librettos," *English Journal* 9 : 71–79, February, 1920.

LATHAM, A. J. "The Making of a Festival," *Teachers College Record* 16 : 44–60, May, 1915.

MILLER, E. E. *The Dramatization of Bible Stories: An Experiment in the Religious Education of Children.* University of Chicago Press.

PEREGO, I. M. "The Little Theatre in the School, Dramatizations of Popular Tales," *English Journal* 7 : 438–446, September, 1918.

RENSHAW, A. T. "Modern Attention to Pantomime Expression," *Quarterly Journal of Speech Education* 7 : 43–52, February, 1921.

SIMONS, S. E and ORR, C. I. *Dramatization.* Scott, Foresman and Company.

STORM, I. R. "The Eighth Grade Play," *English Journal* 7 : 251–255, April, 1918.

WHITMIRE, L. G. "The Class Play," *Quarterly Journal of Speech Education* 7 : 139–149, April, 1921.

WRIGHT, H. S. *New Plays from Old Tales.* The Macmillan Company.

Theory, Practice and Mechanics

BROWNE, V. D. *Secrets in Scene Painting and Stage Effects.* Routledge and Sons.

CHUBB, P. *Festivals and Plays.* Harper and Brothers.

CLARK, B. H. *How to Produce Amateur Plays.* Little, Brown and Company.

GRIMBALL, E. B. and WELLS, R. *Costuming a Play.* The Century Co.

HERTS, A. M. *The Children's Educational Theatre.* Harper and Brothers.

HILLIARD, E. *Amateur and Educational Dramatics.* The Macmillan Company.

MACKAY, C. D. *Costumes and Scenery for Amateurs.* Henry Holt and Company.

MCCLELLAND, E. *Historic Dress in America.* Jacobs and Company.

PASSPON, E. R. and BECKER, B. *Ritual and Dramatized Folkways.* The Century Co.

SARG, T. *The Tony Sarg Marionette Book.* B. W. Huebsch Inc.

TAYLOR, E. G. *Practical Stage Directing for Amateurs.* E. P. Dutton and Company.

YOUNG, J. *Make-Up.* Whitmark Company.

Sources for Lists of Plays

MOSES, M. J. *Treasury of Plays for Children.* Little, Brown and Company.

American Play Company, Inc., 29 West 47th St., New York City.

Baker and Company, 5 Hamilton Place, Boston, Mass.

Bureau of Educational Dramatics, Community Service, 315 Fourth Ave., New York City.

Drama League of America, 736 Marquette Building, Chicago, Ill. *List of Plays for High School and College Production*, Drama League of America. 25 cents.

—— *Selective Lists of Plays for Amateurs*, Drama League of America, Boston Center.

Drama League Book Store, 7 East 42nd Street, New York City.

Dramatic Index, F. W. Faxon, Boston, Massachusetts.

Dramatic League Book Store, 330 Riggs Building, Washington, D. C.

French, S. 28–30 West 38th Street, New York City.

Rumsey Play Company, West 46th Street, New York City.

Sanger and Jordan, 1428 Broadway, New York City.

Charles Scribner's Sons, New York City.

Stage Guild, 1527 Revenue Exchange Building, Chicago, Ill.

Y. W. C. A., 600 Lexington Avenue, New York City.

PAGEANTS

General

ABBOTT, A. "Producing the Festival," *Teachers College Record* 17 : 156–166, March, 1916.

American Pageant Association *Bulletins*, Mary Porter Beegle, Secretary, Barnard College, New York City.

CLARK, L. A. "Pageantry in America," *English Journal* 3 : 146–153, March, 1924.

CRAWFORD, J. R. "Pageant Technique," *Quarterly Journal of Speech Education* 6 : 76–78, February, 1920.

"How to Conduct a School Carnival," *Scholastic Editor*, September, 1924.

MORLEY, E. E. "The High School Carnival; A Coöperative Enterprise," *School Review*, 34 : 281–285, April, 1926.

Russell Sage Foundation, Child Hygiene Department, *Pageants*, Pamphlet 114.

"What the Pageant Does for the Local History," *Review of Reviews*, September, 1923.

WISE, G. M. *Dramatics for School and Community*. Stewart Kidd Company.

Books on Pageantry

BATES, E. W. and WILLIAMS, O.   *Pageants and Pageant Making.*   Ginn and Company.

BEEGLE, and CRAWFORD.   *Community Drama and Pageantry.*   Yale University Press.

—— *Pageants and Pageantry.*   Ginn and Company.

CHUBB, P.   *Festivals and Plays.*   Harper and Brothers.

HATCHER, O. L.   *Book for Shakespeare's Plays and Pageants.*   E. P. Dutton and Company.

MACKAYE, P.   *Community Drama.*   Houghton Mifflin Company.

NEEDHAM, M. M.   *Folk Festivals, Their Growth, and How to Give Them.*   B. W. Huebsch.

RUSSELL, M. M.   *How to Produce Plays and Pageants.*   George H. Doran Company.

TAFT, L.   *The Technique of Pageantry.*   Barnes and Company.

Publishing Houses

Walter H. Baker and Company, 41 Winter Street, Boston, Mass.
David C. Cook, Elgin, Illinois.
Dramatic Publishing Company, Dearborn Street, Chicago, Ill.
Samuel French, 28 West 38th Street, New York City.

CHAPTER VIII

MUSICAL ORGANIZATIONS AND ACTIVITIES

Every one likes music. However tastes may differ as to the kind preferred music in general has a universal appeal. Every one throughout his lifetime will hear a great deal of music. Consequently, it is clear that the school has an obligation in helping to form musical tastes.

VALUES OF SCHOOL MUSIC

It discovers and develops talent. — School music helps to discover and develop the talent which many students have, but which for lack of encouragement or opportunity for its expression never develops. One student sings, another plays the piano, still another may be interested not only in production but also in the appreciation or history of music. All have a right to their interests and all deserve opportunities to cultivate them. These opportunities may be provided through musical classes, organizations, or programs.

It has important cultural influences. — The second main value of school music is in its cultural and broadening influence on young people. The student already enjoys music of some sort, and to teach him to enjoy and understand the better music is a purpose well worth serving.

PROGRESS IN SCHOOL MUSIC

School music was formerly looked upon as an extracurricular activity. If the student desired to take music lessons, he was penalized by the school; that is, he had to spend his own time for practice, in addition to carrying a full load of school subjects.

Consequently, he slighted his music. It is probably reasonable to expect the student to get as much value from a course in music as from any other course in the school. Although expense has hitherto kept many schools from adopting music, they are now recognizing it more and more.

In many communities now, the school gives credit towards graduation for the music taken outside. The school authorities with the help of a committee of professional musicians and teachers draw up regulations and requirements for the music courses. The school then gives credit towards graduation on the completion of these courses. Sometimes the school music teachers examine the students when they have completed this course with the professional musician, and sometimes the word of the latter is accepted. In any case the reputation both of the school and of the teacher is carefully safeguarded. Occasionally some little disturbance is caused by a dissatisfied teacher who is not placed on the accredited list. But even this may be salutary; for it shows the townspeople that the work is of high grade, as only the best music teachers are accredited.

The tendency now, however, is for the school to employ full-time music teachers and supervisors. Formerly, such a teacher would teach a few classes in musical history or appreciation, and direct the band, orchestra, and other musical clubs. To this work is now added lessons in vocal and instrumental music. Many schools buy instruments, especially the larger and more cumbersome, for the students. The expenditure of such money can be justified on the ground used to justify any other expenditure for school equipment.

ORGANIZATION

Music clubs, whether curricular or extracurricular in control, should have some definite organization. For instance, a girls' chorus may sing just as well as a class; but if it is organized as a club, having officers and committees, it acquires dignity, morale, and interest. Moreover, it then adds to its strictly musical activities those of a lighter nature — parties, socials, attendance at musical programs, etc. — and thus increases the number of educational opportunities offered.

Organizing for the production of music. — The more usual organization of this kind is the band, chorus, or orchestra. As its activities are nearer the regular curricular type, credit for its work is usually given towards graduation. Consequently, it must require formal, systematic work and increase in proficiency. It provides music for the school affairs — plays, pageants, programs, and athletics. It should be organized with the necessary officers and committees. A librarian to care for the music and a student director to direct in public performances are special types of officers for which provision should be made.

Problems. — A number of problems always arise in connection with musical production. For instance, in the band or orchestra there may be undesirable instrumentation. More saxophones may be available than are needed. The student's interest must be preserved and his ability used even if not in the usual way. One way to get around this is to organize a saxophone choir. Such a choir was recently organized at Johnstown, Pennsylvania, and proved to be a big success. Usually there is a dearth of altos, baritones, and bass instruments in the band. Students can be encouraged to play these especially if the school furnishes them.

Mandolin, harmonica, banjo, ukelele, saxophone or other choirs, clubs, or orchestras should be encouraged and developed if a few students are interested enough to want them and willing to help to develop them. In other words, musical ability of any kind should not be neglected. The interest or motive of the student who plays the violin, or piano, may perhaps in itself be no more legitimate than that of the student who plays the saxophone or harmonica. Each has his own interest and, within reason, each deserves recognition and respect, and an opportunity to grow.

Frequently stories of the harm done to lips or face by some of the wind instruments circulate in the community, and prevent girls from learning to play them. As they are not borne out by the facts, an assembly talk and program would be of value in combating them.

Another problem which frequently arises is the kind of music to be used. Some directors want classical music only; some want the more popular; and occasionally one will be found who wants jazz. There is perhaps a place for all. A program of all heavy numbers or all light numbers would be monotonous to the average student or patron. On the other hand, it must be remembered that musical organizations to a large extent set the standards of music appreciation for the school, and frequently for its patrons. Consequently care must be exercised. " The students like it " will not justify inferior music. In some schools a " Jazz Orchestra " is organized to take care of the demand for this sort of music as well as to play for school parties, dances, and receptions.

Musical organizations in a Junior High School. — The following quotation from the report (1924) of Mr. L. V. E. Irvine of the New Castle, Pennsylvania schools shows how music is being developed in one junior high school. The school in question is new; consequently, the present schedule does not indicate all that will be done in a year or two.

BENJAMIN FRANKLIN JUNIOR HIGH SCHOOL

New Castle, Pennsylvania

School enrolment, 1656
Three full-time music teachers
The seventh, eighth, and ninth grades each have a chorus under the direc-

tion of the full-time music teacher who does voice work only.   These special choruses meet once or twice weekly.

There are three beginners' violin classes, twelve students in each class, meeting once a week for a period of fifty-five minutes.

There is a beginners' orchestra for the slightly advanced students meeting once daily for a thirty minute period.   Enrolment, 19.

Orchestra A is composed of thirty-nine pieces.   Before being admitted to this organization, a student must be far enough advanced to play at sight very simple orchestra parts.   Rehearsals are held daily from 8 : 45 to 9 : 40 A.M.   This orchestra plays regularly for the school assemblies and is called upon to furnish special numbers for practically every social program.

The Franklin school also has a band of thirty pieces.   It is frequently called upon for special numbers for the chapel programs, but it regularly furnishes music for the school's athletic events.   A near-by college sometimes engages the band for its intercollegiate contests.   Rehearsals are held in the auditorium, which is equipped with a large orchestra pit.

School music festival. — As an example of student production on a large scale the two following programs are presented.   They were given during " Music Week " (in May, 1925) as the " City Schools Music Festival " by students of the Pittsburgh Public Schools under the direction of Will Earhart.   The hall selected was the largest auditorium in the city and thousands of students, parents, and patrons attended them.

Thursday Program

The Thursday afternoon program will be given by the combined Junior High Chorus, combined Senior High Chorus, and the combined High School Orchestra, assisted by soloists.

Following is the Thursday program : —

"L'Arlesienne," Suite No. 1 . . . . Bizet
Prelude. Minuetto. Adaietto . . . . Carillon

Orchestra

"Ave Maria" . . . . Bach-Gounod
"Under Yonder Oaken Tree" . . . . Welsh Folksong
"Song of the Volga Boatmen" . . . . Russian Folksong
"Pilgrims Chorus " from *Tannhäuser* . . . . Wagner

Junior High School Boys' Chorus

"The Dragon Flies" . . . . Rimsky-Korsakof
The semi-chorus is composed of six students from each of the
Junior High Schools

"Solveijg's Cradle Song" . . . . Grieg
Soprano solo by the instructor in music

"The Omnipotence" . . . . Schubert

Junior High School Treble Voice Chorus

"Jutlandish Dance Song" . . . . Danish Folksong
"Holiday Bells" . . . . Mendelssohn

Students of the First, Second, Third, and Fourth Grades

Cantata, "The Village Blacksmith" . . . . Richard Kountz

Students of the Fifth, Sixth, Seventh, and Eighth Grades
and Orchestra

"Hymns of Praise" . . . . Mendelssohn
Soloists, Senior High School Chorus and Orchestra

FRIDAY PROGRAM

Friday afternoon the program will be given by the choruses of students
from the elementary grades and the combined high school orchestra, with
piano accompaniment.

Overture, "Ruy Blas" . . . . Mendelssohn

Orchestra

"The Songs I Know" . . . . Grace Everson
"The Bell" . . . . Jean Loughridge
"Who Has Seen the Wind" . . . . Alys Bentley
"The Evening Star" . . . . Schumann
"Dancing" . . . . Folksong

Students of the First and Second Grades

"Music of the Chimes" . . . . Old French Air
"The Pine Tree" . . . . C. F. Manney
"Signs of Spring" . . . . Henry P. Gilbert
"Flowers, Birds and Babies Sleep" . . . . Taubert
"The Piper" . . . . Bohemian Folksong
"Morning Song" . . . . English Folksong

Students of the Third and Fourth Grades

"Sunrise" . . . . Beethoven
"My Prayer" . . . . Mozart
"The Flower Garden" . . . . Russian Folk Tune
"Lullaby and Good Night" . . . . Brahms

Musical contests. — Many state universities now hold annually an " Interscholastic Meet " or " Rally " in which contests are held in athletics, debating and declamations, curricular subjects, exhibits, and music. In order to suggest the general plan of music contest together with the selections used, the contests held by the University of Oklahoma are described below. Descriptions are taken from the bulletin published by the university.

University of Oklahoma

GENERAL RULES GOVERNING MUSIC CONTESTS

Eligibility: Entrants in these contests must be regularly enrolled undergraduate students in a high school in the state of Oklahoma and must be pursuing successfully three standard high school subjects. No person more than twenty-one years of age at the time of the contest may compete. A first prize winner of a former Interscholastic Meet is not eligible to compete again in the same contest. A second or third prize winner of a previous year may compete again, but in the event of receiving first prize will be given only enough free tuition to complete one full year's scholarship. Not more than four students from the same school may enter the same contest. In contests of musical organizations each school is of course limited to one entry. Contestants who have been enrolled in the University of Oklahoma as special music students are not eligible to enter these contests.

Entry: Application to enter these contests must be made on or before Saturday, April 30, on the official entry blank, copies of which will be sent to the school authorities or will be furnished upon application to the Interscholastic Meet Committee.

Nature of Contests: In all contests except band and orchestra, there is specified a selection to be performed. In addition, each contestant performs also a selection of his own choice. All selections in this contest (except band and orchestra) must be performed from memory. (This shall not be construed to apply to accompanist or conductor.)

Preliminaries: There are no county or district elimination preliminaries for these contests. Each high school may hold a local elimination contest in case there are more than four students desirous of entering the same contest. During the interscholastic meet, if the number of entrants in a contest necessitates it, elimination preliminaries in several groups are held, and the winners from each group then participate in the final contest. Music contests in which this has become necessary are piano, voice, boys' and girls' glee club.

Judging: Contestants shall be designated and graded only by number, and their order of appearance in the contest shall be determined by lot. There shall be three judges in each contest. In contests of individuals, only one of these judges shall be connected with the University of Oklahoma. In contests of musical organizations, all three judges shall be members of the Fine Arts Faculty of the University of Oklahoma.

Prizes: See under "Prizes and Award" earlier in this bulletin.

PIANO, VIOLIN, 'CELLO, AND VOICE CONTESTS

In addition to the general rules stated above note the following:

The time required for the performance of the contestant's own selection must not exceed four minutes.

There are two divisions in the voice contests: (1) girls' voice (soprano and alto) and (2) boys' voice (tenor, baritone, and bass). Separate prizes are awarded in each division.

The points of judging in the piano contest are: tone, technique, clearness with reference to finger work and pedaling, phrasing, interpretation, and stage presence; in the voice contest, tone pitch, technique including enunciation, phrasing, interpretation, and stage presence.

Contest selections for 1921:

Piano: "Alla Tarantella" Op. 39, no. 2, by McDowell. Thirty-five cents postpaid, Arthur P. Schmidt Co., Boston, Mass.

Violin: "Serenade" by Pierne. Thirty-six cents, postpaid, Carl Fisher, 339 S. Wabash Ave., Chicago, Ill.

'Cello: "Sing Me to Sleep" for violincello, by Greene. Fifty-two cents, postpaid, Boston Music Co., Boston.

Soprano: "From an Old Garden" (Key of F) by Grant-Schaeffer. Thirty-five cents postpaid, Arthur P. Schmidt Co., Boston.

Alto: "To an Old Love" (Key of F) by John Prindle Scott. Forty-two cents, postpaid, G. Schirmer, New York.

Tenor: "Thy Heart's A Rose" (Key of B flat) by Claude Warford. Thirty-five cents postpaid. Arthur P. Schmidt Co., Boston.

Bass or *Baritone:* "When All the World Is Young" (Key of E flat) by James Rogers. Twenty-seven cents postpaid, White-Smith Music Publishing Co., Boston.

These contests will be held on Friday morning, May 6th. The piano contest begins at 8:30 in the auditorium of the Fine Arts Building and is divided into preliminary contests, the final being held at 10:30. That in violin and 'cello will be held in Recital Hall on the third floor of the Administration Building at 10:00. Contestants in boys' voice will report at 8:30 to room 105, Fine Arts Building, for preliminaries, and those in girls' voice to room 305, Teachers' Building, at the same hour. The finals in both voice contests will be held at 10:30 in room 305, Teachers' Building.

QUARTET AND GLEE CLUB CONTESTS

In addition to the general rules stated above, note the following:

The points of judging in these contests are: pitch, attack, balance, technical proficiency, interpretation, and stage appearance.

The organization's own selection must not exceed five minutes in length and may be sung with or without accompaniment as desired.

Glee clubs must not have less than 10 singers or more than 24.

Contest selections for 1921:

Girls' quartet: "They Met on the Twig of a Chestnut Tree" (No. 12, 214) by Robinson. Eight cents a copy, not including postage. Oliver Ditson Co., Boston. To be sung without accompaniment.

Boys' quartet: "When the Snowflakes Flutter Low" (No. 216 Stanhope edition) by Geibel. Seven cents a copy postpaid. White-Smith Music Publishing Co., Boston. To be sung without accompaniment, omitting the third stanza.

Girls' Glee Club: "The Night Has a Thousand Eyes" (No. 5250) by Belle Boltwood. Ten cents a copy not including postage. G. Schirmer, New York,

Boys' Glee Club: "Serenade" (No. 1087) by Haydn-Schultz. Six cents a copy not including postage. G. Schirmer, New York. To be sung without accompaniment.

These contests will be held on Friday afternoon, May 6th. Boys' and Girls' Quartets will be held in Recital Hall, third floor of the Administration Building, at 2:30. Directors or representatives of boys' and girls' glee clubs will meet in Dean Holmberg's Office, room 103, Fine Arts Building at 11 : 00 A.M. for drawing and assignment to rooms for preliminaries. The preliminaries will begin in the rooms assigned, at one o'clock for the boys' glee clubs and at 2 : 00 o'clock for the girls' glee clubs. The finals in the boys' glee club contest will be held in room 305, Teachers' Building, at 4 : 00 P.M., and at the same hour the finals in the girls' glee club contest will be held in the Auditorium of the Fine Arts Building.

BAND AND ORCHESTRA CONTESTS

In addition to the general rules stated above, note the following :

A band must have at least two cornets, two altos, one baritone, two trombones, one tuba, and two drums (ten pieces). It should have clarinets, but the minimum stated will pass.

An orchestra must have at least six pieces or players, and must have of course one or more violins in its instrumentation.

Bands or orchestras may have one fourth their total membership from the grade schools.

The orchestra contest will be divided into two classes as follows : Class A, orchestras with a personnel of eighteen or more; Class B, orchestras with a personnel of less than eighteen. Prizes will be awarded to the winning orchestras in each class.

These contests will be held Friday afternoon, May 6th. The band contest will be heard in the Auditorium of the Fine Arts Building, at 2 : 30. The orchestra contests will begin at 1 : 00 o'clock, Class A being held in the Auditorium of the Fine Arts Building, and Class B in Recital Hall, Administration Building.

Beginning with students in the grade school and definitely working with them towards the high school will help to solve many of the perplexing problems which face the director or supervisor. This book is not a discussion of the technical matters of try-outs, orchestration, and seating. These are matters for professional books. All that is suggested here is that the organizations be made educative for their participants, and that opportunities in addition to those of a purely musical nature be included.

Organizing for the enjoyment of music. — The second general type of music club organization is that which has as its main purpose the appreciation of music. It is a club of consumers rather than of producers. It must have producers in its membership, but its main purpose is general appreciation. It should be open to all students who have an interest in music. Its programs should be varied and should aim at a better understanding and appreciation and knowledge of music.

Activities. — Some of the activities of a general music club are the following:

Use of the Victrola for purposes of appreciation, illustration, and demonstration.

Study of harmony, composition, melody, rhythm

Study of the lives of great composers

Solos, duets, quartettes by the members

Group singing

Staging contests, harmonica, jewsharp, "uke"

Organization of choruses, sub-orchestras and clubs

Visiting and reporting on recitals

Promoting music-memory contests

Listening to radio programs

Producing program for general assembly

Staging of operetta, musical comedy

Discussion of:

   History of music

   Music of various countries

      Egypt

      Greece

      Rome

      India and the American Indian

      Mexico

   Evolution of various musical instruments

   Instruments of the various peoples, bagpipe, castenets, tom-tom

   Stories of the operas

   Development of church music. Hebrew poets and prophets

      Music of the Bible, instruments, songs

      Early congregational singing

      Ambrose and his scales

      Gregorian scales

Neume notation

Origin of staff and clefs

Forms of church music, mass, chorale, passion, anthems, hymns, recitative with illustrations

Types of mediæval secular musicians, troubadours, trouvères, minne-singers, meistersingers

Types of instruments, percussion, wind, and string

Contribution of the freaks, kazoos, jewsharps

My favorite song or piece and why

History of the organ, piano, violin

Classical *vs.* jazz music

Music criticism

Music memory contest. — One of the most interesting of the recent developments in public education is the music memory contest. In 1916 Mr. C. M. Tremaine, director of the National Bureau for the Advancement of Music, began the promotion of " Music Memory " contests. Community-Service and other organizations joined in this promotion and as a result several hundred contests are held each year by cities, counties, and states. Prizes are usually offered to excite competition. Bulletins, books, and material are now available for these contests.[1]

The selections used may be suggested by the following table. Professor T. H. Briggs [2] made a tabulation of the numbers used in nine city and thirteen state wide contests. Miss Edna McEachern made a tabulation of the selections used in one hundred miscellaneous contests. The thirteen compositions most frequently appearing in Mr. Briggs' list are shown in the table. The percentages at the right refer to their appearance in the tabulation of Miss McEachern.

[1] Write to the National Bureau for the Advancement of Music, 105 W. 40th Street, New York City. Community Service, 315 4th Avenue, New York City. The various phonograph companies have bulletins available, as have also several of the states.

[2] "Music Memory Contests" (*Teachers College Record*, November, 1924).

Interesting stories about composers or about compositions help to educate the student in the appreciation of music. The following list of selections, taken from the " Clairtonian News " of the Clairton, Pennsylvania, High School, shows a typical list from which contest material is drawn. Note the requirements concerning knowledge of nationality of composer and spelling of his name.

Music Memory Contest List

Below are given the numbers on which the contest is based. Contestants will be required to give the name of the composition, the name of composer and his nationality, with correct spelling.

1. "Amaryllis" . . . . Composer Unknown
2. "Ave Maria" . . . . Bach-Gounod, German and French
3. "Angels' Serenade" . . . . Braga
4. "Anitra's Dance" from *Peer Gynt Suite* . . . . Grieg, Norwegian
5. "Believe Me If All Those Endearing Young Charms" . Old Irish Air
6. "Come Where My Love Lies Dreaming" . . . Foster, American
7. "Lullaby" . . . . Brahms, German
8. "Danny Deever" . . . . Damrosch, German-American
9. "Drink To Me Only With Thine Eyes" . . . . Folk Song, English
10. "El Capitan March" . . . . Sousa, American
11. "Evening Star" from *Tannhäuser* . . . . . . Wagner, German

12. "The Rosary" . . . . Nevin, American
13. "The Land of the Sky-Blue Water" . . . . Cadman, American
14. "By the Waters of Minnetonka" . . . . . Lieurance, American
15. "Good-Bye" . . . . Tosti, Italian
16. "Intermezzo" from *Cavalleria Rusticana* . . . . Mascagni, Italian
17. "Spring Song" . . . . Mendelssohn, German
18. "Invitation to the Dance" . . . . Weber, German
19. "Largo" from the *New World Symphony* . . . . Dvořák, Bohemian
20. "Swing Low, Sweet Chariot" . . . . . American Negro Spiritual
21. "Celeste Aida" from *Aida* . . . . Verdi, Italian
22. "O Sole Mio" . . . . di Capua, Italian
23. "Air for the G String" . . . . Bach, German
24. Sextette from *Lucia* . . . . Donizetti, Italian
25. "Two Grenadiers" . . . . Schumann, German
26. "Moment Musical" . . . . Schubert, Austrian
27. "Pilgrims Chorus" from *Tannhäuser* . . . . . Wagner, German
28. "To a Wild Rose" . . . . MacDowell, American
29. "Träumerei" . . . . Schumann, German
30. "Nocturne" from *Midsummer Night's Dream* Mendelssohn, German
31. "Caprice Viennois" . . . . Kreisler, Austrian
32. "Melody in F" . . . . Rubenstein, Russian
33. "Humoresque" . . . . Dvořák, Bohemian
34. Intermezzo from *Jewels of the Madonna* Wolf-Ferrari, German-Italian
35. *Unfinished Symphony* (First Movement) . . . . Schubert, Austrian

Standards must be set if there is to be discrimination, and the students must be taught to recognize those standards. The music contests will help to fix these standards, and to acquaint the student with some of the finer things in music. He will hear many of these compositions often during his lifetime and will appreciate them the more because of his familiarity with them. These contests should also do much toward making classical music popular. Too often good music is looked upon as dry and uninteresting though fashionable. The question is often suggested as to whether or not cultured people really enjoy classical music. The music contest is an important instrument of education.

Summary

Music is an important part of education and the school should assume responsibility for it. The school should try to discover and develop student talent. It should also teach an understanding and appreciation of music both to the student who is a producer of music and the one who is not. A general music club will be found to serve these ends. The music contest among students who have music ability is a good device for the motivation of music education. The music memory contest is another activity which is rapidly increasing in popularity.

References

BRIGGS, T. H. "Music Memory Contest," *Teachers College Record* 26 : 184–196, November, 1924.

CUNDIFF, H. M. and DYKEMA, P. W. *School Music Handbook*, Birchard and Company.

ELSON, A. *A Book of Musical Knowledge*, Houghton Mifflin Company.

—— *Musical Programs from all Nations*, Houghton Mifflin Company.

TREMAINE, C. M. "Music Memory Contests," *Journal of the National Education Association*, Vol. XV. no. 2, 43–44, February, 1926.

National Bureau for the Advancement of Music, 105 West 40th St., New York City.

Material from
　Victor Talking Machine Company
　Columbia Graphaphone Company.

Community Service, 315 Fourth Ave., New York City
　Community Songs Leaflet
　Christmas Carol Song Sheet
　Easter Carol Song Sheet
　Four Bulletins on Music Week
　Bulletin # 765 — A Christmas Carnival
　Bulletin # 526b — A Festival of Freedom (revised)
　A Stephen C. Foster Program
　C. S. *# 74 — Working out Music Memory Contest*
　C. S. *# 74c — Following up Music Memory Contest*
　Complete Music Memory Selections, List # 1

Second Year's Music Memory Selections, List # 2
C. S. # 110 — *Stories of the Christmas Carols*
C. S. # 117 — *Giving Opera with the Phonograph*
C. S. # 121 — *Stories of the Easter Carols*
C. S. # 132a — *The History of Church Music*
C. S. # 168a — *Music Composed by Negroes*
Harmonica Tournament
Ukelele Supplement, and others.

CHAPTER IX

LITERARY SOCIETIES, DEBATING AND SPEAKING

LITERARY SOCIETIES

One of the oldest activities in the school is the literary society. In one form or another it has persisted ever since the early literary contests of the Greek and Roman schools. Usually these contests were arranged as an exhibition for the patrons of the school. Even in America, similarly, we can all remember the old custom of Friday afternoon " Literary " when declamations, readings, orations, and a debate concluded the day. There has been a change from this type of society, but some form of literary club or organization is to be found in nearly all schools.

The literary club. — One type of general organization is the literary club, a society organized like any other club in the school. The student with literary or debating interests joins of his own volition. Usually no membership requirements are stated — any student may belong. Those who can speak and debate will probably join, but the student who cannot speak and who wants to learn should certainly not be barred. The usual club organization may be followed. The work of the club consists of regular weekly or bi-weekly student programs; and school credit may or may not be given for this work.

Divided school type of literary society. — Another type of organization is that in which the school is divided into two (or more) groups or societies. Each new student joins or is assigned to one of these organizations. He remains a member as long as he is in school. The purpose of this type of organization is to increase interest by competition. These societies have weekly, bi-weekly, or monthly meetings and the usual program of activities. The great event of the year, however, is the final contest between the societies.

This is a contest between the picked teams of the two organizations. The program consists usually of a debate, declamations, orations, and essays. Each side has selected its best material and the contest is usually enlivened by competition for a cup or other trophy. It is held in the school auditorium in the evening and the public is invited. Each society sits by itself on opposite sides of the hall. Each has its own decorations, colors, yells, songs, and stunts. Usually the parents also make an effort to sit near the sides to which their children belong, and perhaps to which they themselves belonged in earlier days. All contestants are seated on the platform with the chairman — the principal or some other disinterested individual.

Such a contest often generates an enormous amount of enthusiasm. Old graduates look upon it in much the same way as upon an important football game. Newspaper publicity, posters, signs, stunts, and even painted streets and walks advertise it. Such advertising may of course result in opposition from the citizens and business men of the town. Painting sidewalks and streets, chalking windows, and the like are not looked upon with favor by the average citizen.

Values of literary societies. — The old fashioned literary society grew out of an honor program, arranged to " show off " the students. The programs themselves consisted of pompous and formal speeches and debates in the heavy and ponderous oratory of earlier days. The purpose was evidently to impress the parents and patrons with the accomplishments of the school or system by this unusual and supposedly intellectual display. As the teachers began to think more clearly and to appreciate the potential value of the organization or program, it became more of an educational and less of an honoring agency. Teachers realized that preparation for and participation in such a program would be educative and consequently good for the student inapt in this as well as for him who needed no practice.

Oral English is important, for it is used constantly. Practice in it can be justified on the grounds that not only is it used more frequently, but also that it improves written expression, other things being equal, more than an equal amount of written work. The student is made to imagine that he is telling the story or describing the scene, and this makes it more personal and interesting. The main values of the literary society may then be summarized: it educates the student in oral expression, teaches him self-control and poise; it teaches him new means of expression and enlarges his vocabulary; it widens and increases his range of interest in the world about him, particularly the literary world.

Objections to literary society activities. — A consideration of the most common objections to the literary society together with suggestions for their removal will define the principles of literary society organization and administration.

Too few students participate. — The first objection to the literary society is that too few students share in its work. This is true in far too many instances. If the group is large the student cannot perform very frequently. Many of the schools having the " divided school " arrangement require each member to appear on the program at least once each half-year. This, of course, is better than if he did not appear at all. However, it is doubtful whether serving in only one or two programs during the year has a very great educational effect on the student. A smaller group or club (or several of them) in which the students take part frequently is preferable for educational reasons.

Competition arouses unsocial feelings in the school. — The objection also has been made to the " divided school " plan that it arouses too intense feeling in the school. Gloating by winners tends to increase the dejection and irritability of the losers, and very serious friction may result. This feeling may even extend to the faculty sponsors of the clubs. Such a contest may be an emotional debauch for the school and leave deleterious after effects which last for several weeks. If such is the case, the contest cannot be justified.

Literary programs are uninteresting. — If literary programs are uninteresting, they are so for at least two important reasons. The first is the kind of material presented in the programs. It has been suggested before that the material with which the student works should be that in which he is interested or in which he can be brought to take an interest. The listener is at least as important as the speaker.

The following general classification of material will suggest large topics of interest.

1. School life, people, events, subjects, and activities
2. Amusements, hobbies, pets, leisure occupations
3. Heroes or favorites in athletics, dramatics, literature, and business
4. Topics of general current interest or unusual appeal

A second reason why programs are uninteresting is that the speech itself is poorly organized and poorly given. The student must be taught to organize his topic and give it in a way that will arrest his hearers. He must appreciate the fact that he has an important obligation to this audience to give it something worth while. He would not go to see a football game for which neither team had practiced, nor has he any right to expect the audience to listen to him if he has come unprepared.

The cabinet of the literary club might well provide a series of talks in methods of organization and presentation, or at least emphasize their importance. The average student is afraid of appearing in public, and consequently this training course must not make him self-conscious or discourage him. He must be shown that it is not expected that he will do all that a great orator would do, that what is wanted from him is a simple, straightforward, interesting talk.

The old-time literary program consisted of more or less successful attempts at formal oratory. Their heavy, dignified, pompous orations would not be appropriate for student clubs to-day because the topics now used are not suited to such a stilted form of oratorical eloquence. The topics now are more prosaic and have to do more with the matter-of-fact world about us. Consequently the student in the handling of them will have factual content, not imaginative; and his speech must be suited to his material.

A third reason why the literary program is uninteresting is the attitude frequently taken towards appearing on it. Students often refuse to take part usually because a wrong emotional attitude has been built up towards such participation. Some sponsors or program committees make up a program and assign the various parts to the students without consulting them or considering their interests in the matter. When the program is posted and the names are noted, the student who escapes feels gay, and ridicules his friend whose name appears on it. The latter's dismay is increased by the jibes of his friends, and he begins to think of ways to avoid appearing. In other words, there is frequently built up an attitude on the part of the students that participation is a type of penalty, or at least that the individual is unlucky in being selected. Every student should be made to feel that it is a privilege to participate, and that the other students really want to hear what he has to say and are not there to ridicule, criticize, or make fun of him. Proper consideration of the student's interests, abilities, and preferences in the matter of program material would do much to eliminate this vicious attitude.

Activities. — The main activities of the literary societies have to do with student programs. The following kinds of material are suggested as usable.

Original stories, poems, essays, scenarios. — There are always good writers in any school. The literary club should encourage them. Usually students' stories are too long, and deal with subjects too large and cumbersome for them. Short stories on simple subjects and suitable themes, in which the student does not try to outdo the old masters, should help to make a program attractive.

Simple dramatizations. — Poetry, fiction, and scenarios may be drawn upon to good advantage in telling or illustrating a story. Dramatization of sections of classics may be made if these are not too long or difficult. Pantomime and shadowgraph add variety. A few properties always help to make a program interesting.

The feature story. — The feature story will be discussed in the chapters on publications. It is a most interesting species of literature and may well be used in the literary program. It may have to do with the unusual in the lives of well-known writers, or with persons about the school. The feature story should be short.

Debating. — The debate has always been an important form of literature and always will be. Debating is not very popular as a high school activity, but it can be made so if the topics chosen are those about which the student knows something, or can readily inform himself. The best topics for the literary society are such as concern the student, in and out of school.

Current events. — A brief review of the most important events of the week may enliven the program. The trouble with the usual current-events feature is that it attempts to present too much and in too small detail. A very few simple topics well managed are better than attempts at a more complete survey.

Book and dramatic reviews. — Reviews of new or widely discussed books, poems, and plays have their place in the work of the literary society. The society is organized for the purpose of increasing interest in and experience with literature, and consequently this method of acquainting the student with contemporary work must not be overlooked. The reviewer's purpose is to arouse the interest of the listener in the book or play reviewed so that he will want to read it.

Declamation and recitation. — The recitation of selections of poetry and also of prose varies a program agreeably. Attempts at high sounding oratory should be discouraged.

Music. — Music must not be neglected in the program — instrumental and vocal — for music is the most universally enjoyed of all the arts. Reports on the history of the opera or of selected songs may offer much welcome material.

Biographies. — The personal side of authors' lives makes good material for programs, especially of contemporaries. Their replies to the society to letters of inquiry sent them are always interesting. A study may be made of birthdays, birthplaces, and hobbies of authors.

Parliamentary law. — The procedure in organizing and handling a meeting of any kind may be discussed, dramatized, and illustrated as program material. Parliamentary law as a subject has little to interest the average student, chiefly because it is rather technical and confusing. A few simple principles of parliamentary law, however, may be welcome and useful.

Public speaking. — Nearly all of the program of the society will be public speaking, but there are many types of speaking in addition to those mentioned. Such forms as " pep " speeches, toasts, story-telling, introductions, conversation, interviews, presentations, and acceptances may be made use of in the program. Wherever possible, the subjects should concern school affairs or people.

Debating

Its value. — One of the most abused of high school activities is debating, though potentially one of the best; for it embraces in itself almost all of the advantages of both curricular and extra-curricular activities collectively, — the development of intellectual capacities and interests, of good sportsmanship, self-reliance, confidence, and poise. It brings fluency of speech, clear logical thinking, and a greater capacity to appraise modern affairs. There are indeed few activities of the school which can offer as much as debating. In athletics the mental phase is somewhat neglected; in publications or strictly literary activity, speaking is little considered; in dramatics logical thinking is subordinated. Debating requires all of these and more.

Objections to debating. — The most frequently mentioned objections to high school debating are:

Winning is overemphasized. — This is a serious charge against debating. Any one would admit that the desire to win is strong in the student and that it is legitimate. But when winning is emphasized to the exclusion of all other values, the debate becomes an end in itself and not merely a means to the larger end of educating the student participant. Evasions and trickery are resorted to in debating, not for the purpose of discovering truth but to gain the decision of the judges. Nearly all of the objections to debating can be traced to the desire to win.

The coach and not the student debates. — The author, acting as chairman of a certain interscholastic debate, noticed during the rebuttal that the coach of one school was displaying to his team small cards with numbers on them. The debate was stopped in order to see what this meant. The coach explained that he was signaling his team which rebuttal to use. The team had " canned " seventeen rebuttal speeches, and the coach, after listening to the arguments of the opponents, decided which of these would make the best refutation and flashed the number of this rebuttal to his team. In other words, the coach was debating for the team. The game was to win the debate, and winning was more important than teaching debaters to select their own arguments to meet those of their opponents. Sportsmanship and the spirit of learning never enter into such a scheme. Many speeches of debaters are written by the coaches. Probably the coach cannot be blamed; certainly not if his job depends upon his team's winning. School principals and superintendents who countenance or permit the practice are responsible, and to them can be attributed the unhealthy conditions of debating to-day.

Debating develops superficiality, insincerity, and glibness. — This objection to debating has been raised many times. It is held that sides are selected or assigned before the student begins to study the question and consequently he must " dope out " an argument for the side upon which he finds himself, whether he really believes in that side or not. Further, it is easy for the student to imagine that because his flow of language is not interrupted he is debating. He frequently " raves " and seems to think that assertion, especially with loud voice and emphatic gesture, constitutes proof. He ridicules opponents and magnifies their little slips in the name of argument.

Too few students participate in the debates. — If debating had no merit, this objection would be less serious than it really is. If debates are good, why should not all students receive practice in them? The student who needs athletic training the least is the one usually who gets most of it, and probably the same can be said for debating.

Debating subjects are unreasonable. — It is held that high school teams debate on topics which even wise and experienced statesmen could hardly handle. In such case the student merely mirrors what the opponents and proponents have said, organizing their material into his speech instead of thinking upon the question very seriously himself.

Suggestions for improving high school debating. — In any case, whether these objections are valid or not, the average high school debate is a rather uninteresting, poorly attended affair. How can it be made to function in the best way? The following suggestions are offered. They are neither new nor original, and are not calculated to work miracles; but they might to some extent help to place debating where it should be considered one of the most valuable activities of the school.

Emphasize the educational values of the debate instead of the winning. — It has been shown that the desire to win is the most pernicious thing about the debates. The fact that the team is not considered successful until it gets the decision of the judges hinders its development. No one would deny that the awarding of a cup or banner or other special recognition for the best team is an incentive. But if this cup only is sought, then all other values may be lost sight of.

In the Oxford or " Open Forum " debating procedure, which has found its way into collegiate circles, the two schools are not opposed to each other. The teams are mixed. If there are two members from each school, then one of these members goes on one side with an " opponent " and the other is joined by an " opponent." Or there may be two and one in case of a three man team. In order to avoid repetition and to make for better articulation of the speeches briefs are exchanged before the debate. There is no rebuttal. The audience votes at the end of the debate for the winner. No award of any sort is given. After this vote the meeting is thrown open, and speeches to the extent of three minutes in length are allowed from the floor. Questions and arguments must be answered by the debaters. It will be seen that this scheme fosters the fairest and purest type of debating. Its purpose is to ascertain the truth, not to name a winner. The debaters themselves for this type of debate must be all the better prepared. There is little probability of the debate's descending to quibbling or losing itself in a display of oratory. It is true that this form of debate may lack conclusiveness and that the public will not like it; but a little publicity, perhaps some " planted " discussions in the audience for the first few times, will help to make it attractive. On the other hand, an audience's partiality to a certain type of debate does not necessarily justify it, especially if the community has had no experience with any other and is consequently not competent to judge. No judgment is exercised where there is no choice.

Make use of extemporaneous debates. — The objection that the student spends all of his time on one side of a subject and with the help of the coach and the English department writes and memorizes a speech can be obviated by the use of the extemporaneous debate, which is becoming popular. The teams representing the two or more schools prepare on both sides of several questions, three, five or more, submitted to them several weeks beforehand. An hour or so before the debate the question and sides are drawn. This has the disadvantage that the debate is not as thorough and polished, perhaps not as interesting to the audience as the more formal type. On the other hand, it might be more educative to the students engaged, and this is more important than pleasing the patrons.

Encourage intrascholastic debating. — There will always be a place for interscholastic debating, but intrascholastic debating is becoming perhaps even more important still, as its values are more clearly discerned. The proper place to begin debating work outside of the curriculum is probably in some form of debating club. It may be composed of those students who are already interested in debating. Probably the most important part of the work of this club will be not its own programs, but those it encourages for the school at large. It will encourage, foster, and organize inter-room, inter-class, inter-floor, inter-club, and other forms of intrascholastic debating in order to increase interest and distribute educational opportunities. It may conduct a debating class, if none is provided within the regular schedule, in which the rudiments of debating are discussed and illustrated. Its critics will criticize all debates held. In other ways this club will help to develop not only a good attitude toward debating but increase participation in it.

Use reasonable topics. — The high school has ever been the imitator of the college, even in the subjects chosen for its debates. That these subjects are frequently of national importance does not mean they are interesting to the average citizen of the school or community. On the other hand, it is not desired to make the debate a show in order to attract an audience. Questions concerning the school and its activities should be used for intrascholastic purposes. The official school team may debate questions of wider import, but it too may well avoid ponderous questions in favor of such as are more in keeping with the age, maturity, and judgment of the students.

Emphasize argument, discourage glibness. — It is probably true that many students debating for the first time imagine because they talk in a loud voice or fluently and with some confidence that what they say is the truth and will be looked upon as such by the judges. Quibbling, trickery, ridicule and the like are often resorted to for the same reason. To eradicate these erroneous ideas the criticisms of the various speakers by a competent judge may be effective. The coach, of course, can do more than any one else to combat them. Further, only experienced debaters of good judgment should be allowed to appear in interscholastic events.

Seek coöperation of the entire faculty. — Too frequently each member of the faculty shuts himself up in his little job and takes no interest in that of another. Debating naturally has as its basis literary expression and public speaking, but the social science department and occasionally other departments may be called upon for assistance. Faculty help in organizing, administering and judging intrascholastic debates is desirable. A good faculty attitude toward debating is essential.

Students can be led to express their convictions in spontaneous debate in the home room and in smaller groups about the school. Such discussion should be naturally upon subjects about which the students know something or have convictions. Such practice will reveal to the student the fact that debating is a mastery of thought and expression instead of an oratorical exhibition, and that it is the debate and not the debater that wins.

Public Speaking

Much of what has been said about debating applies equally to speaking. Only a word more need be added. No one doubts the value of training in speaking. We shall always have the dramatic and the humorous readings and perhaps the oratorical, but these are being emphasized less and less because the more common values of speaking are being recognized. Ability to speak at a banquet, or to a group at a meeting is much more important for the average student than to read a dramatic or humorous piece. The professional will make use of other types of speaking, but the average student will never become a professional. The trend is now away from the formal reading and toward the extemporaneous (not impromptu) type of speaking. Many states now hold extemporaneous speaking contests.

In this type of activity the subjects are not announced until an hour before the contest, when the contestants draw for subject and place on the program. Subjects may be provided in two ways. They may be chosen from any ten (or other number) issues of some current events magazine, say, the *Literary Digest*. The students will read and study these magazines from beginning to end for several weeks before the contest. In some instances the contestant may draw two or even three topics and take a choice. A second plan of this same general order is to place a list of topics in the hands of the contestant several weeks before the event. He prepares a general talk on each of them. An hour or so before the contest he draws for his topic. The value of such a contest is obvious.

The real danger, as has been emphasized before, is that these contests and speaking programs will be made a show for the audience or that winning will be emphasized to the exclusion of nearly everything else. A public speaking club along the same general lines as that suggested for debating will be found valuable. Its duties will be to encourage and develop speaking in the school by the same general means as were suggested for creating a background for debating. Competitions of various sorts, discussions, publicity, will give the students who want to speak the opportunity, and challenge those who do not dare to get upon their feet before a group. Perhaps the name " Discussion Club " would be less intimidating than " Public Speaking Club."

Because literary work, debating, and speaking represent types of activity very closely related to curricular activity it is easy to justify giving school credit for participation in them. The student who plays on the football team is usually excused from gymnasium work. In like manner the student who debates or speaks should receive credit. Thus this legitimate activity would be recognized and encouraged, a high quality of work would be required of the student, and a more systematic and careful attention on the part of the sponsor.

SUMMARY

Literary activities were originally designed to honor students and to show educational progress, but now they are looked upon as instruments of education. The two main types of societies found in high schools are the Club and the Divided School organizations. A great variety of material for programs is available and meetings can be made both interesting and beneficial. Debating is one of the most educative activities about the school. The main objections to it are those centering around the demand for winning. These may be minimized by emphasizing debating as an educational agency rather than as a self-glorifying agency. The trend in both debating and public speaking is towards extemporaneous speaking.

REFERENCES

BREWER, J. M. *Oral English and Guidance for Debating*. Ginn and Company.

BRIGGS, T. H. and McKINNEY, I. *A Second Book of Composition*, Chap. II, "Argument and Debate." Ginn and Company.

CLARK, S. H. "Public Speaking, A New Plan for a School Contest," *School Review* 20 : 379–382, June, 1912.

FOSTER, W. F. *Argumentation and Debating*. Houghton Mifflin Company.

GARDNER, B. L. "Debating in the High School," *School Review* 19 : 534–545, October, 1911.

—— "Debating in the High School," *School Review* 20 : 120–124, February, 1912.

HARTWELL, E. C. "Debating in High School," *School Review* 19 : 689–693, December, 1911.

LEE, A. "Literary Societies in a Small High School," *English Journal* 13 : 35–38, January, 1924.

PHELPS, E. M. *Debater's Manual*. H. W. Wilson Company.

PRINGLE, R. W. *Adolescence and High School Problems*, Chaps. 12, 13. D. C. Heath and Company.

STOWE, A. M. "Student Debating Activities," JOHNSTON's *Modern High School*, Chap. 17. Charles Scribner's Sons.

—— "Motivation of Debate in Secondary Schools," *School Review* 19 : 546–549, October, 1911.

WEAVER, A. T. "Interscholastic Forensic Contest," *Quarterly Journal of Speech Education* 4 : 160–169, March, 1918.

CHAPTER X

SECRET SOCIETIES

The problem of the high school secret society has been bothering school authorities for twenty-five or thirty years. The importance of this subject is evidenced by the abundance of writing upon it; the number of condemnatory resolutions; the passage of state legislation; and the amount of litigation, carried, in more than one instance, to the supreme court of the state concerned.

Definition. — There has been much quibbling over the definition of the secret society. The terms " fraternity " and " sorority " and " Greek Letter Society " have been used most frequently. The law passed by the Illinois Legislature in 1919 prohibiting secret societies defines them as follows:

An Act to Prohibit Fraternities, Sororities, and Secret Societies in the Public Schools of the State and to Provide for the Enforcement of the Same.

SECTION I. Be it enacted by the people of the State of Illinois represented in the General Assembly, that a public school fraternity, sorority, or secret society, as contemplated by this act, is hereby defined to be any organization, composed wholly or in part of public school students, which seeks to perpetuate itself by taking additional members from the students enrolled in such school on the basis of the decision of the membership, rather than upon the free choice of any student who is qualified by the school to fill the specific aims of the organization.

Origin. — The high school secret society originating about fifty years ago, is another one of the high school imitations of college life. A number of elements have combined to bring it into being and develop it. The high school is more or less closely related to the college, especially if the college and the high school are located in the smaller town. It is but natural for the high school student to want to imitate the collegian, especially if he knows a number of former high school students who are now at the college. A second element which has helped to encourage the high school secret society is the fact that in connection with the many meets and conventions held at the college for the high school students, special attractions, lodging, entertainments, and parties are offered by the college fraternities. A third cause is the fact that frequently a high school society is founded and developed by a faculty member. Still another cause is the establishment of the pre-college fraternity, or " pre-pledging," especially in cities where there is a close relation between the high school and the college. Of course all arise from the desire of the student for membership in exclusive organizations.

ADVANTAGES OF HIGH SCHOOL SECRET SOCIETIES

The most frequently mentioned arguments in favor of the high school secret societies are that they give the student a harmless outlet for the instinct of gregariousness; teach social usage and customs; foster fine friendships among the members; inspire loyalty and other desirable virtues emphasized in the ritual; can encourage school activities because of their weight and solidarity; if secret societies are valuable in the college they are valuable in the high school.

The validity of these arguments can be tested best by a consideration of the effects they have caused in schools. Probably the best way will be to deal with this evidence under the head of objections, for all of it is upon the " objections " side. Some of the evidence is in the form of statistical data and some in the form of argument.

OBJECTIONS TO HIGH SCHOOL SECRET SOCIETIES

A great many objections to the high school secret society have been raised, chief among which are the following:

They are undemocractic. — No one would contend that an organization, eligibility for which is based upon the vote of its members, is democratic in its ideals. A democratic organization is one to which eligibility for membership is determined by interest and technical qualifications.

Develop clannishness and snobbishness. — If it is difficult for the college man or woman to refrain from advertising the fact that he is a member of an exclusive organization, surely the high school student with less experience and ability to control his feelings need not be expected to act with more consideration towards the " barbarians " who do not have the good fortune to belong.

Set false standards. — The student is elected to membership on the basis not of what he is, but of what he has. Clothes, automobiles, money, popularity, qualities of a social luminary, looks, athletic prowess, and similar characteristics, are more frequently the basis of candidacy than scholastic attainments or high moral character. The organization, by electing its members on these bases, has set its stamp of approval on their values as those which should be developed.

Carry petty politics into the school. — The part played by petty politics in college fraternities in connection with athletics is well known ; and much distress is occasioned because loyalty to fraternity is placed above loyalty to college. The fraternity encourages selfishness. Its aim is to control as many of the organizations in the school as possible. That is what will make it respected and feared by the school population, and will consequently make membership in it more to be desired. Investigations of the question of office holding in the high school in which fraternities flourish has shown time and again that the fraternity man has many more chances for election or appointment to an office than has the barbarian. It may be argued that this is not a result but a cause of his membership and that the fact that he was competent to hold office is the reason why he was elected to membership. There may be some truth in this, but it would not explain why a large majority of fraternity member office-holders make their reputations after joining fraternities.

Are detrimental to school spirit. — The fraternity pledge cannot be more interested in school than he is in the organization which honors him by election. Consequently, he can have no real school spirit, for the school is a secondary matter with him. The evidence presented by Newlon, Masters, Perkins, and others bears this out.

Have a bad effect upon scholarship. — This has been proved time and again. Beginning with the report made by the committee of the Secondary School Department of the National Education Association in 1905, the discussion of the subject is full of figures on the relative standing of members and non-members. In one of the best of these studies, Mr. J. G. Masters shows the difference between the work of the fraternity and the non-fraternity student and states that " the disparity is so great as to be a cause for concern to the parents and school authorities." [1]

Do not encourage proper use of leisure time. — The college fraternity is the basis of most of the social life of the college. Its parties and its activities must be exciting and the result is often undesirable. The high school fraternity copies its original in organization, ritual, and social activities. Newlon reported that the fraternities in his school even held " activities smokers." A smoker for boys thirteen or fifteen years of age could hardly be classed as encouraging the wise use of leisure time.

Narrow the sympathies and interests of the student. — The student belonging to a group is naturally more interested in it than in any other of which he is not a member. If it is considered

[1] See Bibliography for reference.

a rather important feat to " make " his fraternity, he is all the more interested in it.

Foster habits of extravagance. — No one likes to belong to an organization which is cheap, and inexpensiveness is frequently looked upon as being synonymous with inferiority in general character and importance.

Stir up strife and contention. — The desire to control is important in the life of the individual. If there are two or more contending forces in the school, there will be the more of petty intrigue engendered. Further, probably every college in the country has local fraternities which are organized in most cases by disgruntled or disappointed students who failed of election to some established fraternity. These organizations continue to multiply, and are becoming ever more trifling. Jealousies, competition, and contention are the result.

Dissipate the energies and ambition of the students. — The student who is elected to membership in a fraternity is naturally under obligation to it. It has honored him by election, and he must stand by it. He accordingly spends his time for this club rather than for the school, or upon what should be his main business, school work.

Lower ethical standards. — It has been reported many times that student members of the high school fraternities have confessed that they are supposed to " resign " mentally just before being questioned about membership, and to " join " again immediately after the denial of membership. Greek Letter organizations have frequently changed their names because of laws prohibiting them though they remained otherwise unaltered in any way. Such subterfuge and trickery can hardly be conducive to the development of ethical character.

Cause disciplinary troubles. — It would be impossible for an organization which placed its own interests or those of its members above the welfare of the school to avoid conflict with the authorities of the school, who stand for the school as a whole. And in fact the reports of Masters and others on this point are conclusive.

Nearly all of the above objections were taken from the resolution forming part of the report of the committee appointed by the Secondary School Department of the National Education Association to consider the subject of high school fraternities. The resolution is as follows:

" Whereas, the sentiment of superintendents, principals, and teachers against secret fraternities is almost universal, and their testimony, as disclosed in the foregoing report, coincides with the observation and experience of the members of the committee individually, be it therefore

Resolved, that we condemn these secret organizations, because they are subversive of the principles of democracy which should prevail in the public school; because they are selfish, and tend to narrow the minds and sympathies of the students; because they stir up strife and contention; because they are snobbish; because they dissipate energy and proper ambition; because they set wrong standards; because rewards are not based on merit, but on fraternity vows; because they inculcate a feeling of self-sufficiency among the members; because secondary-school boys are too young for club life; because they are expensive and foster habits of extravagance; because they bring politics into the legitimate organizations; because they detract interest from the study; and because all legitimate elements for good — social, moral, and intellectual — which these societies claim to possess, can be better supplied to the students through the school at large in the form of literary societies and the clubs under the sanction and supervision of the faculties of the school.[1]

So far as the college fraternity is concerned, college heads are not agreed upon its value. True, some colleges provide houses

[1] *Proceedings* of the National Education Association, 1905, p. 451.

and equipment, but other colleges just as large and influential prohibit anything which resembles a fraternity. The high school and the college fraternity have not the same purpose or nature. The college fraternity serves as a home to many students. The high school student lives at home. The college fraternity grew up because the authorities took little or no interest in the social life of the students. High school social activities, however, are more closely supervised. The college, because of its diverse interests, and more highly developed social life, may need fraternities; the high school with less diversity and less development does not. "There is not a good word to be said for the high school secret society." This statement, by Mr. Jesse H. Newlon, epitomizes the attitude of nearly all school administrators, who, on the basis of their experience with such societies, are competent to speak upon the subject.

In this connection it is true that not much statistical evidence has been offered. It is not necessary. A mass of such evidence is, however, available.[1] In the second place, the fact that nineteen states and a number of city boards have legislated against these organizations, and that such legislation has been upheld in supreme court decisions, should remove all necessity for any extended arraignment of the high school fraternity. The arguments have been sketched briefly in the hope that they will be beneficial to any administrator trying to solve this troublesome problem.

How Shall Secret Societies Be Dealt With?

Ignore them. — The first high school fraternity is supposed to have been started in 1876. It is interesting to note that when these organizations began to appear, little or nothing was done by the school authorities to hinder them. School administrators looked upon them as fads which would disappear shortly. As a

[1] See the Bibliography by E. K. Fretwell, *Teachers College Record.*

matter of fact, the influence of these societies was not felt for nearly twenty years. But they did not disappear; they grew in number and developed in strength until the school authorities were roused to take a more active attitude towards them. Ignoring them has not been effective.

Control them. — Naturally, as they grew and developed, some attempt was made to control them. If there might be a value in them, it was up to the school administrator to attempt to control or direct them to the betterment of the school. This of course meant a recognition of them. The following requirements were set by the board of education of Dubuque, Iowa. In this high school there were three fraternities and two sororities.

Pledging of grammar school students forbidden

Wearing of pins or other insignia forbidden

Attempt to use influence in school affairs forbidden

All initiations and other ceremonies which would bring ridicule or criticism upon the school authorities forbidden

Unbecoming conduct or low scholarship might result in the disbanding of each organization

Twice a year a complete roster of the names of the members must be furnished

Exterminate them. — Regulation was not successful, so the authorities began a real war against these societies. This war aimed to prevent the establishment of new fraternities, and to exterminate those which were already established. Naturally, most of the organizations fought stubbornly, assisted in many instances rather ably by parents of members. The State laws declaring against high school fraternities usually leave to the boards of educations or their authorized representatives the methods of prevention or eradication.

The first method of eradication is that used at the Tucson, Arizona, High School. In this instance the members themselves helped to disband the organizations.[1] Two years' observation

[1] See Bibliography.

in this school showed two bad effects of these organizations:
" a lowering of scholarship, and a break up of school spirit and
the establishment of a group spirit in its place." Student leaders
and influential alumni members discussed the problem, and finally
at the end of two years the organizations disbanded and sur-
rendered their charters " without a note of discord." In place
of the two fraternities, one of which had been in operation for ten
years, two clubs were organized for all of the members of the school.
The " Rousers " club was organized for the boys. It met at
night once every two weeks in the cafeteria for dinner and for a
program of interest to boys and of value to the school. Its aim
was " to develop the school spirit and to develop the boy socially
and morally." The " Social Hour Club " was established for the
girls. On every alternate Friday school was dismissed a half-
hour early, and the period from three-thirty to five o'clock
was given over to games, refreshments, and interesting programs.

A second method of abolishing secret societies, represented by
the plan used at Washington, D. C., is to restrict the privileges
of their members. Briefly, the most important provisions of
these regulations are as follows: [1]

The student who is a member of such an organization is disqualified:
1. From holding office or a warrant in the high school Cadet Brigade
2. From holding office or position either elective or appointive on any
school publication
3. From representing his school in competitive athletics, rifle matches,
interscholastic debate, or dramatic performance
4. From being certified as eligible to stand for election to any class office
5. From holding any position in the high school bank
6. From holding office in any organization, club, or activity which comes
under the direction of the school
7. From receiving any honor other than award for scholarship
8. From holding any position as representative of his school

[1] See Bibliography.

Under such a plan, there would be little of interest about the school for the fraternity member.

A third procedure, widely discussed and imitated, is that followed at Lincoln, Nebraska. The records of one hundred and twenty-nine fraternity members were compared with similar records of one hundred and twenty-nine students chosen at random. The following ratio was reported:

	TARDINESS	ABSENCE	FAILURES	MARKS OVER 90 PER CENT
Fraternity Member	802	1386	102	96
Non-Fraternity	412	1085	48	152

The student member was required to sign a pledge of resignation from the fraternity, and asked to deposit his pin or other insignia with the Board of Education as proof of his good intentions. If he did not deposit his pin he had to bring from his parents a signed statement that he would not wear it. A letter was sent to all parents explaining and justifying the action taken, and asking the parents for their voted approval or disapproval. Eighty-five per cent of the parents voted approval, three per cent disapproval, and twelve per cent did not vote. A vitalized activities program for the students was immediately got under way.

The offering of clear evidence of the bad influence of fraternity life upon the school work; the disapproval of it by an overwhelming majority of the parents and patrons of the school; and the development of a substitutionary program, are the three best weapons to be used to exterminate the secret society.

It occasionally happens that an innocent Sunday School group, a Hi-Y club, a dramatic club with excellent social and moral ideals develops into a secret society with all of the ugly attributes mentioned above. Care must be taken to anticipate and prevent any such attempt on the part of the students to head the organization in the general direction of a secret society. Election of members by secret ballot is the first step in this direction.

State laws or board of education rules are worthless unless enforced. Real enforcement is possible only when it is upheld by a strong school and community sentiment, and the best way to secure this is to present the facts and the statistics showing bad results. The community attitude towards the school far too often has an emotional and not an intellectual basis, and favors the student rather than the administrator. A sensible continuous program of publicity should help to alleviate the troubles in connection with secret societies. One of the most promising things in this connection is the rule adopted by Phi Delta Theta and other college fraternities, to the effect that members of high school fraternities will not be eligible for membership.

SUMMARY

The first secret societies originated in the high school some fifty years ago, but only within the past twenty-five years have they been a problem to school administrators. The main arguments advanced for them are that they teach social usage and loyalty, promote school activities, and foster desirable friendships. The main objections to them are that they are undemocratic, set up false standards, corrupt the school, and do not encourage proper use of leisure time. Three methods of dealing with them have been used — to ignore, control, or eradicate them. Proving their harmfulness by means of statistics is the most reasonable method of getting community support for a campaign against them.

REFERENCES

BALLOU, F. W. "High School Fraternities and Sororities," *School Life,* October, 1921.

BROWN, J. W. *American Secondary School Fraternities.* The Maske Brown Company.

Digest of the State Laws Relating to Public Education in force January 1, 1925, compiled by W. R. Wood, S. B. Weeks, and S. Ford. Bureau of Education *Bulletin* No. 47, p. 591-592, 1915.

FRETWELL, E. K. "Bibliography on High School Fraternities and Sororities," *Teachers College Record* 24 : 147-158, March, 1923.

"High School Fraternities," *School Review* 21 : 141-142, February, 1913; 31 : 330-331, May, 1923.

"High School Fraternities and Democracy," *Educational Review*, 157 f., March, 1924.

"High School Fraternities; Legislation in Illinois." *School and Society* 10 : 13-14, July 5, 1919. "Decisions on," *School Review* 31 : 332-339, May, 1923.

"Legislation concerning fraternities in Illinois. State Laws relating to Education enacted in 1918-1919," U. S. Bureau of Education *Bulletin*, No. 30, 1920.

MASTERS, J. H. "High School Fraternities," *School Review* 14 : 422-432, June, 1917.

McDANIEL, M. R. "Laws against High School Fraternities," *Tenth Yearbook*, National Association of Secondary School Principals, 1926, 58-62.

MONAHAN, A. C. "High School Fraternities," *American School Board Journal* 70 : 108, May, 1925.

MORRISON, G. B. "Report of Committees on Secret Fraternities," *Proceedings* of the National Educational Association, 1905, 445-451.

NEWLON, J. H. "High School Fraternities," *Educational Administration and Supervision* 7 : 372-379, October, 1921.

PERKINS, G. O. "High School Fraternities Again," *School Review* 34 : 277-280, April, 1926.

—— "The Elimination of Fraternities and Sororities in Tucson High School," *School Review* 31 : 224-226, March, 1923.

State Laws relating to Education enacted in 1915, 1916, 1917, Bureau of Education *Bulletin* 1918, No. 23, p. 156.

WELLS, A. R. "Secret Societies in High Schools," *Journal of Education*, 73 : 5-9, January, 1911.

CHAPTER XI

STUDENT PARTICIPATION IN CONTROL OF STUDY HALLS AND LIBRARY

To the high school teacher the study hall is a nuisance. The plan of having a study hall developed from the small schoolroom where the teacher heard one class at the front of the room while, at the back, the remainder of the students were supposed to study their lessons. When rooms multiplied and classes became larger it was natural that space should be set aside for the purpose of study. So the quiet and more or less undisturbed study hall was the result. Naturally some one had to supervise this room, and thus the study hall duty of teachers began. The trend now is away from the old-fashioned hall with its group of several hundred students, towards the smaller unit in the general study hall plan, and towards the small group in the supervised study or directed study plan. Changes have come as a result of clearer thinking, but in most schools there is still a general study hall.

In order to do away with control by the teacher, a number of schools have students supervise these rooms. A teacher may be responsible for the room for the period, but the actual administration and supervision of the room is in the hands of the students, and they do the work formerly done by the teacher.

Arguments for Student Supervision of Study Halls

The values claimed for this kind of study hall organization are numerous. In fact nearly all of the values claimed for extra-curricular activities in general pertain to it. There are, however, certain special values.

It makes the student increasingly self-directive. — In another chapter it was suggested that the school is frequently a repressive agency and that the attitudes which the student learns are frequently those of the subject and might not fit him for membership in a society where he has more rights and privileges. The school is likely to develop a negative rather than a positive attitude towards law and order where the student faces and feels no responsibility. No initiative or leadership or special interest in the school will result.

If the student assumes charge of some important act or organization about the school and faces the responsibilities of succeeding, his initiative and leadership are developed. He will, moreover, be more interested in the school and its activities because it belongs to him; that is, he himself has a part in making it. Submitting to authority which he helps to establish prepares the student for citizenship in a community.

Student control is sound psychologically. — In the second place it is claimed that student participation is psychologically more sound than teacher-administration of study halls because the latter practice invites trouble. The student likes to tease the teacher, especially if he can embarrass her in front of a group, and particularly the teacher who flies into a panic or a frenzy. In a large room it is difficult to locate the student who hums, or the one who rolls shot or marbles down the aisle, or the one who brings animals into the school. The student is a gambler. He likes to " get away " with things. Consequently there is built up an unsocial attitude towards the teacher-policeman in the room. It is claimed that the student will sympathize more with his fellow, especially if that fellow is well known, honored, and liked. And if the student agrees to abide by certain rules and regulations which he himself helped to develop and formulate when administered by student friends he helped to elect, his attitude is likely to be good.

More effective use can be made of the study period. — A third claim is that such an arrangement encourages more efficient habits of study.   There may be some merit in this claim, but if so, it is probably small.   Certainly the student monitors can give little direct systematic help in teaching students to study more effectively.   They may be able to do this indirectly by making the hall a quiet place in which to study and work, or in releasing the teacher from this duty to " free " periods when the students may receive individual help, but beyond this there is probably little merit in this claim.   Teachers themselves cannot do much in a study hall to help the students study and if the teachers can do little the students themselves can probably do even less.

Using teachers for study hall duty is uneconomical. — The use of one or two teachers in the study hall is expensive because each such period assigned means a reduction of the teaching program. The teacher does police duty and draws teacher's salary for it. Much might be said along this line.   It seems reasonable to conclude that a teacher's time is too valuable to be spent standing over a group of students to keep order.   It is even worse where the heads of departments are assigned study hall duty. This practice cannot be justified.   A jeweler would not employ a high-salaried diamond setter to wash windows.   Neither will an intelligent principal use a teacher for duty which can be done just as effectively, and more cheaply, by some one else. If the teacher's time can be spent to more advantage outside of the study hall, less expensive help should be obtained to assume the study hall duties.   It has even been suggested that a full time " policeman " with lower qualifications, scholastically, than the teacher and consequently on a lower salary, be placed in charge of the large study hall groups.   The teacher in the general study hall can be of very little direct assistance to the students for obvious reasons.   He can be little more than a disciplinarian.

Objections to Student Supervision

The main arguments against student monitoring are first, that students cannot do it effectively for lack of judgment, prestige, and authority. If the teacher herself can hardly do it, how can the inexperienced student be expected to succeed at it? In the second place it is held that their power will be misused, that they will become tyrannical and officious, and that the plan will fail because students do not like to have their fellows supervise, criticize, or correct them. In the third place it is stated that such a use of the student's time cannot be justified, that the student is there to study and get his lessons and if much of his time is taken up with these duties his work will suffer.

The best way to settle the question of whether student control is effective and desirable is to examine situations in which it has been used. If it has been done successfully it can be done again. If it has never been done successfully the statement that it can be done is not proved.

Plans for Student Participation in Study Hall Control

The simplest and most logical plan for student control is that by which students who make high marks are allowed to go into a student-monitored room upon signing a pledge that they will cause no disturbance there. This is the logical beginning of a plan of participation because in the first place the students who make the high marks show that they can study and that they have studied, and consequently are more to be trusted than those less successful in their school work. In the second place this group would be the last to tolerate any noise or disturbance which would interfere with the keeping up of its high marks. The plan is further safeguarded by the fact that the students feel it an honor to " make " the room. It is a special privilege open only to the students who do good work. If the student falls behind in his work, he forfeits his place in the honor room and goes back to the general study hall. This plan is also safe-guarded further by the fact that the student signs a pledge not to cause trouble and if he violates this pledge he loses his right to a place in the room.

The monitors may be elected by the students or appointed by the faculty or principal. Allowing the room to elect its own monitors gives an added attractiveness. The monitor, or monitors, depending upon the size of the group, arranges the seating chart, takes the roll, signs release slips to other rooms, accepts admit slips, excuses the students, and in other ways handles the routine affairs of the room. If several monitors are necessary, these elect a chairman who acts as head of the group. This group is rather an administrative than a police force; if there is any trouble or disturbance that it cannot handle, it reports to the proper authorities. The faculty or principal admits the students to membership in this room and revokes membership upon the recommendation of the monitors. Such revocation will of course come only after both sides of the case have been heard.

A more extensive application of this principle is found in the East Technical High School, Cleveland, Ohio.[1] In this school a gradual development of student interest was made and at the psychological moment, just after a remarkable speech on " train your mind and will," the plan of the " Concentration Study Hall " was brought forward. No student was assigned to this room. Any student might apply for admission. Each student who applied signed the following pledge:

In order to develop the spirit of self-direction in the school and to " train my mind and will " to their full power, I apply for permission to study in the Concentration Study Hall. In appreciation of this permission I pledge myself unreservedly to refrain from all communication of any kind and to use my influence to prevent any violation of this pledge on the part of others.

Signature

[1] Described by Miss Parmenter in the *School Review* for January 1924.

Student monitors were elected, one for each row, and a general chairman for the group of monitors was chosen. The monitors handled the usual routine details of the study hall. The principal and teachers responsible for a particular period dropped in many times to see how things were going. These were merely " interested friendly visits " and were not in any sense spying trips and were not looked upon as such by the students or their monitors.

In addition to the regular monitors some committees were appointed in each session. A " Fresh Air " committee opened the windows at the end of the period and aired the room for the next group. A " Light " committee attended to the adjusting of shades as more or less light was needed or to prevent any student from sitting in the glare, and turned on and off the electric light as occasion demanded.

The plan worked well the first term and the second term some interesting research work was started by the students themselves. One group, for instance, made a study of attendance before and after holidays, significant events or programs at schools, and the like, and drew graphs to illustrate the fluctuations. Another group of students worked upon a " student self-rating work-habit scale." Still another group worked on the topic of a " trouble chart for weak wills."

If there was disturbance in any part of the room, the monitors checked the proper place for investigation or watching. In most cases the suggestion of the monitor to the offender to " read your pledge " was sufficient to rectify matters. In case this did not accomplish the desired result other means, such as exclusion from this hall, were followed.

A third type of organization is that represented in the Walla Walla, Washington, High School. There the students gradually took responsibility for the study halls. The movement was backed by the Student Council and after the school had been made familiar with the plan and its possibilities and had voted to give it a trial the study halls were organized with the usual student monitors and chairman.

This organization differs from the others in that practically the entire school is under student control and further in the method of punishment for the student who causes disturbance. A " Council Box " is provided into which the monitor drops a brief report on any student in the room who does not observe the rules and regulations.   The disturber is called before the Council at its weekly meeting and is asked to plead " guilty " or " not guilty " to the charge made by the monitor.   In order to avoid friction between students the monitor's name is withheld.   If the offender pleads " guilty," he is sentenced by the Council; if " not guilty," he states his case and is excused to another room while the monitor who made the complaint is called and presents his side of the case.   He is then excused and the offender brought in again.   Naturally nearly all cases of " not guilty " are decided " guilty," and the student receives sentence for his acts.

Punishment for offenses in the study hall are exclusion from assembly programs, forfeiture of certain rights and privileges, the memorization of poetry, the writing of themes, or assignment to the " Pest Room."   This room is governed by a teacher.   Naturally, as it is made up of a group of offenders, being sent to it is looked upon as a disgrace.   The fact that the student is away from his fellows, one of a small group under a teacher who stands for no nonsense, does not increase his relish at being sent to this room.

Mr. H. W. Jones, in writing about the plan after it had been in operation for two years, states that " The results have far surpassed all expectations.   The study halls have been more orderly and better governed under student control than they ever were under faculty supervision."   This statement was made after the plan had been in operation for two years, and is therefore the more worth noticing. By the end of the two years the novelty of the plan had worn off and it was looked upon as the regular custom of the school.

Other plans of student participation are in operation in various schools of the country. In general principles and organization these do not differ greatly from the three types mentioned. Such plans are not limited to any particular size of school. They are found both in small and in large high schools. The fact that they have been successful proves that such a thing as student participation in control is not impossible. The above plan established most recently has been in operation for more than four years.

Principles of Student Control

Certain principles must govern any attempt to organize the study halls under student supervision. Briefly, these principles are as follows:

Student participation must be desired by the students. — The faculty may initiate the movement by helping to educate the student in what is being done elsewhere, or by making suggestions to the council, but surely no scheme of student participation can ever be thrust upon the student. This means that the students must adopt the plan by vote; or if they are to be admitted by personal choice, they must sign a suitable pledge or give other evidence of acceptance and understanding.

Participation must be under close supervision. — Strong and responsible teachers should have charge of the plan and be ready to make readjustments that are necessary for its success. The teacher is not excused from the responsibility of supervision, and may be assigned for a certain period.

Monitors and student-leaders must be carefully chosen. — Age, maturity, prestige, experience, and personality must be considered in the choice of student monitors. While it is probably best for the groups to elect their own monitors, this procedure can be supervised closely enough to insure the selection of good representatives.

Members must be made to feel honored in being under student monitorship. — If any student has the idea that student participation is a cheap plan or a " let down " he will not take pride in it, even though he wants it.   He must respect the plan and those responsible for it.   Naturally, too, he must not feel that the teacher is being excused from responsibility for the conduct of the room or the school.   Nor must the teacher have this attitude.   Further, the student monitor must not be looked upon as a policeman.

The plan should be tried on a small scale. — It is good practice to start with one honor room to which the students with high marks may go, and thus set up the ideal.

Provision must be made for those who violate regulations. — These provisions should not be published as threats.   The student should feel that he is on his honor.   But the heads of the organization should have very clearly in mind what punishments will be given for violations.

The difference between monitoring a study hall and teaching the student to study must be recognized. — The former may be the function of the student.   The latter is the function of the teacher.   The teacher with the help of the student can suggest methods, policies, or practices which will aid the students in their work.   Posters, charts, graphs, themes, publicity of various kinds, assembly and home-room programs, and discussions may be utilized to encourage better attendance and punctuality, higher scholarship, and more effective study habits.

Wherever possible, competition should be utilized. — Competition always adds to interest.   This competition may be between groups, rows, or rooms.   Suitable recognition should be given for meritorious conduct or record.

Student-teacher coöperation is essential. — The plan must not be looked upon as a scheme for excusing teachers from their duties or for providing students with teachers' prerogatives. It is an educational device and as such requires the whole-hearted coöperation of student and teacher.

STUDENT PARTICIPATION IN CONTROL OF THE SCHOOL LIBRARY

The school librarian can be of service to teachers and students in definite school tasks and reference work. Besides, by a proper display of the various interesting books, magazines, and papers, and by means of clever advertising he can help to keep the students interested in school work. In the second place he can be courteous, and this is very important. The real librarian takes pride and joy in hunting up the books and papers which the reader wants. This makes the reader all the more appreciative. To increase the reader's interest is an important part of his business. If he were to discourage interest by short surly answers and discourteous treatment, he would be like the physician refusing medicine to the sick patient. The student may learn courtesy from a good librarian, and because of his encouragement of his interests he can be led to a deeper appreciation of the school and its activities.

VALUES OF STUDENT PARTICIPATION IN LIBRARY CONTROL

The main values to the student who assists in the control of the library come in the form of a training in coöperation, leadership, and other qualities which are developed when he assumes and discharges responsibility. If he recognizes that he has been honored by being made an assistant to the librarian, he will endeavor to do his work as well as possible. For students interested in library work, this opportunity offers a chance to try it out.

Again assistance releases the librarian from the smaller routine duties, which the students can perform equally well, and allows him to give his time and attention to larger and more important duties. The librarian is an expert, and most of his work should be such as requires expert service. If he is smothered under routine and the smaller tasks, he will not be able best to perform the larger duties of which there are certainly enough in any school to require his full time and attention.

Student participation should make the library more attractive, too, because there will be more freedom. Students naturally feel more free towards their fellows than towards their teachers. This should make the library more popular. Further, the fact that there is more help should increase the popularity of the library because the student reader will feel less that he is intruding upon the librarian's time, and in turn more time can be given to a consideration of his needs and wishes.

ORGANIZATION FOR STUDENT PARTICIPATION IN CONTROL OF LIBRARY

Several types of organization for student participation are in use. One of the most popular is the library club. This club may be organized along the usual club lines with such requisites for membership as suitable personality, good scholarship, genuine interest, fondness for books, neatness, and accuracy. The usual officers are elected and the club is formed and conducts its affairs like any other club in the school. Its programs concern the function, work, and structure of the library; library methods, cataloguing, classification, arranging, charging, recharging, library history, references, scrapbooks, publicity, the librarian himself, etc. It organizes for the purpose of helping the librarian with his work. He should be its sponsor. Assignments are made for this purpose as the schedule of the students permit.

A second type of organization is that in which students make formal application as librarians or assistants and are elected by the faculty upon recommendation by the librarian or a committee headed by the school librarian. This type of plan differs from the first in that the student may not be appointed merely because he wants to be appointed. In this sense it is not a club but a team which the student must make by meeting such requirements as high marks, attractive personality, interest, prestige, and ability. The assistants are trained in their various duties by the librarian in regular class, group, or staff meetings. Suitable recognition, probably not money, but a monogram, school credit, or other honor award for the work should be given.

The weakest type of organization is that in which there is no recognized librarian, the work being done by one or several teachers as a part of their regular duties. They are of course mere "handers-out-of-books" and not librarians in any sense of the word. They may or may not have student helpers. This form of organization is probably not any more commendable than that in which only students care for the library. In the latter case the students are assigned to certain periods by the principal or decide among themselves and "keep the library" for their period.

Activities of student assistants. — The activities of a group or club of assistants will be such as are usually performed by the librarian, and include cataloguing, classifying, charging, and arranging the books; making scrapbooks; publicity through bulletins, bulletin board, paper, posters, and the like; publicity in the use of the library by means of home-room talks and discussions and assembly demonstrations and explanations — all of which will help to make the library increasingly attractive and valuable.

Relation of school library to other libraries. — Many schools have libraries of considerable size continually growing larger because of wise provision by the board of education. In many schools blocks of rotating books travel from the city library to the school libraries. In some instances where the city library is not far away it is used as a school library and students do their work there. In other places the city librarian or assistant acts as school librarian either with or without student helpers.

Danger of student librarians. — The danger — and it is a real danger — is that if the students can do the job passably well they may prevent its being done any better. If the community or its school board finds that the library is being handled at least fairly well by students, it will be satisfied with this and will not be particularly inclined to engage a trained librarian. Nevertheless a trained librarian is indispensable to a modern school, and any plan which prevents, discourages, or delays the appointment of such an officer obstructs the progress of the school. No plan of student assistance should ever be justified in the least on the ground that money can be saved by it. The greater the funds wisely invested in the school the greater the profit returned; the smaller the funds invested the smaller the returns.

Summary

Student participation in the control of study halls is a new development which offers many educational opportunities. Many schools have developed successful plans for such supervision. Probably the best way to begin such a plan is with a small group of honor students. Student help may also be employed to good advantage in the control of the school library. However, such employment may be dangerous, especially in the smaller school, because it may prevent the appointment of one of the school's most important officers — the librarian.

References

ABELE, L. "The Organization of Student-governed Study Halls," *School Review* 34 : 777–781, December, 1926.

"Departmental Library Study Halls, *School Review* 33 : 7–8, January, 1925.

JONES, H. W. "Student Coöperation in School Government," *School and Society* 13 : 251–257, February 26, 1921.

MASTERS, J. G.   "Experiments in Democracy," *School Review* 35 : 125–134, February, 1927.

MORGAN, J. E.   "The Library and the School," *Library Journal* 49 : 877–880, October 15, 1924.

PARMENTER, E. M.   "The Concentration Study Hall," *School Review* 32 : 53–59, January, 1924.

PORAY, A.   "Student-Assistants in a High School Library," *Public Libraries* 29 : 208–212, April, 1924.

SATCHELL, J. K.   "Student Participation in School Administration," *School Review* 30 : 733–741, December, 1922.

STOOPS, R. O.   "The School Library on a Modest Budget," *Library Journal* 50 : 222–223, March 1, 1925.

WOOD, H. A.   "High School Library in Relation to Adult Education," *Public Libraries* 30 : 217–219, April, 1925.

CHAPTER XII

CITIZENSHIP AND SCHOOL SPIRIT

The main function of the school is to produce the good citizen and all its activities should contribute to this end. There are far too many aspects of the citizen to be covered in one formal course, for the student must be a good citizen in physical, social, intellectual, moral, and religious characteristics. The purpose of this section is to indicate a few of the ways in which increasing emphasis is being placed upon the development of particular phases of citizenship.

METHODS OF EMPHASIZING TRAINING IN CITIZENSHIP

Morality codes. — Morality codes are of ancient origin. Religious writings held many such codes and creeds. The Proverbs of the Bible are typical of collections to be found in the writings of all of the great religious teachers. This kind of material early found its way into the school. The New England Primer, the most famous of all early American textbooks, was little more than a collection of proverbs. Schoolrooms long have been adorned with adages; the copy book was full of them; and they were used in memory work. Now they appear on cards for birthdays, special days, Thanksgiving, Christmas, and Easter.

Citizenship creeds and pledges. — Quite recently there has appeared in America an increased interest in morality creeds and codes for school purposes. Some of these have been in the form of school creeds or oaths, and many are modeled after the famous Ephoeban Oath. An example is the following from the high school at Ottumwa, Iowa:

OTTUMWA HIGH SCHOOL

CITIZENSHIP CARD

As a citizen of the Ottumwa High School, I promise: I will never bring disgrace upon this, my High School, by an act of dishonesty or cowardice. I will fight for the ideals and sacred standards of my high school. I will revere and obey the high school laws and do my best to encourage a like respect and reverence among those who are prone to annul them or to set them at nought. I will strive unceasingly to quicken the public sense of civic duty. Thus, in all these ways, I will leave this high school, not less, but greater than it was left to me.

TOBACCO PLEDGE

For the good of the Ottumwa High School, I hereby pledge myself not to use tobacco during this school year and as far as possible I pledge myself to discourage the use of tobacco by others in the Ottumwa High School.

TEAM PLEDGE

As a member of any team representing this school I hereby pledge myself not to use tobacco during this school year, and I agree that the good of the school demands that I be dropped from its roll if I should break my pledge.

_____

Signed

Many of these creeds have appeared since the war, owing probably to the influence of the famous " American's Creed." Others are modeled after famous religious creeds or statements.

Work of the Character Education Institution. — Many of these creeds appeared in response to offers of prizes by interested individuals or organizations. One of the foremost organizations in the development of codes and creeds for young people is the Character Education Institution of Washington, D. C., formerly called the National Institution for Moral Instruction. In 1914, a well-known business man offered through this Institution a prize of $5000 for the best children's code of morals. His name was kept secret at his request in order that no one could accuse him of seeking personal glory or advertisement. He was known merely as " The Donor." The " National $5000 Morality Codes Competition " held from Washington's Birthday, 1916, to Washington's Birthday, 1917, was the result, and some seventy code writers, at least one from each state, were selected to write the codes.

The Hutchins' Code. — The winner of this contest was William J. Hutchins, President of Berea College. The winning code is composed of eleven laws, as follows: [1]

1. The Law of Self-Control
2. The Law of Good Health
3. The Law of Kindness
4. The Law of Sportsmanship
5. The Law of Self Reliance
6. The Law of Duty
7. The Law of Reliability
8. The Law of Truth
9. The Law of Good Workmanship
10. The Law of Teamwork
11. The Law of Loyalty

Under each of these headings appears a short, pithy statement explaining and supporting it. For instance, under the " Law of Self-Control " is the statement:

" I will control my tongue, and will not allow it to speak mean, vulgar, or profane words. I will think before I speak. I will tell the truth and nothing but the truth."

Methods of Character Education Contest. — The mere formulation of a Children's Code of Morals was, however, looked upon as being insufficient, for a code is of limited value in itself. Conse-

[1] The Institution also issues two high school "Morality Codes," one by Caroline M. Brevard, and one by Vernon P. Squires. The Character Education Institution is not a commercial but a research organization. It has nothing to sell, takes no royalties, and assumes no business responsibilities. Its publications may be secured from the National Capital Press, 1210 D Street, Northwest, Washington, D. C.

quently, this same " Donor " offered the largest sum that has ever been offered in educational competition, $20,000, for the best method of educating students morally.

The right to compete for this prize was limited. The desire was to effect group thinking. Groups of nine " Character Education Collaborators " were established in nearly all of the states. Other individuals who might be interested were allowed to coöperate by giving advice and suggestions. In order to help these groups get started, The Donor made the necessary appropriation for the gathering of extracts from educational literature having a bearing on the subject of character education. The volume, under the editorship of Dr. Harris L. Latham, contained six hundred pages. It was called " The Donor Library On Character Education, Vol. I." The time allowed the groups was from October 1, 1919 to February 22, 1921. Five copies of each plan were to be sent to an outsider who numbered and sent them to the judges, removing all marks of identification so that no accusation of favoritism might be made. Judges were selected, who read and judged the twenty-six plans which were submitted. The prize was awarded to the Iowa group which was under the chairmanship of Dr. Edwin D. Starbuck, of the University of Iowa. Five thousand copies of this plan were published and distributed to schools at the expense of The Donor. The table of contents of the " Iowa Plan " is as follows:

I. Iowa plan
II. The goal
III. The organization and control of the school
IV. Some ways of preserving, directing, and exercising the entire integrity of the child
V. Fitting the methods and materials to the child's development
VI. A moral curriculum with a progressive plan, a drive, and a goal
VII. Moving progressively towards the objective
VIII. The curriculum by years
IX. Measurements of progress and attainment

This somewhat detailed report of these two contests is made to show the emphasis being placed upon this kind of work. The Character Education Institution, through its board of trustees, composed of heads of public instruction with several other well-known educators, and its chairman, Mr. Milton Fairchild, has produced a number of suggestive plans and programs.

Analytical Study of Ethical Behavior. — A typical study by the Institution of the analytical order is found in the publication, *What Is Ethical Behavior in the Child 9 to 14?* which is set down as " A descriptive list of all the items of personal conduct, occurring before the age of fourteen, which are important to good citizenship in America to-day." These items of conduct, or morality acts as they are called, were obtained from the following sources: personal observation and memory of child conduct situations, memory being aided by a list of the objects and persons of the child's environment, and a list of character virtues; Mr. Milton Fairchild's collection of photographs of child-conduct situations; the fifty-two codes of morality for children of 9 to 14 years submitted in the $5000 prize contest of the Character Education Institution; criminal law; three textbooks on manners and etiquette; several books on moral education; writings on Sociology and social ethics, and on psychiatry and mental hygiene. About twelve hundred of these " morality acts " were collected, classified, and condensed into five hundred forty-six separate statements. Citizenship is made up of acts as elements, and the definition and classification of these are the first steps in the teaching of them.

The Five-Point Plan. — The Institution has devised what is called " The Five-Point Plan for Character Education in Elementary-School Classrooms." The five points are as follows:

1. Uncle Sam's boys and girls	Thirty per cent emphasis
2. Children's morality code	Fifteen per cent emphasis
3. Character diagnosis	Fifteen per cent emphasis
4. Character projects	Thirty per cent emphasis
5. Report to parents	Ten per cent emphasis

The first point has to do with the organization of a citizens' club which shall furnish opportunity for student participation in the activities of the room, its management, discipline, work, and other affairs. Each student receives a badge, at cost. If, at the time of his promotion from the grammar school, he has sufficient points or records in his citizenship work, he is allowed to retain the badge and take the " loyalty oath," which is as follows:

"I am a citizen of the United States of America. I pledge myself to Uncle Sam, to live in Loyalty to my Nation, its Constitution and its laws. In the spirit of justice, I will do my best to establish peace, good will, and happiness, and to increase the benefits of civilization to all humanity."

The room is organized under student officers and committees.

The work of point two in the plan centers around the " children's morality code," mentioned before. Some item in this code is studied and discussed each day. Point three has to do with the teacher's diagnosis of the student on a " character chart." The " character projects " are " projects to be carried out by the club which will give expression to, and tend to form habits in accordance with, important moral ideals." Courtesy, service, prevention of petty stealing, and lying, and the like are material for these projects. A " court of honor " is established to consider the matters of treatment of the students by each other. The " report to parents " gives a marking on the social as well as the intellectual development of the students.

The Collier's Moral Code for Youth. — *Collier's, The National Weekly*, published in 1925 a " Moral Code for Youth " which was the result of a great deal of work on the part of thousands of educators, professional workers, and business men and women, in an effort " to find out those fundamental precepts of right living upon which all men are practically agreed, and which could be confidently set up in our public schools without sectarian opposition." This code is as follows : [1]

If I want to be a happy, useful citizen I must have:

COURAGE AND HOPE

I must be brave — This means I must be brave enough and strong enough to control what I think, and what I say and what I do, and I must always be hopeful because hope is power for improvement.

WISDOM

I must act wisely — In school, at home, playing, working, reading or talking, I must learn how to choose the good, and how to avoid the bad.

INDUSTRY AND GOOD HABITS

I must make my character strong — My character is what I am, if not in the eyes of others, then in the eyes of my own conscience. Good thoughts in my mind will keep out bad thoughts. When I am busy doing good I shall have no time to do evil. I can build my character by training myself in good habits.

KNOWLEDGE AND USEFULNESS

I must make my mind strong — The better I know myself, my fellows and the world about me, the happier and more useful I shall be. I must always welcome useful knowledge in school, at home, everywhere.

TRUTH AND HONESTY

I must be truthful and honest — I must know what is true in order to do what is right. I must tell the truth without fear. I must be honest in all my dealings and in all my thoughts. Unless I am honest I cannot have self-respect.

HEALTHFULNESS AND CLEANLINESS

I must make my body strong — My eyes, my teeth, my heart, my whole body must be healthful so that my mind can work properly. I must keep physically and morally clean.

[1] Copyright 1925 by *Collier's, The National Weekly*, reprinted by permission. Copies suitable for framing may be bought at a nominal price from the owners.

HELPFULNESS AND UNSELFISHNESS

I must use my strength to help others who need help — If I am strong I can help others. I can be kind, I can forgive those who hurt me and I can help and protect the weak, the suffering, the young and the old, and dumb animals.

CHARITY

I must love — I must love God, who created not only this earth but also all men of all races, nations and creeds, who are my brothers. I must love my parents, my home, my neighbors, my country, and be loyal to all these.

HUMILITY AND REVERENCE

I must know that there are always more things to learn — What I may know is small compared to what can be known. I must respect all who have more wisdom than I, and have reverence for all that is good. And I must know how and whom to obey.

FAITH AND RESPONSIBILITY

I must do all these things because I am accountable to God and to humanity for how I live and how I can help my fellows, and for the extent to which my fellows may trust and depend upon me.

Ten life-memberships in the National Education Association, valued at one hundred dollars each, were offered as prizes for the best essays by teachers describing methods of using this code in the classroom. Winners of this contest were announced in the issue of July 18, 1925, under the caption " The Best Moral Code is a Two-Legged Moral Code."

The Detroit Code. — The schools of Detroit make use of an attractive booklet called *A Children's Code of Morals*, which is based upon the Hutchins' code. To each section of the code is appended a rather complete list of references and suggestive readings, suitable for children of the various grades, illustrating that part of the code. The illustrative references were prepared by the supervisors of the local department of instruction.

It has been pointed out before that ideals themselves are not sufficient to make a good citizen, for habits and action must be based upon those ideals. The danger with codes is that the teacher or the student will think that the job is done when the code has been formulated, memorized, or discussed. As a matter of fact, the job is then just begun. The code's real value comes only when it is made the basis of desirable action.

Citizenship balloting. — Another method of setting and teaching the standards of good citizenship is to have the students rate each other. The following account of such a plan, taken from a booklet, *The Student Councils*, issued by the Lincoln School of Teachers College, illustrates this method of naming the schools' best citizens.

INSIGNIA

It has been resolved by the entire school that a high achievement in scholarship, citizenship, and athletics be recognized the third quarter of every year. This recognition is to be in the form of a pin. The honor shall be based on the work during the interval from the beginning of the school year to the third quarter, inclusive. There shall be a difference between Junior and Senior high school pins. The Junior and Senior high schools shall be scored separately in scholarship, citizenship, and athletics. The pins shall be awarded the first Tuesday after the third quarter. To be eligible for a pin in one of the aforesaid subjects, a student must rank in the upper 15 percentile. When pins have been obtained for distinction in two fields of activity, the pin for the third and last field may be obtained when the student attains rank in the upper 25 percentile in that field.

SCHOLARSHIP

The reports covering the three quarters of the year's work in scholarship shall be used as a basis for determining those who rank highest in scholarship. Boys and girls shall be scored, according to the same rules.

CITIZENSHIP

Those ranking in the upper 15 percentile, as determined by a ballot, shall be eligible for the citizenship pin. The ballots shall be given to Junior and Senior high schools the Friday before the close of the third quarter. The boys and girls shall be voted on together.

1. Honesty
2. Pride in appearance of school
3. Followership
4. Courtesy
5. Loyalty
6. Sportsmanship
7. Fellowship
8. Leadership
9. Sense of economic value
10. Obedience
11. Trustworthiness

ATHLETICS

Tests drawn up by the instructors of athletics shall be administered during the year. The results of these tests shall be used as the basis for determining the highest 15 percentile. The boys and the girls shall have separate tests and shall be separately listed.

Each item included on the citizenship ballot was formulated in discussions by the whole high school. None was included that did not receive a majority vote of the student body. The definitions of the qualities were based on the assembly discussions and were put on the ballot to insure uniform and impersonal marking. Insignia were awarded according to the results of the students' votes. The ballots were prepared in secret, signed by each high school student, and counted by the teacher members of the council. A sample ballot is shown on the following two pages.

Another illustration of student-rating is to be found in the Julia Richman High School, New York City. Each class in this school elects one student whose duty is to rate all the other students in the class on the various elements of personal appearance, habits, and characteristics. The teachers also make ratings. The final ratings, which go on the permanent record card, are a combination of the students' and teachers' marks.

CITIZENSHIP BALLOT OF THE LINCOLN SCHOOL

	FIRST CHOICE	SECOND CHOICE
SPORTSMANSHIP Is a good loser; wins without conceit or boasting; knows the rules of the game; plays fair; controls his temper; disdains "squealing."		
FELLOWSHIP Is an optimistic, cheerful companion; values friendships; recognizes and extols the good qualities of others; is tactful and kind regarding others' faults; avoids snobbishness.		
LEADERSHIP Accepts responsibility; inspires confidence; keeps mind on task rather than on self; promotes team work; sees a task through; weighs effect of act on future policy; has initiative; has energy; suppresses grouching.		
HONESTY Is truthful; accepts deserved blame; free from prejudice; rejects gossip; despises thieving.		
PRIDE IN APPEARANCE OF SCHOOL Keeps locker and cloakroom in order; neat in personal appearance; picks up waste paper; discourages crowding in halls and elevator; is helpful to visitors; avoids unseemly haste.		
SENSE OF ECONOMIC VALUE Realizes the value of things; careful of his own property and that of others; realizes that some one has earned and saved to produce all material goods; economizes time; is thrifty.		

CITIZENSHIP BALLOT OF THE LINCOLN SCHOOL (*Continued*)

	FIRST CHOICE	SECOND CHOICE
FOLLOWERSHIP Recognizes responsible leadership; values expert opinion; respects past experience; sacrificing of self for the sake of the task; coöperates cheerfully for the good of the group; works faithfully on committees.		
COURTESY Actions are prompted by an unconscious kindness of heart rather than mere social forms; deference to elders; helpful to those younger and weaker.		
LOYALTY Discourages "knocking"; encourages criticism which purposes to improve; has faith in the possibilities of the group; promotes school spirit.		
OBEDIENCE Abides by regulations of the school; recognition of authorities; namely, (1) teachers, (2) students in charge.		
TRUSTWORTHINESS Has sense of responsibility; keeps his word; can be trusted without supervision.		

Self-rating scales. — The student must see for himself what is being attempted in his education. In this way he can help in the process. He can analyze his difficulties and diagnose his troubles or weaknesses, and his efforts will be the more effective. One of the most interesting scales for this purpose is that of the South Philadelphia High School for Girls shown in Figure VII, pages 208 and 209.

Records and reports. — If developing good citizenship is the main function of the school, it is reasonable that records in citizenship should be kept and sent to the parents. This has not been done to any great extent because it is a very difficult task.

Some very interesting work of this sort has been done at the Horace Mann School For Girls, New York City. Prior to 1917, the usual form of report was sent periodically to parents, but a general dissatisfaction was felt because of the inaccuracy in marking students, the difference in standards of marking used, the undesirable effect of marks upon the students, and the lack of emphasis upon character development. In order to avoid these difficulties and to make the report mean more to the parents, as well as to emphasize the development of character, a committee was appointed and set to work. This committee developed a "Citizenship Scale," which was put to use in 1918 as an experiment. Its main feature was a chart showing an analysis of "habits and attributes desirable for good citizenship." This chart was "an analysis of conduct in terms of the concrete and specific habits and attitudes which should characterize the child who is taking his part as a good citizen in an elementary-school democracy." Later qualities and chart were made into "Eight Short Scales for Measuring the Habits of Good Citizenship." The card used to report "Estimate of Habits and Attitudes" is shown in Figure VIII on page 210.

The Philadelphia High School For Girls incorporated, as a part of the permanent record card, the "Character Record" shown in Figure IX on page 211. It will be noted in this list of character elements, that not one is represented by an array of high marks, necessarily. It is commonly assumed that character is a by-product of scholarship, but this is not invariably true. A student may receive high marks and, at the same time, fail to be neat, courteous, obedient, honest, and industrious. If these elements are important, they must be recognized and developed.

LAST NAME	FIRST NAME	SCHOOL	FIRST RATING	SECOND RATING	THIRD RATING
			192	192	192

DIRECTIONS FOR TEACHERS

1. Give out the form, inviting a general discussion, first, of the five subdivisions, and, second, of each individual question belonging to the grade.
2. The questions that are starred need especially to be discussed carefully and at length with *concrete* illustrations. In grades XI and XII, after collecting the form, discuss the improvement, if any, that the student discovers. It may help the others to have concrete illustrations of such improvements.
3. Give out the form a second time, allowing the student to rate self, by placing a check in the appropriate column.
4. It will not be enough simply to provide the time and opportunity for self-rating. This form ought to be discussed with each student in turn, probably in connection with actual ratings given by the teachers, in the personal interview with those who are in charge of educational and vocational guidance.

1. LEARNING ABILITIES

	GRADE X			GRADE XI			GRADE XII		
	HIGH	AVE.	LOW	HIGH	AVE.	LOW	HIGH	AVE.	LOW

To What Extent Are You Able:

1. To follow directions exactly?
2. To follow directions the first time that they are given?
3. To keep pace with the explanations of your teacher and with class discussions?
*4. To avoid asking foolish questions?
*5. To ask intelligent questions?
6. To recall facts and ideas brought out earlier in the course?
7. To see the relation of these to the newer work?
8. To sum up and explain without aid the point of an assigned lesson?
*9. To weigh the statements of your teachers and of textboooks, not accepting, necessarily, the ideas that are presented to you with authority?
*10. To discriminate, wisely, knowing when you must think for yourself and when it is wiser to accept, at least temporarily, the thinking of others?

2. ATTITUDE TOWARD THE SCHOOL

Have You Been Successful:

4. QUALITIES OF LEADERSHIP

	GRADE X			GRADE XI			GRADE XII		
	HIGH	AVE.	LOW	HIGH	AVE.	LOW	HIGH	AVE.	LOW

To What Extent:

*1. Have you the right kind of confidence (not over-confidence) in your own ability?
2. Have you been definitely helpful to individual students (say, two or more)—
  a. In their studies?
  b. In their club or other social activities?
3. Are you definitely helpful to your teachers?
4. Have you shown a real interest in numbers of other students (say, fifty) in school who are neither in your class or club, as shown—
  a. By knowing their names and speaking to them more than once?
  b. By being definitely helpful to some of them?
*5. Have you succeeded in developing your power—
  a. To suggest practical ideas and workable plans?
  b. To persuade and convince others?
  c. To organize others to carry out your practical ideas?
*6. Have your teachers recognized in you qualities of leadership by selecting you for positions of responsibility?

208

2. In attending on time?

3. In doing the best school work of which you are capable? If not, is it due to—
   a. Lack of industry?
   b. Too many outside interests?
   c. Outside work for self-support?
   d. Duties in the home?

*4. In sticking to problems and plans until completed?

5. In obeying and supporting the regulations of the officers of the Students' Association?

*6. In exercising self-control, so that you are a desirable member of the student body?

7. In acquiring a real and hearty interest in the work and play of the school?

3. TEAM WORK QUALITIES

To What Extent:

1. Have you considered the welfare of the class, instead of your own advantage?

2. Have you considered the welfare of the club, instead of your own advantage?

*3. Have you given hearty support to school activities?

*4. Have you been loyal to your class and clubmates, and to your school, with outsiders?

5. Can you "win without boasting, lose without excusing"?

*7. Have your classmates recognized in you qualities of leadership by selecting you for positions of responsibility?

8. Have you organized or led in activities outside the school?

9. Have you kept physically fit enough to bear the burden of leadership?

5. PERSONAL AND SOCIAL QUALITIES

To What Extent Do People Like You Because:

1. You are clean in your personal habits?

2. You are neat in your dress?

*3. You have no unpleasant mannerism?

4. You are interested either in the work or play of your classmates?

5. You are modest and unassuming?

*6. You are tactful in criticizing others?

7. You are courteous?

8. You have a sensible attitude toward the opposite sex?

9. You are honest—
   a. In your school work?
   b. Towards your classmates and other friends?

10. You realize your responsibility in carrying out plans—
   a. Started by yourself?
   b. Given you by others?

FORM H 85—SELF-RATING SCALE STUDENTS—SCHOOL DISTRICT OF PHILADELPHIA

FIGURE VII. — A SELF-RATING SCALE USED IN SOUTH PHILADELPHIA HIGH SCHOOL FOR GIRLS

1925-26	HORACE MANN HIGH SCHOOL FOR GIRLS																			
	Estimate of Habits and Attitudes																			
										YEAR_____										
Report of_____										SECTION ROOM_____										
	INDUSTRY					DEPENDABILITY					COURTESY					PUBLIC SPIRIT				
	1	2	3	4	5	1	2	3	4	5	1	2	3	4	5	1	2	3	4	5
First Quarter																				
Mid-year																				
Third Quarter																				
Final																				

FIGURE VIII. — THE FRONT OF THE "HABITS AND ATTITUDES" REPORT CARD USED BY THE HORACE MANN HIGH SCHOOL FOR GIRLS, NEW YORK CITY

EXPLANATION

Pupils are rated on four habits or attitudes on the basis of a five-part scale.

The marks record teachers' impressions of the pupil's behavior with respect to these qualities. No assumptions are made as to inner attitudes or motives.

The meaning of figures used in the ratings is given below:

1. Habit or attitude thoroughly established so that behavior is altogether satisfactory.

2. Habit or attitude positively in evidence, but behavior less satisfactory than indicated by "1".

3. Behavior neither definitely satisfactory nor definitely unsatisfactory.

4. Behavior unsatisfactory but to a less marked degree than is indicated by "5".

5. Habit or attitude so slightly developed that behavior is decidedly unsatisfactory.

THE BACK OF THE "HABITS AND ATTITUDES" REPORT CARD OF THE HORACE MANN HIGH SCHOOL FOR GIRLS

	FIRST YEAR	SECOND YEAR	THIRD YEAR	FOURTH YEAR
COURTESY..........................				
NEATNESS..........................				
INDUSTRY				
OBEDIENCE.........................				
HONESTY				
REGARD FOR DUTY..................				
INITIATIVE.........................				
COÖPERATION.......................				
SCHOOL SPIRIT......................				
INFLUENCE ON CLASSMATES............				
QUALITIES OF LEADERSHIP.............				
VOCATIONAL INTERESTS...............				
ENVIRONMENTAL INFLUENCES..........				
SCHOOL ACTIVITIES AND SCHOOL HONORS				
HONORS NOT AWARDED BY THE SCHOOL.				
GENERAL REMARKS...................				

FIGURE IX. — CHARACTER RECORD OF THE PHILADELPHIA HIGH SCHOOL FOR GIRLS

Citizenship awards. — Awarding " Citizenship " prizes of various kinds is becoming more and more common in high schools. Such awards are usually made at the end of the semester or year. The faculty or student body votes on the students most eligible for this recognition. Prizes consist of school monograms, pennants, medals, cups, or other trophies of recognized value and honor. In many communities the American Legion awards annually a prize to the " best citizen." Such award is made at commencement. Many colleges also make similar awards at commencement time.

Such an award has a certain value in that it sets a premium on citizenship. It may stimulate the other students toward the goal or ideal that is set up. The arguments against it are that it affects only one student or at the most a very small number, and second, that it makes no provision for definite training along the lines it represents. It merely recognizes what has been produced. Probably it would be more profitable if the time and attention were spent in attempts to increase the citizenship of the school generally through campaigns, drives, rating, and in other ways.

Citizenship contests. — Another method of emphasizing citizenship is the holding of citizenship contests, such as was recently held in the high schools of Birmingham, Alabama. Mr. Louis Pizitz, a public-spirited citizen of Birmingham, offered one hundred dollars to each of the five high schools as a prize for the development of " Citizenship Contests." A Contest Committee was appointed in each school and each committee handled the contest in its school in any way it chose. In the Phillips High School, for instance, the committee decided upon a contest based upon (1) points awarded for scholarship, punctuality, service, general behavior, extracurricular participation, etc., and (2) a " project." Each class (the contest was between the semester classes) chose its own project. One class established a " Vigilance Committee " to supervise traffic and halls; another class organized a committee of " Housekeepers " for the halls, grounds, etc.; another group saved tinfoil; and another presented a pageant. The class which won the contest presented as its project a mock election, in which all of the usual procedure — holding of convention, nomination of candidates, campaign speaking, and balloting — was followed. The group which won this contest at Phillips spent the hundred dollars prize money for a picture and presented it to the school.

Discussion and dramatization of citizenship. — The home-room or assembly period may be used to good advantage for the discussion, illustration, dramatization, or presentation of the various elements of good citizenship. Posters, newspaper publicity, tags, contests, and other devices may also be used. The following suggestions may be helpful in planning these programs:

The meaning of citizenship; patriotic lessons; history of flag; the flag salute; courtesy to the flag; love of the flag; flag songs. For illustrative material the following may serve:

Makers of the Flag, Franklin K. Lane
"The Man without a Country"
"Home Again," Van Dyke
Nathan Hale
Francis Scott Key
Barbara Frietchie
"The Flag Goes By," and other poems.

The various elements of a code of morals can be discussed and illustrated by use of historical or literary personages and events. The following, for instance, are suggestive:

Washington
Lincoln
Roosevelt
John Wanamaker
The Message to Garcia
Hobson
Robin Hood
Abou Ben Adhem
Roderick Dhu
Stories from Athletics and Sports
Fables and Other Stories

Another group of lessons might deal with such elements as dependableness, loyalty, accuracy, ambition, industry, faithfulness, truthfulness, perseverance, and patience. Such topics might be illustrated by the following material:

Columbus
Burbank
Thomas Edison
The Wright Brothers
Helen Keller
Benjamin Franklin
Mme. Curie

> Bible Stories: Jonathan and David
> Ruth and Naomi
> Damon and Pythias
>
> Dog Stories

Another important group of elements of citizenship is to be found in the ideals of service, and interesting programs may be made out of such topics as the Girl Scouts; Boy Scouts; Girl Reserves; Camp Fire Girls; Hi-Y; Red Cross; Clara Barton; Florence Nightingale; Earthquakes, Fires, and Floods; the Salvation Army; the Y.W.C.A. and Y.M.C.A.; Knights of Columbus; The Good Samaritan; Jane Addams; William Booth; David Livingstone; Samuel Gompers.

Civic truths and the various elements of citizenship are made the more interesting by being dramatized.

Organized courses in citizenship. — Regular courses in citizenship are beginning to appear. A pertinent suggestion in this connection was recently made by the Character Education Institution when its board of trustees passed the following resolution:

Resolved, That it will be wise to try the experiment of introducing into the high school curriculum, as a part of high school character education, a course dealing with the personal rights and obligations of the citizen, this course to constitute the main body of instruction in civics and sociology.

The argument has been made that the average boy or girl is not mature enough for very valuable participation in the discussion of vital sociological and civic problems. However, such a course as that suggested above would take the student as he is, include items with which he is somewhat familiar and which he is somewhat competent to discuss, and would lead him gradually to the larger problems. It is easy to predict that a very significant advance will be made along this line within the next decade. Many state departments of public instruction, as well as the Bureau of Education at Washington, publish material suitable for use in citizenship classes.

School Spirit

A very important element of citizenship is morale. The importance of morale was recognized during the war as it had never been recognized before. A great many devices such as amusements, games, singing, and activities in addition to the more technical activities of war, were used to build up and preserve this spirit of morale. The difference between the well drilled company and the mob is largely due to the presence or absence of this spirit, and in the final analysis is due to the presence or absence of this spirit in the individual member or unit.

Basic elements of morale or spirit. — Morale is based upon a number of elements, perhaps the largest of which is confidence. The individual who is confident is the one who has no fear of the outcome of the undertaking in which he is concerned. The attorney faces the jury, the teacher walks to class, or the player takes his position, in a confident manner because each knows what he can do. The individual who is not confident does not feel at home, and cannot concentrate his attention. His lack of confidence can then easily develop into panic.

True, there is such a thing as overconfidence when the individual miscalculates the size of the job or his own ability to do it. This frequently brings defeat for him; for he is thrown off his guard by the unexpected and cannot readjust himself to the new situation in time to defend himself.

Confidence is based largely upon two things: knowledge and ability; knowledge of what will or may happen, and ability to meet the situation. In short, confidence comes when the individual believes that he is prepared to meet a certain situation. The lawyer believes he will win the case; the teacher knows what he is going to do; and the player takes his place confidently because he knows and feels his ability.

A second element in spirit or morale is pride. The individual not only knows that he is master, but naturally takes pride in it. The desire to master is great in most individuals, and mastery naturally brings satisfaction. The team that knows it is good, or the individual who feels sure of himself cannot but be proud of it. Further, the strength of the beliefs and convictions of one individual are increased when he finds that others share them.

As with the individual, so with the school. School spirit was once defined by a student as " the feeling a school has when it knows it is good." The school that has confidence in its team has the faith that that team will win. True, the team may lose, but even that will not necessarily break down school spirit. The belief that this was a hard game or the consideration of other mitigating circumstances will help to excuse the team and keep up morale. The school that has confidence in its team takes pride in it, and confidence and pride are increased because they are commonly held by all members of the school. The result is solidarity, and the feeling known as school spirit.

It is clear that the student himself, even though not a member of the team, must feel that it represents him, and that he is a part of the team. I have but a passing interest in my neighbor's watch because it is his. In like manner, I have but passing interest in another school because it is not mine. I can never have much of a feeling for it so long as it is not mine. The student must feel that the school is his own : that he is a part of it and consequently *is* it. There will never be any school spirit where this is not true. Consequently the more opportunity for student participation about the school, the greater will be the spirit developed.

Again, the student must be convinced that the school is a good one. It is made up of a great many elements, and toward these proper attitudes must be developed. The more of which the student can be proud, the greater will be his school spirit. These elements may be the football team, band, an assembly schedule, dramatics, or a fine building.

Further, when the student likes his school it gives him pleasure and satisfaction to show this. Every one likes to talk about and show off the things of which he is proud. A wise program will provide opportunities for the student to express his legitimate pride in the school and its achievements.

In a sentence, the formula for creating school spirit is to develop a school of which the student is proud, and to give him opportunities to express his pride.

Methods of developing school spirit. — Indirectly, everything that increases the value or efficiency of school activities is a means of developing school spirit. The more successful the various activities, the more pride the student will have in them. Consequently, school spirit cannot be discussed apart from a consideration of school activities. It is not an end in itself any more than the assembly program is an end in itself. It is a means to making the school a better and more interesting place — a more educative place for the students.

The school as mentioned above, must offer opportunities for the student to share its work. Similarly, when he does a fine piece of work of any kind he should receive public recognition. This not only brings him pleasure, but shows the school another cause for self-respect.

Discussion should help the student to see what is especially good in the school. Informational talks about its most attractive features will be found profitable. Home-room discussion, assembly presentations, and newspaper publicity, of the things of which the school may feel satisfaction convinces the student that he is in a good school. And any school has a great many things about it of which it may be proud.

On the other hand, attention must be given to those elements most readily improved. This must not be overdone, however, for introspection may cause morbidity and dissatisfaction, and discourage rather than encourage school spirit. Several good items must be balanced against one bad. The confidence of the school must be built up and time and attention gradually directed to what most needs improvement. Only a fool imagines that he is always right in everything. It is just as stupid for a school to take the attitude that it has little or no room for improvement.

School spirit has to do with conduct at the games, in the assembly hall, on the street, in the classroom, in the lunchroom, and in the halls and corridors. There is little that the student can do that does not reflect upon his school. He must recognize this and assume the responsibility. His actions must show that he knows he is retailing to his fellows and to the community one part of the life of the school. Sportsmanship, courtesy, citizenship, and all of the other elements discussed express the attitude the student holds towards his school. Everything that he does reflects his school, and he is largely responsible for the attitude taken by the community toward the school.

School songs, yells, and parades in which all of the school participates are good for increasing morale. The assembly is a maker of good morale, for the student sees that he is a part of a large organization and enjoys belonging to it. The groups he usually sees are the small ones in the classes. Feeling himself a part of a large group in concerted activity helps to increase pride and spirit.

SUMMARY

The chief function of the school is to develop citizenship, and all of its activities should contribute to this general end. But direct emphasis may be placed upon the various elements of citizenship by the use of such devices as morality codes, citizenship balloting, self-rating scales, report and record cards, citizenship awards, discussion and dramatization of the elements of good citizenship, citizenship contests, and organized courses in citizenship. School spirit and morale is an important element in training for citizenship. Morale is based upon confidence and ability. Confidence is based upon knowledge of ability and pride in it. The school must provide opportunities for the student to participate in its life in order that he may feel a direct personal interest in it. Its organization, program, and activities must be such that he can take pride in them, and he should have opportunities for the expression of this pride.

REFERENCES

American Historical Association, Committee on History and Education for Citizenship. *Historical Outlook* 11 : 73–83, February, 1920.

BELTING, P. E. *The Community and Its High School*, Chapter XIV. D. C. Heath and Company.

BRADLEY, J. H. "Practicing Citizenship in the Lindsay High School," *Educational Administration and Supervision* 9 : 120–124, February, 1923.

Bulletin on Training for Citizenship, Third Series, no. 2. The National Municipal League, North American Building, Philadelphia.

CABOT, A. H. *A Course in Citizenship and Patriotism.* Houghton Mifflin Company.

DAVIS, C. O. "Training for Citizenship," *Fourth Yearbook*, National Association of Secondary Education Principals, 1920.

DUNN, A. W. "Civic Training through Service," *Teacher's Leaflet*, no. 8, June, 1920. Department of the Interior, Bureau of Education, Washington, D. C.

GOSLING, T. W. "A High School Program for Training Citizenship," *School Review* 28 : 57–65, January, 1920.

HATCH, R. W. *Training in Citizenship.* Charles Scribner's Sons.

Historical Outlook, numerous fine articles. McKinley Publishing Company.

HUBBARD, E. *Citizenship Plays.* I. E. Sanborn and Company.

HUGHES, H. W. "A Rating Scale for Individual Capacities, Aptitudes and Interests," *Journal of Educational Method*, October, 1920.

KITTRELL, C. A. "An Important Factor in Teaching Citizenship," *School Review* 29 : 366–372, May, 1921.

PICKELL, F. G. "Training for Citizenship through Practice," *School Review* 28 : 518–528, September, 1920.

RUGG, H. O. "Is the Rating of Character Possible?" *Journal of Educational Psychology*, November and December, 1921; and January and February, 1922.

SLEEZER, M. M. "Student Citizenship at the Senior High School," *School Review* 32 : 508–521, September, 1924.

TILLINGHAST, C. C. "Criteria for Judging Moral Training in Secondary Schools," *Seventh Yearbook*, National Association of Secondary-School Principals.

UPTON, C. B. and CHASSELL, C. F. "Measurement Scale in Citizenship," *Teachers College Record* 20 : 36–65, January, 1919.

United States Bureau of Education Bulletin. *List of References on Education for Citizenship*.

VOELKER, E. W. "The Organization and Functioning of Pupil Opinion in High School Control," *School Review* 34 : 654–667, November, 1926.

WOELLNER, F. P. *Education for Citizenship in a Democracy*. Charles Scribner's Sons.

WILEY, W. E. "Organization of Extracurricular Activities as a Device for Training in Citizenship," *School Review* 33 : 62–67, January, 1925.

CHAPTER XIII

MANNERS AND COURTESY

Dr. Eliot has said that the teaching of manners and morals is plainly one of the most important parts of education. There is probably little in the original nature of the child which forces him to be mannerly and courteous or a good citizen in a broad sense. In fact, it seems that original nature forces him in the opposite direction. He is so selfish and rude in his manner and so outspoken and boisterous in his talk that he frequently seems to lack all of the social niceties which the adult would like to see in him.

All men must live in a social world, all must take attitudes towards others. The student will not by nature be mannerly; he must be taught. Most of us learn our courtesy at tremendous expense through more or less incidental experiences. The student just picks up his manners if he gets them at all. The result is that he has none to spare.

TEACHING COURTESY

The teaching of manners and courtesy is difficult, for it attempts to change habits which have become entrenched in the student. Consequently, serious study and the most earnest application are required. Certain principles are basic. The most important of these are as follows:

The faculty must recognize and accept its responsibility. — Too frequently the teacher teaches his subject instead of his object. He is too much interested in teaching the material of the textbook to have time to teach habits of good living. It is easier of course to teach facts than it is to teach habits.   Such a teacher's interests are in the subject and not in the student.   Consequently, he can easily escape thinking of the responsibility for these extra duties which lie outside of the narrow confines of his subject. The teacher may not be entirely to blame; the system of education may be responsible.   Work in courtesy has been done largely incidentally — that is, hardly done at all.   The faculty must recognize that its job is to teach the youngster and not merely the subjects, and in doing this to make provision for many things which are not to be found within the limits of the regular subjects.

Students should participate in planning and executing plans. — Sermons and moralizings by the faculty or principal probably have little effect on the actions of the students.   They will set standards for conduct, but that will not make the student elect to emulate them.   They must be helped along by the students themselves, as a part of their problem.   Moreover, if standards are set which the student helps to make, he will tend to follow them more readily because they are his.   Further, students who have an interest in the promotion of any project or purpose, have just so many additional points of contact with the student body. Besides, the student may react in very different ways to the same thing when desired by the teacher or by a respected student friend.   The council or other student representative body should have a great share in the organization and execution of any plan for teaching courtesy and coöperate very closely with the faculty. Such coöperation brings dignity, prestige, and system to the project and makes it more sure of success.

Methods of Teaching Courtesy

A number of methods may be used to teach the student good manners and courtesy.   Perhaps the best single method would be a combination of all of these.   In such a subject as this there is danger of too much moralizing and preaching.   Good advertising and selling methods are essential.

By association and observation. — Every individual learns a great deal from the people with whom he associates.   In like manner the student may learn a great deal from associating with or by watching those who are more courteous and gracious than he.   The teacher must be the example of courtesy.   A teacher or principal who " bawls " at his students or who in other ways violates good usage need not expect to be listened to when he leads the discussion of the topic of good manners.   The many little acts of outsiders being shown about the building, speakers and performers in assembly, etc., may be appropriated for this teaching.   Lists and discussion of " Courteous Acts I Saw To-day " make a good basis for the general improvement of ideals of good manners.

In literature and history. — There are many fine examples of graciousness, heroism, and unselfishness, to be found in the literature the student reads.   History is full of them.   Lofty emotional sentiments are usually found in poetry.   The teacher can employ these to raise the ideal of courtesy if he will.   Such practice is always appropriate no matter what may be the particular aim of the class at the time.   Much may be done in the more or less formal composition work required of the student.

By campaigns and drives. — Education by special drives or campaigns is psychologically sound.   We want the student always to use good English, but we can emphasize this and give it a special interest and effectiveness by conducting an advertising campaign for " Better Speech."   The business man has his goods for sale all the time, but by skilful and clever advertising he emphasizes certain goods and values and increases his volume of sales.   The school campaign does exactly the same thing. Courtesy can be emphasized in this manner.   Naturally this work will not be limited to this one week any more than the storekeeper would limit his sale of one particular article to the one week. The courtesy campaign merely emphasizes and gives added impetus to the campaign continuously being conducted. Home-room talks and discussions, assembly programs, dramatizations, posters, newspaper publicity, contests, compositions in English, and Civics all serve to emphasize this important aspect of school life. The following devices may be used during the campaigns:

Posters. — Good publicity for campaigns may be had through the use of posters, bulletins, and freak advertisements. Such posters may be made by the Art department. A contest held for the best in ideas and in execution would arouse interest, especially if the various home rooms competed.

Tags. — Tags may be used to good advantage in " Courtesy Drives." Each student is given a tag, button, pin, or similar durable device at the beginning of the drive. When he sees or hears a breach of etiquette or good manners he immediately gives his button to the offending student, who must take it and wear it. The offender may receive only one tag for an offense, the first individual " catching " him having the right to tag him. An " honor " or " courtesy " roll is kept in each home room or in the assembly and names of untagged students are posted twice a day. A variation of this is to consider the tag a badge of honor and take it from the student who violates a law of courtesy. A plan may be worked out whereby he can regain it by showing proper respect for others.

Cards. — Each student in school is given a number — say ten — of small " Courtesy Cards." These are to be given to other students for breaches of etiquette. Each student must keep a list of the names of the students to whom he gives his cards. The names of the students who have given away all of their cards are placed on the " Courtesy " or " Honor Roll." A central body or committee is established and to this are referred any cases in which there is a question of whether the alleged breach is a violation or not.

Formulation and codification of rules of good conduct. — The establishment of proper ideals and attitudes by campaigns, discussions, or other means should result in the publication of a set of suggestions for good manners. Copies should be given to all students. The work should not stop with this codification but should continue, the booklet or sheet being used as the basis for further study and improved continuously.

One illustration of this type of code is that adopted at Johnstown, Pennsylvania and shown below. This code was neatly printed in a small folder and distributed to the students of the school:

A Student's Code of Courtesy

I hereby pledge myself to do my best to uphold the standards of my school and to make my conduct on the school grounds, about the building, in the halls and classrooms fitting to my position as a student of the Johnstown Senior High School.

ABOUT THE BUILDING

I will endeavor to be polite in my conduct to outsiders.

I will not throw snowballs in front of, or about, the building.

I will not deface the building by writing or painting anything upon the walls, and will refrain from smoking while near the building.

I will not drop waste paper on the grounds nor about the building.

I will be sportsmanlike and considerate of visitors at all games.

IN THE HALLS

I will remove my hat upon entering the building.

I will assist whenever possible by opening doors for teachers and students.

I will be orderly in the halls, and respect the rights of others by not hurrying, and will refrain from boisterous talking and laughing.

I will refrain from unladylike and ungentlemanlike conduct in the halls.

I will be considerate when in the lunch-line and take my turn.

I will not eat in any part of the building except such places set aside for this purpose.

I will not carelessly drop bits of paper in the halls but will deposit all paper in receptacles.

IN THE CLASSROOM

I will enter classrooms in a prompt and orderly manner.
I will show my respect for teachers by speaking politely and by complying with their requests.
I will assume an attentive attitude during class and will rise to recite.
I will not make annoying noises or indulge in conversation with neighbors.
I will not make my toilet in public.

IN THE AUDITORIUM

I will be quiet and attentive during chapel exercises even if I am not interested or cannot hear.
I will not cause the speaker discomfort by laughing at mistakes he may make during a mass meeting or class meeting.
I will not push or hurry when entering or leaving the auditorium.
I will aim at all times to give outsiders the right impression of the Johnstown Senior High School by being courteous and by being a good loser as well as a good winner.

Making a definite study of courtesy and etiquette. — The many little details of etiquette must be learned. Consequently they can be taught. There are a number of ways of teaching them, the most expedient being the following:

Use of books. — There are now on the market a number of small books designed for use in teaching students courtesy. The larger and more formal are naturally more complete but not so effective in teaching, for they are not closely adapted to school life and school situations.

A very good example of a special book is *Manners and Conduct In School and Out.*[1] It is the result of a constructive piece of work done by the Deans of Girls of the Chicago High Schools. Another suitable book is *Fiber and Finish.*[2] Perhaps the most

---

[1] Published by Allyn and Bacon.
[2] Written by E. E. Dodd, published by Ginn and Company.

attractive for school use is *Everyday Manners* [1] prepared by the faculty of the South Philadelphia High School for Girls. The book is attractively written and illustrated, and each chapter ends with " Problems; who will solve them? " These problems have to do with actual situations.

Assembly programs. — Material on courtesy can be utilized in the assembly-room program in a variety of ways — talks, discussions, debates, dramatizations, and shadowgraphs. The weakness of talks, especially by faculty members, is that the student is merely a listener.

Interesting and attractive assembly talks may be made on " Illustrations of Good Manners That Paid." Many illustrations of the value of good manners can be found in business. A few of these could be mentioned and briefly discussed by a teacher, or better still by a well known business man. Actual situations are always better than hypothetical ones. Such material can be easily obtained from the teachers by one of their number and presented in the assembly program. The inclusion of the name of the teacher who contributed each item would make a more personal contact with the student.

Dramatizations. — The high school at McKees Rocks, Pennsylvania, recently held a program in which " Things as They Are " and " Things as They Should Be " were dramatized. The dramatizations concerned courtesy in the assembly room, classroom, home room, dressing-room, cafeteria, and at the games. A formal " Trial of Bad Manners and Miss B. Havior " can be presented as the climax to a school campaign for better manners.

The fashion show is a very effective way of showing good taste in dress. Girls suitably and unsuitably dressed may walk upon the platform one at a time. Another girl may explain just why the person is unsuitably or suitably dressed. Dresses for signifi-

[1] Published by The Macmillan Company.

cant occasions may be illustrated and discussed. Hats, shoes, stockings, and coats may be considered.

Dress is not the only thing which can be dramatized in this manner. Excessive use of make-up, care of hair, deportment when dressed up are also subjects for the fashion show. Designers from the larger stores in town usually very willingly give their services and supply much fine material for these shows. It is good advertising. Further, the designers are professionals and make the program all the better.

Boys' clothes are so standardized that there can be little variety shown. But such things as soiled collars, mussed hair, muddy shoes, and dirty clothes can be dramatized.

Dramatization may be made of manners at table, at the telephone, in the street, the street car, and elsewhere.

Shadowgraphs. — Shadowgraphs can be used to good advantage in the dramatization of table manners. The table is set behind a screen. Strong light comes from the rear. One student reads or explains in a clear voice what is being done. Where the " right " and " wrong " are being shown the " wrong " should never be shown last. Another good form of dramatization is the dumb show or pantomime.

Home-room programs. — Probably the best place in the school to teach manners and courtesy is in the home room. The group is smaller than that in the assembly, and this means there is less of the mob spirit to disconcert and divert attention from what is being done to some trifling but amusing incident ; and questions can be asked and the students themselves can enter into the discussion. Important subjects suitable for discussion are as follows :

FRIENDSHIP

What do you expect of a friend?
Understanding, loyalty, cheerfulness.
Definition and explanation of friendship and friendliness.

How many kinds of friends can we have?

Relatives, chums, boy and girl friends, mere speaking acquaintances, school friends, church friends, people in need of friendship.

On forming cliques.

Short sketches, illustrating friendliness, on such topics as speaking on the street, visiting lonely people, friendliness to new students, friendliness to country students, friendliness to students in general, friendliness to teachers, talking about your friends, developing a pleasing personality.

COURTESY

IN THE CLASSROOM

Interrupting another; talking in undertone, humming; rustling papers, shuffling feet; eating candy; rushing in or out; slouchiness; being disrespectful to visitors; whispering; snapping fingers; "blurting" or "explosive" answers; mumbling and indistinct speech; being late to take one's seat; ridiculing answers or statements; passing notes; throwing wads, chalk, shot, erasers; drumming on desk with pencil; kicking seat in front; rising in seat to attract attention of teacher; tittering or snickering at the bashful student; dropping or knocking books on the floor; "Smart Aleck" remarks and foolish questions.

IN THE ASSEMBLY

Whispering or talking; tittering and snickering; boisterous laughing or clapping applause; reading or studying.

AT THE GAME

Failure to show good sportsmanship; jeering or ridiculing; "booing" or "razzing" opponents or officials; boasting; petty and childish exhibitions after a victory; losing gracefully; recognizing merit in opponents; "playing hard" *vs.* "unnecessary roughness."

IN THE LUNCHROOM

Throwing material; shouting; noisiness, upsetting chairs; crowding and rushing for places; spilling food on the floor, table, and others; pleasing habits in eating.

AT THE TABLE

Entering the dining-room; being seated; use of various pieces of silver; eating of various foods; passing and refusing dishes; accidents; conversation; leaving table.

IN STREET CARS OR WHILE TRAVELLING

Rushing and crowding; noisy and rude behavior; loud talking; seats for ladies and elders; boarding and alighting with a lady; annoying and teasing conductors or trainmen; asking for information; buying a ticket; courtesy with baggage, bundles, and umbrellas; sharing a seat.

IN CORRESPONDENCE

What is courtesy in correspondence? paper, (color, quality, shape, size, and ink); use of wax, seals, scented paper; invitations, engraving, "R. S. V. P."; order of pages, folding, mailing; salutations and closings; addresses, abbreviations, punctuations; notes of apology and explanation; answers, form and content; exhibit of suitable letters, notes, and invitations.

AT THE THEATER

Punctuality; entering and leaving; boisterousness in talking and applause; precedence going down and up the aisles; removing hat; courtesy in box seats; chaperons; dinner afterwards?

AT THE PARTY

Invitations and acceptances; teasing to stay when closing time comes; incorrect dancing; courtesy regarding "bumping"; courtesies to Hostess, Chaperon, or Patroness; asking for a dance; accepting or refusing a dance; expressing appreciation for a dance; introductions; discussion of embarrassing social duties.

IN DRESS AND PERSONAL APPEARANCE

Extreme or poor taste; conspicuousness; attending to details of toilet in public; excessive rouge and powder; emphasizing "remaking" in make-up; continuous primping, pruning, and preening.

MISCELLANEOUS

Interrupting a person who is speaking; chewing gum; making-up in public; tilting or rocking a chair; boisterousness; lack of respect for superiors; crowding, shoving, and jostling; sitting while being addressed by lady or superiors; giving precedence to girls and ladies; removal of hats by boys; whistling and singing; boys' hands in pockets; use of "Hey there,"

"Listen," "Say, you"; passing in front of people; impudence and lack of tact; cluttering up floor or street with papers; looking over some one's shoulder; snatching books; placing feet on desks or chairs; sitting on desks; tripping; ridiculing others; proper form in salutation; undue familiarities; slang expressions; apologies; "wise cracks"; banging doors; defacing property; studying aloud; indifference to others; borrowing from others; personal cleanliness; criticism; staring at visitors; courtesy in regard to perfume, onions, garlic; rummaging through desks or lockers of others; hazing new students; foolish fads in dress, actions, expressions; cribbing and petty thieving; vulgarity; smoking; gossiping and tale bearing; mimicking pecularities or weaknesses; courtesy in the elevator; on the stairs; courtesy on the street; in the automobile.

Discussion of problems. — Actual situations are valuable in teaching the student courtesy. He must actually practice courtesy just as he must swimming or football. Knowing about it is not sufficient. The following problem illustrates this type of activity:

Mary and her friend Dora are visiting Beulah. At noon Beulah's father comes home. He knows Mary but has never met Dora. Plan the introductions and dramatize them.

In the evening Dora's brother George calls with Will to spend the evening. John has also been invited and arrives late. Plan the introductions and see that each boy is made to "feel at home" as soon as possible.

Many of such problems can be originated by the students themselves. The book *Everyday Manners*, already mentioned, presents a fine set of such problems at the end of each chapter.

Use of question box. — A question box can be used to good advantage, especially just before a party or social event. Questions are written anonymously and dropped into this box. Solutions to these may then be discussed in home room or in informal assembly meeting.

Preparation of "Do" and "Do Not" lists. — A campaign may be divided into parts and one day set aside for emphasis upon table manners, another for classroom manners, another for assembly manners. Lists of "Do" and "Do Not" may be arranged and discussed each day in the home-room meeting, and attractively posted on the bulletin board of the room. This must not be looked upon as the end of the campaign. It merely emphasizes the "knowing" part of courtesy. The habit part comes only by practice.

Preparation of list of objectionable and commendable acts actually seen about the building each day. — One way to emphasize the local importance of good manners is to have each student watch for discourteous or unmannerly offenses about the school. These are noted together with the name of the student, the time, and the place. Each student then brings his illustrations to the home-room meeting and reports them. A discussion follows. Of course when the students know that they are being watched they will be more careful. Naturally each offense should be corrected by suggestion as to what should have been done.

Capital should, also, be made of the courtesy shown by visitors, visiting speakers or performers, or notable examples in games. Such purely local examples which the students can see and appreciate are worth far more than the hypothetical or actual ones which the students do not see. The importance of the cheer leader in the training for good manners at the game will be discussed in the chapter on athletic activities. Discouraging booing, groaning, razzing, and yelling during signals and encouraging yelling for the opposing team, injured opponents, and good plays are important parts of his work. All of this material can be capitalized in home-room discussions.

Collection of quotations. Quotations dealing with manners and courtesy may be collected and posted or distributed, and competition organized between the various rooms or groups. Mere collection must not be emphasized as the main goal of the drive. The following are examples of this kind of quotation :

Life is not so short but that there is always time enough for courtesy.
— EMERSON

The greater man, the greater courtesy. — TENNYSON

Neither a borrower nor a lender be:
For loan oft loses both itself and friend. — SHAKESPEARE

The gentle mind by gentle deeds is known. — SPENSER

Development of slogans. — Slogans and catchy phrases have great advertising values. They are suitable devices to use in campaigns of any kind. Examples of such slogans are:

Mend Your Manners
Courtesy Counts
The Voice with the Smile Wins
Be Polite: It Pays
Manners Are Shadows of Great Virtues

Competition always adds interest to campaigns and drives of any sort. Competition in the development of slogans, creeds, codes, and commandments all make for increased interest. The Irwin Junior High School, Pittsburgh, recently held a competition in the development of a " Ten Commandment " series. Home rooms, groups, or individual students could compete in this contest. Competition between groups, or rooms may be organized around the tag and card devices suggested before. Or the school may, if small, be divided into two or three sections and a contest be held to determine which section is the most courteous. Another possibility would be a contest between upper and lower classes or between boys and girls.

Use of publications. — In addition to the books and codes mentioned, good use may be made of other publication agencies, particularly the newspaper, magazine, and handbook. The topic lends itself very easily to special feature writings and cartooning. During a campaign a regular space may be reserved for " Pertinent Questions " such as " What would you do? "

The following questions on voice, William Penn High School for Girls, Philadelphia, illustrate attractive and interesting publicity.

Is your voice

shrill	gentle?
high-pitched	well-modulated?
rasping	harmonious?
blatant	calm?
raucous	pleasant?
strident	serene?
boisterous	subdued?
vociferous	low?
hoidenish	restrained?
obstreperous	quiet?
stentorian	moderate?

or

Parodies and songs are likewise in order.

The following illustration is typical of what many schools do in regard to calling attention to the fact that the student represents the school, that his every action reflects it:

CUSTOMS AND MANNERS AT SOUTH HIGH

Very often you are not yourself; sometimes you are a person called South High. If you do something rude, people say that South High is rude. If you are very nice and make a good impression, they say South High is nice. Because this is true, everything you do brings credit or disgrace to the school as a whole. Let us try to live well in South High. Let us learn what is fine and good.

DO IT FOR SOUTH

It is not expected at South High that teachers must watch students. You are "on your honor" a large part of the time. If you do things when you are not watched, you advertise the fact that you have little or no honor.

It takes little brain power to be tricky or sly. The slyest people are in asylums or prisons. South High is neither.

Your self-respect is shown in the friends you choose, the places you go to, and in your general conduct.

One who puts on airs is always tiresome company and usually is ridiculous. We admire one who makes his natural self his best self.

No self-respecting person indulges in indecent talk. People who do that should be shunned and made to feel so uncomfortable that they either reform or leave school.

A person who respects himself keeps himself healthy physically, mentally, and morally.

Keep yourself clean by frequent bathing.

See that your breath is not offensive.

Change your underclothes frequently.

A well-bred person is one whose politeness is a habit.

One of the surest ways to measure the good breeding of a person is to watch how members of the family treat each other. Brothers and sisters should be courteous to each other.

A child should always allow the mother to go first through a door, or down an aisle, or into a car. He should never sit down till the mother is seated.

A boy follows his father, opens the door for him, sees that he is seated.

It is impolite to eat when in company. Do not chew gum.

To make fun of another person is always a mark of low breeding.

— THE BOOK OF SOUTH HIGH
Youngstown, Ohio.

Organization of courtesy club. — The formation of a " Prevention of Social Cruelties Club " or some similar organization would be beneficial for those students who were interested enough to want to belong. Its greatest weakness is in that its benefits would be limited to a small group. It could, however, be instrumental in the promotion of good manners throughout the school.

Study in courtesy classes. — In some schools courtesy classes are provided in the regular schedule. In still others, such classes are provided for those who have failed in deportment for the term or period. These students must attend the classes for the following period, prepare assignments, have recitations, and pass examinations at the end of the period. Recognized books on etiquette are used as texts. Such a practice is disciplinary in purpose and probably not educative to any great extent. Knowing what should be done does not mean that the student does it.

Summary

One of the important elements of good citizenship is courtesy. The faculty of the school must recognize and accept responsibility for teaching it. Plans for teaching courtesy should be reasonable, progressive, and continuous. The students themselves should help to develop and execute these plans. Courtesy may be taught through association and observation; by the use of illustrations in literature and history; of campaigns and drives; by formulation and codification of rules of good conduct; and by making a definite study of courtesy by means of books, assembly and home-room programs, problems, quotations, slogans, and publications. A good way to begin this teaching is to establish a courtesy club. Learning about courtesy does not insure courteous conduct. Courtesy implies habits as well as standards, and habits are developed only by practice.

References

Character Education Institution Publications, Washington, D. C.

DEWEY, J. M. *How to Teach Manners to School Children.* Noble, Noble and Noble.

DODD, E. E. *Fiber and Finish.* Ginn and Company.

ELLIOTT, C. W. "Democracy and Manners," *Century Magazine* 83 : 173–178, December, 1911.

HALL, G. S. "Flapper Americana Novissima," *Atlantic Monthly*, June, 1922.

McNAUGHT, M. *Training in Courtesy*, Department of the Interior, Bureau of Education, *Bulletin 54*, 1917.

Everyday Manners, South Philadelphia High School for Girls. The Macmillan Company.

Manners and Conduct, Chicago High School Deans of Girls. Allyn and Bacon.

CHAPTER XIV

ATHLETICS

Physical activities have always been an important part of the education of the child. They date back to the very beginning when the individual was taught to take care of himself. He learned to hunt, swim, fight, and in other ways to use his body to his own advantage. The ideal of physical education was formalized by the Athenians, the Spartans, and the Romans and received a great deal of attention. Later inventions in war equipment made the use of sword, shield, and spear less valuable, but formations and marching technique were always taught. In Europe physical education later took the form of gymnastics and calisthenics.

While formal gymnastics and calisthenics were being used inside the gymnasium, athletic games were in progress outside. Football, baseball, and track events became popular. Soon came interscholastic competition. As athletics became popular, formal gymnasium work became less so and the attention the student gave grudgingly to gymnasium work he gave freely to athletics.

DEVELOPMENT OF SECONDARY INTERSCHOLASTIC ATHLETICS

Period of opposition. — The first period in the development of secondary interscholastic relations has been called the period of opposition, the opposers being the school authorities. The school's function was to improve the student mentally, not physically. However, despite the attitude of the educational authorities, the students played interscholastically under the name of the school. Coached and backed by townsmen who were always seeking a thrill and boosting town enterprises, these teams without training rules, regulations, or restraint brought so much disgrace upon the school that it was forced to recognize them for self-protection.

Period of toleration. — In this second period the school assumed no obligation for teaching the students. The teams were still usually coached by the students and alumni or by the town sportsmen. The school merely provided for the protection of its name. It was not interested in the games or events themselves. But this arrangement was not satisfactory. The teams were not successful; they violated the rules and regulations, and continued to bring disgrace upon the school.

Period of coöperation. — The school now assumed control, employed and controlled the coaches, and did what it could to help keep the games and relations respectable. Interscholastic athletic associations were formed and helped to set the limitations necessary to make the contests reputable. Most schools are now in this third stage. There is now keen competition to secure collegiate stars and competent coaches, the latter commanding ever larger salaries; a wave of stadia building; and the expenditure of sums of money which are enormous compared with those of thirty years ago.

Values of Athletics

Physical values. — Physical development for adults has probably been over-emphasized. Commercial and semi-commercial organizations have combined to magnify adult physical training out of all proportion to its real value. All men need physical exercise, but few need as much as physical-education enthusiasts would have them take. What they need is recreation, maintenance, not developmental work. And maintenance can be had with a great deal less exertion and energy than development.

The student, however, needs a vigorous and developmental activity. Football, basketball, and baseball give this vigorous practice. Efficiency demands, too, that he feel well. He will not feel well if he is not in health. It was probably by no mere chance that the Committee on Reorganization of Secondary Education named health as its first cardinal principle.

Recreational values. — A most important value of physical activities is the recreational. It has been found that a period in a formal gymnasium class takes as much energy as a class in mathematics or language. The student needs a rest from things largely mental. He gets this by temporarily emphasizing things largely physical. He " lets loose," has a good time, and comes back to his work refreshed in mind and body.

Recreational work means games and play of a lighter nature in which the student plays for the fun of it. His recreational interest should be widened. He should be taught those activities in which he can take an interest when he is old. As an adult he will probably never play football, basketball, or baseball. He will play tennis and golf, will swim, hike, and skate. If the school is to teach him to do better the desirable things he is going to do anyway, it should make some attempt to teach or interest him in these activities.

Educational values. — Other values of physical activities are in their mental and social training. The student learns by playing with a team that he is only a part of that team. This teaches him coöperation. He learns to subordinate himself for the good of the group. This is the first step in the building of a public spirit. The students learn both to lead and to follow. As there are many varied opportunities in athletics, nearly all students can do the thing in which they are most interested. Healthy competition for places on the teams will help to draw out the best in the players.

Athletics present many valuable educational opportunities, but these must be utilized. The coach who sits on the side lines and tells his players what play to use, or who in other ways directs the game from the bench is not teaching the students to think for themselves. He thinks for them and they merely have to carry out the mechanics of his thinking. He is robbing them of educational opportunities. True, they may lose the game if they think for themselves. But here again it is a question of relative value between winning the game or educating the players. The professional baseball manager signals his men what to do and where and how to play. This is different, however: it is for business ends — the game must be won. It is not played for the education of the players.

Athletics offer many opportunities for the development of the boy or the girl. Frequently the slow student has found himself or the hot-headed one has discovered that it does not pay to " lose one's head " when in the game. The player explores his interests and capacities and develops them. Moreover, it has been shown that athletics motivate school work.

Good sportsmanship is an important social element that must be developed through competitive play. Good sportsmanship will not willingly let the opponents win and will take legitimate advantage of all of its opportunities, especially those caused by mistakes of the opponent. It will play just as hard as it can; but it will play fairly. Good sportsmanship involves following the rules and playing cleanly. Good coaches emphasize this point.

Attractive codes and creeds help in the education of the students and the building of a sportsmanlike atmosphere in the school. The following are examples of such codes:

CODE OF A GOOD SPORTSMAN

1. Thou shalt not alibi.
2. Thou shalt not quit.
3. Thou shalt not gloat over winning.
4. Thou shalt not be a rotten loser.
5. Thou shalt not take unfair advantage.

6. Thou shalt not ask odds thou art loath to give.
7. Thou shalt always be ready to give thine opponent the shade.
8. Thou shalt not under-estimate an opponent, nor over-estimate thyself.
9. Remember, the game is the thing, and he who thinketh otherwise is a mucker.
10. Honor the game thou playest, for he who playeth the game straight and clean and hard is a winner even when he loses.

— *The Northern Light*, Northern H. S., Detroit.

TEN COMMANDMENTS

Don't yell, "Killum team!"
Don't think you know more than the team. You don't.
Don't forget your manners; if you have none, get some.
Don't forget to cheer all men injured.
Don't cheer or groan on penalties.
Don't forget that the officials are the judges.
Don't make fun of opponents.
Don't cheer during signals.
Don't forget to be a sportsman, winner or loser.

— *West High School Weekly*, West High School, Minneapolis.

One excellent way to help to promote good sportsmanship is to award a trophy. The following article from the *West High Weekly*, Minneapolis, October 20, 1922, illustrates this type of procedure:

J. E. MEYERS AGAIN GIVES SPORTSMANSHIP TROPHY

J. E. Meyers is offering this year as a trophy to the high school displaying the best sportsmanship during the football season, a silk flag and streamer. Should a school win the emblem twice, a streamer will be given.

"It is not so much the value of the trophy that should be coveted, but the honor which is attached to it," says C. W. Boardman.

The school as well as the teams and coaches will be judged in the following manner:

Ten judges will be selected to grade the school as follows:

1. Five citizens not connected with any school will be appointed to each team, and score the players of all schools as they played that team.
2. Five faculty members, one from each school, will score the students of the schools as they meet their own team. These five faculty judges will

circulate about the grandstands, and will consider the behavior of the students of the competing schools, before, during, and after the games.

Points will be scored for or against the contending players, substitutes or coaches as follows:

1. Violation of the rules of sportsmanship or conduct before, during, or after the game. This includes the use of abusive or profane language, deliberate violations of the rules of the game such as slugging, unnecessary rough play, ragging the officials, refusing to abide by a decision, ragging the opposing team, and other acts tending toward unsportsmanlike conduct.

2. Points will be scored for a team for meritorious conduct such as conceding a doubtful point, assisting an injured opponent, orderly conduct, loyalty to own school and team, etc.

A "Sportsmanship Program" recently initiated by Mr Homer L. Thomas, Supervisor of Athletics at Birmingham, Alabama, illustrates a high type of development. The various schools competed in "Sportsmanship" for a loving cup which was finally awarded by a committee of three disinterested citizens. Themes were written on sportsmanship in all schools and the best of these were sent to the judges. Poetry, stories, essays, and plays were written. One group of students wrote a masque. Ideas for this were gathered from the entire group, and one girl then wrote the blank verse, one composed the music, one designed the costumes, and others originated and directed the dancing. Another group of students prepared "The Annals of the Sportsman," a series of tableaux showing the evolution of the sportsman from Cain down to the present as he has been pictured in literature. "Sportsmanship" numbers of the school papers were issued, and a page in the Sunday edition of the Birmingham *New* was given to the topic. The result of such an extensive and thorough program could not but result in improved ideals and practice in sportsmanship.

In some communities the local papers sponsor sportsmanship campaigns or awards. For instance, the Pittsburgh *Sun* gives each year a set of good sportsmanship medals to the players or

Pittsburgh High School teams who are voted by their opponents to have shown fine sportsmanship during the season. These medals are awarded at a banquet attended by all players and coaches.

The cheer-leader is an important individual about the school in promoting good sportsmanship. It is easy to learn that a good sportsman does not groan at penalties nor become abusive of officials and opponents, but during the excitement of the game it is easier still to forget this and to lapse into unsportsmanlike conduct. The cheer-leader, by discouraging groans and jeers and by calling for cheers for opponents, injured players, or even for good plays of opponents, can lessen the demonstrations of poor sportsmanship on the part of the spectators.

In fostering school spirit. — Every student should have something worthy to which he can attach his loyalty; for all students have loyalty in greater or less degree. To have a school interest against a common enemy is a good way to increase school spirit. No matter how much the members of a family may fight among themselves, they all join to attack an outsider who tries to take a part. Nations uniting against a common enemy have many times built up confidence and morale. Interscholastic athletics can accomplish this for the school. And if a school does not teach and emphasize loyalty, it fails in one of its duties.

Advertising the school. — The publicity that comes from interscholastic athletics has been offered as one of its virtues. Some colleges and universities are said to have been " made " by their football teams. That is, students were attracted, and connections were made with influential and wealthy families because of the publicity received. Probably to some degree this is true of high schools. Certainly the average student likes to attend a school which has an outstanding football team. The publicity may cause the school to try to live up to its name and reputation. The responsibility is all the greater when there is a reputation to uphold.

Objections to Interscholastic Athletics

Many objections have been raised to interscholastic athletics The most important of these are as follows:

They benefit too few students. — Interscholastic competition i usually between the first teams. This means that the number o players must be limited. Of course substitute players will b needed, and two or more teams may have been used in regula practice; but in any case the comparatively small number o players remains as one of the greatest objections to interscholasti athletics. Moreover, the student who needs the exercise least i the very one who gets it most; for he is the best player and mus be used to win, while the student who really needs the exercis is the one who does not get it because he is not competen enough to play on the team.

They are expensive in time and money. — More money i raised and spent on interscholastic athletics than on all of th other extracurricular activities combined. This tends to over emphasize the importance of athletics. The epidemic of stadium building which is now sweeping the country in university circle is being paralleled in high schools. One wag has suggested that a university is a " stadium with a college attached." High salaried coaches, expensive equipment, and heavy travelling expenses combine to make athletics expensive in any school.

Further, they require a great deal of time. Football takes from two to four hours each day of the school week. Basketball, track, and other athletics also require a considerable amount of time. The objectors state that while some time may be spent in athletics justifiably, so much as this means the slighting of the regular curricular work of the school.

They encourage commercialism and professionalism. — This is a serious indictment of interscholastic athletics. Basketball, football, hockey, and other former amateur sports have become professional games. This has brought with it a temptation to the amateur who excels in them. The professional must win at any cost. The continuous emphasis on winning is imitated by the amateurs usually to the detriment of the other values of the sport. Where winning is the most important consideration, betting and gambling with their frequent tampering are inevitable. Loans, special favors, and concessions to players are not unheard of even in high school athletic circles. The giving of valuable prizes, cups, medals, watches, sweaters, blankets, and gold balls has a taint of commercialism in it. Further, the true value of the games seems to be lost behind the " winning your letter " idea. This " winning your letter " has been reduced to a system, so that the player knows exactly the requirement he must meet. He knows that he must play for a certain number of minutes, quarters, or innings in order to win his letter. In other words, he buys his letter at a certain definite price. Such a system for the equitable distribution of monograms is definite and may be necessary ; but it, too, smacks of commercialism. School loyalty and patriotism cannot be measured in terms of quarters or number of innings.

They develop an athletic aristocracy. — Spreading the name of a high school football hero across the sporting page of a local paper can hardly do anything else than spoil him. Not in every case of course for there are many athletes who do not let praise and applause turn their heads. The newspaper grades its news on the basis of interest and importance, and indicates them by position, style and number of headings, and length of article. Frequently the most important thing in the paper, on this basis, is the football game. It is but natural that such emphasis should lead the student-hero to think that he is the most important individual about the school. This would not be so bad perhaps if he were the only one who thought so ; but he is not — frequently the other students and even the townsfolk think so and thus perpetuate this foolish idea.   Athletics then becomes the thing for which the school stands.   One such advertisement is probably more publicity than the principal or faculty of the school ever got for work much more important than the execution of a couple of brilliant plays in a football game.

All too frequently such a lionized athlete takes an unsocial attitude towards the school and its work.   He feels that the school should humor him because he has helped to win its victories.   And worse than that, he often gets what he wants and receives favors of various sorts which convince him all the more of his importance to the school.   Thus there is built up in him an unnatural attitude towards society.   When he gets into real life where he is paid and promoted for what he does in his regular work, he is confused and makes his adjustments slowly and painfully, if at all.   He is being miseducated, not fitted for his part in life.

They cause physical injuries. — Student players usually play as hard as possible in " fighting " for their school.   Their spirit is commendable, but it cannot but result in physical injuries. Especially when the players are ordered by the coach to " put 'em down so they stay down."   Probably too many play when they are unfit in order to avoid being called " yellow " by those who do not know their condition.   A great many more players are injured than the average individual supposes.   Moreover, many of the students are " burned out " by such strenuous games as basketball.   Indeed, some college coaches are taking the stand that the high school basketball star is not worth as much as he might be because he has " burned himself out " and will not last three or four seasons of college basketball.

They foster specialization and over-development. — Another objection to athletics is that the student learns to play one position and only one.   He plays quarterback, or end, or forward, or second base and specializes in the technique of playing this one position. He does not get an all-round development. Naturally not, if the main end of the game is to win. There must be specialists to take care of the specialized duties and jobs. If the game were for general educational purposes the players would be shifted around until they learned the job of each position. They would likely never become stars, but they would have an extensive instead of a narrow training.

They develop poor sportsmanship. — There are those who contend that when the main end of the game is to win, almost any means is justifiable. As a result we have evasions of rules, playing of ineligibles, allowing the athlete to slight his school work, lowering of school standards, and trickery of various sorts. The proof that these things exist is in the number of schools which are expelled from the various state and regional interscholastic athletic associations each year. In most instances, probably, the fault does not lie with the school officials but with the townsfolk. The school officials are responsible to the town and will give the townsfolk almost anything they want. The nature of their positions demands a certain support of local interests. If a group of " old grads " get their heads together, they can talk loudly enough to be heard. Worse yet is the situation in which there is an athletic committee on the board of education dominated by an enthusiastic, and not too honest, alumnus or former athlete.

On the other hand, it must be realized that these alumni may be of service to the school. It is good policy to keep them interested. Some day the school may need a new playing field, a swimming pool, or a gymnasium. At that time the alumni association may be a valuable asset. But allowing the alumni, or a few of them, to dictate athletic policy is very different from keeping them interested in school affairs.

They give rise to unsocial feelings. — The gloating and boastfulness of the winner frequently leads to serious trouble. The loser is easily irritated. Rivalry often breeds hatred. Looking upon any one from an adjoining town as an enemy because of a football game is all too common.

They produce the chronic rooter.—Specialized athletics has developed the chronic rooter. Rooting is essential and has its values, but it is certainly no substitute for the play which the students themselves should have. A physical director in a large school system recently said that one of the great values of the interscholastic football game is the emotional thrill it gives the onlooker. Such a stand is hardly justifiable. The emotions of the students are aroused and such shouts as " get the shine," " kill the nigger," " kill the umpire " are heard while the groanings, booings, and catcallings of athletic crowds over penalties are well known. True, the student has a place to " let off steam." He can shout and yell and scream as much as he likes. This may be a value. But the usual emotional effects of the typical thrilling athletic contest combine to make it for the spectators more of an emotional extravagance than anything else.

They benefit only the boys. — Increasing attention is being paid to athletics for girls and the making of opportunities for them to compete in interscholastic contests. But as yet the girls have not had many opportunities in this field.

Teams must win to insure financial success. — Athletics cost money. People pay to see a successful team, one that wins the games. There is the whole story. The more successful the team, the more people will go to see it play. Students will go to see any of their teams play, but financial success cannot be built upon student attendance. Consequently, winning is again emphasized, and all the more so when, as in many schools, athletics is looked upon as the chief revenue producer for the extracurricular program of the school. Hence an unsuccessful team and an unsuccessful financial season mean a curtailed program of other extracurricular activities.

Every one realizes that the desire to win is more or less instinctive and valuable. What we wish to emphasize, however, is that when an amateur high school team which wins is looked upon as successful and when it loses as unsuccessful, we condemn winning. Winning then becomes winning at any price. Nearly all of the troubles with interscholastic athletics can be traced to the demand that the team win its games. A winning team and a team that wins its games may be entirely different. A team which loses its games may be a winner in more important ends and values, while a team which wins may be the loser of values more significant than the mere fact that it ran up a score.

In conclusion, the main objections to interscholastic athletics are that they are ill-balanced, owing in most cases to a misconception of their function and values.

SUGGESTIONS FOR THE IMPROVEMENT OF INTERSCHOLASTIC ATHLETICS

Instruct the school and the community in the real values of interscholastic athletics. — The community must be taught that there are many values in athletics, important and unimportant, that there are greater values in interscholastic athletics than the mere winning of a game or the adding of a trophy to the collection. The educational values to the players must be emphasized, and the mere winning must assume a smaller place than it now holds. This instruction may be carried on in a number of ways: in assembly programs; in the relative emphasis placed upon athletics in the school; in the organization of the school board; and in newspapers.

Win the coöperation of the local newspapers. — The key man in the whole situation is neither the principal nor the coach, but the editor of the local paper. He can probably do more to encourage profitable aims in athletics than all of the coaches and principals. He talks directly to the parents and patrons, supporters of the athletic program. The hours the school officials spend with the editor of the newspaper in arriving at a sane view of athletics are not wasted. This editor can do three very definite things to put sports in their proper place.

First, he can tone down his over-enthusiastic sports writer. This individual is usually a high school graduate himself who had an interest in the games while in high school. He usually has a good motive at heart, too — the encouraging of local athletics and athletes. So he writes stories about them, scareheads their names across his sporting page, and in other ways emphasizes them all out of proportion to their real importance. If the sports editor is limited in space and otherwise restrained, he will not make it appear that the only deserving thing about the school is its football teams.

Again, the editor can separate amateur from professional news in the sporting section, and this will have a salutary effect on high school athletics. In the professional game the sport is the end (for the spectator) while the player is the means. In the amateur type the sport should be the means, the player the end. Few people distinguish between these two. So amateur sports are considered the same as professional, only not quite so good. Classifying the news under two headings, professional and amateur, and keeping the ideas of the two types separate, would help to clarify the interscholastic athletic problem in our schools.

In the third place the editor can help to educate the community by his use of editorial space. Frequent editorials, especially at times when many are thinking in terms of important coming or past contests, will help to avoid overemphasizing these activities.

Eliminate intrinsically valuable awards and gifts. — The line must be drawn between the professional and the amateur. The professional plays for something which is valuable in itself. Sweaters, gold balls, and blankets are valuable in themselves and are in a way not very different from cash. Many schools have eliminated all such valuable awards and have restricted awards to the school monogram, or the right to wear it. It is inexpensive, costing only a few cents. If the student wants to put his letter on a sweater, he must furnish the sweater. Under such conditions he is an amateur in the full sense of the word. It would be immediately suggested that such an award would not be appreciated by the player. He would prefer a more substantial one. Naturally he would and this proves that he is professionally minded, is not playing for honor. A simple award will not only react favorably on the sport, but will save a great deal of money; and it does cost a considerable amount to furnish the balls, sweaters, blankets, or other awards frequently given. Some one has to pay for these things.

Discourage community gifts to athletes and coaches. — This has become a rule of many state athletic associations. It was introduced because many communities have lionized their athletic heroes to absurd limits. There is probably nothing improper about the practice of the Chamber of Commerce, for instance, in giving a banquet to boys who have brought honor to the town. But when local clothing houses give them suits, hats, shirts; barber shops give them haircuts and shaves; pressing establishments press their clothes for a year; and bootblacks promise to shine their shoes for a year, it is time to call a halt. Such lionizing emphasizes athletics far beyond their worth, and the players are being paid for playing. Playing for profit is professionalism. It has no business in the school.

Establish a one-semester rule for interscholastic participation. — In some communities the same incompetent student group enters school each fall, struggles along with the work, plays football, and drops out at the end of the football season. If such " students " were made to carry one semester of school work before being allowed to enter any contest there would be fewer of them. Such a rule would remove one of the opportunities for the most common violations of association rules — playing ineligibles. This would mean that the football player would have to go to the school in question the spring term previously. This would also prevent the moving about of star athletes from one school to another.

Limit participation to two or three years. — Some schools play a star for four full years and then arrange for him to fail in one subject so that he can return and play again. Here again the game is put above the regular school work. Moreover, every student in school knows the scheme to keep the star in school and save him for the game. Imagine a principal or coach in such a school getting up in the assembly and talking about sportsmanship and moral values!

Recognize and develop athletics for girls. — There is a very strong movement throughout the country for athletics for girls. This is good. But many of the games for girls are absurd imitations of the games the boys play. This of course cheapens them, for the girls cannot expect to compete with equal skill. Girls should have their sports, but they should be developed with the ability of the girl in mind and not as cheap imitations of boys' games.

Detroit has done a great deal toward having all students take part in athletics. The following excerpt from the official bulletin shows the " sports calendar " for the girls of the elementary schools for 1924–1925 :

SPORTS CALENDAR — GIRLS' ATHLETICS

1924–1925

Sept. 29 — Field ball tournament starts
Oct.   6 — Begin taking pentathlon records
Nov.   3 — All pentathlon records completed
Nov. 21 — Field ball tournament closes
Dec.   1 — Game tournament meets start
Jan. 23 — Game tournament meets completed
Feb.   9 — Stunt test begins
Mar. 16 — Begin coaching all teams for spring tournaments

Mar. 20 — Stunt test completed
Mar. 23 — Begin taking pentathlon records
April 20 — Hit-pin baseball tournament starts
April 24 — All pentathlon records completed
May 1 — Entry blanks for eleventh annual field day to be in office of
       Department of Health Education
May 16 — Annual pentathlon test, Codd Athletic Field
June 4 — Hit-pin baseball tournament closes
June 5 — Eleventh annual field day, Belle Isle Athletic Field

GIRLS' ATHLETICS

GENERAL PROGRAM, 1924–1925

	SCHOOL ACTIVITY	SPECIAL ACTIVITY
Sept. Oct. Nov.	1. Taking complete pentathlon records according to pentathlon card	Field ball
Dec. Jan.	2. Field ball Game tournament	Game tournament finals
Feb. March	Stunt test fifth and sixth grades	
April May	1. Taking complete pentathlon records according o pentathlon card 2. Hit-pin basebal	Pentathlon Meet Hit-pin baseball finals
June		Eleventh annual field day

The boys' calendar is equally complete.

A number of very interesting contests are held for both boys and girls. All boys and girls are properly classified on a very carefully worked out age and weight plan. A " Decathlon " contest for boys includes the following events:

> Standing hop, step, and jump
> Running hop, step, and jump
> Running high-jump
> Chin, Sit up, Dip

Standing broad-jump
Running broad-jump
Overhead shot
Shot put
100-yard dash

The girls have a Pentathlon Contest which is made up of the following events:

Basket-ball throw	Low hurdle
Dash and throw	Standing broad-jump
Fifty-yard dash	

All girls in the fifth and sixth grades, unless excused, must take the " Girls' Stunt Test." The total score is the school score. The stunts and scoring are described in bulletins issued by the Department of Health Education of Detroit. The stunts and the credit values are as follows:

GIRLS' STUNT TEST

RULES:

****

3. The girls shall be tested only upon the stunts listed below, and the credits obtained shall be as stated here.

Dog Run	1	Bear Dance	3
Front Somersault	1	Crane Dive	3
Full Squat	1	Fish Hawk Dive	3
Stiff Leg Bend	1	Frog Dance	3
The Top	1	Hand Traveling	3
Wheelbarrow	1	Skin the Cat	3
Wicket Walk	1	Through the Loop	3
Ankle Somersault	2	Cork Screw	4
Chair Creeper	2	Eskimo Roll	4
Heel Knock	2	Free Front Rest	4
Jumping Jack	2	Jump Stick	4
Knee Dip	2	Single Squat	4
Stiff (Wooden Man)	2	Cart Wheel	5
Through Stick	2	Jump Foot	5
Arm Bending from Fall Hanging Position	3	Slow Somersault	5

4. For the description of the correct method to be used in doing the stunts, consult only this pamphlet.

Base interscholastic supremacy on many teams instead of one. — If all students could be brought into the interscholastic games, the culmination of socialization in athletics would be reached. Athletic games between second teams is the first step in this direction. The next step will be games between class teams, teams of various weights, sizes, or ages. The interscholastic program of the future will probably find nearly every student in the school representing it in his own way. The use of records, performance tests of all sorts, and classified competition is increasing fast. There will always be the old-fashioned varsity, but it will have company.

The following is an illustration of group competition as promoted by the University of Louisiana. The quotation is taken from the university bulletin describing the athletic and academic contests.

Contests Held Away from the University

These contests are not for individual students, but for the entire class or group. The aim is to bring out the fact that excellent work can be done by the class or group as a whole when the teacher works to this end.

ATHLETIC EVENTS

Girls' Group Athletics

This contest is similar in aim to the literary contests held away from the University. It is to be held at each school at any convenient time before April 5, 1921.

To enter for this contest, report to the secretary, Dr. A. G. Reed, Baton Rouge, Louisiana, the number of girls in your school, whereupon he will send you the necessary number of blanks to be filled out by your local committee at the time that your girls take the test. This report must reach Baton Rouge not later than Tuesday, April 5, 1921.

Each girl taking part in the contest will have her record carefully kept and will be scored according to the requirements shown in the scoring-table below.

In the basket-ball chest throw for height marks will be made (probably on the wall of a building) at 10′ 10″, 14′ 0″, 18′ 0″, 22′ 0″, and 26′ 0″, and each contestant will throw a standard basket-ball vertically in the air and near enough to the marks to enable the scorer to determine the highest mark reached by the top edge of the ball. The throw must be started with elbows sharply bent and ball resting against chest. As the ball leaves the hands the elbows must be straight and the angle at the elbow must steadily increase from a sharp acute angle at the start to a straight angle at the finish of throw. The throw must be a chest-throw without lateral movement.

In the basket-ball throw for distance, the throw will be made from behind a straight line. No part of the person or clothing of the contestant may touch the ground in front of this restraining line until after the distance has been measured and the score announced.

In the balance-board event, the contestant must meet the requirements indicated in the scoring table. The balance board must have the upper edge, upon which the contestant walks or steps, not more than 2″ in width. The length of the board must be not less than 12′ 0″. The height of the upper edge from the ground must be not less than 2′ 0″.

In the 25-yard dash, the starting signal shall be a wave of a handkerchief. The timer shall also act as starter.

In the potato race, there shall be a starting line and a basket twenty yards apart. Between these there shall be three circles, each 1 foot in diameter, placed at five-yard intervals and numbered 1, 2, and 3 in order, circle No. 1 being nearest at the starting line. At the word *go!* the contestant shall start from behind the starting line and running to the basket shall take from it one potato (or stone or block of wood, etc.) and place same in circle No. 1; then the contestant shall return to the basket and take from it a second potato and place same in circle No. 2; then the contestant shall run to the starting line and touch same and without stopping shall return to circle No. 1, take up the potato, and return it to the basket, then shall run to circle No. 2 and return its potato to the basket, and then similarly shall run to circle No. 3 and return its potato to the basket. Finally, when the three potatoes are in the basket, the contestant shall finish by running back to the starting line. The potatoes must not be tossed or thrown. Whenever a potato is to be placed either in a circle or in a basket, the contestant must pass around and beyond the circle or basket.

Only one try at each event will be permitted.

The total score of all girls representing a school will be divided by the number of girls taking part to find the average score for the school. The number of girls taking part must not be less than 75 per cent of all the girls on the rolls of the high school grades. Furthermore, the number taking part must not be less than ten.

If, on official test, all three schools with best reported records fall below the record reported by the fourth best school, this fourth best school becomes entitled to official test. Thereafter the other schools will be tested officially in the order of their rank by reported record until a school is found whose official record is better than any other official record and better than any remaining reported record.

SCORING TABLE

	I PT.	2 PTS.	3 PTS.	4 PTS.	5 PTS.
	I PT.	2 PTS.	3 PTS.	4 PTS.	5 PTS.
Basket-ball chest throw, distance . .	10' 10''	14' 0''	18' 0''	22' 0''	26' 0''
Basket-ball throw, distance	20' 0''	32' 0''	44' 0''	56' 0''	68' 0''
25-yard dash . . .	5⅖ sec.	5 sec.	4⅗ sec.	4⅕ sec.	3⅘ sec.
Balance Board . .	Walk	Walk and return	Change step	Change and return	[1] Polka step
Potato race . . .	63 sec.	58 sec.	53 sec.	48 sec.	43 sec.

BOYS' GROUP ATHLETICS

The following group athletic contest begun in the year 1918 will again be held in 1921.

This contest is similar in aim to the literary contests held away from the University. It is to be held at each school at any convenient time before April 5, 1921.

To enter for this contest, report to the secretary, Dr. A. G. Reed, Baton Rouge, Louisiana, the number of boys in your school, whereupon he will send you the necessary number of blanks to be filled out by your local committee at the time that your boys take the test. This report must reach Baton Rouge not later than Tuesday, April 5, 1921.

Each boy taking part in the contest will have his record carefully kept and will be scored according to the requirements shown in the scoring-table on the following page.

[1] The Polka step equals change step and step, hop.

In the fence vault the bar will be placed at 3′ 0″, 3′ 9″, 4′ 6″, 5′ 3″, and 6′ 0″ successively and each contestant will be permitted to take one try and but one at each height. To touch the bar with any part of the person or clothing except the hands will constitute a failure. By failure at any height the contestant loses his right to try further at the same or greater height.

In the standing broad-jump, chinning and 100-yard dash, each contestant will be permitted to make but one try.

In the running high-jump, the bar will be placed successively at 3′ 1″, 3′ 6″, 3′ 11″, 4′ 4″, and 4′ 9″. Otherwise this event will be operated like the fence vault.

In the chinning event each contestant must raise his chin above the bar and must lower himself to a fully extended position below the bar and must neither swing, "kip," nor wriggle.

The total score of all the boys representing a school will be divided by the number of boys taking part to find the average score of the school. The number of boys taking part must not be less than 75 per cent of all the boys on the rolls of the high school grades. Furthermore, the number taking part must not be less than ten.

If, on official test, all three schools with best reported records fall below the record reported by the fourth best school, this fourth best school becomes entitled to official test.

Thereafter the other schools will be tested officially in the order of their rank by reported record until a school is found whose official record is better than any other official record and better than any remaining reported record.

SCORING TABLE

	1 PT.	2 PTS.	3 PTS.	4 PTS.	5 PTS.
Fence vault (hands only to touch bar)	3′ 0″	3′ 9″	4′ 6″	5′ 3″	6′ 0″
Standing broad-jump	4′ 6″	5′ 6″	6′ 6″	7′ 6″	8′ 6″
Running high-jump .	3′ 1″	3′ 6″	3′ 11″	4′ 4″	4′ 9″
Chinning	3 times	5 times	7 times	9 times	11 times
100 yards	$15\frac{2}{5}$	$14\frac{2}{5}$	$13\frac{2}{5}$	$12\frac{2}{5}$	$11\frac{2}{5}$

Another way of meeting the objection that too few students benefit is through the addition of other activities than the five traditional ones. In the illustrations quoted above it will be seen that novelty races and stunts are becoming more and more common, particularly in athletics for girls. Increased use is being made of golf, wrestling, boxing, tennis, raquets, croquet, swimming (and stunts and novelties), skating, and canoeing. Hiking is another activity which has promise of use in interscholastic competition. In short, football, basketball, track, and baseball will never be strictly eliminated from high school competition; but they will be accompanied by novelty races, stunts, and other games.

Still another way to meet the objection that too few students benefit is to provide opportunities for the student who is not an athlete to help in staging the games and contests. Staging a game involves a great many details. Some one must look after these details. Usually it is the coach or an assistant, frequently a teacher. Here then are many opportunities for student participation. Committees such as the following might be appointed by the council athletic committee to handle the detail of the various tasks:

SUB-COMMITTEES OF THE ATHLETIC COMMITTEE

Finance:
Prints, sells, distributes, and collects tickets
Receives, cares for, and disburses money
Sees that records and audits are made on proper authorization
Provides for proper publicity of athletic finances

Officials:
Provides suitable officials
Meets officials, takes them to games, provides entertainment

Eligibility:
Sees that eligibility lists are made out properly, authenticated, and mailed
Promotes the demand that players keep up their work
Helps players to keep up in work by tutoring and doing outside tasks for them

Schedule:	Helps to make suitable schedules of inter- and intra-school games and contests
	Sees that contracts are properly drawn and cared for
Pep:	Arranges pep and booster meetings, parades, celebrations, and stunts
	Selects and trains cheer leaders
	Develops and collects cheers, songs, and stunts
Entertainment:	Meets and receives visiting teams
	Arranges for entertainment, baggage, and transportation
	Arranges receptions and parties for visiting groups
Decoration:	Decorates goal posts, gymnasium, or field with colors of both schools
Publicity:	Advertises games by posters, newspapers, stunts, window cards, signs, slides, parades, bands, and other means
Disciplinary:	Investigates and recommends action deemed necessary on account of conduct of players, teams, or spectators
Rewards and Honors:	Recommends the adoption of various insignia and honors

Abolish part-time coaches. — The coach who is employed for part-time has only one interest — a winning team. He is on duty for only two or three months. He usually knows little about educational values and processes and has little interest in them. He has been employed to turn out a successful team. His only interest then is in winning. This is the fault of the board which employs him. The coach should be a full-time man, a physical educator with coaching as a side line. He should understand education, physical education aims and purposes, and have a bigger conception of his job than that of being the builder of a successful team. Needless to say, he should be paid by the board of education only.

Build an inclusive health program with interscholastic athletics at the top. — With full-time coaches and physical directors who understand their jobs there will be built up a broad, liberal system of athletic competition. This work will include health and hygiene, remedial, recreational, disciplinary, and educational work, and the competitive side of it will be taken care of by intra- as well as interscholastic activities. Inter-class, inter-floor, and inter-community activities will be arranged and every one will have his chance to compete with some one of his size, weight, or ability. Mass athletics will become the rule, with every one taking part. At the very top of this pyramid will be found the interscholastic first teams. These will be more numerous than they now are, and will include different types for the various sizes, ages, and weights of students.

Abolish board of education athletic committees or limit their work. — A board of education committee may be proper if it knows its place; but it can no more handle athletics soundly than select the textbooks the students are to use. If the committee has respect for expert opinion, it may work to the benefit of all; if not, the result may be disastrous. It has no more right to make an eligibility report, for instance, than it has to come to the classroom and tell the teacher how to teach. The principal is an educational expert; it is his job. The committee or board can offer help and counsel and in other ways make the program a success, even as it does the regular curriculum. But beyond this it has no right to go.

Abolish championships. — Regional, state, and national championships are becoming more and more common. All of the troubles found in the smaller interscholastic contest between two schools are magnified many times in the regional or state championship event — the demoralization of school; the lionizing of the teams by school and community; and the over-emphasis placed upon winning and upon athletics in general. Occasionally in the heat of such an emotional debauch a school board honors the coach who has turned out the winning team by giving him a political plum — the principalship or the superintendency of the system. He may make a fine incumbent for either position or he may not; but certainly he does not deserve the appointment just because he has turned out a successful football team.

Abolish training camps. — The high school training camp is an imitation of the college camp. It is a good place for a boy to be. He gets good training in wholesome surroundings. What is wrong with the camp is that it magnifies the importance of the game. The camp is maintained so that a better football team may be turned out — a team that wins. Thus again winning is over-emphasized.

Let the board of education subsidize athletics. — If, as has been suggested before, a winning team is necessary for financial reasons, in order that there be a team next season, or that needed equipment may be bought, or that the other extracurricular activities of the school may be supported financially, then there is nothing to be done but to have a winning team — a team which citizens will pay to see play. But if the board of education subsidizes athletics it will remove one of the most important reasons for the demand of a winning team, that of finance. The school board which wishes to emphasize the other elements or aims of physical education can start by voting money for their support. A small charge might always be made for regulatory purposes, but this charge would be so small that the revenue coming from it would not be large enough to be influenced by the success or failure of the team.

THE LOCAL ATHLETIC ASSOCIATION

The question arises as to the advisability of having a student athletic association. This question cannot be answered absolutely either way. The answer depends upon local conditions and circumstances. Many schools have an athletic association to which all the students belong. In other schools only students who join and contribute a few cents or buy a season ticket are members. Such an association usually has a constitution, regularly elected officers, and appointed committees. Its officers and committees help with advertising and tickets, receive and entertain teams, hold pep meetings, and in other ways assist in staging the games and contests.

The main objection to an athletic association is that in schools with a student council it parallels too closely the general student organization. This means in the first place that athletics is as important as all of the other activities of the school combined. Interscholastic athletics need little encouragement. In the second place, if athletics has an athletic association why should there not be a dramatic association, a music association, or a French association? These activities are smaller and interest fewer students perhaps; but the athletic association does not interest all of the students. In the plan for council organization it was suggested that there be no athletic association as such, but that athletics be handled in the same manner as other extracurricular activities — through a committee of the council. Even this arrangement is giving athletics more attention than many of the other activities, for a whole committee is devoted to it. However, it is an important activity and probably requires a special committee. The handling of athletics by such a committee guarantees that all phases will be covered; those needing encouragement will be encouraged, those not, not. The committee will have the entire athletic program in mind and will be able to articulate its various elements into a well-rounded program. Athletic associations over-emphasize the interscholastic athletic side of school life. Certainly interscholastic athletics are not as important as all of the other activities of the school combined. A general organization of students with an elected body of representatives at its head interested in the promotion of all of the extracurricular activities is more valuable than an athletic association responsible for but one of them.   If there is a council, interscholastic athletics should be under its direction, as is an interscholastic debate or music contest.   All of the fine work usually done in promoting athletics can be done by properly constituted sub-committees of the athletic committee of the council.

INTERSCHOLASTIC ATHLETIC ASSOCIATIONS

The interscholastic associations of the country, local, county, regional, and state, deserve a great deal of credit for the progress made in athletics and athletic relationships during the past two or three decades.   Various limitations concerning players, officials, expenses, and awards have been placed upon the schools, with salutary effect.   Ineligibles are still played occasionally, unsportsmanlike conduct frequently occurs, but at least not so much as formerly.   It has been a hard fight, and still is in many communities, to put the limitations and regulations through the association meetings; but the men who have done this have benefited every school and every player concerned.

A new type of association, designed to honor the athlete who does good work scholastically, was organized by the National Association of Secondary School Principals in 1924.   This " National Athletic Scholarship Society " may be established in any accredited high school with little trouble.   Any letter wearer of the school whose scholastic work for three consecutive semesters is higher in quality than the average of the school as a whole is eligible to membership.   After becoming a member he may wear the key — a gold charm made up of the letters S and A. Before this organization was a year old, nearly three hundred high schools had joined it.   It promises to exert a beneficial influence in high school athletics within the next few years.

SUMMARY

There are many values attached to interscholastic athletics. On the other hand there are many objections also.   Most of these can be classified under the general head of over-emphasis. These objections are being met by students and workers in this field. It is not an easy battle to fight the tradition, cheap loyalty, and demagoguery usually connected with athletics. It takes time, study, and energy. The trend in athletics is very strong now towards mass athletics, entire class or school competition, and there is a consequent emphasis upon making available for all students the fine educational opportunities of athletic competition.

REFERENCES

BANCROFT, J. H. *Games for Playground, Home, School and Gymnasium.* The Macmillan Company.

—— and PULVERMACHER. *Handbook of Athletic Games.* The Macmillan Company.

BOWEN, W. P. and MITCHELL, E. D. *The Practice of Organized Play.* A. S. Barnes and Company.

BROWNE, E. *Outdoor Athletic Tests for Boys.* Association Press.

Bulletins of United States Bureau of Education. Department of the Interior:
> *Athletic Badge Tests for Boys and Girls.*
> *Dramatics for Health Teachings.*
> *The Continuing Need for Teachers of Child Health,* and others.

CAMP, W. *Athletes All.* Charles Scribner's Sons.

CLARK, H. P. and BEATTY, W. W. "Physical Training in the Junior High School," *School Review* 33 : 532–541, September, 1925.

COX, P. W. L. *Creative School Control,* Chap. VII. J. B. Lippincott Company.

DAVIS, C. O. *Junior High School Education,* Chap. XIX. World Book Company.

DRAPER, G. O. *Community Recreation.* Association Press.

DUDLEY, W. L. "The Proper Control of Athletics," *Proceedings* of the National Collegiate Athletic Association, December, 1922.

FOSTER, C. R. *Extracurricular Activities in the High School,* Chap. X. Johnson Publishing Company.

GILCHRIST, E. P. "Socialized Athletics," *School and Society* 7 : 597–599, May 18, 1918.

GRIFFITH, J. L. "Athletic Organization and Administration." *Athletic Journal,* November, 1923.

HEATHERINGTON, C. W. "Athletics." MONROE'S *Principles of Secondary Education*, Chap. XIX. The Macmillan Company.

HOLMES, P. K. "Is Physical Education Worthy of Academic Credit?" *School and Society* 11 : 160–164, February 7, 1920.

LILLARD, W. H. "The Andover Plan," *American Physical Education Review*, 195, April, 1915.

MEYER, H. D. *Handbook of Extracurricular Activities*, Part IV. A. S. Barnes and Company.

MITCHELL, E. D. *Intra-Mural Athletics*. A. S. Barnes and Company.

MORRILL, R. S. "The Coach and the School," *School Review* 32 : 380–387. May, 1924.

O'KEEFE, N. A. "Organization of Athletics for Girls in the Elementary Schools," *Proceedings* of the National Education Association, 1916, 693–695.

PEARL, N. H. and BROWN, H. E. *Health by Stunts*. The Macmillan Company.

PENDLETON, L. B. "Competitive Athletics in the Junior High School," *American Physical Education Review*, November, 1918.

PRINGLE, R. W. *Adolescence and High School Problems*, Chap. XV. D. C. Heath and Company.

RAYCROFT, J. E. "Educational Value of Athletics in Schools and Colleges," *School and Society* 3 : 295–300, February 26, 1916.

Russell Sage Foundation *Reports*, Child Hygiene Division.

SMITH, C. F. *Games and Recreational Methods*. Dodd, Mead and Company.

Spauldings' Athletic Library of Handbooks on Various Sports.

STALEY, S. C. *Individual and Mass Athletics*. A. S. Barnes and Company.

—— *Games, Contests and Relays*. A. S. Barnes and Company.

STECHER, W. A. Essentials of Physical Education in City Schools, *American Physical Education Review* 25 : 8–10, January, 1920.

THOMAS-TINDAL, E. V. and MYERS, J. D. *Junior High School Life*, Chap. III. The Macmillan Company.

THISTLETHWAITE, B. F. "Citizenship and Athletics." *Proceedings* of the National Education Association, 1918, 183–187.

TRUSLER, H. R. "State High School Athletic Associations," *American School Board Journal* 70 : 40, June, 1925.

WAGENHORST, L. H. *The Administration End of High School Interscholastic Athletics*, Teachers College Contributions to Education, No. 205.

WILLIAMS, J. F. *The Organization and Administration of Physical Education*. The Macmillan Company.

CHAPTER XV

SCHOOL TRIPS AND EXCURSIONS

By the school trip is meant a visit by students in body to some place or event for educational purposes. Such trips are becoming more and more popular as educators appreciate their value. In many instances they can hardly be called extracurricular, because of their close relationship to the regular work of the school. Perhaps they never should be, strictly speaking, extracurricular. If they facilitate classroom work, they should be recognized and provided for on the same basis as maps, charts, models, apparatus — any illustrative or demonstrative material.

Kinds of school trips. — There are two main kinds of school excursions or trips. The first is that in which a small group, a class for instance, visits a bank, commercial house, factory, post office, or museum. The second is that in which a group of students is taken to Washington, or to a neighboring city, for a few days. It is perhaps more strictly an excursion. An excursion implies education by coming in contact with things about which one has read. Probably sight-seeing is a more accurate term. The other is not wholly an excursion or sight-seeing trip. It is the more educational in that it is more closely correlated with the regular work of the school. In this chapter, then, " trip " will be used to designate the short journeys to industrial and commercial plants in the community, and " excursion " the longer, less frequent, trips to more distant points.

Values of school trips. — The main function of the school is to develop good citizens. Being a good citizen implies a membership, interest, and responsibility in a community. This membership must be based upon an acquaintance with the affairs, feelings, and history of the community, its industrial and commercial activities. This knowledge a student may acquire partly in the regular work, and through assembly speakers and newspapers; but it usually is formal and uninteresting, because second-hand. More vital is a direct contact between the prospective citizen and the community. The school trip provides this direct contact.

The adolescent is a wanderer. He wants to be " on the go " physically and mentally. He likes to make trips, to explore, and to travel about seeing new things and new places. If uncontrolled, this wanderlust may develop into laziness, a distaste for substantial things, a mild satisfaction with things novel, and an increased craving to be foot-loose and care-free. On the other hand, if intelligently guided and directed, this nomadic tendency may be utilized.

The usual school procedure of placing a student in a seat and requiring him to sit there for continued stretches of time, is not altogether in accord with the acknowledged principles of educational psychology. Of course, he must be taught to sit still and concentrate, but this need not mean that his migratory instinct should not be capitalized for good educational purposes. History, geography, and language furnish a vicarious experience which helps, to some extent, to satisfy his craving for change. A few trips wisely planned and administered would also help to put this urge to good use.

Principles and procedure. — The most important of the principles of organization of the school trip are as follows :

The trip must have one definite aim. — It would be stupid to attempt to see New York in one afternoon. There is entirely too much of it to be seen in that time. If it were physically possible to see it all in a day, such a procedure would not be psychologically sound, because much of it would have to be skipped over hurriedly. This in itself would be bad, if for no other reason than for the worry and fretfulness it would create in the minds of the seers. More than that, though, the seer could not " digest " it all. World travelers say that the best way to see foreign places is to see only a very few of them at one time. Many travelers make a practice of seeing a few things during the day, and of reviewing them at night. In that way, they are assimilated and remembered.

Having a definite objective does not mean that other things will not be seen. As a matter of fact, a wise trip leader will so arrange that in going and returning other things which should interest the students will be passed or noticed. The youngsters will want to stop, and their curiosity will result in more trips and more interest. For instance, if a group is going to the museum to see old types of vehicles, the wise leader will lead the students around by an indirect way among the cases containing other exhibits, not permitting them to stop to view these. They will want to stop, and it will take good management to keep them all going to the one thing they came to see, but prevention both of satiety and of dissipation of interest will mean better educational results.

Seeing one thing well will take a considerable time; nevertheless, it is better to see one thing well than to half-see several things. There must be efficiency on trips as well as in classroom work. Efficiency makes for dignity and respect. Both are important from the point of view of the student as well as from that of the parents and patrons who may not be able to see the values of such trips.

Solid preparation should be made. — If the student is to get the most out of his trip he must be in the proper mood; his attitude must be right. The atmosphere must be one of anticipation and not merely of suspense waiting for whatever may happen to surprise him next. The student who knows something about the thing to be seen, and who has tried to picture it in his own mind, attempting to visualize its details, how the parts work, etc., will approach the objective with a number of questions in his mind. In short, a trip can be likened to an assignment. The teacher may say " take the next chapter for to-morrow," or assign the reference and then give several questions or problems which the student will be expected to answer when he returns. In the first instance, he will be looking for everything and anything, in the second, for what, in the judgment of the teacher, are the most important elements in the lesson. Merely going to see a cuttle-fish at the museum is not so effective as going to see how a cuttle-fish swims, eats, the position of its eyes, the relative length of its tentacles, or the number, location, and size of the suckers. In the first instance the student anticipates only " seeing " the cuttle-fish; in the second he anticipates learning the answers to some " hows " and " whys." Needless to say, such questions in the assignment should usually be the most significant and not merely the most interesting. The most interesting is not necessarily the most important.

Preparation for such trips should be carried on in the class or group. Material on the objects to be visited will be brought in and textual references, clippings, and stories will be read or made available. A committee may be formed to go over the details of preparing for the trip. It will gather material, bring pictures, arrange for discussion and reports, formulate questions, and in other ways increase the interest of the group not only in seeing, but in seeing " how " and " why." Preparation for a visit to a factory, for instance, might include suggestions as to the conditions to be looked for, machines and machinery, products and by-products, personnel employed, safety devices, stock, equipment, dress and manners of employees, procedures, and practices.

The trip should be definitely planned. — Any trip, long or short, involves many arrangements and adjustments. These can probably be made better by the teacher than by the student, more easily and more efficiently. But we could say the same thing about the teacher's classroom work. He can recite better than any of the students. This, however, would not be very educative for the group. So also with the trip; although the teacher can make the arrangements and see that they are carried out as planned, such a procedure would rob the students of educational opportunities. In the first place, then, planning the trip means that the students will be exercised in facing and having to respond to practical situations.

Definite planning, again, puts a certain dignity and importance on the trip that it would not otherwise have. This adds to the expectancy of the students and to the probability of its success.

In the third place, it interests a larger number of students in the activity. It does this because more have parts to play, and as each is unwilling that his part should be looked upon as a failure he strives hard to make it a success. All this adds to the general mobilization of interest which will make the trip successful.

Committees. — A number of committees may be appointed by the teacher or selected by the students themselves; for instance, committees on Arrangements, Transportation, Preparation, and Values. The first of these makes the necessary arrangements with the individuals in charge of the object to be visited, planning the time, place, and other details in such a manner that neither the group nor these individuals will be inconvenienced. Suppose, for instance, that the group is planning to visit a bank. The Committee would call upon the banker and ask permission to make the visit. Of course, it would be wise for the principal or teacher privately to make all the necessary arrangements beforehand. The Committee calls upon the banker, is ushered into his private office, and seated with all the dignity of a committee from an important commercial enterprise. The Committee, through its chairman or spokesman, explains the purpose of the visit and requests permission to see how a bank operates. The banker, of course, is interested and asks what they want to see, the time most convenient for them to come, and the number that may be expected, and also makes any suggestions or curiosity pricks that he can. Arrangements are made and the committee withdraws, enthusiastic over its reception and success, and passes on its enthusiasm to the main group. After the group has visited the bank, ordinary courtesy demands that the group formally, as well as informally, express its appreciation for the privilege and pleasure of the visit. This not only gives the student training in such courtesy, but also leaves the person visited in a fine frame of mind, and this may facilitate making similar visits later.

The Transportation Committee secures information concerning methods of reaching the place. There may be several ways of going. In the larger cities there may be the elevated, subway, surface cars, or busses. The Committee studies relative costs, compares time schedules, considers convenience, etc., and decides upon a way of going. This Committee may collect the fares beforehand, in case fares are required, and then pay the conductor in one sum for all. This may be good practice with grade school and lower junior high school students. It at least insures all students getting out and back without requiring the Committee to provide fares. It is interesting to note that some schools which conduct regular schedules of weekly trips, require the parents to deposit with the headmaster or principal a small sum each month to pay for carfares.

The work of the Committee on Preparation was discussed under the second principle. A Committee on Values may make a study of the object visited, learning of its importance in commercial, industrial, social, or physical life, and present this view to the group. Such presentation is a part of the duty of preparation and adds to interest in the object visited, and an appreciation of it.

Some schools make use of a regular form in connection with school trips. The following is an example:

TRIPS

Time left building   Date

Time group dismissed

Place

Object

Students taking trip

Results (ground covered)

How used in class work (correlation)

Expense per student

Name of officer, guide, or representative to whom thanks are due

Instructor in Charge

Such a form gives dignity and definiteness to the trip. The educational value is emphasized by requiring from the teacher certain information concerning the purpose of the trip.

The trip should be conducted as planned. — It would be useless to plan a trip carefully and then allow anything to interfere. Of course it might happen that adjustments would be necessary if new situations arose, or unforeseen events demanded changes in original plans. Generally speaking, however, it would be decidedly poor practice to make plans and then abandon them. Naturally, if such plans were not followed, there would be little planning on the part of the students for the next trip.

The trip should be correlated, wherever possible, with classroom work. — Probably many trips that are nevertheless of value and represent time well spent, cannot be correlated definitely and directly with classroom work; but if trips can be related to classroom work they will not only help to motivate it, but will supply the practical contact so frequently lacking in curricular activities. Such things as sewage disposal, police and fire protection, water supply, or movies or dramatics illustrating or representing periods that are studied in history or fiction can be easily related to the textbook work.

FIGURE X. — A GROUP OF STUDENTS LISTENING TO A LECTURE ON BANKING BEFORE BEING SHOWN THROUGH THE BANK.

In such correlation it is important that the students do not over-stress the most interesting or novel, but that they see and appreciate the most important. When watching a film of pioneer life, for instance, boys may be more interested in the strange weapons the pioneers carried, or girls in the funny clothes the women wore, than in its more significant aspects.

Places to visit. — Every community, large or small, has its history and its places of historical interest, if only local interest, its industrial and commercial activities, its interesting and attractive natural phenomona; and few communities there are which do not have public works, offices, and services with which the prospective citizen should be acquainted.

The school trip is an almost unexplored field in education. The teacher who begins a series of trips will be surprised at the reception he will receive from business men. There are industries to which it would not be wise to take students, and the teacher would probably be refused permission to visit them. But there are many places about the town to which groups would be welcomed.

The bank is probably the logical place with which to start a series of visits, and it is one of the easiest and most interesting. Any banker would welcome the opportunity to show his bank to a group of youngsters. Usually this would be done after banking hours. The students listen to simple talks on banking, and they are shown the vaults, and protective devices. Any banker, if it were suggested to him, would be glad to let the group pass around and each member " heft " one of his bags of gold. The sight of a few bills of large denomination would also interest the students. The author was with such a group visiting one of the New York City banks, and saw the bank actually lend a depositor one million dollars. It so happened that the loan was to be arranged while the group was there, and the vice-president, finding the borrower did not object, invited the group in to see just how it was done. Of course, no cash changed hands, but the students saw the signing of the papers which represented the loan.

Another business man who will welcome student visits, especially if he is exhibiting an educational picture, is the manager of a moving-picture house. In the larger cities some of the theaters make a regular business of running appropriate pictures in the morning for the students, charging only a small fraction of the price charged in the afternoon and evening. The manager knows that it is good advertising. Special student rates can also be obtained for almost any dramatic or musical performance.

The following list suggests suitable places to visit :

CITY, COUNTY, STATE, AND FEDERAL

Arsenal
Bridges and other public works
County hospitals and homes
Court house
Filtration plant
Fire department
Incinerator
Jail and penitentiary
Ships
Treasury

Markets
Mint
Navy yards and stations
Police station
Post office
Pumping stations
Road and bridge building
Sewage disposal plant
Water works

COMMERCIAL

Bakery
Banks
Bottling works
Brokerage houses
Bus lines
Candy factory
Cannery
Car barns
Cleaners and dyers
Dairy farms and plants
Dress-making shops
Electric light company

Flower shops and greenhouses
Ferries
Garage
Insurance offices
Interurban offices
Hotel
Ice cream plant
Laundry
Lumber yard
Oil station
Printing office
Publication offices

Railroad stations, yards, shops
Real estate offices
Restaurants
Ships
Shops
Stockyards
Stock exchange

Storage plants
Stores
Tailoring establishments
Telegraph office
Telephone office
Toy and novelty stores

INDUSTRIAL

Automobile factory
Brick yards
Building trades
Cabinet and furniture making
Chemical plants
Coal mines
Coke ovens
Engineering construction
Factories
Gas works

Glass works
Ice plant
Oil and gas wells
Pottery
Quarries
Refinery
Rubber works
Sawmill
Ship yards
Steel, tin, copper plants

EDUCATIONAL

Churches (windows, architecture)
Colleges
Concerts
Dramatics
Exhibitions
Lectures

Musical comedies
Observatory
Opera
Pictures
Y.M.C.A. and Y.W.C.A.
Zoölogical Garden

MISCELLANEOUS

Field trips, birds, flowers, formations
Historical landmarks, graves, monuments
Large estates
Memorials
Museum, conservatory, fishponds
Natural beauties, caves, rivers, mountains
Parks, playgrounds
Rocks, minerals
Sanitariums

The final test of the success of such a trip is not whether the students enjoyed it, but rather whether or not they want more trips, and whether or not they take trips themselves. A visit to the museum should result in the student's taking many trips by himself or with his own crowd. The school group will never be able to see everything worth seeing. Consequently, the school trip may be said to be merely a curiosity-pricker. It merely samples and the test of its success is whether or not the student wants more.

SUMMARY

The school trip is an educational agency as yet little developed by teachers. Its main value is that, by capitalizing one of his strongest instincts, it acquaints the prospective citizen with his community. The trip should be definitely arranged and prepared for, and should be correlated with the regular school work wherever possible. Every community has some places to which interesting and valuable visits might be made.

REFERENCES

BRIGGS, T. H. "The Excursion as a Means of Education." *Teachers College Record* 22 : 415–419, November, 1921.

COLEMAN, L. V. "School and Public Museum," *Journal of the National Education Association* 13 : 218 f., June, 1924.

PUFFER, J. A. *The Boy and His Gang.* Houghton Mifflin Company.

Manuals and books on Scouting will be found valuable for field trips.

CHAPTER XVI

PARTIES

One of the strongest urges in the young is that of play. The young animal plays, runs, jumps, and goes through a great many motions and stunts which have as their immediate end nothing in particular. But the animal enjoys these actions, and they may be of value to him when he grows up. The kitten in its play practices stealth, attacking its mate, retreating from attack, and in other ways acquiring the tactics which, as a cat, it will need.

The party as an expression of the play instinct in the young.— The child likes to play and probably most of his play has some direct bearing upon his adult capabilities and interests. The adult, indeed, demands a different sort of game, but this he enjoys as much as the child enjoys his own. The value of good play and recreation in the life of any one is undisputed. Consequently, if the student is bound to play, the school should teach him to play better. It should teach him more and better games, and in every way improve his playing and increase his fun at his games.

Parties are as much a part of the life of the child and are probably as important in his development as outdoor games and recreation. Young people will have their parties and should have them. We can help them, however, to play better by showing a variety of experience, by encouraging the backward, and by giving all an opportunity to learn the techniques which are essential to the success of any party. A party which " just happens " may be a fine success, but other things being equal, one which is carefully studied and planned for will have far more chances of succeeding.

A typical school party. — Frequently the school party is an exceedingly painful affair. The students stand around awkward and self-conscious in their assumed dignity. Parents and teachers invited to chaperon, not to participate, stand off to themselves in pompous groups smiling superior smiles and watching the children play. The honor and dignity of the school has been carefully safeguarded by set rules and regulations, and the whole party takes on a strained and unnatural atmosphere. It is a time of repression, not of constructively directed fun. Every one is glad when it is over. The student breathes more freely when he leaves; the chaperon is happy because it represents the one evening when she was seen, heard, and feared; and the principal, too, is happy because the affair went off smoothly and without trouble. Little wonder the students did not have a good time. In the main, their evening was probably wasted. Strict regulations, treatment of students like little children, lack of knowledge of party technique, lack of provision for the amusement of all the students, and failure to encourage all students to play — these are what kill a party.

Values of School Parties

They develop the student socially. — Participation in the party prepares the student for the social affairs in which he will engage as an adult. Poise, grace, and ability to hold up one's end of a social conversation are all important. Ability to meet people, the technique of introductions, and the common courtesies all have to be learned. The school usually makes no effort to teach them, but they may be acquired through actual practice at parties. Further, if the students help to plan and conduct their parties, they will receive valuable training through these experiences.

They afford reasonable and healthful amusement. — Every one needs recreation and amusement, and the school party can help to meet the needs of the students in this particular. By being properly conducted, the party can raise the students' standards of amusement, it can make them dissatisfied with the inferior and desirous of the best in amusement. For instance, nearly all high school students are determined to dance. Consequently it is a question of whether we will shut our eyes to this demand and let them dance at cabarets, road houses, or other questionable places, or provide properly conducted opportunities for the expression of this play instinct. In some communities dancing is still looked upon as being vicious. This Puritanic idea is fast disappearing, but still persists here and there. If the associations and organizations which oppose dancing in the school would look at the matter fairly, they would probably have little to say against it. In any case, the majority of students will dance. The question is not whether or not they will dance, but where, and how?

They often motivate and add interest to the life of the school. — It might be stated that the student who stays in school because it has a few parties each year has a poor motive for staying. Probably, however, no student would stay in school just because of the social life it offered. But each one of these little affairs brightens school life, adds to the attractiveness of it. Moreover, a poor motive is better than no motive at all. A social program increases acquaintanceships among students. Adding to the number of friends one has in school means making just so many more contacts with the school and its life, and so many more ties.

Essentials to the Success of a Social Program

If the school party is to be a success, it must follow sound principles. Of course an occasional party might be successful which did not illustrate these principles, but we should not be misled by the occasional success. The student has a right to expect any party or social event to be a success.

The faculty must recognize its responsibility in helping the student to play. — This does not mean that the faculty shall attend the party and stand about and smile superciliously at the attempts of the students to have a good time. Such an atmosphere would chill any party. Neither does it mean that the faculty will arrange the party and play for the students. Doing it for them is not teaching them to do it. The faculty must teach the students to play. This will mean service on social committees. Most of the faculty members have had much more party experience than the students and should be able to make this available. Moreover, they have better judgment. The faculty members can help with suggestions for planning games, decorations, music, stunts, refreshments, and many other things that must be provided.

The success of any party depends in a large measure on the preparation which has been made for it. — Such preparation includes preparation for all phases of it, decorations, invitations, chaperonage, games, and refreshments. Preparation requires serious study. The preparation usually made for parties stops with decorations, refreshments, music, and chaperons. But these do not guarantee the final success of the party. Games, stunts, getting students acquainted, "breaking the ice," and other similar problems which concern the activities of the party are as important as procuring the materials for it.

ORGANIZING THE SOCIAL PROGRAM

The social committee. — The social program for the year should be supervised by a central committee or club. Such a committee might well be a committee of the student council, representing both student body and faculty. Its members need not, probably should not, all be chosen from the council; but its chairman should be. Its membership may be chosen by the council from the school at large. Its faculty members should be recommended by the council and appointed by the principal. Needless to say all of its members should be interested in social affairs. Such a committee should represent the school and not individual classes or groups. Because of its many important duties this committee should probably be rather large.

Its activities. — The social committee is charged with the responsibility of scheduling, arranging, and staging all of the social events of the year. In order to succeed, it must take its work seriously, as it will when it realizes the importance of the social program. It should hold regular meetings, once a week probably, and more frequently if necessary, and must give its time and attention to the serious study of this phase of school work. The more important of its activities are the following:

Make a study of games. — Every party requires games, and needless to say games must be studied and learned. No high school party should be entirely devoted to dancing. Many students do not dance, or they do not dance well enough to wish to dance in public, and provision must be made for them. At many school parties, of course, it would seem as if all students danced, but this is because most of those who do not dance have no motive for coming and so do not come. The program should include provision for all the students who have a legitimate right to be there.

The committee should make a " social " library. It should add new books as they appear. Much material is available in various magazines and may be clipped and made into scrapbooks. Data on refreshments, materials, decoration, programs, and equipment are all a part of party work and should be collected and properly classified so that they will be readily accessible. For instance, material might be indexed and cross-indexed as suitable for " Banquet," " Formal," " House party," " Indoor," " Large indoor," " Outdoor," or " St. Valentine."

The committee should also make a study of foreign, historical, and stunt games.   Variety adds interest.   Not all of the parties should be of the same type.   Students like to dress up in costume for parties and this can be done occasionally.   Colonial, Dutch, Farmer, Forty-Niner, Freshman, Hard Time, Old Folks, and other parties of this kind can be held for which the students can dress the part.   A few games suitable for these periods or countries may be used, but most of the party can proceed in the usual way with dancing.   Students will not relish for very long learning new games when a dance orchestra is available.

Study decorations, refreshments, music, costs, and invitations. — Decorations always help to make a party a success.   A few cents worth of crêpe paper festooned about the room and a few lanterns or other simple and inexpensive decorations add to the attractiveness of the occasion.   Books on decorating are now available, and several companies make a specialty of providing inexpensive and varied decorations for such occasions.

Refreshments may be similarly studied and planned.   Having a different menu each time will arouse the expectations of the student guests.   Cost, menus, arrangements and serving, providing glasses and bowls and maid service must be considered.   The more intelligently this work is done the more chances the party has of success.

Music must be provided.   If the school has an orchestra, it may be used for general music, for stunts, or dramatic performances ; but unless it is very good should probably be superseded by a professional orchestra for dancing.   This may cause some dissatisfaction on the part of the student musicians and their friends, but it will probably be the cause of much satisfaction on the part of the many dancers, and they are the ones for whom the music is provided.   High school orchestras do not have the experience, skill, or repertory to play very successfully for dancing. Poor dance music will kill a party more quickly than anything else.   A few extra dollars can be spent very profitably on better dance music. Three good experienced musicians are preferable to a dozen inexperienced amateurs.

The study of costs is an important part of this committee's work. The program for the year should be carefully studied, planned, and budgeted. The expense must be met. Small fees may be charged — the lowest that will guarantee reasonable expenditures for music, decorations, and refreshments. Receipts from athletics, dramatics, or other revenue-producing agencies may be utilized.

The Committee should collect sample invitations of all sorts in order to be able to furnish ideas for new ones. Unique invitations may frequently be made by the students themselves. Samples and rough estimates of the cost of invitations should be of value to any group getting up a party.

Train leaders. — A successful party requires leaders. There must be some one to " start things." Even in the ordinary dance much time is wasted at the beginning because many of the students have not yet gotten up the courage to dance or ask for dances. Many may not know each other. What is needed near the beginning of the dancing part of a party is a mixer or " Paul Jones." Such a dance mixes up the students and " breaks the ice." Two such dances during the evening should help to increase interest and fun.

Any party will have its " wallflowers," who are not forward in playing. They need encouragement. Most of them would dance or play if given the slightest excuse to start. The leaders should get these people started by introducing them to partners, by urging them to play, and by making opportunities for them to join in without embarrassment.

Where games are played, leaders and choosers of sides are necessary. Such leaders should be trained as a part of the preparation for the party. They should know the games that are to be played and the rules, so that they can lead, choose, and intelligently instruct sides. Leaders are especially needed when new games are to be played. A " leaders play corps " might be a valuable sub-committee of the general social committee. Such an organization not only gives actual help in the learning and playing of the games but inspires the group with the desire to play and to play well. It makes just so many the more contact points between the general committee and the students.

Teach party courtesy. — Perhaps the most important single reason why school parties fail is the students' ignorance of ordinary party manners and courtesy. Knowledge of what is proper and the ability to do it make for confidence and poise. Lack of this and the consequent fear of doing the incorrect thing prevents many students from entering into party activities. Fear of ridicule is a great wrecker of confidence. There are many wallflowers at parties who are such because they do not know just what to do. On one side of the room is a row of boys each one of whom would probably like to participate. On the other side is a similar row of girls, each one of whom would like to be asked to participate. But the boys do not know what to say or do, and of the girls, many would not know what to say if asked for a dance. The net result is that the girls dance by themselves and the boys stand around awhile and go home. The party for them is a failure. How many party failures could be prevented by a little work along the line of party courtesy! The committee or its sub-committee might make party courtesy the subject of several assembly programs. Dramatization could be made of the correct methods of introduction, of asking for dances, of accepting and refusing invitations, and courtesy due to chaperons. Sermonettes on party courtesy are a waste of time. The student must see how it is done. Even this does not guarantee that he will do it. Continual correct practice alone will do that. Homeroom discussions and dramatizations of the various elements of social courtesy are probably better than the general assembly program, for the student can ask questions and enter into the general discussion himself. Suggestions for this work may be found in the chapter on " Manners and Courtesy."

Teach good form in dancing. — The student need not be expected to dance in good form if he has never had practice in it and would probably not recognize it anyway. Many of our so-called dances are frowned upon by dancing masters. The writer, in order to see if this were really true, visited the studios of four dancing masters and asked to be taught a certain dance which at the time was very popular among college people. Each of the four gave him some such answer as this : " We'll teach you to dance, but we won't teach you that stuff. That is not dancing." Any dancing studio in town would be delighted to put on a demonstration of good dancing at an assembly program. Of course it is good advertising for them. But most dancing instructors are interested enough in seeing good dancing — knowing how much that is undesirable is done in the name of dancing — to want to keep the standards high. The American Dancing Masters Association publishes a small booklet on " Good Form in Dancing." This can be made the subject of home-room discussions and demonstrations. A class in dancing might be organized at which the students are taught good form in dancing, as well as party etiquette.

Make social program for the year. — The social committee should be charged with the scheduling of the entire year's program. It represents the entire school and no particular interest. It is its business to see that all legitimate interests of the school are represented. The principal is too busy to attend to this himself. Often he has little sympathy with it anyway and does not want to take the responsibility of seeing that it is carried out. A complete party schedule is as important as a complete football or basketball schedule. The events can be properly distributed throughout the year, so that no one organization gets more than its share, and no group goes unprovided for. Moreover, the dates are set far ahead, so that an event will not be spoiled by hasty preparation. The schedule drawn up by the Committee should be presented to the council for formal acceptance and adoption. If unusual situations demand changes, additions, or withdrawals, these can be made as the occasion arises.

Events which may be held are as follows:

April Fool Party
Boat Ride
Carnival
Circus
Class Parties
Columbus Day (in costume)
Corn Roast
Country Fair
Emancipation Party for Freshmen (kid costumes)
French Club Parties
Football Banquet and Dance
Get-Acquainted Party for Freshmen
Hallowe'en Party
Hikes
Hi-Y Supper

Indoor Athletic Meet
International Party (costumes and games of nations)
Junior Banquet
May Party
Old-Fashioned Party (Colonial costumes)
Picnics
Senior Breakfast
Sleigh Ride
Stunt Day
St. Patrick's Day
Tea Dance
Teacher-Parent Reception
Thanksgiving Party
Valentine Party
"Wiener" Roast

Completely outline the party. — Some one has wisely said, " The party should be completely outlined from the time when the decision is reached to have it to the washing and putting away of the last dish." There are many small problems to be attended to which, if left undone, threaten the success of the affair. The most important of these questions are as follows:

1. Whose party is it? Each class should probably have one party each year. While this is a class affair, yet it should be supervised by the social committee. This committee need not take the initiative in conducting it, but will help to plan and arrange for it. In some schools the classes unite to hold parties. There

are two freshman-sophomore and two junior-senior parties each semester. This arrangement is desirable where the classes are not large. It means that many more students will attend, and often these groupings add to the congeniality of the event. The above groupings are more successful than senior-freshman or sophomore-junior, for obvious reasons. In addition, if the school is not too large, one or two general school parties may be held. No one can say how many parties shall be held during the year, but two general school parties and a party for each class would probably not be an excessive number. The number depends, however, upon local conditions, available places, size of groups, and traditions. Better two good parties each year than two dozen colorless affairs.

2. Who shall come? If the party is a freshman-sophomore event, let the guests as nearly as possible be limited to these classes. Such limitation is difficult because a sophomore brother may bring a junior sister, and other pairings seem frequently necessary for the interest of the students. It is essential, however, that outsiders be excluded! Admitting alumni to school parties has left a train of trouble. These affairs are school parties and should be kept such. It is hard to draw the line, because some alumni are desirable and some are not. Often there arise friendships which connect seniors with alumni of the opposite sex. But in general, the party should be a school party and outsiders should not be admitted.

3. When shall the party be held? For junior high school students the party should be an afternoon affair; for senior high school students evening events are better. Hours of from 8 : 30 to 10 : 30 or 11 : 30 are suitable. Many schools now hold afternoon " Dansants " of an hour or two in length. The school gym is utilized and inexpensive or school music provided. These are pleasant affairs and more in the nature of a social hour than of the more or less formal party.

4. Where shall the party be held? A gymnasium is essential to a modern high school. It is quite a proper place, if suitable in size and general arrangements, for the school party. Occasionally, however, the school board very shortsightedly refuses permission to hold school parties in it. This means that the students must rent a hall, thereby increasing the expense and inconvenience. It sometimes happens, too, that some shortsighted local association objects to having dances in the school building, or a gymnasium instructor or principal refuses to let the gymnasium be used for a party on the ground that it damages the floor. The best place in the world to hold a school party is in the school building under school auspices.

5. What regulations shall govern the party? A party may be killed by too strict regulations. However, it is necessary that some rules be set and that the students be acquainted with them. Such rules would have to do with the time and place of the party, admittance, and invitations. Some schools have a ruling that the students will not be admitted more than half an hour late. Another regulation frequently made is that no student shall leave the party until it is over unless formally excused. Local conditions should determine such special regulations. Within reason the party should not be repressed by laws and rules.

6. Who shall be chaperon, and what are her duties? No party should be held without careful chaperonage. A failure to observe this may hinder social programs for a decade. Chaperons should be selected from the teachers of the faculty and occasionally from interested parents. They should be acceptable to the students. Patronesses are perhaps more desirable than chaperons. The number depends upon the size of the group. Both men and women should be asked to serve.

The chaperon or patroness should have definite instructions as to her duties. Many chaperons consider themselves police officers whose duty is that of catching offenders or of criticising what is going on. The average teacher who does not dance or who has not danced in years and who consequently is out of sympathy with the modern dance as well as out of practice is not competent to chaperon a party. Few things kill a party more quickly than non-dancing chaperons, especially if they are important and somewhat noisy.

The chaperon will be on hand in case of emergency and, if conditions demand, will act and act promptly. But her main duties are constructive. She helps to make students acquainted. She greets them when they come and it is but courtesy for them to bid her good night when they leave. Chaperonage or patronage of the proper sort adds to the dignity and beauty of the occasion.

7. Of what shall the program consist? It has already been suggested that the program should consist of such varied features that all students, whether they dance or not, will be able to participate. The party might well start with a few simple dramatic events or music. These should be short and of a sort likely to be interesting to a gay crowd. Games and stunts should be planned for the students who do not dance, and dancing for those who do. Appropriate refreshments may be served to all.

8. Miscellaneous duties of the committee. This committee might be charged with the arrangement of other activities such as hikes, banquets of all sorts, sleigh rides, " wiener " roasts, and receptions. Home rooms and small groups of students, will arrange parties and social affairs, from time to time. All of these should be sanctioned by the general committee. The committee need assume no responsibility for a home-room party unless asked for help, but it should formally sanction this and the many similar smaller affairs which cannot be scheduled very far ahead. The committee will do well to encourage such parties and picnics by making available materials and suggestions. It will assume no responsibility for students' private parties.

Summary

It is not a question of whether or not the student will dance and will play, but whether the school will recognize its opportunity and obligation to teach him to do better the desirable play he is going to do anyway, and to reveal higher forms of play and make them desirable and attainable. A wise social program is one of the most attractive things about the school. But it must be wise and it must be a program. It requires serious study, whole-hearted coöperation, and intelligent planning. Successful parties do not happen; they are made.

References

Aspinwall, W. B. "How One School Meets the Problem of School Parties," *School and Society* 15 : 51-54, January 14, 1922.

Baker, C. G. *Indoor Games and Socials for Boys.* Association Press.

Bancroft, J. H. *Games for the Playground, Home, School, and Gymnasium.* The Macmillan Company.

Benson, J. K. *Book of Indoor Games.* J. B. Lippincott Company.

Betzner, E. *Special Parties and Stunts.* The Woman's Press.

Burchenal, E. *Folk Dances and Singing Games.* G. Schirmer.

Clark, T. "The Passing of the Chaperon," *Atlantic Monthly*, 516-519, April, 1922.

Community Service, *What Shall We Do? Games and Play for School Morale.*

Crawford, C. *Folk Dances and Games.* Barnes and Company.

Dawson, M. *The Mary Dawson Game Book.* The McKay Company.

Day, L. P. *Social Entertainments.* Moffat, Yard and Company.

Dennison's *Gala Book, Christmas Book, Bogie Book*, and others. Dennison Manufacturing Company, Framingham, Mass.

Elsom, J. C. and Trilling, B. M. *Social Games and Group Dances.* J. B. Lippincott Company.

Geister, E. *Ice Breakers and the Ice Breaker Herself.* George H. Doran Company.

—— *It is to Laugh.* George H. Doran Company.

—— *The Fun Book.* George H. Doran Company.

—— *Let's Play.* George H. Doran Company.

Girl Reserve Handbook. Woman's Press.

GLOVER, E. H. *Dame Curtsey's Art of Entertaining for All Occasions*. McClurg and Company.

JONES, G. "Parties as Projects of Instruction in High School," *School and Society* 17 : 696–697, June 23, 1923.

ROHRBAUGH, L. *Handy.* 510 Wellington Avenue, Chicago.

Six Rehearsal-less Entertainments. Walter H. Baker Company.

CHAPTER XVII

SCHOOL PUBLICATIONS

THEIR VALUES

The values discussed are, in general, common to all types of student publications — newspapers, yearbooks, handbooks, and magazines. The specific purpose of each of these publications will be emphasized in separate chapters of this book. These values are not of equal importance. Neither are they of equal value in all types of publications. The greatest single value of the yearbook, for instance, is its record of the history of the school for the year, while the handbook is less a record of events than of the rules, regulations, and other data, a knowledge of which is necessary to one who would rapidly become an intelligent citizen of the school.

They unify the school and foster school spirit. — An army without morale is a mob, and a school without spirit is bedlam. School publications, because of their function of carrying news, encouraging enterprises, and representing the entire school and its activities, are of inestimable value in unifying the school, and fostering school spirit.

They encourage desirable school enterprises and activities. — All school activities, if they are to thrive, need to be boosted. Even such popular activities as athletics must have meetings, parades, advertising, and ticket-selling campaigns to make them successful. Dramatics, music, publications, honor and scholarship organizations require continuous publicity. This publicity can best be given through permanent printed records. To recognize any organization by publishing its picture in the yearbook, writing up its activities in the newspaper, or stating its membership qualifications in the handbook is to encourage it. During the war the great loan drives could not have been successful had it not been for the persistent publicity given through the press of the land.

They mold and influence public opinion. — In order to have a society or organization, there must be a general basis of common knowledge and ideals. The school population is always changing. New students, new teachers, new organizations, and new issues make for instability and change. This means that if there is to be a stable organization there must be a continuous campaign to integrate this society. This end may be accomplished to some extent by assembly speakers, good books, and lessons, but not so well, probably, as by a direct method, one which can be easily adapted to local conditions and circumstances, and which leaves a permanent record.

They give authentic news of the school to students, parents, patrons, and other schools. — In the average school many activities and events are taking place about which the student should know, even if for no other reason than that it makes him prouder of his school. Many parents, too, know little about the school, and often what little they do know does not form a true picture. School affairs are notoriously misrepresented and wrongly emphasized through second hand information. The net result is misunderstanding and confusion. A school paper carrying recent and authentic news of the school to the parents and patrons is of real value. The alumni are usually interested in the school and they, too, can profit from it.

There is no history of the American secondary school so authentic and complete as the publications of these schools. Reports of activities, events, and new experiments are the news of school papers. The high school publication is of value to the alert school man, because it tells him what other schools are doing and how they are doing it, thus suggesting ways and means of improving his own practice. It is of value likewise to the student, for through its exchanges and news of other schools it shows him new activities and new ways of organizing and conducting old ones.

They serve as a medium of expression of student opinion. — In far too many schools the average student would hesitate to make suggestions for the betterment of the school or its work, because of his fear of the administration. Of course, any teacher or principal would say that such suggestions would always " be welcomed," but their attitudes too frequently would be anything but encouraging to the student who had suggestions to offer. The teacher or principal might well cultivate an atmosphere that would make the student feel free to express his ideas for betterment. His side is often neglected.

Another advantage of encouraging student expression is that it increases his interest in the school and its activities. We are most interested in the things to which we give the most. If a student thinks through a scheme for the betterment of some phase of school life and is given no attention or consideration, he naturally loses interest in it. He should be given a hearing. In no place can he be heard so well as in the school newspaper. Here the record is permanent. It is also dignified. The student feels elated at being recognized in this way. Again, people like to see their names in print. Consequently the student is doubly careful about what is printed over his name.

They give opportunity for self-expression and creative work. — This, to many the most important reason for the existence of school publications, is not such to the author. No school publication can be justified solely on the basis that it teaches the students who issue it to write well or draw well, or that it gives them valuable business training. It does these things, to some extent, but few are in position to profit, and not sufficient practice can be given to justify the expectation of any considerable development therefrom.

Moreover, it is foolishness to say that this work fits a student for a journalistic career. It would be just as true to say that participation in a couple of plays is a training for a dramatic career, or that the work in the algebra class is a training for a teaching career. Where the publication is used as a laboratory for courses in journalism, such a claim has much more to commend it. However, if the publication cannot be justified as being valuable to the school, it cannot be justified at all. The main purpose of any publication is not to honor the writer but to please and to educate the reader.

The publication does offer splendid opportunity for self-expression, and while this is not its most important value, it is one which must not be overlooked. The practice of writing and drawing is furthered by the demand for publishable material. If there is competition among the students for the honor of publishing, the school publications will benefit. Requiring a certain scholarship standing from staff members also tends to promote school work and encourage scholarship.

They develop qualities of coöperation, tact, accuracy, tolerance, responsibility, initiative, and leadership. — Getting out the publication furnishes a surprising array of splendid opportunities for the development of these qualities. In fact, the staff is a small democratic organization in itself. Its members have various responsibilities; they must individually show leadership, initiative, tact, tolerance, and a high degree of coöperation. Not the least of their virtues is their making for better faculty and student relationships. While the training a publication affords those who get it out could not alone justify it, these smaller values may, nevertheless, be mentioned after the more important values to the school at large have been discussed.

They foster cordial relations among schools. — Knowing what other schools are doing may be profitable, and an exchange of school publications is a splendid medium for the giving of such information to the entire school. An exchange of complimentary remarks about the rival school or its players, particularly at times of strenuous athletic or other competition, will not separate the schools, but will draw them more closely together, and make them friends instead of enemies. School intercourse should be mutually beneficial. Schools need not be bitter enemies just because they meet each other in athletics or in other contests. The publication offers a fine opportunity for the making of pleasant interscholastic relations.

They record the history of the school. — This is a value pertaining more to the yearbook than to other publications. Every person is interested in the affairs of his youth, and looking over the publications of his school days will bring many a happy memory. The main function of the yearbook is to preserve this history. Such books will be looked at many, many times during the lifetime of the graduate.

They advertise the school. — This is perhaps a value of minor importance, but some schools have really been " made " because of the advertising they have received from their publications. Advertising leads to inquiries and write-ups, and these spur the school on to greater achievements. Schools often become the center of interest of other schools, when reports of unusual entertainments, new types of student organization, etc., are published in their paper.

There are other values of the school publications, but those mentioned above are the most evident, and they are sufficient to justify the average school publication.

School publications have specific functions. — That the distinct functions of school publications are considerably obscured in the minds of staff, advisers, and school authorities, is shown by the publications themselves. Often the newspaper is made the carrier of literature; the magazine, the carrier of news; and the yearbook, a carrier of both. No such publication can really function. Attempting to make one publication do the specialized work of several would be like trying to use the janitor's shovel to shovel coal, to sweep with, and to paint with; or the teacher's trying to make the textbook in history serve also in Latin, English, and hygiene classes. The function of the publications of the high school are in the main as follows:

Newspaper . . . . To publish news
Yearbook . . . . To record history
Handbook . . . . To supply information
Magazine . . . . To present literature

The following five chapters will deal with these publications respectively, briefly outlining the facts concerning their organization, material, make-up, financing, and distribution.

CHAPTER XVIII

THE SCHOOL NEWSPAPER

The school newspaper is probably the most important of the four types of school publications. Its function is to carry the news of the school. Its material must be news, that is, records of recent events, and so must be issued every one or two weeks. Because of its frequency of issue, the newspaper realizes most of the values discussed in the preceding chapter. For instance, it can unify the school and foster school spirit, encourage school enterprises, influence school opinion, give authentic news, and serve as a medium of expression of public opinion better than any other publication.

Types of School Newspapers

Every school can have a newspaper; not a four-page printed weekly newspaper perhaps, but nevertheless an organ of publication. Newspapers are to be found in every grade of the elementary school as well as in the high school. They occur even in the kindergarten. Local conditions determine the type, size, organization, price, and other particulars. The following types of newspapers are to be found in the schools of the country.

The "told" newspaper. — The simplest form of spreading news is telling it. The simplest form of newspaper is a "telling" one. In this simplest form of school newspaper the little group discusses the purpose and organization of the newspaper and then elects a staff. This staff, with the help of the teacher, studies its problem and plans its paper. All of the members of the group are interviewed and the various contributions — simple personals — are jotted down and with the help of the teacher put into some kind of form so they may be easily recalled.

On the date of the " issue " the group gathers around to listen to the paper. The editor-in-chief tells a few of the main items of interest and then calls upon the other two or three members of the staff who are responsible for other items. The teacher acts as prompter in case any member forgets his items. Such a " paper " may be " published " once a week, each reading requiring five or ten minutes. A new staff may be elected for the next week's paper.

The " read " newspaper. — This type of paper is similar to the " told," but the news is written out by the staff and then read to the group. The editor may read it all, or he may read only the first page and allow the other editors to read the rest. This paper is better organized and can have a greater variety of material than the " told " paper. Short stories, simple editorials, advertisements, and even cartoons may be used. The group should select a name for the paper. After having been read, the paper may be posted on the bulletin board for further reading and examination. A slight variation of this is the writing of two or three copies of the paper and the passing of these around the class until all students have read them. Posting these two or three copies at various places about the room makes them available to everybody. A frequent change of staff increases competition and interest.

The " posted " paper. — The " told " paper is most suitable for the lower grades. Later, when the student can read and write fairly well, the written or " posted " type will be more attractive. One form of the " posted " paper is that in which the news is placed on the blackboard before the class enters in the morning. This may be made up in the usual sections of a paper with the usual paging. News, editorials, society and athletics sections, and humor may be included. Cartoons and headlines help to make it attractive.

A more complicated paper, but of the same general type is written on paper and posted on the bulletin board or elsewhere. It may be in longhand or typewriting. It is in usual newspaper form with headlines and columns. Large sheets should be used and if typewritten, plenty of " white space " left. Headings may be printed in by hand. The columns may be typed and pasted on the back, or a sheet of ordinary paper may be typed in two or three columns. This is more difficult than typing and pasting in the single columns. A good back can be made out of stiff cardboard. This will not tear and can stand upright if necessary. Such a paper should be written on one side only and there should be few " runovers " or continuations to other pages. It may run to several pages. It is more ambitious than the types previously discussed and can have all of the sections or parts of the usual newspaper, departments, cartoons, headings, pictures (snapshots pasted in), drawings, humor, and advertisements. It may also have the usual newspaper staff organization.

Mimeographed and multigraphed papers. — If the school is too large for the "posted" paper, or if mimeographing facilities are available, the mimeographed paper may be issued. Mimeography is inexpensive and nearly everything that can be done in a printed paper can be done in a mimeographed one. Cartoons, drawings, headlines, and columning can be included. Cuts for the heading or name, and departmental headings and other blocks to be used again can be drawn, and stencils made of wood or heavy cardboard. The wooden stencil can then be traced on the paper stencil. It can be used many times. A stylus, or blunt-nosed instrument, and a sheet of celluloid or a pane of glass is all that is needed for drawing, printing, or cartooning.

Extra-length paper may be used with long stencils and thus a

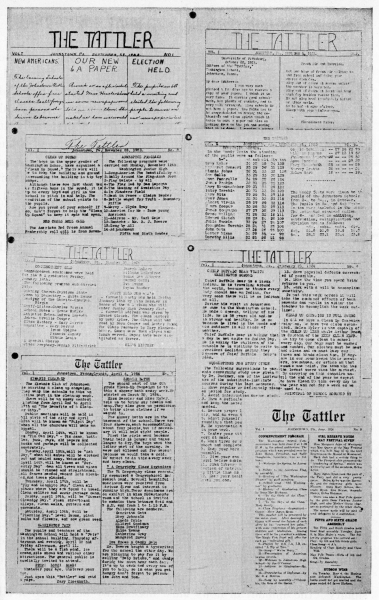

FIGURE XI. — THE EVOLUTION OF AN ELEMENTARY SCHOOL NEWSPAPER
This Newspaper was developed by a Sixth Grade group in the Washington School,
Johnstown, Pennsylvania, under the leadership of Miss Marie Hessler.

longer page be produced. Only one side of the paper should be used, as this makes a neater and more pleasing job. If desired, the paper may be columned. Columning is rather difficult to do, but makes the paper look more like a newspaper. If several pages are used, they should be stapled together, preferably at the side. Liberal margins, short paragraphs, and plenty of space between stories make for general attractiveness.

In addition to the usual staff of a regular newspaper, a more or less expert stencil cutter and mimeographer will be needed. Their duties are not difficult to learn and can readily be acquired where experienced help is not available. Ordinary mimeograph paper is most suitable because the typing dries more quickly and does not smudge as easily as on glazed paper, and is inexpensive. Such a paper should have a business staff to finance and distribute it. A small subscription price should be sufficient to pay for the ink, stencils, and paper used.

The printed paper. — *Part of local newspaper.* — The simplest form of the printed school paper is the one which is a part of the local newspaper. A space for school news is reserved usually once a week. There are two types of this paper. The first is the one which includes the news of all of the schools of the town. This is a " News of the Schools " paper and not a " High School News " paper. In this first, the news is usually written or at least compiled by the editor of the paper or some member of his staff. The superintendent rarely has time to write this material himself. The main advantage of this type of paper is that the people of the town are given the news of the schools. Its chief disadvantages are that the news items are often insignificant, unimportant, and of little interest either to the students or the parents ; the students receive no training in getting out the paper and the school has little interest in it because of its lack of responsibility ; the amount of news must necessarily be limited if all schools are to be represented ; and the high school students frequently do not like to be associated in their publicity with students from the elementary schools.

In the second instance, a certain amount of space is turned over to the school each week and the student-staff has the entire responsibility for what goes into it. Names of staff members are usually published; the page or section is appropriately named; and in other ways the paper resembles an actual newspaper with the exception that there are no advertisements. It is a good plan to have the editor assign to the school two sides of one sheet so composed and set up that the student can cut this sheet (or part) out, fold it, and have a four-page paper of school news.

Any local editor probably would be glad to give space in his paper once a week for such a purpose. This page carries interesting news to the community, and educates the children in learning to read the paper, thus furnishing the paper with an increased list of readers and possible subscribers. Of course, if a student-staff is responsible for the paper, it should be given full responsibility and its copy should not be rewritten or reëdited.

School-system newspaper. — Another type of school paper is one which is gotten out by the superintendent's office and represents the entire school system. Frequently the school vocational shop prints it. This paper has some merit as a carrier of news to the parents. However, the usual student letters or stories about little nothings are not particularly interesting to the average school reader, and expensive publication for them cannot be justified. Such a paper is frequently only a thinly veiled propaganda sheet. Frequently much " filler " is required to make the paper look respectable. Moralizings, sermonettes, and stray bits of information never make a valuable school newspaper.

The usual printed newspaper. — The printed school paper is the most common of all types and will be the basis of discussion in this and the following chapter. All of the types of papers mentioned are " newspapers " to the students whether printed,

FIGURE XII. — TYPICAL HIGH SCHOOL NEWSPAPERS

mimeographed, written, or merely read. Nearly all of the suggestions for the printed paper can be applied or at least adapted to these other types. The larger and more modern the school, the better newspaper it should have. There are a great many fine school newspapers in this country. It is interesting to note that some of the best of them come from fairly small schools.

Typical high school newspapers are illustrated on page 306. These vary greatly in size, shape, number of pages, type of material, and general organization. The paper is a relatively new school activity but a rapidly developing one. Its development is being greatly aided by High School Press Associations which have, as their purpose, the improvement of these publications. They hold contests, publish magazines and bulletins, arrange conferences, and in other ways help to promote good publications. Every school which issues any kind of publication should belong to one or more of these press associations. The largest of them is the Central Interscholastic Press Association, with Headquarters at 1 Folwell Hall, University of Minnesota, Minneapolis, Minnesota.

News

Definition of news. — The function of the newspaper is to carry news to its readers. The question at once arises, What is news? News has been defined as " anything that happens in which people are interested." Naturally, the more people it interests, the more news value it has. The most important news of the day — that found on the front page of the paper — is the news which will interest the largest number of people. That is why it is placed on the front page. Other forms of writing are to be found in the paper — editorials, correspondence, discussion, stories, sports, poems, and advertisements — but the main function of the paper is to present news.

Elements of interest. — News is based upon interest. If no one had any interest in what was going on in the world, there would be no newspapers. The most common elements of interest in news are timeliness, strangeness, familiarity, nearness, and appeal.

Timeliness. — We are usually more interested in what has taken place this morning or to-day than in what took place last month or last week. News is not news unless it is fresh. The most glaring violation in school publications of this principle of timeliness is to be found in the usual high school magazine. This publication frequently attempts to carry news a month or six weeks old — stale accounts of games, parties, and events long since forgotten. Such attempts can never be successful.

Strangeness. — The extraordinary event or happening is always interesting. Discoveries or inventions of new machines or contrivances are always welcome news. Frequently unusual happenings occur about the school which make interesting material for the newspaper.

Familiarity. — The event which concerns people or places with which the reader is familiar is interesting. Movie, athletic, and dramatic stars know the value of keeping their names before the public, and many are the schemes and artifices of the professional publicity man.

Nearness. — Events which occur near by are more interesting usually than those which occur farther away. The school paper should deal with school facts, and not with national, state, or even community affairs, except where these affairs very directly affect the school and its life.

Human appeal. — Every one is interested in what other people are doing. Especially those well known, either personally or by reputation. Lincoln is perhaps the most " human " of our presidents because of the hundreds of little humorous and pathetic stories told about him. The professional publicity man knows the value of this kind of story, and the papers constantly tell what athletic and dramatic heroes like, dislike, wear, eat, believe, what are their pets and their hobbies. Pathetic or amusing, or merely unusual incidents concerning individuals unknown to us are interesting. A " human interest " story is usually called a " feature " story.

Other elements of interest. — Amusements, romance, adventure, children, animals, and instruction make their own appeal. The emphasis being placed just now upon children and animals in the movies shows that the producers recognize the interest inherent in these subjects. The elements of appeal in these subjects affect the newspaper less, however, than those mentioned previously and consequently are not so important.

In short, the best news for the school paper is that which is recent, unusual, nearest at hand, most significant, and " human." Excessive humor, long stories, abundance of literary material or syndicated " filler " does not make live news and should be used sparingly. It must be remembered that the paper goes far beyond the school, into the homes of parents and patrons and to other schools. It must therefore represent the best in the school. The reporter and writer should ask himself the following questions about each bit of news : How many readers will it interest ? To what extent will it interest them ? Is it important or trivial ? Is it really timely news ?

Sources of news. — Every person is a potential source of news — he may know of things or may do things which would interest other people. News comes from a great variety of sources. For the metropolitan daily the various press associations, police courts, railroad stations, hotels, meetings of various sorts, athletic contests, etc., are the main sources of news. In short, news may come from anywhere.

In the school there are many possible sources of news — the principal, administrative officers, faculty, and students; there are meetings, athletic events, functions, organizations, and activities. In addition to the regular sources of faculty, student officers, etc., every student in the school is potentially a source of news. A " morgue " or filing case containing the record of all students in the school is valuable. This is especially so where the advisers and staff change frequently. A good source of material for a morgue is the school yearbooks. The records and pictures may be cut out and filed away and any additional material added to the card or envelope as it is found or published. The cuts used in the yearbook can be filed for future use. Needless to say, the publications office should have a complete file of all publications of the school as well as a good library of exchanges.

Gathering the news. — News does not just come in. It must be dug up. As has been suggested, it comes from a large variety of sources, and these must be diligently covered.

Regular beats. — For the city paper runs or beats are covered daily. A beat might include, for instance, the police stations, court house, and hotels. In like manner, the staff of the school paper should be organized and assigned to cover certain beats. Thus one beat might comprise the faculty, or, if too large, a certain section of it. Another might include the officers of a certain list of organizations.

Special assignments. — The editor should have a calendar in which coming events are noted with such additional information as time, place, purpose, etc., and all such activities should be made the subject of special assignments. This calendar is the " Futures " of the city editor of the daily newspaper. By having a definite system of this sort, all events are covered by responsible persons.

Incidental gathering. — Each member of the staff should be on the lookout for any material in the school. Nothing should be too small for the staff member to see. One might not see the significance of some small item but another might follow it up and get an interesting story out of it. The slogan of the paper might be " The truth, the whole truth and nothing but the truth."

Qualifications of the newsgatherer. — News is the most important part of the paper, and those who gather and prepare it for publication have no slight responsibility. Bleyer says, " No ordinary untrained person can do it. The job makes rigid demands upon those who do it successfully. To be a competent newsgatherer, a reporter and correspondent must have (1) "a nose for news," the ability to recognize news and determine its value; (2) a wide range of knowledge; (3) good judgment; (4) a sense of responsibility; (5) accuracy; (6) the ability to work rapidly; (7) initiative and resourcefulness; (8) perseverance; (9) tact and courtesy." [1]

While this refers particularly to workers on our great daily papers, it applies no less, relatively speaking, to those on our school papers. The newsgatherer is responsible for the character of the paper. If he is careless or inaccurate, the paper will not be worth the attention of the school. If he is careful, responsible, accurate, and industrious, the school will have a paper of which it can justly be proud.

MATERIALS OF THE SCHOOL NEWSPAPER

The school news stories are as varied as the activities of the students of the school. The paper must have variety, for all readers should find something of interest in it. Its contents may be roughly classified thus: (1) news stories; (2) editorials; (3) feature stories; (4) correspondence; (5) advice and helpful information; (6) illustrations; (7) humor; (8) fiction; (9) advertisements; (10) miscellaneous.

[1] *Newspaper Writing and Editing,* 62.

News stories. — The main kinds of news stories found in the school newspaper may be classified as (*a*) regular, (*b*) athletic, (*c*) social, and (*d*) personal.

Regular news. — By regular news is meant the usual news items, results of elections, reports of accidents to school people, publication of honor roll, report of assembly speeches, interviews, etc. These should be written in such manner as to bring out the most important points and should be classified and allotted space according to their importance. Nearly all papers make provision for bits of news too small to have separate headings. These may be arranged under such headings as " Happenings in School," " Odds and Ends," " Do you Know," " Have you Heard," " Side Swipes," " Listen," or " Look'ee Here."

Athletics. — More space is given to athletics in the school newspaper than to any other single topic. This is because the average school has a considerable amount of athletic activity and also because this news has a sensational appeal to the high school student. In many school papers athletics is probably overemphasized, the large headlines and extended space often giving to the outsider the impression that nothing else worth reading about exists in the school.

Social events. — Reports of parties, receptions, dances, picnics, and weddings may be carried under a department of " Social Events," or if important enough, be distributed throughout the paper. Many of these events may be written up at length as feature stories. Private parties should not be written up in the school paper.

Personals. — The great friendmaker of the newspaper is the " personal " column or department. People like to see their names in print, but most of them rarely do anything or have any experience of sufficient importance to justify a newspaper story. Here is the value of the personal column. It records small items which otherwise would not be published. A good column of personals — news, not attempts at humor — is an interesting part of any paper.

Editorials. — The main purpose of the editorial is to interpret the news of the day. It differs from the news story in that it admits of personal opinion, comment, and interpretation. The reporter must not express his opinions in his news story but may express them in an editorial. The editorial policy of the newspaper is determined by its management and ownership.

The school newspaper must represent the whole school if it is to retain its character and dignity. Its policy should be that of encouraging and boosting the best in all school activities.

Types of editorials. — Nearly all of the editorials in the school newspaper may be classified, according to purpose, as (*a*) boosting, (*b*) reasoning, (*c*) commenting, and (*d*) explanatory. The first, as is sufficiently explained by its name, is the usual form of school editorial. The next usually presents both sides of a question and shows how one side is better than the other. Formerly the editorial page was largely argumentative. Now it is rarely so except at election time. In school there will be frequent occasions when a reasoning editorial will be appropriate. The commenting editorial is an expression of opinion upon matters of interest or significance. After a subject is explained the editor takes an attitude towards it, or suspends judgment until more information is available. The purpose of the explaining editorial is largely to explain and pass upon matters of importance for the benefit of busy readers. Besides these, biography, sermonettes, and pleasantries may also serve occasionally.

Subjects for editorials. — A very frequent criticism of high school editorials is that they are sermons or essays on the various virtues and too seldom concern themselves with specific events in the life or work of the school. Editorials should not all be of one type but should be varied in form, topic, and scope. The following list of topics is suggestive of variety.

What does a high school education pay?
New courses in the programs of studies
Cleanliness
Care of personal property
Progress made by our school
Quitters
What have you accomplished this year?
Paddle your own canoe
New order of the board of education
Fads and superstitions
Our library
Good sportsmanship
Teachers as friends
Smile and "hello"
At the game
Are you an abuser?
Training cheer-leaders
The lameness of an excuse
Alibi Ike
Conduct in the halls
The student council
Our football teams
Knocker or booster?
What will you do next year?
Dress, its use and misuse
Self or service?

Feature stories. — Feature or " human interest " stories are short articles about interesting or amusing incidents. They are not to be confused with " special feature " stories appearing in the magazine section of the Sunday newspaper. " Human interest " stories are usually written about incidents which are in themselves unimportant. Such stories are written to entertain the reader. Whether tragic or humorous, they appeal to his emotional sense.

Many incidents occur around the school which might serve for feature stories. Athletics, dramatics, and other public activities can be advertised well by clever stories about them. Such topics as the following are suitable. Others will be found in the chapter on magazines.

> Birthplaces of faculty members
> Methods of coming to school
> Carving desks
> Courtesy
> History of the building
> Favorite dishes of cafeteria
> Reminiscences by old graduate
> Where our statuary and pictures come from
> Story of our cups and banners
> Kinds of candy sold
> Incidents on the athletic field
> Nicknames
> How faculty members spent their vacations
> Favorite books, plays, cars, foods, games, hobbies, slogans
> Special days and their origin
> Free textbooks
> Happenings in the laboratories
> Ambitions of seniors
> What the office clock sees

Correspondence. — The school newspaper serves as a medium for the expression of student opinion. This expression, outside of staff and editorial writing, can best be done by the use of a correspondence department in which are published letters, queries, answers, and other correspondence from students, alumni, or friends. Such a column can be made extremely interesting and valuable by proper encouragement and sound judgment in the selection of correspondence for publication. This is an " opinion " column and must be recognized as such. The newspaper does not necessarily subscribe to the opinions presented and must make this clear. A short statement to this effect at the top of the department or column is good practice. Often parts of communications are not significant, or should not be published, or the letter may be too long to be printed in entirety. In such cases the unimportant or offensive part may be omitted and this omission indicated with the usual marks. However, care must be taken not to " kill " parts of correspondence except where absolutely necessary. The purpose of the column is to encourage frankness and strict editing will not encourage it.

Useful or interesting information. — This kind of news is interesting and instructive, but is usually used as " filler," to fill up space after all news stories are in. The use of much of it shows that the staff has been unsuccessful in getting enough news to fill the paper. Very little of it should be used on the first page. This material may be taken from such sources as " Almanacs " or any one of a dozen books of the " what you ought to know " order.

Illustrations. — Newspaper illustrations are mainly either halftones or " cuts," which are reproductions of photographs; or cartoons, graphs, etc., which are reproductions of drawings. Both types of illustrations are very widely used. They add variety and interest to the paper. Only the most important items should be illustrated, and each illustration should be the best one attainable. The ideas or topics used should have to do with school life and activities.

Humor. — An important part of most publications is humor. It has its place in the school newspaper, whether in a separate department or scattered through its pages. The latter arrangement is preferable. Many school administrators frown on school publications because these have degenerated into sheets of nonsense. This is due, usually, to the fact that an efficient humor editor was on the job and his department expanded out of proportion to its importance. Jokes should be used after the main obligation of the newspaper — purveying news — has been discharged, and then not between news stories or at the top of the page, but at the bottom and wherever required for filler.

A joke which does not concern school people or school activities is out of place. The usual " he-she " joke does not appeal to the student so much as one in which the characters are students known to him. Moreover, it should rarely be necessary to use clipped and threadbare jokes. Many humorous remarks and incidents occur about the school and may be used. Jokes which ridicule students are not in good taste. Short poems, parodies, and other verses make good humor material.

The strip cartoon is an important type of humor. Every school has some student who can draw and he can be used to good advantage. A series of strips with the same characters is a good investment. These should not ape the strips of the daily newspapers, but should be distinctive and have as their subjects items and events of school interest and knowledge. Such strips should be placed at the bottom of the page rather than at the top.

Fiction. — The function of the newspaper is to present news, and news is concerned with facts. Fiction is not concerned with facts. It is imaginative writing. Hence fiction is not the material of which the newspaper is made. However, a bit of it may be used for the sake of variety, *e.g.* a short-story, a poem or two. Filling up the paper with amateurish and puerile stories and poems shows that the staff is incapable. The newspaper is not the laboratory of the English department. It may, however, be the laboratory of the department of Journalism.

Stories and poems used should be on subjects with which students are familiar. Long poems should never be used and long stories but rarely. If used in a weekly, long stories should be run in sections. In a biweekly paper the value of continued stories is doubtful. Stories and poems by outsiders, no matter who they are, should not be used unless they are of direct interest and value to the average student of the school. A school newspaper is no place for Shakespeare, Browning, or Longfellow, no matter how estimable their works may be.

Advertisements. — Advertisements are not as valuable or important as the most important news, and so are rarely found on the front page of a school newspaper. They occur on all other pages. Classified advertisements are rarely used in the high school newspaper.

Advertisements are usually " pyramided " up the side of the page, nearest the seam on the left hand pages and nearest the outer edge on right hand pages. The pyramids are made by using the large advertisements at the bottom and tapering off with the smaller ones. The pyramid need not cover the entire bottom of the page nor should it reach to the top. Its top should not be more than two columns in width. It is bad practice to run advertisements across the middle of the page, thereby cutting the news of the page in two. Neither should they be scattered over the page; they should be grouped. Good judgment and practice are required to arrange advertising in a pleasing manner. Small boxes or cards are frequently used in advertising professional men — doctors, lawyers, and dentists — whose business ethics prevents them from using the large advertisements which the business man uses.

No advertisements of the " compliments of," " by courtesy of," or " space donated by," type should be used. They imply that the paper is of no value as an advertising medium and publishing them is a corroboration of this view by the staff of the paper! Many advertisers do not or cannot write good copy; hence this work must be done by the advertising staff. The staff by making a study of stories can also help to sell space by writing pleasing advertisements and showing them to prospective advertisers. Well-written and well-placed advertisements add to the attractiveness of the paper, in addition to serving the important function of helping to finance it.

Miscellaneous contents. — Alumni notes are of value in interesting graduates and also the members of the school who know them. A well-kept alumni column is an asset both to the paper and to the school.

Exchange news or notes can be made important and valuable in the school paper, but as it appears in many high school papers or magazines it is a waste of space. The following are illustrations from school newspapers of this absurd material:

"*The High School Times:* — A good little paper with plenty of nonsense. Your news items are well written up."

"*The Boyertown School News:* — A fine biweekly school paper filled with school activities. Why not have a literary department?"

Such material is written for the eyes of the editor of the other paper and not for the student readers and subscribers. If these little comments are important, they might be typed and mailed to the other editors and staffs. They certainly have no interest for the student who pays for the paper and who never sees the papers referred to. The exchange editor can make his column interesting by presenting bits of information about what is being done in other schools. A " What Other Schools Are Doing " column is much better than an " Exchange " column. Examples of good use of the exchange column are the following:

"A biweekly Spanish paper is being published by the first and second year Spanish classes of Abilene High School. The purposes of the paper are to stimulate interest and enjoyment in the work and for the help it affords in translation." — Abilene *Booster*.

"Speaking of service, the athletes of Edison High School, Minneapolis, Minnesota, surely have it. A school service committee composed of certain enterprising young ladies has been formed for the purpose of mending the athletic boys' socks."

Other miscellaneous types of news may be arranged under such departments as the " Inquiring Reporter," " The Question Box," and the like. These, if not over-emphasized, add to the attractiveness of the paper.

Writing the News

The average newspaper contains an enormous mass of material. As this material comes in the shape of facts it is unclassified and unreadable. The function of news writing is to take these facts, arrange them under appropriate headings and in the order of their importance, and make readable " stories " of them. The importance of news writing is obvious. The average reader spends little time on his paper. He reads nearly all of the head-lines, picks out what interests him, looks over some of it, reads some of it, and probably studies some of it. The first duty of the newspaper man is to see the picture : the second is to tell it in such manner that the reader can see it.

Style book. — The " style book " or " style sheet " is a set of rules governing such details as abbreviation, capitalization, punctuation, quotation, use of figures, etc. Newspapers do not agree on many of these usages and the result is that each paper has a style book of its own. The reporter must therefore become familiar with the style sheet used and follow it closely. The school newspaper should also have a style sheet in order to secure accuracy and uniformity.

The lead. — The beginning of a news story is its most important part. It is called the " lead." This lead summarizes in a sentence or two the facts of the entire story. If an event happens the reporter is concerned with the following.

What happened ?
When did it happen ?
Where did it happen ?
Why did it happen ?
Whom did it concern ?

These five " w's " are usually answered in the sentence or two which constitute the first paragraph of the story. In long stories separate leads may be written for each paragraph.

Examples of leads. — The following illustrations of the various types of leads are taken from typical school papers.

" What " leads. The most commonly used lead begins by answering the question, What happened?

The election of cheer leaders was conducted in Munhall High by the method suggested by the student body. September 9, 1924, was the day set aside for the candidates to perform on the stage before the assembly. — *Munhisko*, Munhall, Pa.

" Who " leads. — In the great daily papers stories concerning prominent people are often begun with " who " leads. Where the individual is unknown the lead seldom begins by answering the question Who?

Ruth Zeigler has been selected to represent York High School in the state oratorical contest at Harrisburg this evening. She was chosen from a group of thirteen contestants who participated in the local tryout last Monday evening. *York-High Weekly*, York, Pa.

" When " leads. — " When " leads are rarely used unless the time bears some unusual relation to the story that makes it important.

On Monday, in chapel, a set of simple traffic rules which had been adopted by the Student Council were presented to this student body. The Investigating Committee of Traffic conditions was in charge of chapel and explained the rules. *The High Post*, Latrobe, Pa.

" Where " leads. — Leads beginning with the location of the event are also comparatively rare.

In the auditorium meeting held Monday, October 22, Mr. Faucett Ross, a Central alumnus and graduate of the 1919 class, delightfully entertained the students with skilful demonstrations of magic. *Central Outlook*, St. Joseph, Mo.

" Why " leads. — Every event takes place because of certain causes. A knowledge of these causes helps the reader to understand and appreciate the event itself.

To honor members of the North High Chapter of the National Honor Society, a special meeting was called Wednesday, March 19. *The Polaris*, North High School, Columbus, Ohio.

" Unconventional " leads. — Other types of leads, used less frequently and hence " unconventional," are illustrated below. It will be noted that in these the five " W's " are not answered immediately, that you have to read into the story to find out what it is about. To be effective such leads must begin with some statement or question which will lure the reader into going further. The reporter must use a great variety of leads if he would avoid monotony in his stories. Notice the interest the following leads arouse.

What would you do if you met a caleopterist? Haven't you seen one? Then come to "Clarence." *Coyote Journal*, Phoenix, Ariz.

If one had been a mouse backstage at the American theater Wednesday just before the beginning of the afternoon performance of the Anna Pavlowa company, he would have seen strange sights. *The North Central News*, North Central High School, Spokane, Wash.

Back in Schenley again after two months of freedom from restraint. There comes a sigh for the vanished leisure, the long sunny days, and the idle evenings of summer. . . . *The Schenley Triangle*, Schenley High School, Pittsburgh, Pa.

Only twenty-two years of age, yet a student of Harvard University in the day time and feature story and book-review writer for the Boston Transcript at night, is Daniel Rockford, former editor of the West High Weekly, and son of Mrs. W. I. Rockford, West history teacher. *West High Weekly*. Minneapolis, Minn.

Strut your stuff. Here's a chance to have a dance. The mighty seniors will gather Friday evening, May 16, in the girls' gym for one of the biggest hops of the year. Many original features will predominate, colored lights 'n everything. Snappy music and a good program will be the best bets. *Manual Arts Weekly*, Los Angeles, Calif.

Can you believe it? All our self-confidence returned after the team, working hard and in clocklike fashion, made this a reality. *The Forum*, Dubois, Pa.

Job said, " Oh that mine adversary had written a book " and ever since people who manifest no other particular sign of devoutness have been quoting the phrase as illustrative of the peril inherent in print and paper." *The Mountain Echo*, Altoona, Pa.

The goal has been reached. Long and tedious effort has been necessary to produce Clinton's first attempt in opera for many years. To-night will witness the first evening of the *Pirates of Penzance* and everything points to a great success. *The Clinton News*, De Witt Clinton High School, New York City.

The number and variety of leads used, in fact, depends upon the resourcefulness and ingenuity of the staff. And in the newspaper variety means interest, and interest success.

Order of leads. — After the reporter has gathered the facts for his story, he must determine which phase of it is the most important or the most interesting. He will then give this first place. It becomes the " feature " of the article. The " W " corresponding with it will be answered first.

Body of the story. — The lead gives a brief outline of the story ; the body completes it by filling in the details. As will be realized, the body must be interesting to the reader if he is to be induced to read it, for the story has already been told both in the headlines and the lead. The body is a connected logical story of the event from beginning to end. It is in narrative form.

Paragraphs. — Newspaper paragraphs are short, for the average reader of papers has only a short time to give to them. Long paragraphs appall him ; short ones encourage him to continue. Consequently the average newspaper paragraph is rarely longer than twelve or fourteen lines, and usually more often averages from six to ten lines. One line of typewritten material makes two lines of print in column. Paragraphs of from one to three sentences are used most frequently. The beginning of each paragraph should contain the most important element of that paragraph.

Sentences. — " If a sentence of a newspaper story has to be reread it is a poorly constructed sentence." Newspapers must be read hurriedly. They are read silently. In reading silently we read much faster than we do in reading aloud. As a matter of fact silent reading is more scanning than it is reading. We hurry to get the thought and pay little attention to words. Since this is the case, anything the reporter can do to make the paper more easily scanned will be profitable. Using short paragraphs is one method of increasing readability. Using short sentences is another. Newspaper sentences should not be long, but neither should they be so short as to produce a choppy or disconnected style.

Words. — The first aim of the reporter should be to have his reader see the picture as he sees it. In other words, he must " paint " it accurately and completely. The newspaper writer must have at his command a large fund of words because he writes a great deal and consequently is in danger of using some words too frequently. Proficiency in the use of words comes through practice and study. It is good practice after writing a story to go over it and polish it by rearranging its structure, and by substituting more accurate and forceful words wherever possible. Another method is to put in parentheses after every possible word all the synonyms that can be thought up or looked up. Similar practice with antonyms is valuable. Changing the story from passive voice into active and vice versa is also a valuable means of increasing fluency.

News *vs.* opinion. — It is rarely justifiable in news writing for the reporter to express his own opinions, and never in regular news stories. The reader is interested in the story and not in the reporter's opinion concerning it. Opinions of eye-witnesses and bystanders may be quoted, however. It is hard for a person reporting an interview or a speech to refrain from agreeing or disagreeing with it, nevertheless he must not show his own feelings in the matter. Readers are not interested in them.

Preparation of copy. — The style book has been suggested as a requisite in newspaper work because of the necessity for uniformity. In a similar manner all copy must be uniform if errors are to be avoided and loss prevented. Uniformly prepared copy also saves the time of the editor and the printer. A set of rules should be drawn up by the staff and all copy be prepared in accordance with them. The following rules are suggestive only:

1. Place your name in the upper left-hand corner.
2. Typewrite if possible; use double spacing.
3. If you write the story in longhand, write slowly and very legibly and leave plenty of space between the lines.
4. Use only one side of the paper.
5. Begin the story halfway down the first page so that headings can be written above it.
6. Leave a liberal margin at the sides, top, and bottom of paper.
7. If the copy is more than one page in length, paste the pages together in order. Do not use pins; they fall out.
8. Indent each paragraph, or use printers' sign (¶) for it.
9. Use the proper printers' sign at the end of the story to show it is finished.
10. If pictures or illustrations are to be used with your story, indicate the fact at the top of your first page. A simple description and identification such as "one-column cut — President Coolidge" is satisfactory.
11. Follow your style book for punctuation, capitalization, abbreviations, etc.
12. In making corrections in copy do not erase, but cross out and rewrite.
13. Occasionally stories are written in which unusual spellings, constructions, etc., are used. In that case write "Follow Copy" on the page.
14. Adopt accuracy as your watchword.

Summary

The newspaper is probably the most valuable of the four types of school publications. Newspapers are to be found in all grades of the school. The main function of the school newspaper is to present interesting and significant news about the school and its life. News may come from anywhere and the first job of the staff is to provide for the efficient gathering of it. A number of different kinds of material go to make up the newspaper. Not all students have the same interests, and variety adds to its effectiveness. The news writer must not only see the event but must be able to present it in such manner that the reader can see it.

CHAPTER XIX

THE SCHOOL NEWSPAPER (*Continued*)

The first impression the reader receives from the paper is important. If it is poorly or carelessly made up, he will be prejudiced against it before he begins to read it. If it is well made up, he will be favorably impressed and will have a better attitude towards it as he reads it. This first impression depends upon a number of items, the name, paging, size, columning, balance, classification of material, and use of illustrations. While the newspapers of different schools will not all be made up alike, there are yet fundamental principles in make-up which must not be violated.

MAKE-UP OF PAPER

Name. — It must be remembered that school newspapers often travel far and that their circulation is rapidly increasing; consequently the name must be dignified and worthy. Such names as " Talebearer," " Tattletale," and " Gossip," are not appropriate. They suggest flippancy. Many schools name their paper after their school colors, " Red and Black," or " Green and White." While these names are better, they are not particularly suggestive, and lose some value because dozens, if not hundreds, of other schools have the same colors. There is nothing distinctive about them. Such names as " Tribune," " Weekly," " Pilot," " Register," " Hi-Post," and " Hi-News," are good. They are dignified and suggest character. However, they do not indicate the name of the school which publishes them. Such names as

" West High Weekly," " Manual Arts Weekly," " Central Outlook," " Lewis and Clark Journal," " York High Weekly," and " Shadyside News " are appropriate and definite. Names composed of abbreviations, or names with the school name worked in, are frequently found : " Munhisko " (Munhall High School), " Travalon " (Avalon), " Belle Hop " (Bellevue High School), illustrate this method of naming the paper. If the school is just starting a paper, much enthusiasm in the student body can be worked up by balloting on a name for it.

Once the name has been chosen it is important also to see that it is attractively made up to head the paper. Usually this is set up in type each time, but frequently a " headpiece " is made and used. Such a piece is necessary if the name or the make-up desired is complicated or unusual.

The school and city from which the paper comes should always be designated. It is exasperating to pick up a school newspaper and find that nowhere in it is the name of the school or city suggested. Each number of the paper should also be designated or identified by " volume " and " number." " Issue " is not as good as " number " for this designation.

" Ears." — " Ears " are small " boxes " at the top corners of the front page in which are printed designations, news or comment. The " Home Edition " or " Final Edition " of the daily newspapers are carried in the ears. In school newspapers the ears usually carry exhortations to beat rivals, boost campaigns, etc. If the name of the paper does not take all of the space at the top of the page, the ears help to fill it up and give a pleasing effect.

Size. — The size of the paper is understood to include such elements as dimensions, number of columns, and number of pages. Size depends upon two main factors, the amount of news to be used, and the cost of the paper. Needless to say, before a paper is issued a budget of probable income and expenditure should be carefully planned and the latter made to conform to the former. This budget will determine the size of the paper. Size of circulation and size of paper may vary directly.

Dimension. — The school newspaper should look like a newspaper. The magazine page is small; the newspaper page is large. On the large page it is easier to have variety in make-up than on the small page. One large page is less expensive than two pages half as large. Some schools print their own papers and their presses cannot handle a large page. This, however, is no justification for a small page.

Number of pages. — Some schools publish a newspaper in magazine form and size. It is not to be confused with the regular school magazine, to be discussed later. It consists of a number of small pages stapled together. This form for a newspaper is decidedly bad. It suggests literature, not news; it allows but little in the way of pleasing variety of page make-up; and it is expensive because of the necessity of cutting, printing, assembling, and stapling. Newspapers whose number of pages are not in multiples of four are bad because of the inconvenience of the extra sheet. For the average school a paper of four large pages is preferable to any other form.

Columns. — The newspaper column is narrow and the newspaper sentence contains about one half as many words as the average book or letter sentence. This is to make it more readable. School newspapers vary from one or two columns in smaller mimeograph or printed papers to seven or eight in the papers of larger schools.

Usually an odd number of columns is preferable, for it is easier to balance such a page. For instance, most " boxes " and " cuts " will be of one-column width and if the paper is odd-columned, say of five columns, these boxes or cuts may be placed in the middle or third column and there will be two columns on either side of them. If they were used in a four-columned paper and put in column two or three, there would be one more column on one side than on the other.

Classification of content. — The importance of material in the newspaper is shown, first, by its location or position in the paper, second by the space allotted to it, and third by the headings used to advertise it. Not all of the happenings about the school are of equal importance; so they must be rated and placed accordingly. The first page of the paper is most important and on this page will be found all of the most important news stories. Not all of them will be finished on this page; many will " break over " to the inside pages and will be completed there. The importance of the story frequently bears some direct relation to its length, but not always. Often many of the most important stories are short, while features and others may be long.

The duty of judging importance falls to the editors. They must decide which activities or events are the most important and which are the least significant. This will usually not be a particularly difficult task, but it must be carefully and fairly done. The paper must be as unbiased and fair in its classification of news as in its stories of it. How shall the importance of a story be judged? The scales by which the relative importance of stories is measured are those used for measuring news. In general, that which is interesting or significant to the largest number of students should be placed in the most important part of the paper. The report of a fine assembly talk or an important football game or a notice of an unexpected vacation concerns every one in school and should be started, at least, on the front page. The report of a meeting of the French Club or Radio Club, a " personal," an alumni item, or a story of interest only to a restricted group should rarely go on the front page.

The relative importance will vary, too, with each issue. For some numbers there will be a great deal of important news, possibly too much for all of it to be placed on the front page. Or

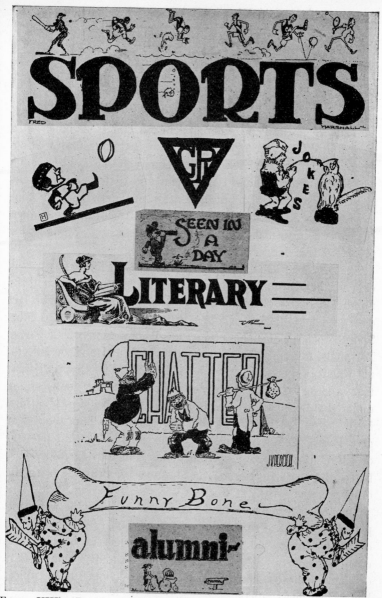

FIGURE XIII. — DEPARTMENT HEADINGS TAKEN FROM HIGH SCHOOL NEWSPAPERS

there may not be enough of it to fill the front page. Thus it will be seen that importance is always relative.

Sections. — City newspapers are usually organized into sections — society, sports, etc. — and many school papers are similarly organized. Such a classification of news makes for directness and definition, and where each reporter is assigned to a section it makes for efficiency in newsgathering and writing. There is a danger, however, that there may not always be enough news for some particular department and that, as departments appear insignificant with but little news, they may fabricate some news. Such a practice cheapens the department and the paper. If care is used in making sections, allotting space, and assigning reporters, this danger should be largely eliminated.

The sections used, as well as their placement in the paper, will depend upon the size of the school, the size of the paper, and the number and size of organizations; no general rule can be laid down. The following sections are typical: Editorial, Clubs, Sports, Society, Class News, Fiction, Poetry, Humor, Exchange, Personals, Alumni. To each department is assigned the individual who is best acquainted with and best fitted for that particular task, and he is held responsible for furnishing the news coming under that designation. Such an individual should be identified in the paper, so that the school will know to whom to send or give items. A few schools carry the name of such a reporter or editor at the top or bottom of his column. Probably it is better to place it in the masthead above the editorials with the other members of the staff.

Departments may be made attractive, as also the page and paper, by the use of headpieces or cartoons. These may be drawn by some student about school or may be bought from engraving houses. They can be used over and over again. The department heads shown on page 331 were clipped from typical high school newspapers.

Occasionally in the departments there will be news stories deserving first-page prominence. For instance, an important athletic contest which will be significant news to the school, deserves front-page display. Such a story may be started there and completed under the sports or athletic section on the third or fourth page. Care must be taken not to over-emphasize any one department. Athletics especially is likely to be over-stressed.

Editorials and staff placement. — In a four-page paper the masthead containing the names of the members of the staff is usually placed at the upper left hand corner of the second page. The names should be listed opposite the office held and usually in rank beginning with the most important and running down to the least important. The block or cut showing membership in press associations is also placed here, and the statement regarding mailing as required by law. Making the masthead and editorial section two columns wide is good practice. It gives more space for names and official positions on the paper, and the editorials are then only half as long because twice as wide as in a single-column arrangement. This encourages reading, especially if the type is larger than that in the body of the paper. The editorial page is often called a page of opinion and consequently is the proper place for special letters or correspondence.

Advertisements. — Advertisements should not be placed on the first page unless they concern some very important school interest. They may be placed on all other pages of the paper. In a four-page paper a few are usually placed on the second page. Some editors claim that the last page of the paper is second in importance, and reserve it for news. In this case few advertisements would be placed on the last page. They are usually built up the side of the page in the form of a pyramid with the base at the bottom of the page. The top of the page is the most important and consequently should be reserved for news. Scattering them through news or vice versa is bad practice. The

DROPLINE

High School
Development
Very Great

**BUILDER ASSURES
NEW AUDITORIUM
FOR CLASS PLAY**

*Annuals Enter
Spring Contest*

CROSSLINE

PRESIDENT STRESSES DUES

PRES. MEES TO LECTURE

Fine Program Arranged

FIGURE XIV. — FOUR COMMONLY USED

Science Club Is Active Body

Y. W. Conference To Be Held At Central Y

Three Delegates Are Picked To Go to Convention At Mankato

HANGING INDENTATION

Tryouts Which Will Be Held Next Week To Be Conducted on Different Plan From That Used Other Years.

Mrs. Jenkins and Mrs. Harris Entertain Better Students of School in Auditorium Held Tuesday

All American C. I. P. A. Annual Ratings to be Made This Spring Instead of in Fall of Year.

TYPES OF NEWSPAPER HEADLINES

advertising dummy is built up, and each space numbered and sold according to number.

Balance. — The page must be made attractive. It would not be so attractive if it were printed solid. Headlines help; but if all headlines were of the same size and style of type, it would still lack variety. Nearly all papers try to balance the first page. For instance, the most important topics are balanced against each other by being placed at opposite sides of the page and under somewhat similar headlines. As two heavy headlines set together would not make for variety, a short or small headline is set next to a heavy or long one. This emphasizes by contrast the importance of the long headline. Some papers go to the extreme of matching each article and heading on one side of the page with one of the same type on the other side. Such mathematical perfection is not desirable, if for no other reason than it subordinates news values to mechanical make-up. The right hand outside column on the front page is usually considered the most important. Some headlines should be placed below the fold of the paper. The inside pages are not balanced as much as the first page. The staff should make the dummy; place the stories and allot space to them; write the headlines; and designate the type to be used. The make-up of the paper is too important to be left to the printer.

Headlines. — The headline of the newspaper is not a label. It has, in fact, a fourfold function: to advertise the news; to summarize it; to classify it according to importance; and to increase the attractiveness of the paper through variety.

Types of headlines. — To avoid monotony and to emphasize by contrast, several kinds of headlines are used. Each head is made up of groups of lines called " decks " or " banks." The four most commonly used are as follows.

Dropline. In the dropline head each successive line is indented.

Crossline. The crossline is a line straight across the column. Frequently it does not fill the column.

Pyramid. The pyramid is usually of smaller type than the dropline or crossline and contains more words or statements. It is made in inverted pyramid or half-diamond shape.

Hanging indentation. In this type of headline the first line begins at the left side of the column and runs entirely across it. The lines following are indented equally a letter or more.

The four kinds of headings are illustrated on pages 334 and 335.

The illustration on page 339 shows complete headings taken from typical high school newspapers.

Special kinds of headlines. — Spread head or layout. Ordinarily the newspaper headline extends one column in width. When it is more than one column in width it is called a spread or layout. It may be any number of columns wide. It is usually in large type, frequently boldface. Its subordinate decks may spread its entire length but usually they do not.

Streamer or banner. This headline spreads across the entire page. More than one story may be " streamered," the streamers being of different kinds and sizes of type. This head is purely an advertising head designed to sell the newspaper. The passing reader can take in the news at a glance, and the big attractive head helps to interest him further in it. Such a head probably has little place in the school newspaper. In the first place, it would not help to sell many more papers, and in the second, as the paper is issued but once a week or once in two weeks, the large headlines are not bulletining recent news but news which took place several days ago and which every one in school knows already.

Jump-heads. When a story "breaks over" or "runs over" to an inside page, a "jump-head" is used, this headline usually being the first phrase of the top deck as it appeared on the front page. This helps the reader to find it readily.

Subheads. In order to break the monotony of long solid columns of text, subheads are used. These are usually simple statements of crossline form and are placed at irregular intervals.

Overlines. The overline is a printed title which is placed above a picture or an illustration. It is short, containing usually only the name or label. It frequently starts the story or relates the picture or illustration to the news of the day.

The legend is an explanation or exposition longer than the overline and is placed below the illustration or picture. It completes, in some detail, the story which the overline started.

Single deck headlines should rarely be found on the front page because nearly all first-page material is long and important enough to demand more. Headings usually contain more than one type of headline, the longer, more important stories having perhaps all four, while shorter stories contain but one or two. The display lines or top deck are commonly crossline or dropline, while the subordinate heads are made up of pyramid and hanging indentation types. The first and third decks are the most important in a four-deck head. Very rarely is one kind of head followed immediately by another deck of the same kind. There must be a contrast. This is secured by a difference in kind of heading and in the kind and size of type used.

Rules for headline writing. — Headline writing requires study and practice. The headline writer must know the story and its details, its news values in general, be able to judge significant features, and have skill in the technique of writing headlines. The main rules to be followed in writing headlines are as follows:

1. The headlines must be symmetrical. The headline will depend first of all upon three things, the space allowed for it, its length, and the size of type desired. The space will be the width of the newspaper column, which cannot be widened or narrowed. It is measured in units. Each letter is one unit in width except M and W, which are one unit and a half each,

Co-operation Stressed
At Fathers' Meeting

Dr. Prosser and J. E. Meyers Speak to Fathers On Improvements

---

DINNER HELD TO FORM VOCATIONAL ADVISERS

Invitations From the Students To District Fathers Bring Results

SIX GIRLS CHOSEN TO LEAD EXERCISES

Four Seniors, One Junior and One Sophomore Will Head Ranks in Exhibition Tonight

---

STUDENT GOVERNMENT MOVEMENT
HAS APPROVAL OF MR. NOONAN

Recommended by Teachers at Faculty Meeting — Success Depends on Students Alone

---

Lowry Gives His Opinions About School

Transit Company Head Declares Boys Work Better with Men

BUSINESS MAN HAS FAITH IN CLASSICS

Education Consists of Problems of Knowledge, Accuracy, Society

Ellsworth House Hallowe'en Party

UNIQUE ENTERTAINMENT

CICERO CLASSES PLAN PROGRAMS

DEMERITS WILL TAKE PLACE OF DETENTION

System Proves Big Success In Other High Schools Where Attempted

DETENTION DAYS OVER

Finally Passed After Long Sojourn in Student Body Council and Faculty

Legion Trophy Presented To School

CHAPEL TALKS GIVEN BY COLONEL CRONIN

Bellevue Varsity Visits

FIGURE XV. — HEADLINES TAKEN FROM HIGH SCHOOL NEWSPAPERS

and I, which is a half unit. The figure 1 and punctuation marks are a half unit, excepting the dash and double quotations, which are one unit. The spaces between the letters count as one unit each.

Letters have the same width in units no matter what type is used. In other words, a unit is a unit, whether in big or small type. The number of units which may be put into a line depends upon the size or point type used and also the face used. This means that the writer of headlines must know his type and how many letters of each is required to fill the column. He can then write his headlines so that they will be symmetrical; that is, will fill the space comfortably and " pile up " nicely.

The printers will have to know what kinds of type are wanted in every head; consequently it will save time if a chart or sheet is made on which are designated the various sizes and kinds of type. Each may be numbered, lettered, or named. Then the headline writer composes the head in the kind of type he wants used, and specifies this on his copy. In the smaller schools, and often in the larger, the writing of heads and the selection of type for them is left to the printer. Such procedure is never satisfactory. The character of the paper is indicated by the headlines more than by anything else, and this matter is too important to be turned over to the average job printer, who frequently has had no experience in setting headlines at all.

2. The headline must be a complete statement. This means that it must contain a subject and predicate. The active voice is preferable to the passive, as it is more forceful. Occasionally the main story is told in the top deck of the headline, and the remaining decks are dependent clauses or phrases and not really complete statements in themselves.

3. The present (or future) tense should be used. What is happening is of more interest than what has happened. The present tense makes the news news, and not history. It shows its

timeliness. The same tense should be used throughout the heading.

4. Short, concrete, vigorous words should be used wherever possible. The heading must tell the story in a few words. Space is limited. Hence short words are preferable. Vigorous, forceful words make the reader want to read further.

5. Articles should be used rarely in the headline. A, an, the, etc., take up valuable space and weaken the statement. Such words are understood.

6. Important words should not be repeated in the headline. Repeating words weakens the headline. Synonyms may be used.

7. Headlines must be accurate and complete. The lead tells the main points of the story and the headline should be a summary of the lead. It should tell the most important or significant features of the story. The headline must not tell something that is not in the story. This frequently happens where the headlines have been made up for a story and some of the story has been cut out later by the editors.

8. Subheads should be used in longer stories. Newspaper paragraphs are kept short in order not to discourage the reader. Consequently subheads are used at intervals of one hundred to three hundred words, or every two or three inches of space, according to the length of the story and the ease with which it breaks up. Subheads should come at natural, not at artificial breaks. The use of only one subhead in a story is not good practice.

9. Jump-heads should be used where the story runs on to another page.

10. Punctuation should be used as little as possible. Periods are rarely used. Occasionally they appear at the end of pyramids and hanging indentations. Semicolons or dashes are sometimes used in place of conjunctions or for independent clauses. Commas seldom occur.

11. Abbreviations used should be those of the style sheet. Probably nothing detracts from the form of a paper more than a lack of uniformity in spelling or abbreviation.

12. Quotations may be used occasionally if authority is immediately specified. A dash is frequently used instead of quotation marks for this purpose.

ORGANIZATION AND DUTIES OF STAFF

Methods of choosing staff. — The character of the newspaper depends upon the staff selected to issue it; consequently the staff should be chosen with great care. The staff may be chosen in the following ways.

Popular election. — The weakness of this method of selection is at once apparent. Popularity does not necessarily mean ability to do the work. Petty politics, personalities, the favoring of friends in the paper, and other possibilities may easily result.

Another method of election is that in which the various staff positions belong to the various classes, the most important being filled by the senior class, the least important by the freshmen. This has the advantage that the editorship and managership are in the hands of older students who know conditions better and who have had opportunities to serve on former papers in less important capacities.

Appointment. — In many schools the staff members are appointed by a Board of Publications. Any student in school may be a candidate for any position by making proper application and having his candidacy approved by from one to three teachers who know him best. The Board considers all candidates, their qualifications and general scholastic standing, and selects those it considers the very best, irrespective of their classifications. After a publication has been running for a year or more, it will have the assistants of the previous year, if they have done their work satisfactorily to consider for the main jobs of their departments. The students taking courses in journalism, if such are offered, will have a considerable advantage. A permanent Board stabilizes the publication and by its experience will serve to prevent serious errors.

Sponsor. — The function of the sponsor is to supervise the production in all of its phases — composition, make-up, financing, and distribution. He will work hand-in-hand with the editor-in-chief. His duty is not to write or rewrite. Neither is it to proofread. He should be a severe but sympathetic critic, and should not assume the task of passing upon everything that goes into each issue. He will help the editor-in-chief to delegate responsibility and will see that such responsibility is faithfully discharged. He should help to educate the members of the staff in the various jobs that fall to them. If they cannot do them or learn to do them acceptably, he must not substitute for them. In such instances provisions should be made for getting some one who can carry the assignments. The sponsor, because of his experience and better judgment, acts as a counselor and adviser for the publication and not in any way as a glorified editor or manager of it. Naturally, he should be a teacher who knows publications and the making of them, who has a good comprehension of purposes and values, and is one whom the students respect, and with whom they will coöperate.

Editor-in-chief. — The editor-in-chief is what the name signifies. He should probably be an upper classman; one thoroughly familiar with the school and its activities; a hard worker; the possessor of good judgment; and a student whom the school and faculty respect in every way. He carries in his position an enormous responsibility, for he has a great deal of power. Tact, diplomacy, thoughtfulness, fairmindedness, and appreciation are other qualities he must have.

The editor-in-chief must have the good of the school at heart.

He must see things that need to be done. He will act as legally appointed student opinion and must be careful in his exercise of this function. He represents the entire school, not merely himself, the faculty, or any particular organization or body in the school. He is the school itself.

His main duty is, of course, to see that a good paper is published. He should delegate most of the work to his subordinates; not because of his power and authority, but because there will be many big issues which will need his attention so that he will have little time for proofreading or rewriting. He will hold staff meetings at which times the various problems will be threshed out. He will write editorials, perhaps not all of them but many of them, and will see that those to whom he assigns the writing of others write them to suit him. He may write headings. He will certainly help to make up the dummy. He will decide what shall be in the paper if there is any question of conflict or if something has to be omitted. His most important duties, however, relate to the members of the staff. He will prescribe duties and hold every staff member responsible for the faithful and complete performance of them. Of course, the sponsor will help him whenever possible; but he must take the responsibility for the paper. He is editor, and if the paper is not of value, he officially is held responsible.

Associate editor or managing editor. — This editor is an assistant to the editor-in-chief. He frequently has special duties such as assigning reporters, making up the dummy, checking over advertisements, or writing headings. He will be assigned his work on the basis of special interests or abilities. He must learn the editor's duties, so that in case of emergency he will be able to fill his place acceptably.

He should keep an assignment book in which are entered all assignments. This book will show all events to be covered; the reporter assigned; the date the story is due; the date checked in; what number it is to be used in, etc. In this way he has a close check on each reporter, and can locate immediately any error or delinquency. Responsibility is definitely charged.

Assistant editors. — There may be any number of editorial assistants in accordance with the size of the school, paper, and distribution of work. They are assigned whatever tasks the editor and sponsor decide upon. Copyreading, proofreading, writing headlines, and editing copy are some of them.

Business manager. — A newspaper is a business and must be conducted in accordance with good business principles. It cannot be published if it is not financed. The job of the business manager is to finance it. As a later section will be devoted to the problems of business management, it will be enough to state here that the business manager must be a student with good business ability, one who has good judgment, industry, and integrity, and is respected by students, faculty, and business men. He must know how to handle his assistants, for they are the direct contact points with the business world. He may not perhaps solicit advertisements, but at least he will plan with his advertising manager for the soliciting of them and the distribution of them in the dummy. He will plan with his other right-hand man, the circulation manager, for subscription campaigns and for the efficient distribution of the paper. He must work hand-in-hand with his superior, the editor-in-chief, on all matters of finance, circulation, advertisement, or policy.

Advertising manager. — The advertising manager is an assistant business manager whose special duty is to solicit advertising. He may or may not collect for it, according to the local conditions and the method of collection decided upon by the editor, adviser, or the Board of Publications. This individual must know students and their needs, and use good judgment in selecting business houses to be solicited. Other qualities obviously necessary are business ability, tact, enthusiasm, and persistency.

Circulation manager. — This officer is another assistant business manager and twin of the advertising manager. His main duty is to sell and distribute the product. He is responsible for subscription campaigns, booster campaigns, and other methods of increasing the sale of the paper.

Auditor. — The auditor should keep all records. He may collect all bills, check and discount them, and send them to the treasurer to be paid. He receives all money and turns it over to the treasurer. He makes monthly reports to the business manager. He accounts for every copy of the paper. In addition, he sees that all of his accounts are properly audited.

Sports editor. — The sports editor is responsible for stories of all athletic contests in which the school is interested, write-ups of former athletes now making good at universities, etc. He should know athletics well or should have competent assistants for games with which he is not so familiar, girls' games, for example. Fair-mindedness and accuracy should be his watchwords.

Exchange editor. — The paper should exchange with a large number of other high schools. The function of the exchange editor is to get lists and make the exchanges. He can run a very interesting exchange column if he makes it a " what other schools are doing " column. If, however, he makes the usual remarks about the other papers or publications, he should either be educated or relieved of his position.

Alumni editor. — The alumni editor collects the news regarding old graduates or former students. A good alumni editor is an asset to any paper, for he keeps the alumni informed about the school. This editor can find much material in the " morgue." He can also get a great deal more by calling up the parents of the various alumni, and watching the daily papers.

Society editor. — The society editor covers all the parties, receptions, picnics, and other society events not covered by special or regular reporters. She may use the stories of other reporters in her department, if desired.

Feature editor. — If the paper is a large one, it may be well to designate a feature editor. His duty will be to collect subjects suitable for feature articles and either write them himself or assign them to assistants. He must be a wide reader and must have the insight necessary to pick up and follow insignificant leads into interesting stories.

Art editor. — This editor is responsible for cartoons, cuts, and all illustrative material used in the paper. His office can do more than any other to make the paper interesting. He may have several assistants, such as cartoonist or photographer.

Other editors. — There may be as many editors as there are departments of the paper. Each department may have an editor if the paper is a large one and if several reporters are employed in it. Humor, Personals, Clubs, Music, Reviews, Dramatics, Literary, and Junior High are examples of such departments.

Equipment for the staff. — The staff of any publication should have a suitable permanent office in which to work. This office should have desks, tables, chairs, filing cabinets, shelf space, typewriters, bulletin board, and other necessary equipment. It should be kept clean to avoid loss of copy. It should be under lock and key.

BUSINESS ORGANIZATION

The professional newspaper is a business proposition. It must return a profit to its stockholders or owners. The school paper similarly is a business proposition, for it must be financed if it is to be published. It costs money to put out a school paper. Consequently the business administration and organization of the paper is as important as the newswriting or the organization of the paper in its news-presenting capacity. There are two main sources of income — subscriptions and advertisements.

Circulation. — The paper must be sold. In a few instances it is financed independently and given to the students, but such instances are rare. The ideal is, of course, to sell it to every student in school and to many alumni and friends. The next best thing is to sell it to as many students, friends, and alumni as possible. Often the success of the paper depends upon the success with which it is circulated. A larger circulation means a larger income; for the advertisements will be more valuable and can be sold at a higher rate.

Price of the paper. — The subscription price of the paper must be reasonable. It usually ranges from fifty cents to a dollar and a half. Probably a dollar a year or fifty cents a semester would be the average price for a biweekly paper of average size. The lower the price, within certain limits, the greater will be the circulation.

Subscription campaign. — " All things come to him who waits " is nowhere a more glaring untruth than in the matter of school newspaper subscriptions. It takes a great deal of work thoroughly to sell the school its own paper. Many students would subscribe for it whether or not they were solicited; but these in any school will not be enough to finance it. The paper must be sold by means of efficient drives and these drives must reach every student in school as well as alumni and other friends.

The proper time for a subscription campaign is in the fall after the paper has been organized, and probably just before the first number appears. A few schools give the first number to all students and then start their campaign. This has the advantage of interesting the student in something he can see and read, but it may also have the disadvantage of making him expect to receive the paper again without paying for it. It is probably better to conduct the campaign before the first number appears. This will also give the staff an idea of how well it will be supported and how much income it may expect. The campaign should be thoroughly organized — a real " drive." It is a good plan to set aside the home-room period, or some other period, for this purpose to bring about, if possible, a solid concerted drive throughout the school.

The staff, and other students if necessary, should together work out the outline of the selling talks to be used. These would naturally deal with the proposed paper, its departments, interests, and organization as well as its price. They should emphasize the desirability of having every student subscribe to it. It should, however, not be placed in any light that gives him the impression that he is subscribing to charity. Such arguments or slogans as " save the paper " or " show your spirit " should not be used. If the paper is not worth subscribing for, it should not be allowed in the school. The use of the slogan " Show your school spirit — subscribe for the paper " is a confession that the paper is not worth buying. The talk used should show that the paper will be worth every cent that it costs. After this talk has been thoroughly gone over and explained to each member of the staff who will speak, he should be given a brief outline of it. The speakers are then assigned so that every part of the school is carefully covered. The groups to which speakers are assigned should be relatively small.

Following the talk, subscriptions should be taken. A simple duplicate receipt book showing the amount paid, the name, and date should be used. It will always be necessary to take partial payments for the paper. If the student has the money to pay the entire price he should be urged to pay it at once. Probably twenty-five cents should be the smallest partial payment accepted. The remainder should be paid as soon as possible. It should be the policy of the staff to collect all money at the earliest opportunity. Allowing a student to pay half at the beginning of the semester and half at the end is bad policy and unnecessary. The average student spends each week for candy and sodas more than enough to pay his entire subscription, and as the price is not high he should be expected to pay immediately. In case he does not pay within a reasonable time and presents no good reason to the collectors, his paper should be stopped at the end of a certain time, proportionate to the amount he paid.

The bookkeeping list of subscriptions depends upon the size and organization of the school. For a smaller school a simple alphabetical list of all subscribers with the amounts paid, the number of the receipt book, and the number of the receipt, may be sufficient. In a larger school not only the above accounts will be kept but other details such as room number, floor, etc., may be necessary in order to locate students promptly.

Distribution of papers. — The home-room period probably is the best time for the distribution of the papers. The use of this period also helps to interest the student who has not subscribed for the paper. Some schools distribute papers during the last period of the day or just following the last period. The main argument for the use of such a time is that reading the paper does not disorganize the school, as it occasionally does where the paper is distributed earlier in the day. Another argument is that the student will take it home and read it there, thus making greater the probability that his parents will see it. Again, at this time of day the student will be less likely to give his copy away to a potential subscriber. Attempts to issue the paper in the morning just before school opens have been made, but for obvious reasons have not been very successful.

When it has been decided at just what time the papers shall be distributed the circulation manager and his assistants will prepare lists showing where the subscribers are at that period. Lists are then made up in duplicate for each room, and the papers assorted and stacked accordingly. At the time for distribution the designated assistant, or an officer from the room, takes the bundle of papers with the list of students to whom they go to the room and there the teacher or the proper officer of that room distributes them. He should check the names of the students off the list as each receives his paper. He then returns the list, showing what students have not received their papers, together with these papers, to the circulation manager or his assistant. In this way every paper is accounted for. There will probably be a few students who prefer to buy the paper each time rather than to subscribe for it for the term or year. It will be necessary to have a stand to accommodate such students. Such buying should be discouraged as much as possible. It makes for additional trouble and means a half-hearted reader.

Mailing the papers. — Papers will be sent to exchanges, alumni, patrons, advertisers, and others. There are certain postal regulations concerning wrapping, postage, etc., which the assistant in charge of mailing should learn from his local office.

Advertising. — A large share of the financial support of the school paper will depend upon the amount of advertising space sold. If no advertising were sold the price of the paper would be prohibitive. As a matter of fact there are papers in the United States which are practically given away, because of the large amount of advertising carried. The school paper must not develop into a collection of advertisements, but it should carry some. It was not originated to make money and any attempt to make a big surplus by the use of many advertisements will only cheapen the paper. The budget should be figured out as closely as possible, allowing say fifteen per cent extra for emergencies and shrinkage. The amount of space sold will depend upon the advertising estimate in the budget. In advertising there are three processes: selling the space, writing the advertisement, and collecting for it.

Selling space. — The business man advertises because it pays, seldom for any other reason. He could not be expected to contribute space or advertising to a daily paper just because that paper needed money. Neither can he be expected to do so for the school paper. In far too many localities the business man looks upon such advertising as charity and contributes for that reason. A great many student advertising managers look upon it similarly and solicit advertisements with the arguments that " it will help us to publish the paper," " it is a good cause," or " show your interest! " Such policy is absolutely wrong and should not be tolerated in any community or by any school. In fact, in many communities it is not tolerated and school publishers have been violently brought to light by the Chamber of Commerce or other business men's organization's voting against advertising in school publications. Any business man will advertise if he can be shown where it will bring him business. A good sound advertising policy and businesslike procedure in this connection will not only get more results but it will leave the business men of the town in good humor.

How can this be done? The first thing for the advertising manager to do is to list all the stores or commercial houses in the vicinity which carry goods used by students. Such will include clothing stores, shoe stores, drug stores, candy stores, flower shops, banks, and others. These make good prospects. In some schools a questionnaire on " what would you like to see advertised in our paper? " is prepared and given to all students. The returns make good advertising sales-talk material. The list of houses should be graded and the most important advertiser, from the student's point of view, should be placed at the top and the others roughly in the order of their importance below. These stores will then be solicited in this order. Advertisements of poolrooms, bowling alleys, and cheap restaurants should not be solicited and should be refused if offered. New stores are always anxious to advertise, and consequently should be noted.

The advertising staff will hold meetings and prepare a good

selling speech. The strongest individuals should be the only ones to attempt to solicit advertising. Two students should always go together. Boys in short trousers are not as effective as boys in long ones. Most schools look with disfavor upon the solicitation of advertising by girls.

The talk should be straight business and not charity. For instance, a reasonable talk in soliciting the owner of a shoe store, would be something like this:

You are interested, of course, in advertising where advertising will return the greatest profit. At the high school there are five hundred students each of whom will wear out or buy at least one or two pairs of shoes annually. There are five shoe stores in town, and placing them all on an equal basis each will sell some one hundred pairs of shoes each year to or for these students. With a little advertising before these students your store should sell considerably more than it is selling now. All you need is your name and an attractive ad where the students will read it. Even if you sold only twenty-five pairs to high school students more than you now do you would not only be increasing your sales by that much but you would be increasing the size of your custom, for each boy or girl probably represents a family. Moreover, high school students are just at the age when they are beginning to buy their own shoes, and if you can make a satisfied customer of a student you will have first bid on his permanent trade. One additional customer really means more than one, for this indiviudal has friends and relatives who need your wares. We are going to accept only one shoe ad because our space is limited and we want to make our ads as varied as possible. You have been selected by our staff as being the most important shoe dealer in this community. Consequently we are giving you the opportunity of buying this space.

The solicitor must be courteous always, no matter what the storekeeper may say or do. Even though the solicitor does not get the order, he must leave the man as a friend. He may get it next time. Moreover, the storekeeper may remember what was said and after he has time to think it over and has seen the logic of it he may want to buy space. Tact and good judgment are requisites of a good salesman. He should not pester or worry the storekeeper nor resort to subterfuge to win him.

The price of ads. — The prices charged for ads depend upon the size and circulation of the paper, the size of the school, the community, the business represented, and other considerations, and so cannot be definitely stated. This matter is one for the staff and adviser to decide. It may be that the rates have been fixed by previous issues and, if so, it would probably be best not to change them, except for good reasons. Ads are sold by the " inch " and by " column." The " inch " denotes the height of the ad and the " column " denotes its width. For smaller papers and magazines space is often designated as " page " " half page," or " quarter page." A discount should be given for ads running a longer time than for one number. Some ads might run unchanged for several numbers or they might be changed each issue and the space still be kept by the one concern. In such cases discounts might be offered. If, for instance, the price of one insertion were fifty cents an inch, forty-five cents for the semester or forty cents for the year would be a fair rate. Running long-time ads may make for a little less revenue per inch but they save trouble in several ways. As ads are more easily obtained the first semester than the second, more should be used the first. A simple yet businesslike contract form should be printed and used.

Ads are rarely paid for at the time of solicitation. If the storekeeper wants to pay for his space, no one would refuse to take the money. But it is best to let him see his ad before he is asked to pay for it. Most businesses pay their bills once a month by check, and so it will be better to make up the bills about the last of the month and mail them to creditors. They should be made out on a neat business form and sent to the business address of the firm. No letter or other inclosure is required. Some papers clip the ad and enclose it with the bill ; but if the man has received a copy of the paper with the ad marked, such procedure is not necessary. The business man appreciates businesslike procedure, and he will be pleased by the efficient manner in which the business details of the paper are conducted.

The advertising manager should keep a book showing the name of each advertiser, the size of the ad, the numbers to be run, the cost per inch, and the total cost. The business manager (or the advertising manager) will then make his monthly statements from this. If ads are not paid for promptly — and not all of them will be — solicitors may be assigned to collect the amounts due. A complete list of such assignments together with the amount to be collected, should be kept by the advertising manager, or the business manager.

It occasionally happens that a business man wants a certain space. He may offer a good price, more than asked, if given a strip of space across the middle of the page or across the top of it. Such an advertisement should not be accepted. Breaking up the news with ads or arranging them in bad form, even for an extra price, only tends to cheapen the paper.

Writing the ads. — Frequently the advertising staff will have to write the advertisements for the business man. He may not be able to write them or may not have the time. Many advertising departments sell space by writing advertisements and including these in the advertising dummy for exhibition to the prospective advertiser. Advertisements written by the business man should be checked for accuracy in composition and in form.

Other methods of financing the paper. — Other methods of helping to finance the paper are the giving of entertainments, dramatic performances, athletic contests, and musical programs; the holding of "bake" sales, candy sales, pennant sales, and lotteries; and the use of tag days. In a few instances a part of the school fund is set aside for publications. In still other instances the school board helps to support the paper. All of these methods may be necessary occasionally, especially in a smaller school where circulation and advertising are limited.   However, in the average school such methods of support are not feasible.

There is, however, a legitimate way of helping to finance the newspaper.   That is by the use of a " special edition."   Once or twice a year, after a football season, for instance, a " Football Edition " containing the summarized results of the season may be issued.   Pictures and cartoons of the various games and sidelights, render it attractive.   It may take the form of a small magazine and thus be in shape for permanent keeping.   Such a magazine should be sold, not given to regular subscribers.   It is an " extra " issue and the student should pay for it.   There should not be many of these editions, however.

Budgeting. — *Following a budget necessary to a better paper.* — Good business methods in handling the newspaper include the making and following of a budget.   This is all the more true if the paper is a new one.   The paper should not be a money-making proposition, but there should be a reasonable surplus rather than the opposite.   Now if a budget is followed, the staff can estimate more closely the amount to be spent and thus avoid closing the season with a large surplus.   In other words, it can anticipate the surplus and can distribute it over several numbers of the paper, thereby making a better paper.   On the other hand, the budget will prevent the staff from spending too much, and, as frequently happens, forcing it to reduce its size or number of issues.   It may be good business that causes a large surplus at the end of the year, but the policy that permits it is wrong.   The purpose of the paper is not financial profit-making.   On the other hand, it is neither good business nor good policy to start a program which has to be abandoned before the end of the year.

The budget based on estimated income from subscriptions and advertising. — The budget of the school newspaper should be built upon the principle that expenditures are based upon income. This income will be estimated, not too liberally, on possible circulation and advertising. For instance, suppose there are five hundred students in the school. As some students will not take the paper, and some families are represented by several children, a fair estimate of the number of students who would subscribe and pay for the paper would be about two hundred and fifty or three hundred. It is quite probable that a hundred more will subscribe, but it is better to under-estimate than over-estimate. In the former case, additional funds can be easily applied in increasing the size of paper or in issuing more frequent numbers; but in the latter, additional revenue must be provided or the paper reduced in size or number of issues. The price both for the year and per copy should be placed at a reasonable figure. The estimated income from subscriptions is now easily computed.

The estimation of advertising for a new paper should be on the basis of about one fourth, or one full page of a four-page paper. As the size of the paper has not yet been determined, the estimate for advertising cannot be made accurately. However, a rough estimate, not too liberal, can be made and the total yearly income computed from this. This together with the estimated subscription income will give an estimated total income. Dividing this by the proposed number of issues will give a rough estimate of the amount available for each issue.

Adjustment of expense to estimated income. — A rough dummy should now be made and taken to the printer for his estimate of cost. He will probably quote a price per issue. He should reduce this price if he takes it for the whole year. If the price is higher than the estimated expense, the size or number of issues will have to be reduced or plans made for raising additional funds. If there are several printers in town, bids from each should be secured. If there is only one printer and he has had little experience in printing such a paper, his bid will be high rather than low; for he does not intend to lose money and so places his bid high enough to insure against loss. Allowance for cuts, mailing, and unseen expenditures which always come demands a rather liberal allowance, say 10 to 15 per cent of the regular expenses.

Once the budget is made it should be followed as closely as necessary. The expense of each issue should be computed and by comparing this with the average amount allowed for each issue the staff can check its expenditures. If the cost has been over-estimated or the income under-estimated, the paper may be enlarged, a special issue may be published and given away, or other increased value be given to subscribers. On the other hand, if the cost has been under-estimated or the income over-estimated, suitable adaptations of program must be made. The rule should be " no surplus and no deficits."

A word of caution. — Starting small and growing big is better than the reverse. Many school newspapers just being started try to imitate or outdo papers long established in neighboring schools. Frequently too ambitious plans are made regarding size, number of pages, and number of issues. In such cases the staff can only beat an undignified retreat. The following quotations clipped from front pages illustrate this apologetic retrenchment.

TO THE CUSTOMER

We are sorry, but there will be but one more issue of the . . . making thirteen in all. Owing to delays in appearances of numbers and time out for vacations there is not time enough to publish fifteen numbers as originally intended. Money will be refunded to advertisers who have paid for 15 insertions.

TO MERCHANTS

We are sorry to say that the lack of advertising has forced us to curtail the size of our publication. We have tried to set our standards high enough to make our paper a desirable advertising medium. To date we have published five numbers, the first four of which, at least, we believe, were big successes. But in spite of their unquestionable success our business department is able to secure only enough advertising for an eight-page paper.

What contest judges will look for. — The question of what makes a good newspaper cannot be answered better probably than by considering what the judges in a newspaper contest look for. The following quotation is pertinent, taken from the article, "What Contest Judges Will Look For," by Dr. Grant M. Hyde, Chairman of Contest Committee of the Central Interscholastic Press Association (*Scholastic Editor*, October 1924):

MERITS SOUGHT IN NEWSPAPERS

Some of the particulars to be looked after in newspapers are as follows:

School News — How fully the various activities of the school are covered — How many subjects and school departments are mentioned — How much there is besides routine news — Ingenuity in developing news field — Personal news items.

General News — Covering of related news outside the school house, such as will interest parents, alumni, and other interested persons.

News Writing — Structure of news stories — clearness, conciseness, and originality in writing — Good leads — Well-developed features — Coherence, well-outlined, well-paragraphed stories — Use of direct quotation and other devices of news writing.

Sport Writing — Absence of extreme partisanship in accounts of games — Fact articles instead of "dope" — Good English with a minimum of slang and colloquialism — Enough real copy to fill space rather than valueless padding.

Editorials — Well-written discussions of school affairs, indicating careful thought and careful writing — Informative, helpful discussions.

Special Feature Articles — Skill shown in developing articles on unusual subjects within the news field — Inclusion of some good fact articles on matters of interest to the school off-setting the many essays and fiction stories.

Literary Features — Quality of literary material published — Evidence that entire student body is encouraged to contribute — Fiction, essays, poetry, etc.

Quality of English — Clearness, readability — Avoidance of slang and trite expression — Achievement of originality by legitimate means.

Departments — Number, variety, typography, contents, evidence that each is kept up to "par" and not allowed to be padded out.

Humor — Whether the jokes are local school jokes and not clipped or rewritten "old-timers" — Whether they are not excessive in quantity — Whether they warrant the space taken — Whether borrowed jokes are properly accredited to sources from which they are obtained.

Headlines — Form and typography used — Careful balance of lines and decks — Use of verbs and statements in headlines — Avoidance of many common errors.

Subheads — Also Captions, Overlines, and other display of news columns.

Name of Newspaper — Whether it is a sensible name or simply a tongue-twister.

Illustrations — pictures, cartoons, comic strips, etc. — Appropriateness, subject, size, quality, relation to school news.

Typography — (considering the conditions under which paper is published) Judgment in selection of type, paper, form, column width, etc.

Make-up — The knowledge of typography and make-up evidenced — Indication that paper is made up by staff rather than by printer — General appearance of front page and other pages — Arrangement of advertising — Use of boxes, etc.

Advertising — Quantity and variety — Evidence that the field has been studied and canvassed — Effective copy that will bring returns to advertiser. — Attractive typography and make-up — Absence of "charity" advertising. (For publications that do not carry advertising a grade will be given on the impression of the publication as a unit. This is done so that publications may not lose a grade and so be handicapped.)

General Considerations — Evidence that the school as a whole is supporting the paper — Evidence that the staff is large and not a small clique — Indication that the teacher-adviser is not doing most of the work — Initiative and originality on part of student staff — Is it good advertising for its school?

These two chapters on the newspaper were written more particularly for the school having no courses in journalism. A rough outline of material and procedure is all that could be attempted here. In schools having courses in journalism the newspaper should be the laboratory of the department. The staff should have a growing library of suitable books and magazines, and the school paper should hold membership in the Central Interscholastic Press Association as well as in the state or local press association.

SUMMARY

The school newspaper must be attractively organized. Make-up is concerned with such items as name, size, number of pages, columning, classification of content, sections, advertisements, balance, and headlines. These items must be handled in accordance with well-established principles. Headlines are used to advertise, summarize, and classify the news, and to increase the attractiveness of the paper through variety. The four most commonly used types of headlines are dropline, crossline, pyramid, and hanging indentation. The use of the various kinds of headlines increases the interest of the student in his paper. Headline writing must follow definitely prescribed rules. The staff may be elected or appointed, the latter being preferable. Staff meetings held each week or more frequently are desirable. The sponsor is responsible for the paper but should not do any of the rewriting, proofreading, or similar work. The staff should be carefully organized and each editor or reporter intelligently assigned. The paper is a business proposition and must be conducted in a businesslike manner. The price should be reasonable. A campaign may be used to get subscriptions. Papers should be distributed systematically. Advertising may not only be used to help to finance the paper, but may be made interesting to the readers. The business man should be approached with a business, and not a charity, proposition when being solicited for advertising. The staff should prepare and follow a budget. Good ideas of what constitutes a good high school paper may be gotten by noting what is considered by judges in newspaper contests.

References

GENERAL

Magazine Articles

BLEYER, W. G. "Journalistic Writing in High Schools," *English Journal* 13 : 276–279, April, 1924.

DIMORIER, W. W. "Newspaper Week," *English Journal* 6 : 170–174, March, 1917.

FRETWELL, E. K. and O'NEIL, MARION. "Bibliography on High School Publications," *Teachers College Record* 26 : 59–73, September, 1924.

GUILFOIL, K. "Correlating the School Paper and English Composition," *English Journal* 13 : 269–271, April, 1924.

HARRINGTON, H. F. "Teaching Journalism in a Natural Setting," *Educational Administration and Supervision* 5 : 197–206, April, 1919.

HARTLEY, B. "Motivated English," *Education* 94 : 425–428, March, 1924.

LEWIN, W. "The Business of Running a School Paper," *English Journal* 11 : 8–13, January, 1922.

NIXON, O. F. "The Cost and Financing of Student Publications," *School Review* 31 : 204–212, March, 1923.

—— "Student Publications in High Schools," *American School Board Journal* 67 : 47–127, December, 1923.

OTTO, W. N. *Journalism for High Schools.* Harcourt, Brace and Company.

PERRY, F. M. "The Supervision of School Publications," *English Journal* 8 : 299–308, May, 1919.

REAVIS, W. C. "Student Publications in High Schools," *School Review* 30 : 514–520, September, 1924.

RYAN, C. M. "Project in High School Journalism," *English Journal,* 15 : 129–130, May, 1919.

SHERWOOD, H. N. "Value of High School Publications," *Educational Review* 67 : 20–21, January, 1924.

THALHEIMER, J. A. "School Publications," *Education* 44 : 429–436, March, 1924.

The Scholastic Editor, the files of, University of Minnesota, Minneapolis, Minnesota.

Books

BLEYER, W. G. *Types of News Stories.* Houghton Mifflin Company.

—— *Newspaper Writing and Editing.* Houghton Mifflin Company.

—— *Writing and Feature Story.* Houghton Mifflin Company.

BRIGGS, T. H. and McKINNEY, I. *A Second Book of Composition*, Chap. III. Ginn and Company.

DILLON, C. *Journalism for High Schools.* Noble, Noble and Noble.

FLINT, L. N. *The Editorial.* D. Appleton and Company.

—— *Newspaper Writing in High Schools.* Noble, Noble and Noble.

HARRINGTON, H. E. and FRANKENBERG, T. T. *Essentials in Journalism.* Ginn and Company.

HARRINGTON, H. F. *Writing for Print.* Ginn and Company.

HUFF, B. M. *How to Publish a School Paper.* Mentzer, Bush and Company.

HYDE, G. M. *Newspaper Reporting and Correspondence.* D. Appleton and Company.

—— *Newspaper Editing.* D. Appleton and Company.

—— *A Course in Journalistic Writing.* D. Appleton and Company.

—— *Handbook for Newspaper Workers.* D. Appleton and Company.

MEYER, H. D. *Handbook of Extracurricular Activities.* Part V. A. S. Barnes and Company.

OPDYCKE, J. B. *News, Ads, and Sales.* The Macmillan Company.

ROSE, C. G. *The Writing of News.* Henry Holt and Company.

SPENCER, M. L. *News Writings.* D. C. Heath and Company.

ADVERTISING

BLANCHARD, F. L. *Essentials of Advertising.* McGraw-Hill Book Company.

HALL, S. R. *Advertisers Handbook.* International Correspondence Schools.

STARCH, D. *Advertising.* Scott, Foresman and Company.

PRINTING

PHILLIPPS, F. K. *Army Vocational Three Year Course in Printing.* American Type Founders Company, Jersey City, New Jersey.

STILWELL, K. M. *The School Print Shop.* Rand McNally and Company.

CHAPTER XX

THE MAGAZINE

The school magazine is a bound booklet or bulletin, composed of a number of pages, smaller than a newspaper in dimensions, and usually issued once a month.

CONTENT

The following table shows the kind of content and the proportion of each as found in two hundred typical high school magazines. The figures are approximate only. Extreme variations are occasionally found. For purposes of general presentation, however, the approximate figures are sufficient. The " approximate average range " is the average proportion of content found in the magazines. The " approximate average " is the one figure which most nearly represents the average. All figures are percentages.

The table on the opposite page shows that the average high school magazine is composed of one third news, one fourth advertisements, one fourth literature, and one eighth humor.

CRITICISMS AND CORRESPONDING SUGGESTIONS

A great deal of criticism has been aimed at the high school magazine during the past five or eight years. A part of this criticism has been due to the development of high school press associations over the country and their fine work in calling attention to purposes and values of publications as well as to methods of attaining these values. Possibly the best way to discuss the magazine will be to consider the main objections to it and to

THE KINDS OF CONTENT AND THE PROPORTION OF EACH FOUND IN TWO HUNDRED HIGH SCHOOL MAGAZINES

KIND OF MATERIAL	APPROXIMATE AVERAGE RANGE (Percentage of Total)	APPROXIMATE AVERAGE (Percentage)
NEWS Athletics Alumni News Notes Social Exchange Pictures, etc.	20–40	31
LITERARY Poems Stories Interviews Book reviews, etc.	12–32	24
HUMOR Jokes Stories Poems Cartoons, etc.	7–18	12
EDITORIALS	4–10	6
ADVERTISEMENTS	20–30	24
MISCELLANEOUS Table of Contents Names of Staff, etc.	2–4	3

make suggestions for the elimination of them, in so far as possible. Most of what has been said in the two previous chapters of the newspaper regarding the organization and function of the staff, business procedure, selling, distribution, etc., is equally applicable to the magazine. Consequently, it will not be repeated here. The most common defects of the magazine will now be considered.

It attempts to carry news. — From the above table, it will be seen that approximately one third of the content of the magazine is " news." This concerns athletics mostly and usually it is a rather detailed summary of the games written in newspaper style. It is always stale when published, for the average magazine is issued only seven times a year. News is what happened to-day or yesterday, not what happened last month. A glance through the typical magazine will reveal many futile and uninteresting " news " stories about events which the students have long since forgotten.

If the magazine cannot avoid carrying news, then reduce this news to a minimum. Omit trifling bits of news which might go well in the newspaper. Reduce stories of games and other events to brief summaries. In other words, make no attempt to carry them as news stories. They can never be made such. Write them up from a different or unusual point of view or in an unusual manner. Pictures, cartoons, and other illustrative material may help in this. But be sure to distinguish between news and history.

Its content is uninteresting to the students. — It is asserted that most of the material of the magazine is uninteresting and moreover is not read by the average student. This statement is a popular generalization which probably has some merit, but as yet no one can say whether the student reads the publication or not. It is doubtful whether the average story or poem written by the high school student is very interesting to his fellow beyond the interest which is based on friendship or acquaintanceship. At any rate, the literary material is less interesting to the average individual than the more personal items of the newspaper. The main reason is that it is frequently nearly all of the same general sort. In the average magazine the literature is usually of two kinds only, poems and fiction.

There is no reason why the magazine should not be interesting to the student.   It is free from the restrictions of the newspaper and hence can be made as original and unusual as the ingenuity of the staff permits.   Variety makes for interest.   The magazine need not be looked upon as a carrier of imaginative writing only. Interviews, descriptions, travel stories, book reviews, features, correspondence, alumni notes, and other kinds of writing should be used.   There are a great many sources of fine feature stories around the school.   Mr. O. H. Miller mentions six types of feature stories which are usable in the school magazine.[1]   These are as follows :

The personality sketch
Methods and information stories
Historical articles, local, state, and national
Personal experiences
Sports stories
Miscellaneous, and unclassifiable

In order to suggest possible feature subjects, the following list of topics mentioned by Miss Helene Foellinger of the South Side High School, Fort Wayne, Indiana as having been used in the *South Side Times*, is presented.[2]

Youngest boy and girl in school
Weekly birthdays
Plans of graduates
Amount of food used in the cafeteria daily
What we owe our advertisers for our paper's success
Manual training and domestic science work
Improvements made on our school
Cæsar in modern English or slang
Hobbies of teachers
Colors worn by visiting basketball teams
Most popular flavor of ice cream used in cafeteria
Number of steps and strokes taken by janitor in cleaning gym
Words exchanged among freshies at the office

[1] "The Feature Article", *The Scholastic Editor*, February, March, April, 1925.
[2] See *The Scholastic Editor*, April, 1925.

Number of windows in the rooms
Amount of fuel used each day
Travels and experiences of student visiting Europe
Home brighteners or worries of the teacher (children)
Origin of St. Valentine's day; methods of celebration
Addition to the school
Rules and origin of basketball
Origin of smallpox, what it is.   During smallpox scare
What our advertisers think of the yearbook and newspaper
Eligibility rules of state athletic association
Sports of the Greeks and Romans
The school slogan, its history and development
Trips taken by school groups
Work required to make the student's programs
New teachers' impression of the school spirit
Conveyances required to bring students and teachers to school
Lessons first or last?
Tips from janitors on how to keep the school "spic and span"
Biographies of men for whom streets are named
Calories swallowed each day in the cafeteria
Story composed of students' names
Journalists on the honor roll
Sports which interest our teachers
Preferences in places for study
Most popular names in school
Ministers' opinions on effects of cheating
Number of strokes required to fold and prepare newspapers for mailing
Faculty member's opinion of cross-word puzzles

Another suggestion is to run a questionnaire through the school, inquiring as to the kind of material the students would like to see published.   This will give a lead which may result in a more interesting booklet.   Another plan is to have the students vote on the relative interest of various kinds of articles.

Its organization is uninteresting to the student. — Often it is true that the magazine is a heterogeneous collection of material, hastily thrown together.   If twenty magazines are examined probably no two of them will be found to use the same general plan of organization. There is perhaps no reason why they should, for there is a freedom about the magazine which is not possible in the newspaper. However, if we examine them more closely, we shall find that in many of them the material is not classified or organized but scattered and mixed in a manner which would never attract the student.

Make a serious study of the form and organization of the magazine. Classify all material. Place the most interesting story first. In general, place the literature in the first part of the magazine and the news, humor, etc. after it. Separate these sections with the editorial pages including the names of staff members. In making the dummy, first make it approximate only. That is, do not set aside a certain number of pages and then, if sufficient material for filling these pages is not available, hastily " get up " something to fill them. Make them short rather than long, so that material will have to be cut rather than stretched.

Have some uniformity in headings and general typographical make-up. The headings and titles should be interesting. The title of the feature story, for instance, has been called its " show window." Leave plenty of " white space "; do not crowd, and allot liberally to interesting headlines. A liberal supply of cartoons, pictures, and department heads will make the magazine more interesting. A good cover in attractive colors also adds to interest.

The literature is not worth publishing. — The complaint is very frequently made that the teachers of English, judging by their activities, are interested more in making producers than consumers of good writing and that consequently the magazine is organized, endured, and justified on the basis that it offers motivation to the student taking English. In general, it would appear that there is some truth in this statement that the English teacher uses the magazine too frequently as a laboratory for her work. About one fourth of the average magazine is devoted to literature. The argument is made that this material may be good for high school students but does not justify expensive publication. If the student wants to read literature, he can buy it at any news stand, produced by professionals. He does not have to read the amateurish and puerile stories and poems written by his classmates. Another frequent criticism along the same general line is that the student tries to write on themes too deep for him, and the result is all the more atrocious.

The student reader of the magazine has a right to expect good literary matter, as good as students can write, because of the infrequent appearance of the magazine. With a whole month in which to prepare, it would seem that plenty of good material could be made available for publication. Make the period of planning and writing a month instead of the week before issuance. Do not have a regular staff of story or poem writers, but get the entire school interested in writing for publication. Develop the idea and tradition that it is a real honor to " make " the magazine. Competition for this honor will be a great incentive. Do not allow the teachers of English to hold mortgage on one inch of space in the magazine for their classes or groups. Place their students on the same basis as all others. Judge all material on a competitive basis and allow no one to have the inside track to any space allotted to the literary section. Offer prizes or special mention of some sort in order to increase competition. Encourage the student who has written acceptable material to continue. Post a list of names of students whose material has been accepted for publication. See that the writers hold to reasonable and sensible subjects and avoid favoritism, artificiality, and amateurish imitation. Encourage originality and the development of the particular field of one's own choice. Do not print too much, for this only cheapens what is published.

FIGURE XVI. — COVERS OF TYPICAL HIGH SCHOOL MAGAZINES

So-called humor is largely clipped. — This is a serious criticism of almost any high school publication. *Life, Judge,* and similar humor magazines as well as magazines and papers of other schools are the sources of most of the jokes and humor used. The table shows that about twelve per cent of the space of the average magazine is devoted to such " humor."

Avoid clipped jokes. If the humor staff is not capable of furnishing good, fresh school humor, get a new staff or abolish the department. Have students compete to " make " the magazine. Songs, parodies, verses, cartoons, and a great variety of " what would happen if " and other types of material can be worked out. Have jokes concern school affairs and school people. See that the magazine does not deteriorate into a book of nonsense.

The editorials are sermons and moralizings of no particular value. — This is often true of high school editorials. They usually transcend the experience even of the student who writes them. They seem to be written usually for the eye of the Sunday School teacher or minister, who use a great many of such sermonettes themselves, rather than for the average student of the school and the reader of the paper. Sermonettes on the various virtues are probably of little value in producing desired actions in students.

Eliminate the sermonettes and make use of other types of editorials — explanatory, biographical, boosting, reasoning, and commenting. See that they are on school topics or topics which are interesting to students. Keep them short. Make them attractive by printing, interesting headings, etc. A " principal's page " can be an asset to the school and the magazine if it does not degenerate either into a patronizing or a moralizing column.

Too few students participate in the benefits of publishing the magazine. — Probably no extracurricular activity can be justified on the basis of benefit to participants only, whether athletics, student council, or assembly program. The activity which gives the greatest good to the greatest number is to be preferred to one which educates only a chosen few. The magazine staff is small, therefore but few students can share the benefits.

The staff of the magazine should not look upon itself as the final source of all or even much of the material for the publication. It should rather look upon itself as a board of publication whose duty is to discover, encourage, and develop talent along the various lines represented by the material of the magazine. In this way the number of educational opportunities will be multiplied, the interest of the students will be increased, and the material published will be more varied and interesting than if produced by a small board or staff.

It represents productively only a small part of the school. — That is, it is argued that the magazine represents only the English and Art departments of the school. The literary side is overemphasized.

From the very nature of the material the magazine must be produced by those who write English. It is but natural that the English department should be more interested in it than, for instance, the mathematics or science departments. There is no reason, however, why other departments should not be represented in its work and material. Material for feature stories and interesting reports are to be found in all classes and all subjects.

The magazine is expensive. — This is true. It is expensive to make and consequently must be expensive to buy. About the same general proportion of space is devoted to advertisements in both the newspaper and magazine, usually a little less in the former. Binding, cutting, artistic covers, good paper, etc., are costly. Consequently the usual price of fifteen to fifty cents may seem a bit high to the average student.

Keep the size of the magazine down to a reasonable minimum. The number of pages does not always mean quality but it always does mean expense. A small attractive magazine is preferable to a large one, the material of which has been stretched to fill it. Better cut and omit material than to have to invent it. A liberal supply of good advertisements will help to carry the expense. Do not spend too much in covers and cuts. They beautify the magazine, of course; but there is a point of diminishing returns. Do not cover the magazine at the expense of seriously limiting or cheapening what is inside.

MERITS SOUGHT IN MAGAZINES

The question of what makes a good magazine can at least be partly answered by a consideration of what is looked for in magazines by the judges in the annual contest of the Central Interscholastic Press Association. The suggestions made by the Contest Committee of this Association are as follows: [1]

Some of the characteristics to be looked for in magazines are as follows:

Form and Typography — Do selection of paper, type, and scheme of make-up indicate knowledge of printing and publications in general? Does it appear to be designed by the students or by the printer?

Cover — Character and relation to the general purpose of the publication.

Reading-matter — Quality and scope of selection. Evidence of a definite aim and desire to live up to it. Number of contributors. Quality of writing. Evidence that it is trying to publish some of the best writing in the school and is not merely a perfunctory organ of a small clique.

Departments — Number, variety, make-up, typography. Effort to fill them with material.

Special articles — Inclusion of some fact articles on matters of interest to the school offsetting the many essays and fiction stories.

Verse — Evidence of effort to encourage production of good verse.

Headings — Wording and typography. Use of type or cut.

Illustrations — Size, variety, quality, relations to reading-matter.

Editorials — Well-written discussions of school affairs.

Humor, Advertisements, make-up, and other considerations will be considered in same light as those in student newspapers.

[1] *The Scholastic Editor*, November, 1923.

THE MAGAZINE vs. THE NEWSPAPER

There has been considerable discussion regarding the relative merits of the newspaper and the magazine. Some schools hold tenaciously to the magazine, while others drop it to adopt the newspaper. Very few schools ever give up the newspaper for the magazine. A comparison of the two on the main general values of publications may help to throw some light on the relative worth of each.

The newspaper deals with the facts of school life, while the magazine is concerned with imaginative material. Unifying the school, fostering school spirit, encouraging desirable school enterprises, molding and influencing school opinion, giving authentic school news to school and community, and fostering cordial relations among schools all have to do with facts — the material of the newspaper. Further, the newspaper is issued more frequently than the magazine and timeliness and continuous publicity are essential to the development of any desirable school attitude.

The magazine, because of its freedom from journalistic form, is probably more effective in developing self expression and creative work than the newspaper. Art and literature are its chief concerns. Newspaper work must follow definitely prescribed rules. Making a magazine story has less to restrict it. Consequently, there are probably more opportunities for originality in the magazine than in the newspaper, and more opportunities for students of widely differing abilities and interests to produce the type of material in which they are most interested.

A comparison of the two publications on the basis of the last three values mentioned, developing personal qualities of the staff members, recording the history of the school, and advertising the school shows little advantage of either type over the other. One is probably as effective as the other.

It will be seen therefore that a comparison gives the newspaper a wide margin of superiority over the magazine.

While not all of the values may be mentioned here, perhaps, at any rate all are included that could be found in writings on the subject. In the second place, it may be held that the values are not of equal worth, that one might be worth twice as much to the school or the students as another. This is true, but there is no way to equate them except by common sense. Common sense would tell us then, that the one value in which the magazine leads, expression and creative work, is not so important as fostering school spirit, molding public opinion, or promoting worthy enterprises, because the latter are of value to the entire school, whereas the former concerns only a small portion of it. Further, even though these values are not all equal, a preponderance is in favor of the newspaper.

It is argued by those in favor of the magazine that because of its infrequent appearance, undue demands are not made upon either sponsor or staff. The newspaper indeed appears more frequently, but is much smaller than the magazine. However, no publication should make undue demands of the teacher or student. Credit toward the programs of both should be given for either newspaper or magazine work. In the last place, the criterion of value of the publications is not to be found in the amount of time the teacher or staff spends on it, but rather in the effects or results it accomplishes in the average student reader.

In summary, the newspaper is more valuable to the school than the magazine. This does not mean that the school should not have a magazine. It means that if it can have one publication only, this should be a newspaper. After the school has a well-established newspaper, it may have a magazine if it is large enough to support it. In such a case each staff must recognize that the publication has a very specialized function, and must limit its material and effort to that function, — news for the newspaper and literature for the magazine.

SUMMARY

The average high school magazine is composed of one third news, one fourth advertisement, one fourth literature, and one eighth humor. The most frequent criticisms of the magazine are that (1) it attempts to carry news, (2) its content is uninteresting; (3) its organization is uninteresting, (4) the literature is not worth publishing; (5) the humor is largely clipped; (6) the editorials are sermons of no particular value; (7) too few students participate; (8) it represents only a small part of the school; and (9) it is expensive. Suggestions for improvement are made under each of these criticisms. The most common suggestions are to make the publication a publication of the school and not of the staff; to create variety; and to omit material of a type uninteresting to students. Interest may be enhanced if the English department ceases to look upon the magazine as a motivational scheme for classes in English. A comparison of the newspaper and magazine on the basis of values will show that the newspaper is much more important and valuable. A magazine may be supported and established in a school, but should come after the newspaper. In such a case each publication must recognize its own function — news for the newspaper, and literature for the magazine.

REFERENCES

A great deal of the general material in the references on "The School Newspaper" is equally applicable to "The Magazine." The best material for both of these subjects, properly classified, distinguished, and specialized, will be found in the files of the *Scholastic Editor*, published by the Interscholastic Press Association, at the University of Minnesota, Minneapolis, Minnesota.

CHAPTER XXI

THE YEARBOOK

The yearbook is another of the many activities of college life which the high school has imitated. This publication is a comparatively new addition to the activities of the high school. Fifteen years ago there were relatively few high school yearbooks being published, and most of them were in the larger schools. Now nearly every school issues one. Even many of the small schools which cannot support a printed book issue a mimeographed yearbook. This rapid development has brought with it an increasing number of commercial houses which specialize in yearbook engraving, printing, and binding.

TYPES OF YEARBOOKS

Three types of yearbooks are more or less common in American high schools. These types are not entirely exclusive but each emphasizes particular kinds of material. Two of these distinctions are made on the basis of material and function while the third is distinguished by the limitation of material to one class or group of the school. These three types are " Literary," " Historical," and " Senior " or " Upper Class."

Literary. — This type of yearbook emphasizes original writing. Its material consists of stories, essays, editorials, poems, and other miscellaneous student compositions. The author reviewed recently a yearbook of some eighty or ninety pages which gave twenty-three pages to one story. This book would be classed as a literary yearbook no matter what else it might have had in it. One reason why there are so many yearbooks of this type is that in many schools the official publication is a magazine, and the easiest way to make a yearbook is to make a larger edition of the regular magazine and add the pictures and records of the seniors, and also perhaps a few pictures and accounts of athletics or other activities. The second reason is that the English department is usually looked upon as the official " adviser " of the book, and it is to be expected that a teacher of English will want to motivate work in composition by publication.

Historical. — The historical type of yearbook is one which deals with history. The material of which it is made is historical in type — pictures, summaries and records, chronologies, cartoons, caricatures, and other accounts of what actually took place in the school during the year. Because it is historical, it concerns the entire school, not one particular section only. Seniors may have special panels, but if the book is to be history it must represent all of the activities and organizations about the school which are recognized. It may deal with some organizations and activities to less extent than others, but it fairly represents, on the basis of importance and interest, all of them.

Senior. — The " Senior " or " Upper Class " or " Classbook " type of yearbook cuts across the other two types more or less horizontally, in that it may be either largely literary or historical in general make-up, but its records and material have to do almost entirely with the senior class or the senior and junior classes. In the strictly " Senior " type the junior class is usually mentioned to some extent, but little or no space is devoted to sophomores and freshmen.

Purpose of the Yearbook

A partial answer to the question, What constitutes a good yearbook? can be found in a consideration of its main purpose. The main value of the yearbook is in the presentation of the history of the school for the year. The real value of the yearbook is not to be found in its appeal to the student at the time it is issued; it comes to him ten, twenty, or thirty years later when he picks it up, looks it over, and recalls old days and old friends. The " good old days " can be brought back very vividly by pages of snapshots, photographs, calendar records, cartoons, and other definite accounts of actual happenings about the school. Such memories would never be brought back by stories and poems, because these represent imaginative writing and do not concern facts. In the second place, it is probably true that many students never read, for the first time even, many of the stories and poems published in student publications. In the third place, a reader rarely rereads stories. Imagine how uninteresting a story written by a student would be to a graduate some ten, twenty, or thirty years later! And on the other hand how interesting the pictures and records of old times and events would be to him. While people do not reread stories, they do look and look again many times at pictures.

The biggest argument of the adviser who believes in the literary type of yearbook is, naturally, that it motivates the writing of those who are responsible for it. As was suggested before, no publication can be justified on this basis, because so few students will benefit and, further, because this benefit will be relatively small because of the limited practice the student receives. In all cases, the consumer is far more important than the producer.

In short, the function of the yearbook is historical in nature and history is not much concerned with imaginative writing. It is concerned with facts — in this case, with school facts. One or two short stories and as many prize poems are enough of formal composition for the high school yearbook.

There is little or nothing to commend in the " Senior " type of yearbook. It may be that in a small school a special edition of the paper or magazine may be issued which will consider only senior students. But that, of course, is not a yearbook at all. To be a school yearbook it must represent the entire school and reflect all of its activities.

This Senior type of yearbook is expensive to publish because of the small interest the school has in it. Deficits in finances are found far more frequently in this type than in any other. The reason is obvious. It concerns only a small part of the school, and the remainder of the school rightly has little interest in it. It has nothing to interest the freshmen and sophomores and consequently these students very properly refuse to buy it. The yearbook should be the history of the entire school.

ORGANIZATION AND MATERIAL OF THE YEARBOOK

The average yearbook contains a great deal of material, which might be effectively organized in several different ways. There are general principles of building which must be followed in the construction of any house, but arrangements, plans, and details may legitimately differ in many ways. Similarly with the yearbook; general principles hold for all yearbooks, but organization, arrangement, and details may differ. In fact, one of the qualities of a good yearbook is its originality. In any case, to catalogue and describe all the methods of organizing a yearbook would be impossible.

All of the material of the book may be classified in a few main divisions, under each of which fall smaller divisions. Such arrangement will make the book more pleasing and interesting than if the material were just thrown together without any attempt at system. The " divisions " of a yearbook are the " books " into which it is divided. Usually the number of such " books " or divisions is relatively small. " Section " is the term used to designate particular activities or interests. For instance, " Dramatics " might be a section of the division on " Activities." The following organization is frequently used:

I. PRELIMINARY PAGES
  Cover; Flyleaf; Title page; Dedication; Table of Contents
II. FACULTY AND CLASSES
  Faculty; Senior; Junior; Sophomore; Freshmen
III. ACTIVITIES
  Athletics; Publications; Dramatics; Music
IV. ORGANIZATIONS
  Student Council; Clubs
V. LOOK HERE
  Alumni; Snapshots; other unclassified or miscellaneous material
VI. HUMOR AND ADVERTISING
  Jokes; Cartoons; Parodies.

The divisions are usually separated by attractive pages of cartoons, photographs, or artistic material in color. If a general *motif* or theme runs through the book, the material on the division pages and usually the section pages reflects it. These pages may be drawn by the students, or may be photographic work, or line drawings or color work purchased from the engraver at low cost. All title pages should be on the right-hand side of the book.

Questions regarding the classification of material under " Activities " and " Organizations " may arise. The " Activities " are the more or less general, large or public affairs, while " Organizations " are the less inclusive, smaller, or more private affairs such as the French Club, Radio Club, or the National Honor Society.

Another question will arise as to the disposition of pages of snapshots and " stunts." These may be gathered into sections under " Classes," " Activities," " Humor," or in the " Look Here " section; or they may be scattered throughout the book. The latter is probably the best arrangement. Variety and contrast mean increased interest, and four or five pages of snapshots in one place would not be as interesting as those five pages scattered through the book where each presents a contrast or something pleasingly different from the main topic of such a division or section. A few of these pages scattered through the advertisements help to make the latter more attractive. The question will also arise concerning the " Literary " department of the yearbook. The purpose of the yearbook is historical and not literary in character. Consequently we can suggest but one thing for the " Literary " department — that there be none. A short story or two and a prize poem or two may be inserted here or there without harm; but if a department is established, it becomes necessary to make it respectable in size and consequently too much is included. This does not refer to reports of literary societies or clubs nor to accounts of activities and organizations. It refers to the publication of imaginative literature, stories, essays, and poems. An " editorial," an " exchange,"or "news " is as much out of place in the yearbook as it would be in a history book.

Preliminary pages. — *Motif.* — Many high school books have a *motif* or central theme. If this theme has to do with local situations, it is all the more appropriate and interesting. An industrial motif might be adopted by a staff in an industrial community. Knighthood, Mountains, Norsemen, Animals, Astronomy, Marine, Desert, and other motifs are suitable. This motif is reflected in the cover; division, sectional, and other title pages; in the senior panels; in head and tail pieces; and elsewhere where there is a possibility of introducing it in a pleasing manner.

Cover. — The first impression the reader has of the book will be gained through the cover. A cheap uninteresting cover will give one impression, while an artistic and pleasing cover will give an entirely different impression. The cover should be interesting and pleasing, but not too beautiful or too expensive. The material within the cover is far more important than the cover. A happy medium between the finest manufactured cover and the cheap stock of the printer should be found.   Some schools spend far too much on covers; others spend too little.

In general there are two main kinds of covers suitable.   The first is the " paper cover " made from the stock of the printer. This cover, if durable and attractive, may serve all the purposes of the more expensive one.   The other type is the manufactured cover sometimes called " artificial leather " and known commercially by other names.   Artificial leather is very generally used for high school yearbook covers.   It is a very finely woven cloth material with a thin coating applied to give it a finish. This material can be embossed under heat, and decorated with colors.   It does not have a tendency to dry up and crack after being in use indefinitely, which is true of genuine leather.   College and university books have beautiful manufactured covers. This practice should not be followed too closely by the high schools, for they do not have the source of income the college has, in price of books, volume of sales, amount of fees or assessments from groups, or price and amount of advertising space. The book should be well bound, for it will be used a great deal.

Ex-libris design. — Nearly all yearbooks make use of an *ex-libris* design.   If this design is original, unusual, or interesting, it contributes to the book.   An ordinary design is of little value. If the book makes use of a motif or central theme, this theme can be worked into the *ex-libris* design very effectively.

Title-Page. — The title-page should show the name of the yearbook; by whom it is published; the name of the school; city and state; the date of issue; and the number of the volume. These items may be made up in any one of several effective ways. The first items — name, by whom, where, and when — are usually grouped together about the middle of the page.   The title-page should always be the right-hand page.

Name. — The name of the book is important.   In schools in which yearbooks have been issued before, a traditional name has

usually become established. The book should represent a dignified effort, but dignity and beauty frequently receive a severe jolt
because of the use of a flippant name. A cheap name and a
beautiful cover make an anamolous combination. The name
may be distinctive but need not be foolish. Such names as
" Mirror," " Memories," " Reflector," " Review," " Record,"
" Indicator," " Quill," " Periscope," and " Round-Up " are good.
Many schools use a name containing as a base the name of the
school. Illustrations of such names are " Bucyrian," " Tuc-
sonian," " Nor'easter," " Glahision," " Medillite," " Clinton-
ian," " We-La Voca," " Clairtonian," and " Cornelian." A
variation of this is the name of the school spelled backwards
or the syllables transposed. Illustrative of such names are
"Novaneb" (Ben Avon) and "Senrab" (Barnes) and "Oradon"
(Donora). Another variation is the use of the initials of the
school spelled out, as for example " En Em " (North Manchester).
A number of foreign names such as *Les Adieux*, *Réchauffé*,
Tabula, *Madrona* are now being used. Such names as " Tatler,"
" Spice," " Lampoon," " Chaff " are not suitable. Naming the
book after the school colors is not particularly suggestive or
interesting because of the fact that many schools have the same
colors. The name of the book should be distinctive, dignified,
suggestive, and relative.

Foreword. — Very frequently a short, pointed foreword adds
to the attractiveness of the book. Such a foreword may deal with
the spirit with which the book is issued, the purpose, aims, etc.

Dedication. — Nearly all high school yearbooks are dedicated.
Dedication may be made to an individual, such as the superintendent, the principal, a teacher, an adviser, or some distinguished
friend of the school ; or to a group, such as the board of education,
the faculty, parents, or citizens of the town ; or to a spirit, such
as " Service," " Good citizenship," or " Humanity." The usual
dedication is to a single individual, most frequently the class

adviser of the group issuing the book. Such a dedication is fitting, especially if the group has had the same adviser during all of its stay in the school. If the senior class is responsible for the yearbook, the class as a whole and not the staff alone should decide to whom it is to be dedicated. The superintendent, principal, faculty, or competent outsiders may give suggestions and advice but should not have the final say either directly or indirectly.

If dedicated to an individual, a good photograph should be used. The usual arrangement is to use one page for the photograph and the page facing it for the dedicatory remarks. These two items should never be on opposite sides of the same sheet. If a whole page is utilized for the picture, a large one should be used. If a picture of medium size is used on a whole page, a design or border should be used. If the dedication is to a group such as the school board, the picture may be either a single group or individual picture. The latter can be arranged more effectively than the former.

Building and campus scenes. — An interesting preliminary page can be made out of pictures of the buildings, inside and outside, or scenes, winter and summer, about the campus. Pictures of interiors, auditorium, gymnasium, or laboratory, should show these rooms in use, not empty. Interesting scenes about the city or community may be used if related to school life and activities. Careful photography is essential to a good scenic page. Hastily taken snapshots are inadequate and disappointing.

Table of contents. — The yearbook should contain a table of contents. This table should list only the major groups of activities or divisions of the book, not details. Distinctive designs may be suggested by an engraving company.

Staff. — The names of the staff members responsible for the book are usually published in these preliminary pages. Issuing a yearbook is a big job and the group deserves honor. However, many yearbooks have a section on " publications " later in the book, and there list the staffs of the various publications, including that of the yearbook. A good picture of the members of the staff is desirable. A group picture may be used if distinctive, the group seated around a table in suggestive attitude, for instance. A picture of the staff standing in line or in formal group is not particularly interesting. Individual pictures may be tastily arranged. A good page may be made with stunt pictures showing the staff members on a cartooned train or automobile bringing the book; climbing about the book; carrying the book; or busily engaged in the various duties of the offices. Such pictures are made of the heads of snapshots placed on cartooned bodies. Staff pictures should be good. Baby pictures or snapshots of the various members should not be used.

Faculty and classes. — *Faculty*. — Many yearbooks do not publish the names or pictures of the teachers. There is, however, every reason to believe that these should be included, especially in the yearbook of the smaller or medium-sized high school. The student in later years will like to have the pictures of his teachers and faculty friends. The chief objection to the use of faculty pictures comes, strangely enough, from the faculty members themselves. It has to do principally with the pictures and comes from the women more than the men. Some members of the faculty prefer not to use new pictures but to use older ones and consequently serious matters of make-up, background, and shape are involved. The picture of any faculty member who does not want to coöperate to the extent of having a recent picture taken should be omitted from the book. " Pasted-in " pictures are not practicable. The following methods of using faculty materials are possible :

Names of faculty members
Faculty autographs

Group picture
Kodak pictures
Individual pictures on one page, the name opposite
Individual pictures, labels underneath
Silhouettes of members of faculty

The best arrangement is probably a page of individual pictures, each of which is properly labeled and identified.

Special whole-page pictures of the superintendent and the principal probably do not add much to the book except expense. These may just as well be of the same size as those of the other members of the faculty and be placed with them. Unless there is some special reason, or unless the board of education members are very close to the student-body, their pictures should not be used. Few of the students know them. Such inclusion may honor the board of education, but that is not the purpose of the book. Including the names and pictures of the janitors is a token of appreciation and can be justified on the grounds that the students know them, and that they are a very important part of the administrative force of the school.

Senior Section. — The senior class is usually responsible for the issuance of the book, and it is no more than proper that this class should receive special honor and recognition. Extra space, the front of the book, individual write-ups, and special emphasis are the devices used to honor the graduating class.

Panels. — Individual pictures of the seniors are usually included. Because of the large number, these pictures are most frequently arranged in " panels." Paneling is uniform, neat and economical. A panel is merely a strip of background material upon which are placed the pictures of the seniors. This strip is then photographed and a printing plate made which is used in the actual printing of the page. There are a number of ways in which the panels and sketches may be arranged on the page. The most common of these are as follows :

Single panels on one side of page with sketches on other side of page.
Double panels, one on each side of the page with sketches in the middle.
Double panels in the middle with write-ups on each side.
One full page of pictures with write-ups on opposite page.
Single or double panels at top and bottom of page with sketches in between.
Double or triple panels on upper half of page with write-ups on lower half.
Single pictures arranged separately over page with write-ups under each.
Portrait of each senior with small snapshot or cartoon alongside.
Panels in form of school letter or class numeral.
Large panel composed of small-size individual pictures with write-ups.
Group picture with names underneath or on opposite page.

An important principle in publication of pictures is convenient labeling. A picture which has no label does not have the interest it would have otherwise. All senior pictures should be labeled, and labeled so closely that a stranger could identify them. Several of the methods suggested above violate this principle. Probably the best arrangement is the first one suggested. Such a page is well balanced and the sketches are convenient. The pictures in such cases should always be at the outside of the page, farthest from the seam. The use of cartoons or snapshots as a part of the senior picture is expensive in both time and money and not always successful because of the differences in quality of the snaps, backgrounds, size, etc. The use of them also detracts from the artistry of the page.

Sketch. — The following material is frequently used in the sketches or write-ups of seniors:

> Activity biography, activities, offices, honors
> Appropriate limericks, funny verses, etc.
> Birthplace, and "biography," humorous or serious
> Choice of college or occupation
> Nicknames
> Appropriate quotations from famous authors

The best write-up of a senior is the one which seriously gives his school history. His nickname may be mentioned, but a per-

manent record of the activities he engaged in, the offices he
held, the honors and awards he received, etc., is more desirable
than anything else. Appropriate limericks, funny verses, and
quotations are of no value and, more than that, they are hard to
get or arrange. Choice of college or occupation, either serious
or humorous, is of no value. If it is serious, it is not accurate,
for students do not know what they are going to do; and further,
to avoid embarrassment, students who know they will not go
to college or engage in the more polite occupations frequently
give false information. Humor on this sketch may often degenerate into undignified slams and occasionally cause serious friction
and hard feelings.

Other senior section material. — In addition to the space given
to individual write-ups, a number of additional pages may be
reserved for senior activities and records. The senior sketches
are more or less serious, and a part at least of the senior section
should be of the lighter variety. The following material was
gathered by the author from an analysis of four hundred high
school yearbooks; items questioned are, in the opinion of the
author, of questionable value in these pages of history:

Baby pictures ("Life's Little Jokes"; "A While Back")
Comic page of seniors
Commencement program
Commencement orations (?)
Class directory (Offices held and activities engaged in)
Class history
Class motto, color, flower, yell, song
Class opinion of last year
Class parties
Class plays and programs
Class poems
Class prophecy
Class statistics
Class teams
Class will and testament

Epitaphs
Essays and Short Stories   (?)
Group pictures — "As they entered" and "As they left"
Honor seniors and marks
In memoriam
Jokes
Oration   (?)
Program of class exercises
Senior alphabet
Seniors and their song hits
Senior classics
Senior prescriptions
Senior slams
Snapshots
Superlatives
Trophies, records, triumphs
Valedictory   (?)

Material for the " Senior Horoscope," " Statistics," or " Bureau of Information " may be classified under some of the following heads :

Attached Appellation	Danciest
Adherent Adage	Pet Saying
Amazing Aptitude	Pet Peeve
Ardent Aspiration	Most Dignified
Anticipated Achievement	Most Carefree
Appearance	Venus
Always is	Apollo
Likes	Beau Brummell
Dislikes	Biggest Gossip
Disposition	Biggest Bluffer
Besetting Sin	Most Sophisticated
Philosophy	Coyest Maiden
Fame won by	Huskiest
Recognized by	Biggest Eater
Type	Biggest Crammer
Favorite Expression	Wittiest

Ought to be	Biggest Talker
Would be	Biggest Alibier
Will be	Highest Highbrow
Chief Virtue	Biggest Joke
Prized Possession	Biggest Clown
Seen	Slowest
Woman Hater	Fastest
Man Hater	Noisiest
Teacher's Pet	Quietest
Best Politician	Sleepiest
Flirtiest	Modestest
Vampiest	Grouchiest

Autographs. — Many students, especially seniors, like to have the autographs of their classmates and friends. If autograph sheets are used, they should be placed in the back of the book. They soon present a dirty, scrawly, and messy appearance and continued handling of the pages and the pressure of writing on them will cause undue wear and tear and consequent weakening of the binding. These pages should never be placed in the middle of the book, and the front of the book is too important to be spoiled with a messy page of autographs. One way of preserving the autographs is to have each member of the class autograph a sheet and then have this sheet engraved and printed as one of the regular class pages. While not as interesting as the other method, this method means a much neater book.

Material of other classes. — The write-ups of the other two or three classes of the school will not be as detailed or as extensive as that of the seniors. However, each class should have some recognition. The junior class should have probably more than the sophomore, and the sophomore more than the freshman. Individual pictures of all of the members of any of these classes are not desirable. The following list of material, taken from yearbooks, is suggestive of what these class pages may contain :

Cartoons and caricatures
Class chronicles
Class motto, flower, colors, yell, and song
Class numeral in outline with autographs on it
Class rolls
Diary
Famous Freshmen
Freshmen's Fits
Jaunty Juniors
Jokes and Comics
Junior Jazz
Junior Jingles
Junior Jinks
Monologue
Pictures of class (usually group)
Pictures of class officers (group or individual)
Pictures of class teams and records
Poems and short stories
Receptions and parties
Rogues' Gallery
Simple Sophs
Snapshots
Sophomore Scandal
Sophomore Slams
Sophomore Slush

The larger the group of students, the less valuable will be the group picture. There may be no other way of representing the class except by means of a large group picture. What such a picture lacks in detail it will certainly make up in mass. Folding pictures are being used to some extent in presenting large groups, and while more satisfactory in material than a single page picture, they are far less satisfactory for printing and binding. Such pictures are easily torn, and easily torn out, and of course will soon fall apart where they are creased. With such large classes, perhaps a list of the names, and a picture of the officers is more practicable than an attempt to photograph the entire group.

Activities. — The purpose of the yearbook is to present the history of the school for the year and most of this history will be found in connection with activities and organizations.

Athletics. — Many yearbooks give athletics a separate department. It is true that a great deal of the activity about the school has to do with athletics; but it is hardly logical to rank it as a separate department or section and to rank music, for instance, as only a small part of the division on " Activities " or " Organizations."

Two weaknesses are very common in yearbook treatments of athletics. The first is to be found in the reports of the season. Too frequently yearbooks repeat verbatim the newspaper reports of the games, listing the line-ups, noting substitutions, and in other ways giving detailed reports of the games or contests. The place for this material is in the newspaper and not in the yearbook. The write-ups in the yearbook should be short summaries of the season for each type of athletics, football, basketball, etc. A table should show the scores of all the games. In this connection it might be appropriate to suggest that season's totals be omitted. It is usually customary for each school to total its own score and its opponent's scores and to show how very much larger its own score was than its opponent's. There is no logic or value in showing such totals. It is possible, for instance, for the team to have lost every game it played and yet to have in total score twice or three times as many points as the total score of all of its opponents.

The second weakness has to do with the pictures used. In probably half of the yearbooks issued, one or more of the athletic teams are shown in citizen's clothes, lined up in front of the entrance to the school. There is no suggestion of the activity in such a picture. If the printer lost the label, for instance, there is no reason why he should not call such a group a Hi-Y Club, Boys' Club, Boys' Chorus, or Radio Club. The picture should suggest the activity wherever possible. The main reason why the football team is so frequently shown in citizen's clothing is that the school does not begin to think about organizing for the yearbook until January or February and of course there is then no chance to get football pictures.

The football pictures, especially, should be suggestive of football. Individual posed pictures of the various members of the team may be used, but because of the nature of the game this type of picture had better be left for basketball. Real action pictures cannot be taken of basketball, but can of football. One real action picture showing open-field running, forward passing, or tackling is worth a dozen posed pictures. Pictures showing piled-up heaps of players are not much better than none. Bright descriptions of the scenes with the names of the players make them all the more attractive. These descriptions should of course be written, or at least checked, by some one who knows the game.

The following material is suggestive of the possible content of the athletic pages:

Cheer leaders, pictures, and activities
Comics, caricatures, and silhouettes
Football, camp pictures, and write-ups
Interclass teams, and records
Names of members of teams, managers, and coaches
Pictures of teams, players, and groups
Poems and parodies on athletics
Season's records
Snapshots of "action," crowds, parades, and pep meetings
Statistics of teams, height, weight, records, positions played by individual members, points scored
Superlatives of the teams
Wearers of letters. Often in panels forming the school letter
Who's who in athletics
Write-ups of athletic banquets
Write-ups of games (very short review)

In addition to the usual summaries of the year, there are always high lights, interesting events, and unusual happenings which make good material for the athletic pages. Cartoons and caricatures of these events, if they are of humorous nature, are appropriate. These pages would not be complete without the names of the students who won their letters. Prospects for the next year may be suggested. Alibis and similar apologetic writing cheapens any athletic page. Statistics showing the athletic finances belong in the newspaper and not in the yearbook. Care must be taken not to over-emphasize athletics.

Dramatics. — Dramatics is another one of the public functions which should have reasonable recognition. If a great many plays are given during the year, it may be expedient to do little more than list the names of the casts, and give very brief write-ups. However, it is well to include a few pictures of the most notable dramatic events of the year. The most common weakness in dramatic write-ups is to be found in the pictures presented. Too frequently, as with athletics, the cast is lined up in front of the building in citizen's clothes and a picture taken. Such pictures do not suggest in any manner the activity represented. It might be held that not all of the cast would be in any one part of the play at any one time and a picture could not thus be made of it. If so there is no reason why the entire cast should not be grouped on the stage for the picture. Pictures showing scenes in which two or three principals only are represented cannot be justified. It is more difficult to get good pictures on the stage than out of doors, but one of the former is worth a dozen of the latter. Publishing pictures of teams, dramatics, or musical organizations in unsuggestive costume or grouping suggests one of two things to the reader: that the staff either does not know good picture organization, or was so inefficient that no thought was given to the question of pictures until it was too late to get suggestive ones.

Music. — Music plays an important part in the life of the school and should be adequately represented. The book should include short write-ups of activities, programs, and personnel of the various organizations. The records of operettas, musical comedies, programs, and contests are valuable material for it. Short synopses may be used occasionally to good advantage. Pictures of operetta or comedy casts, bands or orchestras should be taken in suggestive costume or pose.

Society. — Brief write-ups of social events, parties, and receptions may be used. If these are class affairs, the proper places for them is in the appropriate class section. A very extensive department or section on society is not advisable.

Organizations. — All recognized organizations of the school should be represented in the yearbook. Many of these will be small perhaps, but even size is not necessarily a criterion of importance and interest. Uusually one page will be sufficient space to allow to the average organization. One half of the page may be given to a picture and one half to activities, list of officers, personnel of membership, or other interesting material about the organization and its work.

Clubs. — These should be written up and pictured as suggested in the above paragraph. They should probably be listed alphabetically in order to avoid trouble regarding placement. If it is desired to place them in the order of importance, a rough estimate of their relative importance may be made by considering size of membership or scope of activities. Another method of placing clubs is classifying them under such heads as " Science," " Literary," " Historical," or " Civic." Such classification is not always accurate or even possible, and moreover is somewhat objectionable because the classifications themselves must be placed.

Publications. — A unique and interesting way to represent the staffs and activities of the various publications is to use the individual pictures of the staff members with the publication as a background. A short review of the year, and the names of the staff is all that is necessary for presenting the history of this phase of school life.

Student council. — A brief account of the history, aims, organization, and a summary of the work of the council for the year is sufficient. A picture of the council together with a record of its internal organization should be included.

Other Organizations. — Other organizations of the school may be written up and illustrated. Care must be exercised on the one hand to see that all organizations are represented, and on the other hand to see that the foolish and outside organizations of students, which frequently go under the school names, are not included. Some schools have clubs which are traditional and which may not be particularly detrimental to school life and work, but which at the same time are not recognized by the authorities. These should receive no attention in the yearbook.

Look Here. — The " Look Here " division is merely a division set aside to care for the material which is not readily classifiable into the other divisions. It is a department of miscellaneous material called by a more arresting name. The organization of the remainder of the book will determine whether or not such a section is necessary.

Alumni. — An alumni section is frequently found in the yearbook. This may be interesting to the alumni and therefore be the cause of the sale of a few more books. It has little historical value, however. Most of these alumni are unknown to the students of the school, and consequently these pages are of no interest to them. Lists of alumni classified by years, showing occupation or residence, is the usual method of treatment. " News " stories about the alumni are not practicable.

Snapshots. — One of the most important elements of any yearbook is the snapshots. Such pictures represent history, facts, events, and personages. They are always interesting. Liberal use of such pictures increases the demand for the book because of the number of students who are represented. A very good way to get many of these pictures, and thus increase the value of the pages, is to have a snapshot contest. Announcement should be made in the early fall of this contest. Several cash prizes should be offered for the best sets of pictures. This should mean that a great many more pictures will be turned in than can be used, and naturally a wider variety means a better selection of the ones which go into the yearbook. In addition, more interest will be aroused.

Suggestions on the taking of these pictures should be made by the committee. Several of the following suggestions to the snapshot editor are equally applicable to the student photographer:

Use only those prints which have a story value

Use only those "shots" which will be in "good taste"

Use only snaps which will reproduce well, those too dark or too light will not reproduce well

Do not try to place too many on a page

Remember that the snaps must reduce proportionally

Allow some of the background to show in making up a page

Do not spoil the page with too much designing

Label all pictures. See that these labels are good

If flashlight pictures are to be used, have your official photographer take them

Have the prints of about the same general size

Prints on semi-glossy paper reproduce well

A medium background such as gray is usually best

Don't forget that this is art work and that your engraver knows much more about it than you do

Chronology of the year. — A "Calendar," "Chronology," "Events of the Year," or "Log of the Good Ship —— " may be used to record the main events of the year.

Humor and advertisements. — Humor may be of a variety of types; jokes, parodies, verses, limericks, cartoons, and caricatures.

Jokes are better suited to the advertising pages than cartoons because of the contrast. Cartoons contrast well with text. Jokes should be fresh and should deal with school events and school people. The humor element in the book is important but must not be over-emphasized.

Stunt pages. — A most important part of the humor of any yearbook is to be found in its " stunt pages." These are pages of interesting stunts or devices built around actual school events and school people. Several pages of these stunts distributed through the book will add very greatly to its interest and attractiveness.

The following stunts were noted in a study of four hundred yearbooks. Of course not many of them were taken from any one yearbook. The list suggests ideas and material which staffs can make use of for many years. It would be impracticable to try to use very many of them each year.

Athletic Glimpses. Cartoons and freaks of athletics
Beauty, Brains, and Brawn.   Students listed under each caption
Believe It or Not.   Unusual imaginings on school affairs
Can You Imagine This Faculty? Teachers and subjects rearranged
Class Inventory. "Freak" items; most clothes, least sleep
Could It Be Possible For? Prominent qualities of students rearranged
Crippled Careers. Cartoons. Unsuitable Careers
Day Life in School. Cartoons depicting routine; exaggerated
Familiar Signatures. Take-offs on signatures, or bona fide signatures
Find Misspelled Words. Names of students freakishly (phonetically) spelled
Freak Newspapers. Few pages of newspaper, past or future, with outlandish news, ads and editorials. Names — "Cracked Mirror," "Futurist," "Last Gasp," "Literary Bigest," "Plunkettville Gossip,"
Glimpses of the Past. Baby Pictures, often unnamed, key in back or among ads
Guess Again. Silhouettes of faculty and prominent students
Haunted Bookshelf. Students named after prominent books
If Students Had Their Way. Cartoons depicting paradisiacal school

Ink Dabs.   Cartoons

In Their Youth.   Baby or Childhood pictures of faculty and students

In the Observation Ward.   Comics on students and their hobbies

Jest Spose.   Students and teachers with prominent characteristics lacking

Mind in the Making.   Cartoons depicting school tasks

Not so Long Ago.   Baby or childhood pictures

Nursery Players.   Students named and cartooned after nursery characters

Our Gang Railroad.   Train loaded with students, picture heads, cartoon bodies

Peeps into the Future.   Cartoons showing students at future tasks

Reincarnations.   Students named after famous persons, Nero, Cleopatra

Review of the Year.   Cartoons of high lights

Seniors Writing Home about Their Jobs.   Cartoons

Some Notables in our School.   Cartoons, exaggerating characteristics

Stairs to Success.   Cartoons.   School tasks and hurdles

Staff Automobile.   Cartoons and pictured heads in and about the auto

Suggestions for New Building.   Cartoons

Superlative Degrees.   Best looking, best dressed, most popular

Theatrical Bills.   Students named after famous plays and pictures

Ten Years Hence.   Cartoons depicting seniors at future tasks

Tid-Bits.   Cartoons of school and events

Things Worth Seeing.   List of distorted imaginings

Topics of the Day.   Cartoons of school life

Training for Efficiency.   Cartoons of athletes in strange positions

Try These on Your Victrola.   Students named after song hits

Weather Forecast.   Students named for weather signs, "Fair," "dark"

What's Wrong Here?   Cartoons of folks minus prominent characteristics

What We Want (one page of words clipped from magazine advertisements) "Pierce-Arrow," "Vacation," "Money"

What We Get (opposite page) "Pain," "bun," "medicine," "work"

What Would Happen If?   List of folks with prominent characteristics missing

Who Are They?   Cartoons or silhouettes

Whom Book Titles Remind Us Of.   Students named after "best sellers"

Who's What and Why's Why.   Cartoons or text or both

Why's Who in United States in 1944.   Names of Students and professions or fame

Idealism *vs.* Realism.   "How they should be" and "How they are" cartoons

Current Mythology.   Cartoons of students named after Venus, Apollo
Hall of Fame.   Superlatives cartooned
Hall of Fame.   Cartoons showing students as famous statues or pictures
Tremendous Trifles.   Cartoons or snapshots
Flower Basket.   Students named and cartooned as flowers
One Thing and Another.   Snapshots or cartoons
Wouldn't It Surprise You?   Individuals minus characteristics
Vegetable basket.   Students named and cartooned as vegetables

Humor must not be offensive, in poor taste, nor undignified. Humor about the faculty may be used if carefully safeguarded and censored.

BUSINESS MANAGEMENT

Financing the yearbook. — The yearbook is expensive and much effort will be needed to finance it adequately.   The usual methods used for raising money for the yearbook are as follows:

> Subscriptions or sales of copies
> Advertisements
> Assessments of seniors and organizations
> Entertainments, sales of candy, etc.
> Gifts from alumni or friends, or grants from school board
> Miscellaneous: refunds, rebates, sales of material

The most businesslike ways of raising the funds — sales, advertisements, and assessments — should, if at all possible, provide sufficient funds for the issuance of the book.   Entertainments, sales, and gifts may be necessary to some extent in the small school.

The amount to be expected from the various sources can be estimated only approximately.   Possibly a fair estimate for the hypothetical average yearbook in the average high school of the average community might be somewhat as follows:

Sales of books	40–60 per cent
Advertising	30–50 per cent
Assessments and Fees	10–20 per cent

Price of the yearbook. — The price of the book should be reasonable; that is, within easy reach of all. This will mean that the staff will have to be economical. Some schools have a rule that the book shall not cost more than a certain amount. In cities where there are a number of schools, a maximum price is usually set in order that needless and expensive competition between schools shall not be started. The aim of every staff is always " bigger and better than ever " and this frequently means disaster. One disastrous year will handicap yearbook production in that school for a decade.

Probably a dollar and a quarter is enough for the average high school yearbook. The author once heard of a high school yearbook that sold for twelve dollars a copy. The same report suggested that so few copies were sold that the book was a colossal failure. It should have been a colossal failure. A staff which was so stupid as not to appreciate the value of the yearbook any more than that should have failed. A three- or four-dollar yearbook is out of place in the public high school. Reasonableness of price will mean reasonableness in expenses, material, size, and particularly in cover. Individual photos, art work, particularly two-color work, and tables of statistics or other material requiring hand setting, is also expensive. Cutting down expenses should mean cutting down the price of the yearbook.

Advertisements. — Advertisements usually fill one fifth or one fourth of the book and pay about one third or one half of the expenses. For instance, if the budget calls for a yearbook to cost about $1200, plans should be made to get seven or eight hundred dollars worth of advertising. There is always some shrinkage, owing either to inability to sell the ads or to collect, or to canceling of contracts, and shrinkage should be allowed for. The methods of securing advertisements for the newspaper and magazine also hold for the yearbook.

Because of the size of the page and of the book, there will be many more full-page ads than in the newspaper. The price for them cannot be stated because this will depend entirely upon local conditions. Ten to twenty dollars is the usual price charged. The price of a half-page should be slightly more than one half of the full-page price. If the latter is $20.00, the half-page price may be $12.50; the price of the quarter-page $7.00, etc. If jokes and humor are distributed through these pages of advertising, the pages will not be full, half, or quarter pages. Their technical name remains full, half and quarter page, however, and no advertiser will grumble because a joke takes a little part of his space. An attractive "Advertisers' Index" is a good device for calling attention to the advertisements.

Assessments. — If individuals, groups, and organizations have space devoted to them, they should help to pay the expense. This applies more to clubs and similar organizations than it does to such activities as athletics or publications, where the interest is a school interest and not a mere personal one.

Expenditures. — While any estimate on the expenditures for the yearbook is at best only a more or less intelligent guess, even such a guess may help to give a general idea of the proportion of expenses which go to the various items. One such guess would be as follows:

Photography	3–8 per cent
Engraving	30–45 per cent
Printing	35–50 per cent
Miscellaneous	4–8 per cent
Reserve	10–15 per cent

Good business demands carefully estimated budgets and as close a following of these as is advisable and expedient.

Contracts for engraving and printing. — Great care should be exercised in letting contracts for engraving and printing. Many high school yearbooks are produced each year which are hardly complimentary to the school issuing them. Most of these books are produced in the smaller community by local firms. In such communities the local photographer usually knows little about engraving or engravers' requirements; the engraver does not specialize in this type of work; and the printer probably knows as little about the printing and binding of a yearbook as the others know about its photography and engraving. Naturally the result is a book of inferior quality.

There are in America a great many companies which specialize in the production of high school and college yearbooks. These concerns employ editors, artists, engravers, printers, and binders who do nothing else but study these books. All such concerns of any size have representatives whose business it is to visit the high school, help the staff to plan a book, and make an estimate on it. Most of these concerns lend to the staff contracting for their services a very complete set of guide books and composite yearbooks which discuss in great detail the duties of the various members of the staff, procedures, etc., and supply all other information necessary for the production of the yearbook.

THE STAFF

The staff of the yearbook will not differ greatly in general organization or type of work from that of the newspaper or magazine. The usual staff of officers, editor-in-chief, associate and assistant editors, business manager, circulation and advertising managers, etc., is elected or appointed.

Policy of the staff. — The staff must determine and adopt a policy for the year. This policy must be based largely upon finances, for financial support will determine size, type, cover, engraving, and other details of the book. The following questions suggested by Mr. Herbert H. Brockhausen should be seriously considered by the staff.[1]

[1] "How to Make a Yearbook Dummy," *Scholastic Editor*, May, 1925.

"Here are a few of the things to be considered before you actually begin work on the dummy and, incidentally, they prove the scope and importance of a dummy.

1. Will your budget allow

        a. A larger book than last year?
        b. The same size book as last year?
        c. A smaller book than last year?

2. Analyze the general theme and plan of your predecessor's book. Can you improve upon it? What new theme or treatment can be used to make your book different?

3. Can you afford color in your introductory pages, division and section pages, and a colored border? Get this information from your predecessor, printer, and engraver and decide at once as the matter of color will vitally affect the art, and consequently, the theme of your book.

4. What kind of paper stock can you afford? Will you be able to select a paper to fit a special theme and color scheme or will you have to decide upon a theme or color scheme to fit an inexpensive grade of paper?

5. Can you plan on a specially manufactured cover or will it need to be an ordinary cover from your printer's stock?

6. Do you want to feature a particular division, such as scenic or athletic, by a special handling or by more pages?

Make notes of ideas regarding these things as they occur to you and when you have exhausted every source of ideas, study your material, make your decisions, and you will have arrived at the policy for your book."

Special technical assistance. — There are two organizations with which the staff, new or old, experienced or inexperienced, should make contact. The first is The Art Crafts Guild,[1] a research association whose purpose is the improvement of art work in school publications. This Guild is not a producing or selling organization but an association of the leaders in this field of art work. It publishes a monthly magazine, *The Art Crafts Review* which is " devoted to the improvement of school publications." The second organization is the Central Interscholastic

[1] 500 North Dearborn, Suite 720, Boyce Building, Chicago.

Press Association.[1] This association is the largest of all such associations in America. It holds yearly competitions in newspapers, magazines, and yearbooks, and several hundred contestants are entered each year. The magazine, the *Scholastic Editor*, has sections devoted to the newspaper, the magazine, and the yearbook, and service departments for each. A new department, " Annual Loan," was recently established for further service to yearbook staffs.

Time schedule. — The yearbook should be started as early as the spring of the year before it is to be issued. The following time schedule suggested by Mr. E. M. Johnson shows how the work may be distributed over the entire year to the general improvement of the product.[2]

SUGGESTED TIME SCHEDULE

April 15 — Elect next year's editor and business manager

April 20 — Complete plans for spring work

May 1 — Preliminary staff appointments, especially art editor. Take baseball and track pictures. Start taking pictures for scenic section. Spring is the most beautiful season of the year and the best outdoor views are then to be obtained.

May 15 — Build up a collection of good exchanges; study them for suggestions that may be adapted to your school

June 1 — Decide on central theme and art motif of book

June 15 — Prepare dummy of book and complete working-budget. Base budget on this year's book

June 20 — Start selection of engraver, printer

August 1 — If possible, make final selection of printer and engraver. They are able to give you additional assistance at this time of year, and additional discounts are given to books that get work in early. Continue the development of details in dummy with assistance of engraver and printer

[1] The official publication of this organization, *The Scholastic Editor*, is published at 1 Folwell Hall, University of Minnesota, Minneapolis, Minnesota.

[2] "Hold Yearbook Elections in April." *The Scholastic Editor*, April, 1925.

September   1 — Approve all art work for color plates and border, opening pages, and make final selections for view sections

September 15 — Appoint and organize complete staff

October   1 — Take football pictures

October   15 — Start publicity campaign. Start taking pictures of all organization groups

November   1 — Start advertising solicitors to work. Start taking individual senior pictures, etc. Start first intensive circulation campaign

November 15 — Start editing of copy for printers — senior write-ups, organizations, societies, etc.

December   1 — Second circulation campaign

December 15 — Complete preparation of snapshot sections

January   10 — Take winter athletic team pictures — basketball, swimming, etc.

January   20 — Deadline for all pictures, except special events

February   1 — Final circulation drive

February 10 — Last of copy sent to engravers except special events

February 15 — Last of copy to printer except special events together with final order for number of books to be printed, etc.

March   1 — Drive to collect all outstanding circulation pledges if installment payment plan is used. Last of special copy sent to printers and engravers.

April   15 — Start distribution of books

Library. — The staff should build up a library. By exchanging its yearbooks with other schools each year, a rather complete library of books may be built up within five or ten years. Not all of the ideas found in these yearbooks could be used each year, but many of them could be used or adapted in later years. Hence this shelf of books should be a gold mine of material for several years. What other schools do is not necessarily the best thing to do, but an inexperienced staff does not have nearly the wealth of ideas or material that is represented in a number of books already issued. The library should include complete files of the *Scholastic Editor*, catalogues of engraving and printing concerns, and other books and material which deal with the subject.

No attempt has been made in this chapter to outline or discuss the more detailed mechanical and technical processes by which a yearbook is produced. Such discussions would fill a big volume. The purpose of the chapter has been to state reasonable principles and purposes and to suggest ways and means of attaining these aims and purposes. The technical matters of engraving and printing; binding and photographing are handled best by the commercial concerns which specialize in these processes. Expert service in this connection is as advisable, logical, and essential as expert service in the coaching of an athletic team, a dramatic club, or a musical organization.

SUMMARY

There are three main types of high school yearbooks, the Literary, the Historical, and the Senior or Classbook. The main purpose of the yearbook is to present the history of the school for the year. The book should be well organized and all material classified. The classifications suggested are (1) Preliminary Pages, (2) Faculty and Classes, (3) Activities, (4) Organizations, (5) Look Here, (6) Humor and Advertising. All of the recognized organizations and activities of the school should be represented. A yearbook is an expensive activity and much careful work will be required to finance it. The main sources of income are the sale of copies, advertisements, and assessments. Good business methods demand that the staff make and follow a budget. This budget will depend upon the policy of the staff regarding size, material, cover, art work, etc. Special technical assistance should be obtained from the commercial houses which specialize in yearbook making. The book should be organized for in the spring of the year before it is to be issued. A permanent library of suitable material should be built up by the staff.

REFERENCES

Practically nothing has been published in this field except material appearing in magazines for the improvement of school publications, and the various bulletins issued by the engraving, printing, and binding companies. In the files of the *Scholastic Editor* will be found much material of value to the yearbook staff. State and local press association publications will also be found valuable.

CHAPTER XXII

THE HANDBOOK

This is the age of handbooks. They are to be found in business, industry, transportation, the professions, religion, the army, and many other organizations and activities where there is a demand for accurate and concise information by means of which the individual will be better able to carry on his work, buy his goods, plan his trip, operate his car, or understand organization and administration. Common among such books are time-tables, tourist folders, guidebooks, directories, hints, directions, and small catalogues. The more diversified and specialized our civilization becomes, the more demand there is for such books. When a person goes from his own field into another, he must obtain information with a minimum expenditure of time and energy. To give this information in concise and convenient form is the function of the handbook.

The same is true of educational institutions. The universities have had handbooks for some time, but it is only recently that they have appeared in the high schools. With the rapid growth of secondary schools and the increasing complexity of their educational and social offerings, not to mention organization and administration, there has come a demand for such books. This originated in the larger high schools, but now many smaller schools are issuing manuals and finding them useful. The rapidity with which this newest type of school publication has developed in the high schools may be readily seen when it is considered that a decade ago there were probably not a dozen of these books in existence. There are now a large number of them in this country, and most of them have appeared since the war.

The wide use made of handbooks and manuals during the war undoubtedly gave impetus to the high school handbook movement. It is not improbable that within a decade the handbook will be the most common of school publications.

Purpose of the Handbook

In far too many schools the life of the new student, especially the freshman, is an unhappy one. He is " strung " by the upper classmen; is sent off on wild goose chases in search of the elevator or escalator; is sent to " Mr. Jones " (the janitor) for advice on his schedule; is made to shine shoes, carry the books of the seniors, violate unwittingly rules and customs, and do many other humiliating things at the request of the seniors or other students in the school. The old jokes of the " left-handed monkey wrench " in the shop, " rain-bow ink " in the office, and the " check-stretcher " in the bank are outdone in many ways by the jokes in the modern high school. This hazing does everything but what the school has a right to expect and demand — that the new student will be welcomed to the school and will be made to feel at home as soon as possible. Instead of welcoming him and making him glad that he is here, such a reception does the opposite. It gives a wrong direction at a most critical time in the life of the student. Such pranks are self-perpetuating, because it is natural for an individual who has been a victim to victimize others. So the freshman, when he becomes a sophomore, takes delight in hazing the new freshman, often carrying the treatment far beyond what he received. Thus is this vicious circle ever widened.

The new student enters a new world, one that he probably knows little or nothing about, and naturally he is tense with excitement. He knows little about the school or what is expected of him. He does not know the teachers, the rules and the regulations, the customs, the school traditions, what programs he is eligible to take, the social organizations to which he may belong, the school songs, yells, etc. In short, he is ignorant, and his ignorance must be dissipated before he can become a real citizen of the school. Knowledge of laws, customs, and regulations is, of course, no guarantee of their observance, but it is the basis on which intelligent observance is built. Considering the entering class as a whole, with its members from many different homes, schools, and social and occupational backgrounds, it is evident that the making of this mass into a homogeneous group is no small task.

The main purpose of the handbook is to hasten assimilation of the new student. It endeavors to give him, in a concise and compact form, the information which will aid him most rapidly in becoming a real member of the school. It codifies the various rules and regulations of the school; introduces the student to the school system; explains the purpose of the school; shows what is offered in educational and social activities; offers counsel and advice; and informs the student of what is expected of him. So far as values, as distinguished from purposes, are concerned, the handbook helps to educate the parents of the students and the patrons of the school; trains the students engaged in preparing it for publication by demanding investigation, initiative, responsibility, and coöperation; establishes confidence in the student council or other organization responsible for its publication; unifies the school; and clarifies the ideals and principles of the various school organizations and activities.

CONTENT OF THE HANDBOOK

A basis for a discussion of the answer to the question " What material should the handbook contain " can be gotten from an analysis of the material the books now published contain. Table I shows the frequency of each item which was discussed in at least one paragraph in ten or more of the 212 books analyzed.

Many of these items were mentioned in other books, but no record
was made of an item unless at least one paragraph, of any size,
was devoted to it. No attempt was made to catalogue and
classify the numerous student organizations and activities.
In most cases where these were discussed, a paragraph was
given to each one, describing it and stating the qualifications for
membership or participation. Table II shows the items which
were discussed in fewer than ten books. Thus the two tables
give a complete list of all topics, exclusive of specific student
organizations, discussed in the 212 handbooks.

TABLE I

FREQUENCY OF MENTION OF EACH ITEM

DISCUSSED IN TEN OR MORE OF 212 HIGH SCHOOL HANDBOOKS

ITEM	FREQUENCY	ITEM	FREQUENCY
Student organizations	188	History of school	60
Program of studies	154	Student schedule blank	59
Date of publication	148	Marks and marking	59
School songs	145	Index	59
Names of faculty members	140	Lost and found information	58
School yells	138	Scholarships	58
Attendance regulations	121	Promotion and classification	57
Student's constitution	98	Honor roll	56
Daily schedule	92	How to study	55
Cafeteria or lunchroom	86	Reports to parents	52
Requirements for graduation	81	Registration rules	51
Organization publishing handbook	80	Medals and prizes	50
College entrance requirements	78	Traffic regulations	49
Fire drill regulations	72	Manners and courtesy	49
Table of contents	71	Blank memorandum space	48
Library information	70	Introduction and foreword	47
School calendar	64	Names of handbook staff	47
Rules for athletics	62	Athletic schedules	46
Directory of building	61	Care of building	45
Lockers and wardrobes	60	Home work	45
		School counselors	45

TABLE I. — *Continued*

ITEM	FREQUENCY	ITEM	FREQUENCY
Vocational guidance	45	Flag salute	26
Study-hall rules	44	Employment	26
Working papers	42	Pass slips	25
Pictures in handbook	41	Members of school board	25
Textbooks	40	Office rules	24
Examinations	38	Daily calendar	23
Athletic records	38	Anti-fraternity rule	23
Names of club officers	37	Elevator regulations	23
Space for owner's name	36	Use of stairways	22
Transfer and discharge	36	Book exchanges	21
Bulletin boards	35	Reading lists (English)	20
Regent's examinations	35	Special equipment (school)	20
Principal's greeting	35	Hospital room	19
Visitors	34	Alumni association	18
School colors	34	School and student creeds	17
Letter wearers	33	Trophies	17
Admission regulations	32	Care of books	16
Telephone regulations	31	Dress (usually girls')	16
Aims of the school	31	Definition of credits	15
School building (not directory)	31	Evening school	14
Advertisements	30	Fees and tuition	13
Entering and leaving school	29	Special examinations	13
Rules for organizations	28	Motto	12
Rules for office holding	28	Commutation tickets	12
Dedication of books	27	Self-examination scale	11
Smoking regulations	26	Parking bicycles	10

TABLE II

ITEMS DISCUSSED IN FEWER THAN TEN
OF 212 HIGH SCHOOL HANDBOOKS STUDIED

A look ahead	American's creed
Academic letter	As others see us
Addresses (spaces for)	Athletic heroes
After school what?	Athletics
Aids to success	Auditorium rules
Alumni loan fund	Autographs (spaces for)

TABLE II. — *Continued*

Banks
Be square
Big sisters
Book room
Books and supplies
Broadening influences
Caps and gowns
Cardinal principles of secondary education
Care of valuables
Cartoons
Certificate of understanding
Chant
Chaperons
Character pledge
Character records
Choosing a college
Choosing an occupation
Choosing your course
Citizenship
Class mottoes, 1918 —
Class rolls
Classroom procedure
Coaching room
Coat-of-arms
Code of a good sport
Collections
College choices
Color day
Commencement
Comments on the work of the various departments
Committees of board of education
Community agencies
Conduct
Conduct board
Conduct on the street

Coöperation of parents
Correction theme symbols
Courtesy to flag
Cuts
Dance program
Dancing regulations
Deans' systems
Discipline
Do you know
Does it pay to go to school?
Do's and don't's
Editorials
Educational guidance
Election board
Elections
Endowment fund
English in the school
Entering and leaving classroom
Examination days
Excess work
Expulsion
Famous alumni
Fathers and sons
Fees
Field trips
Finances
First aid
Food for thought
Form for written work
Freshmen mixers
Gifts
Girls' clubrooms
Girls' uniforms
Girl's wish
Good sportsmanship
Graduates, 1913 —
Graduates who lose

Table II. — *Continued*

Graduates who win
Greenhouse
Gum chewing
Health hints
Hints to lower classmen
Home rooms
Honor banquet
Honor code
Honor points
Honor system
Housekeeping regulations
How to become a booster
How to do school work successfully
How to enter college
How to reach school
Ideals
In memoriam
Interscholastic athletic association
Keeping fit
Leadership pin
Letter from teacher
Letter requirement
Loafer rules
Loan fund
Location of high school
Look for the Blue Triangle
Loyalty pledges
Make-up work
Marks (effort)
Marks (standards for)
Medical report
Meetings of board of education
Memory selections
Menu suggestions
Monthly calendar
Motto of school
Moving pictures

Neatness and cleanliness
Notice to graduates and alumni
Number of graduates
Number of students
Nurse
Office hours
On holding office
Open house
Out of town students
Our school
Parent-teacher association
Parties
Pass slips
Past captains
Patriotic songs
Patrols
Permanent record card
Phonograph
Pictures and statues
Placement
Pledge to school
Postscript
Preparation for professions
Price of handbook
Procedure on first day
Program-making
Pronunciation
Purpose of school
Purposes of courses
Quotations, poetry, etc.
Recommendation to college
Rehabilitation work
Requisites for success
Rules for parties
School emblem
School grounds
School laws

TABLE II. — *Continued*

School spirit
Score cards
Seal
Senior room
Senior traditions
Sequences
Service opportunities
Setting up exercises
Slides
Social distractions
Social life
Special excuses
Special students
Stage regulations
State records (athletic)
Stores
Student aid
Student's prayer
Study periods
Substitute and new teachers
Suggestions for poor spellers
Suggestions to teachers
Suggestions for writing exams
Summer schools
Tardy room
Teachers' council
Teachers' office hours
Term colors
Theater

Thrift
Tickets
Time limit for use of building
To the student leaving school
Traditions
Training rules
Tuition
Tutoring regulations
Typical programs
Use of gymnasium
Useful information
Ushers
Vacation advice
Value of education
Vocational books
War work
Watch your English
Welfare committee
What the city may expect
What the college catalogue tells
What the colleges say about our course of study
What's what at ——
Who's who at ——
Whom to see and why
Why go to high school?
Words often misspelled
Words to the wise
Write-ups of principal and teachers

Material not appropriate for the handbook. — If the purpose of the handbook is to hasten the assimilation of the new student, the material used should answer the many questions he has in mind as he enters the school. An examination of these books shows that many of them are written for the student already in the school who knows the school, its regulations, and its life. The following items selected from those mentioned are typical:

College entrance requirements
Notices to the graduates and alumni
Names of members of board of education
Lists of former students
What the college catalogues tell you
What the colleges say about our course of study
Reading and reference lists
Words often misspelled
Number of graduates yearly
Popular and religious songs (not school songs)
Memory selections
Excessive use of poetry and quotations
Dedication
Jokes and humor
Seasons summaries, usually athletics
Medical reports
Excessive discussion of curricula

The use of these and other items of similar nature indicates that the committee issuing the book does not have a clear conception of the purpose of the handbook.

It might be argued that the discussion of colleges and entrance requirements is of value to the average student; but when the small proportion of students who will enter college is considered, such justification dwindles considerably. A page or two of general suggestions may help or encourage the student, but detailed reports of the entrance requirements of various colleges, especially if these colleges are conveniently situated, is not good practice. Jokes and humor are out of place in such a handbook, as also are popular songs, religious songs, and memory selections. Many of these books resemble college catalogues. The larger high school should probably issue a catalogue. However, organizing a catalogue should be the work of the faculty and not the students; and further, the school has no more right to charge for such a book than the college has to charge for its catalogue. It is probably true that the school of the future will issue both a catalogue and a handbook. The catalogue with its program of studies, curricula, etc., will be issued to all students, while the handbook will be issued only to the new students.

Space for memoranda, addresses, and notes is of little value. The book is not a notebook. A page or two of such space, especially if placed in the middle of the book shows poor organization. Space in which the student may write his schedule is occasionally made. Such blanks are not necessary and probably add nothing to the book.

Many of the books include paragraphs on the reasons for the study of the various high school subjects. Suggestions and hints for study, if given in short clever manner may also be useful. Such attractive headings as " At Grips With Your Studies," " How To Get Ready To Graduate," " How To Pass Your Subjects," help in this connection. " Graduates Who Win " and " Graduates Who Lose," and " Personality Efficiency Tests," are other types of topics discussed for the direct purpose of aiding the student in his work. Not a great deal of such material should be used, however.

Criteria for the selection of material. — In order to help the staff to decide on matters of inclusion or exclusion the following questions are suggested. Each item may be weighed or evaluated on the basis of the answers to these questions concerning it.

What is the purpose of our handbook?

For whom is it, in the main, intended?

On the basis of purpose, can this item be justified?

Would it be missed by the proper student if it were omitted?

Can it be justified as written?

Will it have to be rewritten or changed each year?

As written, will it look well in print?

If included, where will it best fit?

ORGANIZATION OF THE HANDBOOK

The handbook is a new venture and naturally as yet is not as fully developed and matured as it will be in ten or fifteen years. Few high school handbooks exhibit any great attempt at a systematic organization of the material presented. The arrangement is important; the book is to serve for inspirational as well as for informational purposes. As yet no one can say whether " student organizations " should precede or follow the " program of studies," but it is certain that all of the material must be accurately classified under appropriate headings if it is to be readily accessible.

Typical organization. — The books which are definitely organized usually follow some such system or plan as this, though not always in this order:

   I. General Introduction
  II. Organization of School
 III. Program of Studies
 IV. Student Organizations and Activities
  V. School routine, customs, traditions, etc.
 VI. Miscellaneous

Some books contain a larger number of sections, divisions, or parts, and also make use of other headings; but in general the material may be classified as designated.

Detailed organization. — In order to give more detailed suggestions as to organization, the following plan is presented. Some of the less important topics have been included with the more important in order to suggest possible classifications. This plan is probably too incomplete for some schools and too complete for others. It is offered merely as an elastic arrangement which the individual school may adapt to its own needs. Items under each heading are classified alphabetically and not in the order of their importance:

SUGGESTED ORGANIZATION OF THE HIGH SCHOOL HANDBOOK

1. INTRODUCTION

Aims of the school
    Creeds, American's and student's
    Date of publication
    Flag salute
    Identification spaces
    Introduction or foreword
    Location of school and how to reach it
    Names of faculty members
    Names of handbook staff
    Picture of school
    Principal's greeting
    School emblems, motto, colors
    Table of contents
    What the city has a right to expect from you

2. ORGANIZATION OF SCHOOL

Advisers
Assemblies
Attendance
    Compulsory-attendance laws
    General and special excuses
    Tardiness
Building and grounds
    Directory, floor plans, etc.
    Lockers or wardrobes
Calendar of school year
Daily schedule
Examinations, regular and special
General regulations, traffic and fire
Library, information and rules
Marks and marking
Registration
    Admission
    Enrolment
    Transfers and discharges
Reports to parents

Signal bells
Study hall regulations
Textbooks

3. PROGRAM OF STUDIES

Admission requirements
Classification and promotion
College entrance requirements
Credits
Curricula and courses of study
Required and elective courses

4. STUDENT ORGANIZATIONS AND ACTIVITIES

Clubs and organizations
  Alumni association
  Athletics; records, regulations, schedules, etc.
  Band
  Council
  Debating
  Dramatics, etc.
Constitution
Names of club officers
Names of letter wearers
Recognitions
  Honors
  Letters and numerals
  Medals
  Prizes
  Scholarships
Regulations for organizations
Rules for office holders

5. GENERAL USAGES, CUSTOMS, AND TRADITIONS

Anti-fraternity rule
Book exchange
Bulletin boards
Care of books and personal property
Care of building and school property
Dress and personal appearance

Home work
Hospital room
How to study
Lost and found bureau
Manners and courtesy
Office rules
School songs
Smoking
Telephone rules
Trophies
Visitors
Working papers and certificates
Yells and cheers

6. MISCELLANEOUS

Addresses (spaces for)
Index
Memorandum (spaces for)
Student-schedule blanks

Name. — The most commonly used types of names of handbooks contain the following factors:

Handbook: Used with the name of the school issuing it.
Initial: Initial of school, " N," " M," " B," " W."
Colors: School colors, " Red and Black," " Red and Blue."
Suggestive: " Pathfinder," " Guide," " Pilot."
Miscellaneous: " Circular of Information," " Life of ——,"
" All About ——," " Freshman First Aid," " Blue Book,"
" Green Book," " Rules and Regulations," " Handy Book."

Such names as suggested under " Initial " and " Suggestive "
names are probably the most interesting and suitable. School
colors mean little because of the large number of schools using
the same colors, while such names as " Manual," and " Rules
and Regulations " are formal and unattractive. Needless to
state the name of the school issuing the book should always be
included, if not on the cover at least on the flyleaf.

Cover. — The book should be attractively covered and bound. The first impression is important, and nothing is so disappointing as a dusty, dirty-looking cover. Brown covers, although they do not soil easily, usually give such an impression. Many books are bound in the school colors. Such colors usually make a pleasing combination. Gold and silver names and seals on blue covers also make an attractive dress. The covers are usually of paper, although a few are issued in imitation leather. Probably nothing should go on the cover except the name of the book, and perhaps the date and identification of the school issuing it. Rounded corners and invisible stapling help to give a favorable first impression.

Size. — The handbook should be small, so that it may be easily carried. It has been suggested that the best test of proper size is the measurement of the boy's most convenient pocket. The dimensions of 212 books vary from $2\frac{1}{2} \times 4$ inches to $6\frac{1}{2} \times 9$ inches, as follows:

TABLE III

DIMENSIONS OF 212 HIGH SCHOOL HANDBOOKS

DIMENSIONS IN INCHES	NUMBER OF BOOKS
Smaller than 3×5	18
3×5	30
$3\frac{1}{4} \times 5\frac{1}{2}$	32
3×6	15
$3\frac{1}{2} \times 6$	61
4×6	35
Larger than 4×6	21
Total	212

As might be expected the number of pages varies with the dimensions of the book, the size of the school, the size of the type used, the number of activities represented, etc. This item therefore is of value only in giving a general idea of the size of the book. Table IV shows the number of pages and the frequency of each classification. In most instances the books could have been a few, and in many instances many, pages smaller. Extra pages found in many of the books were left blank or designated as " memorandum," " addresses," etc., and in some cases were probably due to the arrangement of signatures by the printer. A number of half-pages found in nearly all of the books examined might have been eliminated with a little more care in organization. The larger books are usually those issued by the schools in the larger cities. The " median " book would be one of about 65 pages.

TABLE IV

NUMBER OF PAGES IN 212 HANDBOOKS

NUMBER OF PAGES	NUMBER OF BOOKS
1–20	24
21–30	18
31–40	20
41–50	17
51–60	15
61–70	21
71–80	19
81–90	22
91–100	17
More than 100	39
	Total 212

Style. — The book must be written in clear and comparatively simple style. The student for whom it is intended is the eighth grader or the lower classman and consequently any attempt to be literary will hinder rather than help. The paragraphs should be short, the headings clear and in large or boldface type, and plenty of " white space " should be allowed. A good quality of paper should be used. One bad fault of many books is that the type used is too small. Small type gives the impression of crowding, and being more difficult to read discourages the reader.

General attractiveness. — A number of other devices may be used to make the book interesting. A picture of the building may be included as a frontispiece. Pictures of the coach, an empty classroom, or the auditorium, are not only useless but also needlessly expensive. Small, clever cartoons, bits of poetry, quotations, etc., interspersed throughout the book help to make it attractive. Care should be taken not to use very much of this material. In some books, especially those edited by the " Better English Clubs " or similar organizations, pointed statements about English usage, examples of incorrect and correct grammar and spelling are used. The usual trouble with these is that too much is included. Lists of " reminders " or " remembers " afford a non-catechetical way of calling attention to pleasing social and citizenship qualities. Items about the school under the head of " do you know " may give interesting features, but such items as the number of windows in the building, and number of lights in the corridors, are of no practical value.

In such a book there is danger of too much moralizing. It is easy enough to write a sermon on citizenship, and perhaps it will be read, but it will probably not affect as many students as the same material written in some such form as " If you wish to be thought well of at ——," " A worthy —— it is ——," or " How to become a —— high booster," found in a number of books. Manners and courtesy may be lectured about but probably not so well presented as in " Do it for —— High," or " The —— High gentleman." An article for sportsmanship may be good, but such articles as " Code of a good sport," " A receipt for athletics," or " Diary of a true sportsman " are of more value because of their directness. Facts and figures on " Does it pay to go to school? " are worth more than many lectures about it. "Loafers' Rules," " Don't Get Anywhere Clubs," or " Never Will Be's," bring regulations to attention admirably by means of clever and witty remarks about them.

Every handbook should have both a table of contents and an

index. The table of contents should be short, only a page or so in length, and should show the major divisions of the book. The index, arranged alphabetically, should be in the back of the book and should show all items included in the book. In some books examined the " table of contents " was placed in the back ; in others it was called an " index "; still others make use of a combination " table of contents " and " index " by listing all items as they appear page by page; and some omit entirely one or both of these devices. All of such plans show lack of clear thinking in terms of organization, accessibility, and attractiveness.

The major divisions of the book should be begun at the top of the page in each instance. Beginning an important article at the bottom of the page detracts from its importance and appeal. Divisions or chapters may be prefaced with small appropriate cartoons or short quotations. Such a practice probably adds to the attractiveness of the book.

Cost and Financing of the Handbook

Data on the cost of publishing handbooks are not very valuable because the cost is so variable, depending as it does on the size of the book, the number of pages, the number of copies printed, the type used, etc. A few schools publish the book each year. Most of them publish it every two or three years. If a school uses a single edition for more than one year, such material as the names of faculty members, club officers, team captains, calendar, and schedules must be changed each year or left out entirely. Probably the best way for the school to meet this problem is to purchase the plates of the " regular " material from the printer, thus saving the expense of resetting it each year. The material which is to be changed or reset can then be composed at relatively small cost because there is not a great deal of it.

Financing. — Handbooks are financed, at least in part, in a number of ways. Nearly every school makes a charge for its book. The prices range from ten to twenty-five cents. Some schools receive contributions from those who get copies of the book, others urge each student to contribute ten cents toward financing it, and still others make a straight cash sale at a uniform price. In the instances where contributions are taken, a book is given to each student regardless of whether he contributes or not, the collection of contributions being usually discontinued when the total expense is met.

Another method of financing the book is to have the student council, general organization, or any other student organization sponsoring it raise funds by means of fairs, shows, candy sales, tag days, or sale of arm bands and pennants, and then either give the book outright to all students or make a small charge for it. In a few instances the high school fund is used to pay the expense of the book, any deficit being met by it, or any profit being added to it. A variation of this procedure is found where the student becomes a member of the general organization or student association, paying a small fee as dues, and the book is given to him, being paid for out of the treasury of this organization.

In some cases the board of education assists in financing the book. The entire obligation may be assumed and the books given to all incoming students. In other instances, the board assumes only a part of the expense, usually one-half, and the balance is assumed by the school or some organization of the school. In the latter case a small charge is usually made to meet the school's share of the expense.

A few books make use of advertisements to help meet the expense. The price of advertisements in the books studied range from six to thirty dollars a page. Such a method adds to the income of the book but probably detracts from its dignity and effect. The few dollars added in such manner probably would not be missed if not obtained, and the advertisements certainly do not add to the attractiveness of the book.

BOARD OF PUBLICATION

About one-half of the handbooks studied were published by the student council or other central representative body. In other cases the books were issued by such individuals or organizations as Hi-Y, English club, senior class, parent-teacher association, board of education, alumni association, faculty and students, and principal.

The issuance of such a book is a fine project for the council. A special committee appointed about the middle of the year previous to the appearance of the book should be charged with this job. This committee obtains copies of such books from other schools; studies the problem; the number of activities to be covered; the amount of space to be devoted; publication costs; and then adopts a policy. Sub-committees are appointed, each to be responsible for a certain section or part of the book. Outsiders may be used as well as student committee members for financing and distribution. A healthy competition is started, and some recognition or honor given to the student who writes up the best article on such general school subjects as " school spirit " or " sportsmanship." Write-ups of organizations and clubs should be uniform and should cover such points as name, purposes, meeting, eligibility, time and place of meetings, and general activities or work. The central committee acts as a final board of editors and managers, articulating the various parts supplied by sub-committees, and preventing misemphasis. Naturally, the faculty should be well represented in this work. The first book issued should be small rather than large. The smaller the book, the fewer the mistakes.

DANGERS

While there may be no really serious dangers, nevertheless there are a few possibilities which should not be overlooked. The first one is the possibility that the book will be written in too boastful a manner. The book must reflect the students' pride in the school, but this can be done without boasting. A second danger is that of emphasis. No one can say what activities should have the largest amount of space. The best opinion and judgment of the staff must decide. The board must consider the activities on the basis of their importance. Interest is not necessarily synonymous with importance. A third danger is that of misrepresentation. Giving the new student a wrong impression of the school is starting him off wrongly. A fourth possibility is that the book will be so complete and full that the new student, instead of being encouraged and helped, will be overwhelmed by the mass of material presented. This is the case if the book is a dry, uninteresting circular of information. It must be alive and attractive; this will help to prevent the student from being swamped by a mass of things he is expected to learn and to do.

SUMMARY

The publication of a handbook is a rapidly developing activity in the high school. The main purpose of the handbook is to hasten the assimilation of the new student. The content of the book should be such as will answer the many questions the new student has in mind as he enters the school. The material should be classified and organized in order to make it accessible and attractive. The book might well be financed by the board of education and the student council, and copies given to the new students. A capable board of publication should be responsible for it.

References

Jones, G. "High School Freshmen at Lincoln, Nebraska," *School and Society* 22 : 527–530, October 24, 1925.

Kershaw, W. L. and Carback, C. H. "The High School Student Handbook," *School Review* 32 : 587–597, October, 1924.

McKown, H. C. "The High School Handbook," *School Review* 32 : 667–669, November, 1924.

—— "How to Produce a High School Handbook," *The Scholastic Editor*, March and April, 1925.

Rohrbach, Q. A. W. *Non-Athletic Student Activities in the Secondary School*, 199–201. Westbrook Publishing Company.

CHAPTER XXIII

HONOR SOCIETIES

The competitive spirit and consequent demand for special recognition early found its way into schools and their activities. The ancient Chinese system of education was built upon a system of competitive examinations. The early Greeks held contests in physical activities, poetry, and music. The Romans had their contests in physical combats, races, and oratory. Prizes, honors, and scholarships in the purely academic field of education are as old as the universities themselves. Later came organizations for the awarding of these honors, organizations of more than local significance. The oldest of the strictly academic honor societies is Phi Beta Kappa, which was organized in 1776. It was designated to honor the student who did especially good work in the college. At this time most of the work of the college was " classical," and consequently this honor became known as an honor for students of the classical curricula. It was not long until imitators of this society developed, and now in the average university there are honor or professional organizations in science, education, journalism, law, medicine, dentistry, engineering, and many other special phases of university life and work. Comparatively recently the demand for recognition has spread to the activities of the colleges and now we find " Mortar Board " and similar organizations designed to honor those who have achieved distinction in the social and extracurricular activities of the institution. No one would deny that these various organizations help to motivate work and are useful.

It was but a natural step from the development of honor societies in the college to the development of comparable organizations in the high school, the imitator of the college. The first of these imitations had to do with commencement, special honors in courses and athletics. Honors in athletics, for instance, have long been customary in high school. The most usual of such honors has been the well-known monogram. This recognition spread rapidly to other activities and now in many schools the honored students are allowed to wear monograms of varying sizes and designs for meritorious work in music, debating, dramatics, publications, and other school activities. The final step in this development will be made when the student is honored for doing exceptional work in the various studies themselves, and we may, for instance, have a monogram for History, one for English, one for good work in Domestic Science, etc. Why not?

Typical Formal High School Honor Societies

Within the past twenty-five years a number of organizations somewhat imitative of Phi Beta Kappa have appeared in the high school. Probably the first of these scholarship honor societies was Phi Beta Sigma, founded in 1900 by Dr. W. B. Owen, then principal of the South Side Academy, Chicago. This organization was imitated and copied by many schools. Six years later the Cum Laude Society was founded at the Tome School, Port Deposit, Maryland, by Dr. Q. A. Harris. This organization was first called the Alpha Delta Tau Fraternity, but the name was soon changed to avoid confusion with Greek letter fraternities of an entirely different character. This same year the Oasis Society was founded by W. E. Golden at the Polytechnic Preparatory Country Day School of Brooklyn. In 1910 Dr. W. B. Gunnison founded the Arista Society at the Erasmus Hall High School, Brooklyn. In the same year the Mimerian Society was founded in the Manual Arts High School of Los Angeles, California. One result of this was the recent organization of the California Scholarship Federation including over thirty high schools of the state. In 1916 Pro Merito Society was established by the headmasters of a number of the secondary schools of Massachusetts and now has about seventy schools in its membership. In 1917 Dr. Shields, then Superintendent of Schools, Los Angeles, led in founding the Ephoebian Society, which was to be composed of graduates from the different high schools who stood in the highest ten per cent of their classes. In 1919 the Marcelleans Society was organized at Fargo, North Dakota.

In this same year a committee was appointed by the National Association of Secondary School Principals to consider the advisability of establishing a national society. This committee was later empowered to draft a plan for such an organization. It presented its report in 1921 and the American Torch Society was founded. The name was later changed to National Honor Society. There are now (1927) more than six hundred chapters with a total of more than eighteen thousand members in American secondary schools. This organization promises to become within a decade the largest of the interscholastic associations or organizations. Some of the honor societies discussed, Cum Laude and Pro Merito, for instance, have as their qualification for membership the marks made in the regular school subjects. Others, Arista, Marcelleans and National Honor Society, base membership eligibility not only on marks in regular subjects, but also on ratings in such qualities as citizenship, service, character, leadership, etc.

Typical Local Informal Honor Societies

Honor Roll. — The Honor Roll has long existed in American high schools. This roll, containing the names of the students who have made high marks, is posted, read, or published at the end of each report period. A slight variation or perhaps an extension of this plan is to be found in the organization of the " AB " Club.   In schools using the letters for marks, those students who have no marks lower than " B " or whose average is no lower than a " B " are given the " AB " pin, a small, inexpensive pin in school colors.   An " A " and a " C " will average a " B " but no lower marks than " C " must be found.   The student is entitled to wear this pin as long as his marks remain on the AB average. When they drop below this average, he must return his pin to the office.   If he maintains his AB record until graduation, the school allows him to retain the pin or presents him with a more expensive one.

Still another practice of this same general type is that in which the honor students wear a small two-colored bow, made up in school colors.   The student may wear this bow as long as he retains his standing.   If he fails to meet the requirement for any period, he removes one of the colors.   Wearing the other color shows that he was once a member.   This wearing of the one color may thus become a strong incentive again to add the other color.

Honoring seniors. — Various methods are used to honor the senior.   Frequently the names of honor students are starred or underscored on the commencement program.   The school seal is also being used rather widely.   For instance, if a student in the Long Beach, California, High School wins honors in eleven of his sixteen quarters and these include two of the senior quarters (one of which must be the last), the " Honor Scholarship Seal " is placed in his diploma and also on his college entrance certificate if he goes to college.   Soldan Senior High School, St. Louis, and other schools make use of the seal of the school for the special honoring of graduates.

Honor point society. — The student in order to be eligible for honors must make a certain number of points or credits in the curricular and extracurricular activities of the school.   Points in scholarship are determined by the marks he makes. Only " A's " and " B's " count, and each " A " can be matched against a lower mark to make his net " A " and " B " marks. He is given credit in points for playing on a varsity team, participating in music or dramatics, or holding office. Such an organization provides that a few pupils might be eligible when they are sophomores, more would be eligible as juniors, and of course many more would be eligible as seniors, because of the increasing total of their credits. Limitations are placed upon the number of credits which the student may use in each field in order to demand a well-rounded program. Included in the general qualities are sociability, qualities of character, citizenship, and service.

Honor Societies in the Junior High School

Many interesting and unique honor societies are to be found in junior high schools. The following three illustrate somewhat different principles of organization and purpose.

Principal W. G. Lambert of the College Hill Junior High School, College Hill, Pennsylvania, and his faculty and student committees have worked out the following interesting system of class honors.

College Hill Junior High School

College Hill, Pa.

AWARD OF CLASS HONORS

I. Character	Blue Star	95–100 per cent "Good Americans"
	Red Star	90–95 per cent
	Green Star	80–90 per cent
II. Attendance	Blue Star	Not more than three excused absences
	Red Star	Not more than six excused absences
	Green Star	Not more than nine excused absences
III. Punctuality	Blue Star	No tardiness of any kind
	Red Star	Not more than one case of tardiness
	Green Star	Not more than two cases of tardiness

IV. Thrift   Blue Star   Over 90 per cent
                      Red Star   80 to 90 per cent
                      Green Star   70 to 80 per cent

V. Special Merit   Special recognition may be given to any class that has
                   rendered service to the school of such character as
                   to deserve special mention [1]

GOOD CLASS CHARACTER DEFINED

I. In the Class Room

1. When a student has endeavored to be physically fit for his daily work by observing the laws of health
2. When a student controls his tongue, temper, and thoughts
3. When a student listens to the advice of older and wiser people
4. When a student learns to think for himself, choose for himself, and act for himself, thereby obeying the law of self-reliance
5. When a student decides that he will not do wrong in the hope of not being found out; when he will not take without permission what does not belong to him; that he will do promptly what he has promised to do
6. When a student obeys the law of duty so that there are not shirkers or willing idlers who live upon the labor of others; by doing what he ought to do, whether it is easy or hard; by taking an interest in their work; by not being satisfied with slipshod and merely passable work; by doing the right thing in the right way, even when no one sees or praises him
7. When a student is cheerful and works in friendly coöperation

II. In the Corridors

1. Between classes
   When all of its members pass quietly from room to room in single file on the right side of the corridor (unless instructed differently by a School Community Deputy)
2. During Fire Drill
   When a student obeys promptly the signals and passes at a brisk walk, without talking

---

[1] Once in seven weeks, time is to be allotted on an assembly program for honorable mention of those classes attaining one hundred per cent awards. All awards shall be given by a central council consisting of the School Community president, vice-president, secretary-treasurer, and three members of the faculty.

III. During Assembly

    When a student comes to immediate and respectful attention at a given signal and remains so during the entire assembly [1]

Another type of honor society is that illustrated by the Ben Blewett Junior High School, St. Louis, " B club." This " B " is gained by students who have attained marked success in citizenship, scholarship, and extracurricular activities. The student must have satisfactory records in all three divisions. He can earn three of such " B's " in his three years at the school. The first is a bronze pin, the second a silver pin, and the third is a felt monogram which he may use on a sweater. Regular marks are given for citizenship and the student must earn a mark of at least 85 in order to qualify. The right to wear the " B " may be revoked by the council for unsatisfactory conduct or record.

The Junior High School of Corry, Pennsylvania, has an "Honor Code " which is described by Superintendent Milton L. Brown as follows :

Any student from lowest to highest grade may earn a term honor by conforming to the conditions of the Code of Honor set forth below.

A first term honor is symbolized by a four-inch letter "C." In successive terms the remaining initials of the school name — Corry Junior High School — may be added until the complete C J H S has been earned.

Each semester the home room winning the highest percentage of honors will be awarded a banner to be held for one term. The banner will contain the Star of Honor and the Letters C J H S, symbolizing that the room possessing it is the honor room of the school, and that the five points of the star correspond to the five points of Honor.

The student council of the Senior High School is considering the Code of Honor pending its adoption with modification.

---

[1] A class or section is considered to be of good character when it passes in single file to the right of the corridor. A student may talk quietly to the student in front or behind him (exception — fire drill). Each teacher ought to insist on a section's coming to immediate attention in the classroom.

CODE OF HONOR

I. Scholarship: Nothing below 75 per cent

II. Citizenship

    A. Attendance. Not more than four half-days excused absence for the term

       Exceptions: A prolonged absence caused by personal illness or serious family trouble will not be counted against the record of a student, if he is able to meet the scholarship requirement. In such cases, a special recommendation from the home-room teacher and approval of the council are required.

    B. Punctuality. Not more than four tardinesses per term for unavoidable cause, such tardiness to be excused by the home-room teacher

    C. Service. A recommendation from the home-room teacher for service willingly rendered is required

III. Character

    Self-Control
    Reliability
    Coöperation
    Courtesy
    Certified by all teachers with whom the student comes in contact

IV. Health

    A. Cleanliness. A recommendation from the home-room teacher is required

    B. Vigor. A recommendation from the health teacher is required

V. School Activities

    Athletics   Clubs
    Orchestra   Assembly Programs
    Home-room meetings   Student Council

    To receive credit a student must have participated in *one* of these and receive a recommendation from the director

There are a number of other different kinds of junior high school societies but the general principles or plans used are variations and combinations of those mentioned above. Frequently these organizations take such names as "Round Table," "Knights and Ladies of King Arthur's Court," and "Hiawatha Society."

THE NATIONAL HONOR SOCIETY

The National Honor Society was established in 1921 as the American Torch Society. The committee of the National Association of Secondary School Principals had as its goal the formation of an organization which should include the better elements of the older organizations and also the activity elements which many of these organizations did not include. Because of its national significance and promise of great development the organization will be considered somewhat in detail.

Purposes. — The purposes of the society have been defined as follows:

1. To create enthusiasm for scholarship
2. To stimulate a desire to render service
3. To promote leadership
4. To develop character

Membership requirements. — Members are elected by the faculty or by a properly authorized committee on the basis of records in four items.

1. Scholarship (Student must be in top third of his class)
2. Service
3. Leadership
4. Character

Not more than fifteen per cent of the graduating class may be members of this society. Not more than ten per cent of the 12 B class may be members and not more than five per cent of the 11 A class may be elected to membership. A member who falls below the standards may be dropped by a majority vote of the faculty on recommendation of the council. The council is the governing body of the local chapter and consists of the officers and sponsor.

A Key of the accompanying design is worn by members.

Definition of membership requirements. — A number of questions would arise immediately concerning the interpretation of "top third of the class," "Service," "Leadership," and "Character." In order to assist in this matter a committee was appointed by the National Council to set standards and this Committee reported in 1924 the following methods, definitions, interpretations, and standards.

FIGURE XVII. — THE KEY OF THE NATIONAL HONOR SOCIETY.

Note the letters around the base of the design.

SUGGESTED METHODS FOR DETERMINING STUDENT MEMBERSHIP IN THE NATIONAL HIGH-SCHOOL HONOR SOCIETY

I. The principal submits, either to the entire faculty or to a faculty committee, an alphabetical list of seniors comprising the highest thirty-three per cent of the class in scholarship rank. In case a school uses a letter scheme of grading, it is well to use a weighted value as follows: 5 for grade A; 4 for grade B; 3 for grade C; 2 for grade D; etc.

II. Usually the executive committee of the local honor society defines for the faculty or faculty committee the meaning in their school of service, leadership, and character. The following definitions are suggested:

   1. Service is interpreted to mean:

      (*a*) a willingness to render cheerfully and enthusiastically any service to the school whenever called upon

      (*b*) a willingness to do thoroughly any assigned service in school procedure or student government, such as acting as proctor, citizenship committeeman or serving voluntarily on the staff of the school publication, etc.

(c) a readiness to show courtesy to visitors by acting as guide, selling tickets, looking after concessions, acting as big brother or sister to underclassmen, or assisting students behind in their work

(d) a willingness to offer oneself as a representative of his class or school in interclass or interscholastic competition

(e) a willingness to uphold scholarship and maintain a loyal school attitude

(f) a willingness to render any other worthwhile service to the school, or through the school to the community

2. Leadership is interpreted to mean:

(a) demonstrating a degree of initiative in the classroom activities which leads to higher scholarship for all

(b) showing initiative in prompting any high school activities

(c) successfully holding school offices, committee chairmanships, and other positions of responsibility

(d) contributing ideas which may be incorporated in the civic life of the school

(e) exerting a type of leadership which actively and wholesomely influences toward a fine leadership

3. A student may gain recognition in character:

(a) by meeting his individual obligations to the school promptly and completely

(b) by demonstrating an honest spirit in his class work, and a spirit of cordiality and sincerity toward his teachers and student associates

(c) by actively helping to rid the school of bad influences or environment

(d) by upholding the ideals of the Christian organizations of the school whenever occasion affords opportunity

(e) by constantly demonstrating such qualities of personality, honesty, reliability, promptness, achievement, and morality as are indispensable to the finest young manhood and womanhood.

In presenting the alphabetical list of eligible students to the selective agencies arranged in your schools, it is well to ask that a percentage grade be given in character, service, leadership, and scholarship. 80% may be considered as average; 85%, 90%, 95%, etc., as above the average; 75%, 70%, 65%, etc., below the average.

No school is obligated to elect 15% of its graduating class. Teachers should be asked, in addition to grading candidates, to state, in writing, detailed accounts of the definite qualities revealed by students in leadership, service, character, and citizenship. They should, likewise, state any known facts which might operate to keep any of the upper 33% of the class out of the society.

After having the initial grading by the faculty and having then determined the initial ranking of the candidates, it is well to resubmit to one's faculty or faculty committee the list of the 15% having the highest general standing from among the highest 33% in scholarship ranking. The faculty might then decide to eliminate several of the candidates of lowest rank in order to uphold high standards in their school, and to be sure that every candidate elected is worthy of membership in the National Honor Society.

Constitution. — The Constitution of the National Honor Society is as follows:

CONSTITUTION OF THE NATIONAL HONOR SOCIETY

Revision of Feb. 1923

ARTICLE I

NAME AND PURPOSE

Section 1. The name of this organization shall be the National Honor Society of Secondary Schools.

Section 2. The purpose of this organization shall be to create an enthusiasm for scholarship, to stimulate a desire to render service, to promote leadership, and to develop character in the students of American secondary schools.

ARTICLE II

GENERAL CONTROL

Section 1. The general control of this organization shall be vested in a national council.

Section 2. The National Council shall consist of nine members elected by the National Association of Secondary School Principals. The secretary of the National Association of Secondary School Principals shall be a member, *ex-officio*.

Section 3. The nine elective members shall be chosen for a term of three years, three being chosen annually. Immediately after the first election they shall be divided into three classes for the one, two, and three year terms.

Section 4. Five members shall constitute a quorum of the National Council.

Section 5. The National Council shall each year nominate three members to be elected by the National Association of Secondary School Principals to succeed those whose terms expire.

ARTICLE III

LOCAL ORGANIZATIONS

Section 1. These organizations shall consist of chapters in the secondary schools of the United States, supported by public taxation or endowment, with standards equal to those accredited by such agencies as the North Central Association of Colleges and Secondary Schools, the New England College Entrance Certificate Board, the Association of Colleges and Preparatory Schools of the Middle States and Maryland, and the Southern Association of Colleges and Secondary Schools, etc.

Section 2. Each chapter, before its admission to the National Honor Society, shall have its organization approved by the National Council.

Section 3. Each chapter shall, for continued membership, conform to all rules made by the National Council.

ARTICLE IV

EMBLEM

Section 1. This organization shall have an appropriate emblem, selected by the National Council, and this emblem shall be uniform throughout the United States.

Section 2. This emblem shall be patented.

Section 3. The distribution of the emblem shall be under the exclusive control of the National Council.

ARTICLE V
Dues

Section 1. Each chapter of this organization shall contribute whatever amount may be assessed by the National Council, not to exceed five dollars ($5.00) annually.

ARTICLE VI
Membership

Section 1. Members of chapters shall be known as active and graduate.

Section 2. Membership in any chapter shall be based on scholarship, service, leadership, and character.

Section 3. Candidates eligible to membership in a chapter of this organization shall have a scholarship rank in the first third of their respective classes.

Section 4. To be eligible for membership the student must have spent at least one year in the secondary school electing such student.

Section 5. Not more than fifteen percent of any senior or graduating class shall be elected to membership in a chapter.

Section 6. The election of not more than five percent of the 11 A class may take place during the last month of the sixth semester. The election of not more than ten percent may take place before the end of the seventh semester. The remainder may be chosen during the eighth or last semester before graduation.

ARTICLE VII
Officers

Section 1. The officers of each chapter shall be a president, vice-president, secretary, and treasurer.

Section 2. The secretary shall certify to the National Council the number graduated in each class and the names of those elected to membership in the chapter.

ARTICLE IX
Faculty Supervision

Section 1. All meetings shall be open meetings and shall be held under the direction of the principal or of some member of the faculty selected by him.

Section 2. The activities of the chapter shall be subject to the approval
of the principal.

ARTICLE X

EXECUTIVE COMMITTEE

Section 1. The executive committee shall consist of the officers of the
chapter and the faculty sponsor.

Section 2. The executive committee shall have general charge of the
meetings and business affairs of the chapter, but any action
on the part of the executive committee shall be subject to
review by the chapter.

ARTICLE XI

AMENDMENTS

Section 1. This constitution may be amended at any meeting of the
National Council, or by mail by an affirmative vote of seven
members.

Initiation of new members. — The induction or initiation of
new members should be a serious and impressive ceremony.
It is frequently open to the public. A committee reported to the
National Council 1924 concerning this matter as follows:

PUBLIC PROGRAM FOR INDUCTION

The request from many Chapters for a form or ceremony to be used in
the reception of new members has led the Council to submit the following.
It is intended to be merely suggestive. Some schools may wish to elaborate
and enlarge upon the ceremony, introducing symbolical characters and employing costumes, properties, and electrical effects to make the ceremony
more dramatic and spectacular. Such freedom is left to the schools with
the reservation that mysticism and secrecy ought not to be introduced.
The ceremony here given is simple, dignified, and contains the essential
features to be held continually before the members. The Council, however,
does not make this or any ceremony mandatory upon the Chapters.

As soon as the Chapter is called to order by the president, the secretary
will read the communication from the Faculty formally certifying to the
election of new members. The new members will take places before

the Chapter.   The Principal will then address the Chapter emphasizing the place of honor held by the Chapter in the schools and colleges, and the honor attained by the members in their election to the National Honor Society.

He may say in substance:

"No honor conferred by the school excels that represented by this Society.   It represents the fundamental objectives for which schools are instituted and gives recognition to those who have attained most nearly the desired ends.   Other honors at the disposal of the school are only partial in the sense that they recognize specialized ability, skill or talent, but this Society looks upon education as a total product measured by the four dimensions of life.   Throughout history man has recognized the value of such distinction and in one way or another has marked for special honor those who excel.   Ancient and mediaeval universities established their honor societies.   In modern times the coveted honor of election to Phi Beta Kappa outranks all other distinctions.   In your election to this Society the Faculty is honoring you for the attainments already made and for the promise they contain of continued excellence in the cherished ideals of this school."

The president, or one of the faculty advisers, will then explain the purpose of the Society as set forth in the Constitution.   He may say in effect:

"The Constitution of this national organization recognizes four cardinal objectives as fundamental in all educational practice: Scholarship, Character, Leadership, and Service.   To exalt these objectives and hold them ever before the school as goals towards which all should strive, is the purpose of this Society.   We seek nothing for ourselves beyond the strengthening of our own resolves coming from the bond of union which this Chapter establishes between us.   Our aim shall be to hold before the school such motives as shall induce others to aspire to scholarly habits, enlisting in worthy service and leading forward in all things that shall advance the welfare of the school."

Some member of the Society may be assigned the duty of explaining the symbolism of the emblem.   For this purpose a large replica of the emblem may be made in wood, carved exactly as the emblem of the society.   It may be made in such a way that the torch may be superimposed upon the key-stone so that the torch may be used separately in the closing part of the ceremony.   The member may speak as follows:

"The emblem of this Society is the keystone and flaming torch.   The keystone bears at its base the letters S, L, C, and S, which stand for the four cardinal principles of its organization: Scholarship, Leadership, Character, and Service. As the keystone is placed by the builder to hold the perfect arch in perpetual stability, so the structure of our education must be held firm and true to the purposes of life by the virtues represented in this symbol. Scholarship is the power of the mind to dispel ignorance and superstition through scientific investigation of truth; Leadership is the power of personality that blazes the trail for man's upward climb; Character, the composite of all the common virtues, sets the seal of righteousness upon our every endeavor, while Service is the beginning and end of our education, the altar of altruism from which God's blessings to man have been vouchsafed. Thus the keystone symbolizes the high ideals of our Society. The flaming torch is the emblem of our purpose. To bear forward the searching light of truth, to lead that others may follow in the light, to keep burning in our school a high ambition for the enduring values of life, and to serve, these purposes are symbolized in the torch."

The President may now direct the new members to form a hollow square or keystone with himself in the center, the old members taking their positions just outside the figure, all facing the center. The president will hold the torch aloft in his right hand, the others extending their right hands in the same manner as if holding a torch. In this form the president will administer the following pledge, the new members repeating it after him, phrase by phrase:

"I pledge myself to uphold the high purposes of this Society to which I have been elected, striving in every way, by word and deed, to make its ideals, the ideals of my school."

The secretary will then read the Constitution of the Chapter and each new member will sign the register.

Advantages of the national honor society. — The main advantages of the National Honor Society are as follows:

1. *It defines and sets standards for the ideal high school student.* — Nearly all of the older organizations stood for scholarship alone. But the high school itself does not stand for scholarship alone. It stands for football, music, dramatics, club, and many other activities. These are recognized as a part of its life. Consequently they should be included in its recognition of the student who is its product. The student who should be honored is the student who most nearly represents the ideal of the school.

The good citizen must have ideals of service, must have character, must be able to assume and discharge responsibility, and lead and follow his fellows in work for the betterment of his community. Consequently if the school is to make the " good " citizen it must educate the student morally and socially as well as intellectually.

The student who makes high marks does not necessarily have these characteristics of a good citizen. In the first place, he may show lack of character in the very act of getting his high marks. He may choose easy courses or teachers, or he may be downright dishonest in accomplishing the end of ranking high scholastically. In the second place, when he thinks only of himself and of what he wants he is not thinking in terms of service to his school or to his fellows; he is practicing selfishness. Service is recognized as one of the ideals we should develop in the student. In the third place, if the student is interested only in what he makes in his classes, other qualities will probably be slighted and whatever potentialities he may have in other activities are likely to go undeveloped. In short, if the school emphasizes only scholarship it fails to give recognition to other qualities which the good citizen as such must have. Academic excellence is an important phase of the school work, maybe the most important, but it is not by any means the only phase.

It may be held that the school does honor the student in the other lines of endeavor. That the athlete receives his monogram; the actor or musician receives the publicity and applause; the officers of the various organizations receive recognition. This is true and there is no reason why the student who receives the high marks may not be honored in similar and comparable ways. His name or record may be published, posted, or read in the assembly. Thus he may receive honor for doing exceptionally well the thing in which he is interested. Many schools which have chapters of the National Honor Society also make use of the Honor Roll. Nothing is said against this practice. What is said is that the student who excels only in athletics is not the ideal product of the school and neither is the one who excels only in the classroom work.

2. *Rank rather than marks determines eligibility scholastically.* — A mark in itself means little. Standards of teachers as well as of schools are different and are consequently more or less uncomparable. An average of " B " in one school would not mean, necessarily, the same thing in another school. A student who fails to make a certain percentage in one school might easily excel it in another. The rank method of determining eligibility is reasonable because in all schools the top third means the same thing.

3. *It is very flexible.* — The sample constitution shows how flexible this organization is. It is called a " National " society and was designed for all of the schools of the nation; consequently it had to be made flexible. Almost any local honor society or plan of recognizing merit can be very easily incorporated in the organization of a chapter of the National Honor Society. The steps in the organization of a chapter of the National Honor Society as suggested by the National Council, are as follows :

1. Write to the Secretary, Mr. H. V. Church, J. Sterling Morton High School, Cicero, Illinois, for a sample constitution for chapters. It is not necessary to adopt this, but the chapter constitution must conform to the constitution of the National Honor Society.

2. Adapt the sample constitution or write a new constitution.

3. Send three copies of this to the Secretary with a check for five dollars.

4. If the Council approves the constitution a charter will be sent by Secretary Church. The charter is authority for the school to elect its members. A list of members must be sent to the Secretary, after every election, by the secretary of the chapter. The pins or fobs or emblems can be obtained only through the Secretary. They will be sent C.O.D.

4. *Its national scope gives it significance and prestige.* — We all like to belong to organizations which are well known. This fact helps to make the National Honor society attractive. It is National in scope and it is fostered by the National Association of Secondary School Principals which means that it has a wealth of experience, judgment, and prestige behind it. National Honor keys are becoming more and more in evidence and this too helps to extend and develop the usefulness of this society.

5. *It is an educational agency because of the opportunities in its constructive program.* — One of the main criticisms of the organizations which " honor " only, especially those which honor the senior on his commencement night, is that they have no constructive program. The senior receives his seal or his star on the program as he " goes down the steps." Looked at both from the point of view of the school and of the education of the student it would seem that all of the fine ability represented in such a group should be capitalized for the betterment of the school as well as for the development of the ideals of service, leadership, etc., within the organization. Because of election before commencement night, the organization can assume tasks and programs which will benefit all concerned. The responsibility for such tasks as the following might be assumed by the organization :

Monitorial and study hall duties
Assembly programs promoting society ideals
Study coach work for weaker students, absentees
Big Brother and Big Sister work
Purely social meetings, dances, parties, picnics
Campaigns of service, study, courtesy, "broaden your interests"
Issuing of a handbook
Public initiation service
Presentation of cup to class of highest merit
Encouraging scholarship by various means
Setting the examples of the high ideals for which it stands
Welcoming strangers, visitors, teams

Members act as proctors, assistants to teachers

Assist in mechanics and details of commencement

Discouragement of commercialism in subjects, athletics

Banquet for graduating senior members

Reception for parents

Entertainment of students on Honor List

Establish Class Honor Lists

Inter-class competition in various qualities of citizenship

Reception to freshmen and their parents

Responsibility for assisting substitute teachers

Publicity of commendable work

Exhibitions of fine work on bulletin boards

Recognition of students who have raised their marks over last term's

Letters and encouragement to students, deficient or discouraged

Establishment of Tutor bureau

Special recognition for those intending to teach

Assist faculty in giving and scoring intelligence tests

Hold "assimilation" meetings for Freshmen

Help in the planning and holding of "Academic" contests

Act as substitute teacher

Visitation of Junior high and elementary schools for purposes of encouraging students to come to high school

Encourage participation in activities for the "grind"

Emphasize all around development of the student

Visitation to and reports from other high schools and societies

Increasing interest in going to college or continuing education

Make college entrance requirements available, give information concerning scholarships

Leading in campaigns to abolish undesirable activities, cribbing, dishonesty in home work, cheating, cigarette smoking, gambling, defacing or destroying school property

Substituting programs for "Round Neck Day," "Class Scraps," "Rag Day"

Improving of appearance, and language

Caring of school honors or trophies

Planning, organizing, and executing for the wholesome influence of the schools

Summary

The custom of recognizing merit is as old as the race itself. Honor societies have long existed in higher educational institutions. Recently they have multiplied rapidly. During the last two or three decades imitations of college organizations have appeared in secondary schools. While the earlier organizations recognized and honored the student for academic work, the trend in late years has been in the direction of honoring the student who not only makes good marks, but who excels in certain other important characteristics, such as citizenship, service, character and leadership. The largest of the honor societies in the secondary school is the National Honor Society which was founded in 1921. There are over six hundred chapters of this society in American high schools. It is doing much to define and set the standards of the ideal high school student. A chapter of it should be in every recognized secondary school.

References

Boyd, P. P. "Extracurricular Activities and Scholarship," *School and Society* 13 : 158 — 166, February 5, 1921.

Fifth Yearbook of the National Association of Secondary School Principals, p. 29–38.

French, W. "The Selection of Honor Students, *School and Society* 15 : 589–591, May 27, 1922.

Kittrell, C. A. "An Important Factor in Teaching Citizenship," *School Review* 29 : 366–372, May, 1921.

Lewis, G. T. "Incentives to Higher Scholarship," *School Review* 33 : 131–138, February, 1925.

McKown, H. C. "Recognizing Academic Heroes," *School and Society* 20 : 23–24, July 5, 1924.

Miller, M. E. "Value of Honor Societies in High Schools," *The High School Teacher*, October, 1925.

"National Honor Society for High Schools," *American Educational Digest,* September, 1923.

PETERS, H. A. "Honor Systems in Secondary Schools," *School Review* 32 : 36–39, January, 1924.

RYNEARSON, E. "Honor Societies of the Secondary Schools," *School Review* 36 : 456–466, June, 1922.

TERRY, P. W., NAGIE, C. E. and PIEPER, C. J. "Honor Societies," *Twenty-Fifth Yearbook* of National Society for the Study of Education, Part II, Chapter XIII.

Sixth Yearbook of the National Association of Secondary School Principals, p. 172–183, 1922.

"A System of Honors Used in the Decatur (Ill.) High School," *School Review* 31 : 647–648, November, 1923.

WILLIS, M. M. "The National Honor Society," *School Review* 34 : 129–136, February, 1926.

CHAPTER XXIV

COMMENCEMENT

Whatever is, is not necessarily wrong. Neither is it necessarily right. It may be either at different times in its development. If based upon reason it is probably right. If it has for its basis only tradition it is probably wrong. Traditions " just grow up " and come to be accepted as gospel irrespective of their appropriateness or usefulness. Frequently the fact that they have existed is apparently sufficient justification of their continuance. Education is replete with traditions. Where competition is keener and where more definite results are demanded, as in business and the professions, progress is required and practices and procedures must be justified on some other basis than tradition. One of the most unchanging events of school life, and one which should represent the most progress because it represents the results of the educational system, is the high school commencement.

The average high school commencement, like a number of other high school functions, came from the college. A formal service in which the graduates are officially honored has always been customary in colleges. When the high school assumed the rôle of " peoples' college," it was but natural that it too should have its formal graduation exercises.

OBJECTIONS TO TYPICAL HIGH SCHOOL COMMENCEMENT PROGRAM

The typical formal commencement has its salutatorian, valedictorian, prophet, statistician, poet, historian, and what not, whose duties range all the way from telling humorous anecdotes to wailing tearful good-byes. The program is stilted and the atmosphere is one of artificiality and striving after the impressive. What is wrong with it? The main objections to such a program are as follows:

It is not a distinct high school ceremony. — The typical commencement program is an imitation of the college program. Imitating anything good may be of value to the imitator, but it may also have a formality and a lack of adaptability which unsuit it for his purposes. This may be said about the typical high school commencement program. The high school and the college are different in aims, purposes, material, and atmosphere, to say nothing of the degree of educational advancement. The futile imitation by the high school of something which is different in aims, support, organization, material, and atmosphere, can only mean incongruity.

Oration topics are not suitable. — The following anecdote is quite typical of the man-of-the-street's attitude towards the average commencement program:

First man: " There are certainly a great many big problems facing the world to-day."

Second man: " Well, don't worry; it won't be long now until they'll all be settled; Commencement time is almost here."

How frequently commencement speakers select topics about which they know little and about which the audience knows nothing and cares less. Often these speeches are written by the coaches of these students. Evidently the purpose of such speeches is to prove to parents and patrons, by the use of big words on the printed program, and by the use of high-sounding phrases of the youngsters, that the money spent on high school education is well spent. Illustrative of this kind of topic are the following taken from typical high school commencement programs:

- Present Day Perils of American Life
- The Race Problem
- Nihil Sine Labore
- World Peace
- The Ideal Successful Career
- Law Enforcement
- A Deduction from Psycho-analysis and Quadronometric Calculus
- Tax Reduction
- The Clarion Call
- The Call to Political Altruism
- The Salvation of Democracy
- Plus Ultra
- The Age of Jazz
- The Balance of Power
- Fiascos of Political History
- Ut Prosim
- When a Man Wills

This list might be increased indefinitely. Little wonder that the high school commencement speaker is burlesqued as an inexperienced stripling with solutions for knotty problems which baffle even the wise and experienced!

It is too much an exhibition of graduates. — Commencement frequently turns out to be a " show " for the graduates. No one would deny that the seniors should have honor for their achievement, nor that this occasion should inspire other students to want to graduate, yet there may be other values which are as much worth while, if we do not overlook them in our zeal to glorify the graduating class.

Frequently there is extravagance. — The usual commencement activities are too expensive in time and money. Seniors are usually excused from school for one, two, or three weeks before regular closing time on the plea that this time must be used for preparation for commencement, or that the teachers must have the time to compute marks, in order that commencement speakers can be selected or for other equally simple reasons.

Competition in commencement finery, dresses, and flowers undoubtedly works a hardship on many students. In many schools a senior reception or party is held and, for the girls at least, this requires another new dress. Assessments and other expenses, such as those for invitations, yearbooks, and pictures, all combine to make commencement a time of expenditure. " Show " again is emphasized because " one graduates but once." The purse strings of those able to pay are loosened to the discomfiture of those who are not able to pay. That this expense is no small sum is attested by the practice of some schools of encouraging the freshman or sophomore to start a " Graduation " savings account.

Content is repeated. — Another objection to the average high school commencement program is found in the repetition of material from year to year. The same general " We are glad to see you " will be found in the salutatory; the same tearful " friends, we bid you a sad farewell " is found in the valedictory; and in the usual history, prophecy, and poem, almost the only changes required from year to year are changes in the names of the students. About the only redeeming feature of this oft-repeated program is the fact that the orators change.

VALUES OF THE COMMENCEMENT PROGRAM

It honors the graduates. — Students who have gone through the high school have accomplished something that deserves recognition. They should be honored.

It emphasizes the necessity for a new program. — The realization that graduation time is near means a realization by the student that he will have to consider seriously his future because he is leaving school. Of course he will have been thinking about this important matter many months before commencement, but this final experience crystallizes the demand that he plan a new program of education or activity.

It acts as an incentive to the other students. — Seeing his friends graduate acts as an incentive to make the underclassmen wish to complete the course. The word " graduate " possesses rare magic in motivating school work.

It offers an opportunity to enlist community interest in the school. — Commencement is a time par excellence for school observation and stocktaking by the community. There is no other time during the entire year that offers so golden an opportunity. When persons attend a football game they think in terms of athletics; when they attend a theatrical they think in terms of dramatics; when they attend a musicale they think in terms of music, but when they attend a commencement program they think in terms of education. The average community knows its school only through second hand reports, from the students, and these are often colored. School administrators and teachers are notoriously poor advertisers. How many much needed buildings and how many educational programs have been delayed or defeated only because the community was not sufficiently enthusiastic about its school! A part, at least of the commencement program, can be put to good use here.

Suggestions for the Improvement of Commencement Activities

1. **Use care in the selection of commencement speakers.** — A very troublesome problem is the selection of commencement speakers. The usual method is to count up the marks and assign the valedictory to the student with the highest average and the salutatory to the student with the next highest average, irrespective of whether or not these students can be said to be representative graduates, and irrespective of whether or not they

have been unethical in securing their marks. The student who makes all " A's," thinking only of himself and of his own honor, and caring nothing about service to the school or to his fellows, should certainly be eliminated from the program, in favor of a more typical student whose marks may not have so high an average, but whose service to the school has been significant. It seems reasonable that commencement representatives should be selected on some such basis as the eligibility requirements of the National Honor Society discussed in Chapter XXIII, and that the practice should be abandoned of selecting them on the basis of doubtful averages to the fraction of one percent, based upon the more or less unreliable measures implied in teacher's marks. The student speakers represent the class and consequently, the school. The school should stand for more than instructors' marks in academic subjects.

Outside speakers add to the attractiveness of the occasion if carefully selected, limited as to time, and restricted as to topic. The subjects of such speakers naturally should be related to one or both of two things—education and the future of the graduates. Topics on Peace and War, Law Enforcement, and League of Nations are out of place on the commencement program. If the speech is aimed entirely at the graduates, it is likely to be more or less inspirational in nature and to leave nothing definite to remember after a few days or weeks. If the address is aimed at the parents and patrons of the community, and if it deals with concrete educational problems it can be of untold value to the school and its supporters. The school has the right to suggest to the speaker his general topic. It is a good plan for him to talk both to the parents and to the graduates. A discussion of educational matters with the parents and a congratulatory and exhortatory charge to the graduates are proper. The following topics are suggestive of suitable material for such speeches by outsiders:

1. Education, a life process
2. The study habit, after finishing school
3. Three of the most promising types of careers for the next generation
4. How do you entertain yourself? A test of education
5. High School commencement and the dawn of civilization
6. The trial of Career versus Marriage
7. The nobility of labor
8. If knowledge were diamonds
9. Knowledge versus wealth
10. The chances for success of the eighth grade, the high school, and the college graduate
11. From iron ore to the razor blade; from first grade to the graduate
12. Education minus science or scientific methods
13. Teachers or policemen
14. Business methods applied to learning
15. If teachers sold knowledge the way the storekeepers sell commodities
16. Thoughtless thinkers in education
17. Education, luxury, and necessity
18. Finding yourselves
19. Carry on
20. The cultural benefits of the high school
21. The public library — the peoples' university
22. The high school and democracy
23. Does education pay?
24. The meaning of graduation
25. Pleasures of education
26. Power of a great ideal
27. Significance of commencement
28. Commencing what?
29. American ideals in the high school
30. Young America at the bat
31. Education versus knowledge
32. The younger generation
33. Laziness and the lash
34. What price education
35. The marks of a man
36. Education: investment versus charity
37. After commencement, what?

38. Qualities requisite for success in life
39. Successful living — a money proposition?
40. This community, investor in education

2. Require that the topics used by student speakers be reasonable. — The incongruity of the picture of the inexperienced youth with his adequate solutions to the world's perplexing problems is easily seen and appreciated. It will be to the credit of the high school to require that its commencement speeches deal with subjects with which the student has at least had a chance of becoming acquainted, and subjects which have an interest for the community at large. The following list of topics is suggestive of reasonableness. Note that most of them deal with the school itself. Why not?

1. What's right with the school?
2. Products and by-products of school life
3. Moral influence of the high school
4. If we go no farther
5. Value of the Commercial Department
6. Cultural value of high school subjects
7. Why we are graduating
8. Our four years forty dollars a day job
9. Crowded out
10. The zero hour. Why students fail
11. Are we good enough for our town?
12. What we hope to return to the high school
13. Recognizing merit in the high school
14. One day in our high school
15. The student who will graduate
16. Our school — a laboratory of citizenship
17. Athletics and the town
18. The student who will not graduate
19. Amusements, their uses and misuses
20. Home Economics in the school
21. The aim of this school
22. Pioneer settlers in this town
23. The cost of failures in our high school

24. Evolution of our high school band
25. Plea for improved study conditions in our school
26. Our Alumni Association and what it has done for our school
27. Our faculty, our friends
28. Practical values of various high school subjects
29. Physical education in the high school
30. Study habits of the high school students
31. Absences of the high school students
32. Teachers versus policemen
33. Clubs in the high school
34. Important changes in our high school program
35. What the town owes the school
36. What the school owes the town
37. Why we have athletics
38. Should I go to college?
39. High school — a citizenship training camp
40. Traditions in our school
41. What a high school senior should represent
42. What I have gained in four years at high school
43. Our new school library
44. Good music and its value
45. Comparison of this high school with that of a decade ago
46. Improving our school
47. Our assembly
48. Drop outs — their cause and effect
49. Social life in the high school
50. Evolution of the high school
51. Academic contests and their value
52. The italics in high school
53. Our school counselor
54. What our Cafeteria means to us
55. History of our town
56. Industries of our town
57. Places of interest of the community
58. Development of our schools
59. Future development of our schools
60. What the school has done for the community
61. Needs of the school
62. Education and our community development

63. Our town's health
64. Our town's civic pride
65. What our town offers in education
66. What our town offers in self-development
67. How can I make our town a better place?
68. Coöperation of civic bodies of our town
69. The future of our town
70. How students may aid in improving our schools (or our town)
71. Law observance on the part of our students
72. Our town's ideals
73. Our town and its relation to the world
74. Our school's organizations and what they are doing
75. Fire protection in our town
76. The boy scouts and the community
77. How our schools build for citizenship
78. Our school a community center
79. The building of a school library
80. The cost of education in our town
81. My opportunity for an education
82. What our schools train for, and what I received
83. What the state and nation are doing for education
84. What I owe the community
85. Our interest in our school after graduation
86. How the parent-teachers' association has helped us
87. Value of singing in the school
88. Trophies won by the school
89. The high school as a workshop
90. Mathematics in everyday life
91. Relation of notable current events to the high school
92. The money invested in our high school faculty
93. If our bulletin board could talk
94. A conversation between my report card and my attendance record
95. "If marks were wages ——"
96. The high school and health
97. The new day in our high school
98. What we need most
99. What we do here .
100. The high school and recreation

3. Vary the type of commencement program. — Traditionally, speaking has been the main part of the commencement program. There is no real reason why it should be. Music, exhibitions, and demonstrations are all practicable. The following are variations from the usual type of program.[1]

a. Unified theme program. — A new type of program which is becoming very popular is the " unified theme " type. In this type of program the topics are grouped around a central theme or subject. The following program of the Senior High School, Johnstown, Pennsylvania, June, 1923, illustrates this type of program. Only the topics are shown :

Salutatory : The Indian and Pioneer of Johnstown
Johnstown as a Commercial Center
The History of Transportation in Johnstown
The Problem of More Homes in Johnstown
The Future of High Schools in Johnstown
Valedictory : A Plea for Better Recreation and Health Conditions in Johnstown

It will be noticed that at least the salutatory and valedictory transgressed the usual traditional lines of subject matter for such speeches. The last two topics, in particular, represent school interests and needs and undoubtedly are worth much more to the school and its community than a speech by an outsider, or than speeches by students on unreasonable topics. Probably a better program of this same general type is one in which the central theme is some phase of the school itself. The following program (Joliet, Illinois) represents a school theme :

GENERAL TOPIC : PRODUCTS AND BY-PRODUCTS OF HIGH SCHOOL LIFE
This High School as an Americanizer
Effect of Teachers upon the Student
Development of Physical Education in the High School

[1] *The Commencement Manual*, listed in the bibliography, contains excellent material for commencement purposes.

The Desirability of a Knowledge of Chemistry
Some Practical Values of History and Literature
The Social Training of our High School Course
The Moral Lessons of High School Work

Dr. Cameron Ross, Superintendent of Schools at Doylestown, Pa., was instrumental in having the old fashioned program abolished several years ago. Since that time the programs have centered about investigations in the school and its work. In 1921, for instance, the theme was " The Reading in the Homes of High School Students." Material was gathered from questionnaires from the students. In 1924 the main topic was " Study Habits." The investigation was made by the seniors themselves. The main program was as follows:

Study Habits of High School Students of the Doylestown High School
Explanation
Facilities for Study
Study Habits and Methods

In 1925, the main theme was " Tardiness, Absence, and their Excuses." The material was obtained from records and also from actual excuses which had been saved during a period of five years.

Tardiness, Absence, and their Excuses
Introduction — Purpose and Method of the Survey
Tardiness
Absence

The concluding paragraphs of the student speeches are worthy of quotation as illustrating the results of these investigations. The concluding paragraphs of the talk on " Tardiness " were as follows:

This study reveals then that in spite of bad conditions the rural student is almost as punctual as the town; that over fifty (50) percent of the tardiness could be prevented by proper parental control and that seventy-five (75) percent of the cases of tardiness are inexcusable.

We appeal to the pride of the student body. Think of it — six hundred (600) little children in the grades, through all the conditions of weather have contributed during the current year less than one case of tardiness per student — we, in the high school, with a little more than half the enrollment of the grades, have caused three times as much tardiness. In one grade, the fourth, there were only nine cases all year; surely if we value the importance of good habits and the importance of punctuality, we will all highly resolve to reform.

The summary paragraphs of the talk on " Absence " were as follows :

From these facts you can readily see the significance of the problem. Nearly one-half of the time lost can be salvaged. Parent responsibility is paramount. Irregularity of attendance is a great problem confronting parents, teachers, and the student himself, since it is he who loses the opportunities and can never make up the time wasted.

The compulsory attendance law now in effect in Pennsylvania is not sufficient to compel boys and girls to go to school. The moral support of the parents and the community is the agency needed to reduce these staggering figures and losses.

Dr. Ross states that he has material from several hundred students covering a period of six years on " Vocational Preferences and Changes," and that this topic will be used soon. Regarding the change from the old type of program to the new, Dr. Ross states in a letter to the author :

There was no difficulty in 'putting over' a new type of commencement. I made my faculty see the inaneness of the old type of commencement which was a bore to the public and a joy-killer for those entrusted with its preparation. We started out by eliminating "class day" for a trip to Washington on the ground that it was less expensive to go to Washington than it was to buy fine dresses and waste money on "class gifts" to individual members. Caps and gowns helped the thing along. They are less expensive and they hide a multitude of sins.

I have never heard any objections on the part of the students or patrons. Parents welcome the change since they are put in touch with real live school issues, as the sample programs will show you. Give the public something that contributes to their knowledge of school problems and they will be with you.

Let me stress the real educational value of getting a group of seniors working on a simple project that requires some research and analysis. They like it.

The real difficulty in breaking away from old tradition is that it requires some thinking on the part of those entrusted with making commencement programs. Assigning themes on platitudes is the least difficult thing to do — it follows the lines of least resistance.

One of the most interesting commencement programs the author has seen was given at Knoxville, Pennsylvania, in February, 1926. The main part of the program is indicated below :

A MEETING OF THIRTY PUBLIC SPIRITED CITIZENS CALLED TO CONSIDER THE NEED FOR A NEW HIGH SCHOOL BUILDING

(Only the topics are indicated)

The Chairman
The Secretary
The Principal of the High School
The Head of the Science Department
The Head of the Commercial Department
The Dean of Girls
A Chronic Objector
An Intelligent Mother
An Intelligent Young Mother
The Principal of the Grade School
A Practical Man
A Slow Judicious Citizen
An Interested Citizen
The Idealist
Manager of Boy's Basketball Team
Manager of Girl's Basketball Team
The Y. M. C. A. Representative
A Physical Education Student
A Teacher
Women Voters' League Representative
Ministerial Ass'n. Representative
Business Men's Ass'n. Representative

Literary Club Representative
Legion Representative
The President of Council
U. H. S. Alumni Representative
U. H. S. Alumnae Representative
A Taxpayer
A Citizen

The most interesting thing about the program was that every member of the class spoke at least once (some of them spoke several times) and this entire section of the program lasted only about thirty-five or forty minutes. The most valuable thing about it was that the patrons learned more about their school and its needs in that half hour than they would learn ordinarily in a lifetime.

Other illustrations of this unified theme type are as follows:

1. Art:

Value of Art to the Historian
Art in Industry
Art of the Book
Art in the Theaters
Art in the Home
Queen Fashion
The City Beautiful

2. Books:

Books are keys to Wisdom's treasure;
Books are gates to land of pleasure;
Books are paths that upward lead,
Books are friends. Come, let us read.
The Birth of the Book
The Growth of the Book
The National Library — Its Form and Function
The State Library — A Supplement to Local Libraries
The Public Library — Pleasure and Profit
The School Library — Life and Literature
The Home Library — Children and Cheer
The Future of the Book

3. Our High School:
    Our Aims
    Our Teachers
    Our Equipment
    Our Student Body
    Our Program of Studies
    Our Marking System
    Our Clubs
    Our Athletics (Music, Dramatics)
    Our Publication
    Our Needs

4. The Value of the Educated Man:
    To Himself
    To the Home
    To the Community
    To the State

5. The Product of the High School:
    Mentally
    Socially
    Physically
    Morally

6. Our School — a Laboratory for Developing Citizenship:
    Duties of the Citizen
    Training for these Duties
    Training for Specialized Leadership
    Responsibility for Continuing Community and School Progress

7. History of Our High School:
    Ancient
    Medieval
    Modern
    Future

8. Our School — A Community Center:
    In Education
    In Music, Dramatics
    In Athletics
    In Interest
    In General Importance

9. How Our School Trains in Citizenship:
   Elements of Good Citizenship
   Materials of the Student
   Methods of Utilizing Materials through
      Class and Home-Room Organizations
      Student Council Organizations
      Dramatics, Music
      Clubs
   The Product

10. Then and Now:
    Then
       Old Songs sung by clubs in costume
       Pompous Salutatory by student in costume
       Bombastic Oration by student in costume
       Tearful Valedictory by student
    Now
       Music by clubs
       What's Right with Our School
       Some Accomplishments of the Year
       Crowded Out — a Plea for More Room

11. Our Mountain Climb:
    Preparation
    Going Up
    Difficulties
    The Rainbow
    At the Top

12. Great Men and Our School:
    (Each topic illustrated by students)
    Taft and Bryan, and Public Speaking in Our School
    Chopin and Foster, and Music in Our School
    Edison and Pasteur, and Science in Our School
    Raphael and Michael Angelo, and Art in Our School
    Our School's Father — Horace Mann

13. Do You Want Progress in Education?
    Valedictory — Explanation
    Inadequacies of Our Present Equipment
    Equipment We Really Need

Why Schools Are Financed by Serial Bonds Instead of Direct Taxation
Why All Men and Women Should Vote "Yes" for the Bond Issue
An Equal Chance for Each Child in the City
Salutatory — What are YOU Going to Do About It?

14. Mortality in Our School:

Mortality of the Graduating Class
How Mortality of the Class Compares with that of Other Years
Where the Greatest Mortality in Our School Occurs and Why
Sacrifices which have kept Our Mortality Down
What the Parents Can Do to Decrease School Mortality

15. Our School Twenty-Five Years Ago and Now:

Building and Equipment
Enrollment and Personnel
Curricular Offerings
Extracurricular Activities
Teachers and Teaching

16. Our School Mother:

Her Responsibilities
Her Methods
Her Difficulties
Her Successes
Our Benefits

17. Our School a Republic:

Explanation
Student Participation in Control
Aims
Organization
Activities
Values

18. Crowded Out:

Explanation
Brief History of the School
Increase in School Population
Expansion of Curriculum
Congestion at School
Needs of the School
Plan for Meeting Needs

19. Beauty:

> Explanation
> Beauty in Art
> Beauty in Character
> Beauty in Religion
> Beauty in Music
> Beauty in Literature

20. A Commencement Allegory:

> Explanation
> The Birth of the Brook
> The Song of the Brook
> The Path of the Brook
> The Meeting of the Brook and the River

21. The War:

> Songs of the War
> Poetry of the War
> The War in Posters
> War Facts Dialogues
> Our School and the War
> Our Town and the War

22. Extracurricular Activities Program:

> Explanation of Extracurricular Activities
> Demonstrations
>> Music . . . . Orchestra
>> Student Council Meeting
>> French Songs . . . . French Club
>> Ceremonial . . . . Girl Reserves
>> Music . . . . Chorus
>> Initiation Ceremony . . . . Honor Society
>> Story of School Publications
>> Music . . . . Music Clubs
>> Athletics and Common Sense
>> Music . . . . Orchestra

23. Extracurricular Activities Program:

> Introduction and Explanation . . . President of Student Council
> Demonstration and Contest in Typewriting

Playlet . . . . By French Club
Songs or Other Music . . . . By Music Clubs
Style Show . . . . . . By Home Economics Department
Scouting Demonstrations
Physical Exhibition

On the program of the William A. Cochran Junior High School (Johnstown, January, 1923) were the following five talks:

Study Methods in Cochran
The Cochran Building of Today
The Cochran Buildings Now Under Construction
Pasteur, His Life and Work
Stephen C. Foster, America's Best Folk Song Writer

Interspersed with a variety of music such topics should make an interesting and reasonable program.

b. *Demonstrations and exhibitions.* — Another type of commencement program and one particularly suitable to the Junior High School is that consisting of demonstrations of school work or activity. The following program (Irwin Avenue Junior High School, Pittsburgh, January, 1924) is typical of this demonstration-exhibition type.

DEMONSTRATION OF SCHOOL WORK

Explanation
Making a drafting room table
Making a stool for a drafting room table
Making an assembly chair
Making a cafeteria stool
Making a lamp

Another program of this type is as follows:

PARTS OF OUR SCHOOL AT WORK

The Way to a Man's Heart: Demonstration of serving by students of Home Economics Department
The Vestal Virgins: Classical drill by girls of the Latin Department
Music Hath Power: Short program of types of music with explanations, by students of Music Department

The Model Husband :   Demonstration and illustration of manual training activities, repairs

Our Business World: Demonstration of dictation, typewriting, speed tests

There are a number of fields in which demonstrations and exhibitions might be made.   The most practicable are :

Art	Home economics
Club work	Manual training
Commercial work	Music
Gymnasium activities	Special activities

An interesting exhibition program was held at the Liberty School, Pittsburgh, in January, 1925. The program began with half an hour of music. A short explanation was made by a student of the purpose and material of the program and then the meeting adjourned to three classrooms in which were exhibits of pictures, dresses, and woodworking. Each member of the class had something on exhibit and each item bore the name of the producer.

Such demonstrations and exhibitions are probably more applicable to the work of the junior high or the elementary than to the senior high school. But some of them are applicable to any type of school.

4. Abolish senior vacations. — Excusing seniors one, two, or three weeks before school is out cannot be justified. First, it is reasonable to state that all of the preparation required for the gala event can be done in a day or two. Second, it is logical that if the teachers have not learned to know the students in 142 weeks an additional two weeks spent in contemplation of their academic rank will not be particularly valuable. In the third place, it would seem that if anybody at school should continue to the very end, it should be the student who will leave shortly never to return. In the fourth place, giving the seniors a couple of weeks of vacation may be an old tradition, but any tradition which does not have as its foundation some real basis of thought and judgment, cannot be justified. Speakers and performers, of course, need coaching and training but this may be taken on the side, or at least the entire class need not be dismissed in order that five or six members may " practice their pieces."

5. Adopt caps and gowns or other uniform dress. — In order to avoid the usual competition in commencement finery, caps and gowns may be worn. Gray caps and gowns are preferable to black. Some schools use white, but these are probably needlessly expensive. The school may either buy or rent caps and gowns. Probably the latter is cheaper. Attempts at making students wear uniform dress have not been very successful.

6. Distribute senior activities over a period of time. — Frequently the senior's last week is one dizzy round of parties, class nights, receptions, class plays, and banquets. These activities should be distributed through a longer period and before the last week.

Class night is a popular " stunt " night for seniors. The following program of Latrobe (Pennsylvania) High School for 1924 illustrates one very interesting type of program :

President's Address . . . . . President of Class

THE CLASS NIGHT PAGEANT

IN THE REIGN OF GOOD KING BUD

ACT I

INTRODUCTION TO THE PROBLEMS OF COMMENCEMENT

King . . . . Student
Prime Minister . . . . Student

ACT II

THE KING HOLDS COURT

Astrologers	Court Beauties	Court Venders	Optimist
Class Flower	Court Dancers	Donors	Pessimist
Class Poet	Court Editor	Historians	Prophets
Class Song	Court Musicians	Jester (statistics)	Pages

Other stunts suitable for class night are:

Biography	Ancient history
Class convention (political)	*Commencement Times* (newspaper)
Class debate	Freshman Class
Class drama	Journey
Class reunion	Musical program
Class trial	Stunts and games
	Voyage

7. Have a promotion exercise for the junior high or the elementary school, not a graduation. — The junior high school and the elementary school should have a " Promotion " exercise. A " Graduation " exercise " finishes " the students but a " Promotion " exercise, while it may be large and spectacular, merely " promotes " a student from one section of the school to another.

8. Avoid dictating to the graduating class. — Help the class to make its decisions by giving counsel and advice, but avoid dictating to it. The details of arranging the baccalaureate service, for instance, often needlessly troubles a community. Ministerial associations in many communities seem to control this event and bring pressure to have the honor passed around among the ministers. Or the principal or faculty decides who shall have the service and in what church it shall be held. This service (also handed-down from the college) does not exist in order that ministers shall be honored; it exists for the students and it is only reasonable that the class shall select the minister and the church, and that ministerial wishes in regard to the matter be not considered. The same may be said regarding the principal and the faculty.

9. Take advantage of this opportunity for the education of the community. — The school is supported by the community and the community should know what it is getting out of its investment. The principal might well make a brief review of the progress the school has made during the year; some school official might outline some unusual phases of the work to be done next year; or some one else might recount a few interesting and significant happenings of the year. A brief review of five- or ten-year periods is also appropriate. These talks might be made by the students but would probably carry more weight if made by the administrators of the school. The following subjects are suitable for such talks:

Progress in Education
Our School Building Program
Outstanding Accomplishments of the Year in Our High School
New Departments or Work
What Our School Needs Most
Importance of Keeping High School Accredited
How We Compare with Others
Place of Art and Music in the Curriculum
Our School Program for Next Year
Coöperation of School and Community
This School Ten Years from Now
The Need for a Counselor or Dean of Girls in Our School
Explanation of Some Innovation or Change in Work of the School
How Your Dollar for Education Is Spent

Many schools print on the back of the programs or somewhere within the folder interesting items about the school under some such heading as "Pertinent School Facts."

Summary

Commencement activities are extremely important not only for the student but for the school as well. They represent very large opportunities. Naturally, these opportunities should be capitalized as much as possible. But only by the use of rational and reasonable methods will the graduation exercise be removed from the plane where it is so frequently ridiculed, to a plane where it is looked upon as the most significant annual educational event in the life of the community.

REFERENCES

BUCK, G. "College Commencements, Today and Tomorrow," *School and Society* 2 : 734–743, November, 1915.

BUNCE, E. F. "A Wartime Commencement," *Educational Administration and Supervision* 5 : 41–42, January, 1919.

"Another Sort of Commencement," *The Independent* 69 : 1452–1453, 1910.

CARTER, W. A. "New Kind of Graduation Program," *Industrial Arts Magazine* 7 : 234–235.

"Commencement Orations," *World's Work*, June, 1911.

"Commencement Programs," *School Review* 21 : 260–262, April, 1913.

DAVIS, H. C. *Commencement Parts*. Hinds, Hayden, and Eldridge.

KESTER, K. "Day of the Diploma," *Journal* of National Education Association 14 : 117, April, 1925.

MEYER, H. D. *Handbook of Extracurricular Activities*, Part VI. A. S. Barnes and Company.

MACKAY, C. "Graduation Plays," *Woman's Home Companion*, April, 1923.

MARTIN, S. "Commencement Reflections," *Harper's* 49 : 277–280, July, 1924.

PAINTON, E. F. A. U. *The Commencement Manual*. T. S. Denison and Company.

"Sweet Girl and Boy Graduates," *Collier's* 71 : 15, June 16, 1923.

CHAPTER XXV

SUPPLEMENTARY ORGANIZATIONS

THE GIRL RESERVE MOVEMENT

Purpose. — When a Girl Reserve was asked what she thought the Girl Reserve Movement was, she replied : " It is something that helps a girl to grow." This is perhaps as good a statement as one can give in a few words of what the Girl Reserve Movement of the Young Women's Christian Association is trying to do among girls. This definition has as its center that which is most important in a girl's movement, namely, the girl herself. It also includes the equally important element of growth. This idea — the girl and her growth — the Y.W.C.A. has tried to make the center of its girl movement.

Work with girls, twelve to eighteen years of age, has been done by the Y.W.C.A. since 1866, all work for high school girls being originally under the direction of the Student Department of the Y.W.C.A. In 1916–17 all work for girls under eighteen years, including the High School work, was brought together in a department known as the Girl Reserve Department, and unity but not uniformity attempted through the underlying purpose in the work and through such external elements as a name, slogan, code, and a costume to be worn on certain ceremonial occasions. The name " Girl Reserve " implies that a girl is constantly storing up, putting in reserve, more and more of those qualities which will help her take her place as a Christian citizen in her home, her school, her church, and her community. A Girl Reserve Club therefore becomes a re-serve force in any school in which it is organized.

Membership. — Any girl between the ages of twelve and eighteen in any school or in any community, who is interested in the following purposes, may become a Girl Reserve, by taking this oath :

As a Girl Reserve I will try
To face life squarely and to find and give the best and I will try to be :
>   Gracious in manner
>   Impartial in judgment
>   Ready for service
>   Loyal to friends
>   Reaching toward the best
>   Earnest in purpose
>   Seeing the beautiful
>   Eager for knowledge
>   Reverent to God
>   Victorious over self
>   Ever dependable
>   Sincere at all times

In many schools the above code serves as a guide and each girl is asked to write her own interpretation of the principles in it, and to try to live up to her own expression of it.

Organization. — Both organization and program are flexible, depending upon the needs and conditions in a school. Girl Reserve work should never duplicate other school activities. It should supplement and fit into the school plan as a whole.

Local organization. — The junior high school or 7th and 8th grade school organization is on the basis of a small group, fifteen or twenty girls being included in what is known as a " Triangle " with an adult adviser, preferably a teacher. The senior high school organization, which consists of either the sophomore, junior, and senior classes, or where there is no junior high school of the freshmen class as well, is a self-governing club with the four regular officers and three standing committees, membership, social service, and program. The club officers, plus the chairman of committees, plus one or more adult advisers, who may be part of the school faculty or women of the community chosen by the school, form the cabinet.

Inter-School Council. — In a community with several high schools a Girl Reserve Inter-Club Night School Council is always organized. This is composed of the presidents, sometimes other officers, and one elected member from each club. It provides through its meetings for contacts and friendships between girls from different schools and as Chicago says, " is the only inter-school organization which does not bring our girls together on a competitive basis."

In Chicago such excellent correlation between Girl Reserve and school life has been worked out, and such excellent girl leadership has been developed in consequence, that a large share of the school's service work is delegated to Girl Reserve Clubs. Chicago has about 6000 Girl Reserves in high schools, with a club in every high school meeting on school time.

The Registered Girl Reserve Plan. — Owing to the numbers of requests for the organization of high school clubs from high schools throughout the country in communities where there is no organized Young Women's Christian Association, the National Board of the Young Women's Christian Association through its National Girl Reserve Department administers what is known as " The Registered Girl Reserve Club Plan." This is a plan by which there is formed in any community where there is no Association an advisory committee of women who are made responsible for work with high school girls. The high school club thus formed, together with the advisory committee of women, is related directly to the National Girl Reserve Department.

Program. — The programs are based upon a belief that underlying all activities must be the purpose to help a girl find abundant life in the finest sense of the word. The words work, fellowship, recreation, and spirituality, are the terms used in program planning with leaders. The girls, as they plan their own programs, use the terms health, knowledge, service, and spirit. The philosophy underlying all Girl Reserve work is that of an adolescent movement which, if it is to be a successful one, must be based upon two factors: girl initiative and adult guidance. It is the combination of these two elements which the Y.W.C.A. believes makes possible a movement that really develops a proper girl leadership.

Relation to Y.W.C.A. — Every school girl Reserve Club has one or more faculty advisers chosen by the school. These advisers work with the Girl Reserve secretary of the local Y.W.C.A. The relationship between this Girl Reserve secretary and the school advisers varies according to circumstance. The Y.W.C.A. has an advisory relationship to any Girl Reserve club in a high school. Club meetings are usually held at the school building, often on school time. Supplementary meetings worked out in coöperation between the faculty advisers and the Girl Reserve secretary are held at the Y.W.C.A.

Activities. — The following program of the Bryan High School Girl Reserves (Dallas, Texas) shows how each meeting is made constructive in its relation to student activities.

BRYAN HIGH SCHOOL PROGRAM 1925–1926   DALLAS, TEXAS

October

   7th   Jolly G. Rs. — Freshman Party
  14th   Do It Up Brown — Business
  21st   Plumb the Line — Health
  28th   Hallowe'en Party

November

   4th   Follow the Gleam — Recognition of New Members
  18th   Station B. M. Broadcasting — Business
  25th   Bring a Bite — Pack a Xmas Box for Indian Girls

December

2nd   Ride Your Hobby — Hobby
9th   To Do or Not to Do — Business
16th Sh! Sh! Santa Claus — Service for Xmas (Home)

January

6th   Adios Señoritas — Senior Party
13th My Lady's Finger — G. R. Ring Standards
20th Turn a New Leaf — Business
27th The Best of Friends — Books

February

3rd   Pick Your Star — Movie Discussion
10th Have a Heart — Freshman Party
17th A La Palomar — Friendship Meeting
24th Facts and Figures — Business

March

3rd   Ring Discussions
10th Bringing Up Father — Dad and Daughter Party
17th An Apple a Day — Health
24th Scrap Books
31st "Que Voulez-vous?" — Business

April

7th   Facul-Tea — Faculty Tea
21st Election of Officers
21st Installation
28th Camp Meeting

May

5th   "Cinco De Mayo" — Honoring Seniors
12th Mother and Daughter Tea
19th Palomar — Election of Conference Delegates
26th Goodbye

Theme, Carlyle: "How were friendships possible?
Through mutual devotedness to the good and true."

Other activities of Girl Reserves, selected from reports are:

> Assisting at registration
> Locker and hall duty
> Acting as hostesses
> Coaching weaker students
> Welfare activities
> Foreign missions activities
> Traffic and lunch room duty
> Care of hospital room
> Supervision of playground
> Problems of boy and girl relationships
> Settling difficulties over nationalities
> Encouraging worthy ideals of fair play
> Discouraging cribbing
> Caring for younger children
> Welcoming new students
> Various religious activities
> Assembly programs
> Vocational and other conferences
> Holiday celebrations
> Start student loan fund
> Recreational activities
> Conducting hikes, trips, and excursions
> Social activities [1]

THE HI-Y MOVEMENT

The Hi-Y is a Christian movement of high school boys fostered by the Young Men's Christian Association. Local branches are usually known as " Hi-Y Clubs " and the national organization in the United States is referred to as the " Hi-Y Movement." There are now (1926) more than 2000 of these clubs in the United States with a total membership of more than 60,000 boys.

Membership. — Membership in the Hi-Y is open to mature students, generally of the junior and senior classes of the high

---

[1] Information, materials, books, and other supplies may be obtained from the Girl Reserve Department, National Board of the Young Women's Christian Association, 600 Lexington Avenue, New York City.

school. Membership is not restricted to members of the Young Men's Christian Association or to any religious creed, but to those who subscribe to the purpose and objective of the club. A similar organization for the freshmen and sophomores and for the junior high school boys under the name of Junior Hi-Y is also available. In schools where racial groups that are not potentially Christian exist in large numbers, additional chapters are organized, similar to the Hi-Y, among boys of these groups and federated with the Hi-Y in what are known as " Character Clubs." By this means the campaigns and activities for general helpfulness are conducted jointly, while at the same time the various religious interests are conserved.

Description.—*The Purpose:* " To create, maintain, and extend throughout the school and community high standards of Christian character."

The Slogan: " Clean living, clean speech, clean athletics, clean scholarship."

The Dynamic: " Contagious Christian character."

The Objective: " Health betterment; mind acquirement; soul enlargement; social advancement; and service achievement."

Organization. — The genius of the Hi-Y lies in its adaptability to all types of high schools and situations. This is because it is more a spirit than an organization. Local autonomy, local control, and local adaptions are the guiding principles.

Advisory Council. — A group of three or four men generally stimulate and guide the organization. A secretary from a city or county Y.M.C.A. is usually responsible for supplying the expert counsel needed. He joins with himself either the principal of the school or one or more members of the faculty of the school, one of whom becomes the " faculty adviser," and some leading Christian layman of the community all of whom are willing to give the organization of their time and leadership. Thus it will be seen that an advisory council is made up of five or seven men who are willing to accept general supervision of the work of the local club. The president of the club is often added as a member ex-officio of the advisory council.

Dynamic Group or Inner Circle. — The " Inner Circle " is a cabinet made up for the purpose of influencing high school boys through the instrumentality of a small group of consecrated, virile, active, and genuine boy leaders. This group is usually started by the selection of one or two boys by the Advisory Council and the gradual addition of other members as these seem to be available. It is under the leadership of a competent teacher, committeeman, or pastor appointed by the Association or by the Advisory Council. Its programs consist of devotionals and discussions for the further development of the Hi-Y and its activities.

Officers. — The usual officers are elected by the Club.

Committees. — The number and names of committees are left entirely to local discretion. Executive, Bible Study, Service, and Membership are the committees most commonly used.

Activities. — The program of the Hi-Y is suggested by the following activities :

1. *Bible Study.* — Formerly Bible Study was conducted largely as an information getting procedure and regular courses and diplomas were given for the completion of these courses. The point of emphasis has changed, however, so that now Bible Study and Life Problem discussions center around the interests and purposes of the club.

2. *Campaigns with talks and help from outside.* —
   High standards of scholarship
   Clean speech, clean living, clean athletics
   College and university education
   The campaign of friendship
   Anti-cigarette campaign
   Grade school campaign

Join the Sunday School or Church
Earn and give
No crib, no copy
Stick to school

3. *Life Work Problems.* — Vocational guidance and education
Fundamental principles in the choice of a life work
How I may know for what I am fitted
The requirements, preparation, opportunity, work, and rewards of a lawyer, physician, minister, teacher, and business man
The boy who must leave school to work
The boy who is going to college or university

4. *Topic Discussions.* — Good sportsmanship; appreciation; good manners; doing my best; practical Christianity; procrastination; school standards; smut; giving and taking; friendship; and citizenship; What is a man?

5. *Unselfish Tasks.* — Coach younger boys
Conduct outings or hikes
Tutor backward students
Lead various study groups
Teach English to foreigners
Conduct clubs or socials
Provide music, teach classes
Form and lead reading groups
Conduct observation trips
Assist playground and gym leaders
Plan Father and Son banquet
Raise money for worthy objects
Urge grammar graduates to high school
Various church activities
Serve on welfare activities
Make posters, signs, and charts

6. *Camps, Conferences, and Institutes.* — Many states have summer camps with suitable physical, religious, and educational activities. Older Boys' Conferences are popular.[1]

---

[1] Information regarding the development of Hi-Y Clubs, books, and supplies may be obtained from the National Director for Work with High School Boys, the National Council of Young Men's Christian Association at 347 Madison Avenue, New York.

Dangers. — A few possible dangers of this organization need to be pointed out. In the first place there is a danger that the organization may develop into a secret order or fraternity. This is especially true if its members are elected to membership; if meetings are held at night; if these meetings are held in the Y.M.C.A. or other building than the school; and if an elaborate ritual is used.

A second danger is due to a too narrow interpretation of the term " Christian " with resulting friction with religious groups or denominations. There has been some trouble in schools along this line. There need not be. The author was once leader of a group which had a Catholic boy as its president and a Jewish boy as its treasurer.

A third danger is that friction may develop between the school and the Association authorities. The school administrator is properly jealous of his rights as head of the school. He is responsible for everything that goes on in or about the school and naturally hesitates to divide responsibility. The association must clearly recognize this responsibility.

These dangers are possible and it is the duty of those in charge to avoid them. If the organization becomes undemocratic or exclusive, or if it creates friction between the school and the Association, it had better be abolished. Its purposes and general organization are sound, but like anything else it must be developed slowly by individuals capable of seeing the school program of activities in proper relationship and perspective.

THE JUNIOR RED CROSS

The Junior Red Cross is an organization of elementary and secondary schools in 42 countries. In the United States there are approximately 5,200,000 members and 150,000 teachers coöperating in the program.

Purpose. — The outstanding aim of the organization is to develop the spirit of service and an attitude of world friendship among the children and young people throughout the world. One of the best definitions of the purpose or aim of the Junior Red Cross was formulated at an educators' conference called by the League of the Red Cross Societies in Paris, July, 1925:

The Junior Red Cross is a voluntary organization through which children and young people find opportunities for self-expression; the motive which it brings to any classroom appeals to the imagination and will of children in such a way as to transmute knowledge into action; this motive is being especially used by those who are directing the movement, to promote health, to develop the altruistic tendencies in children, to give practice in good citizenship and to promote international friendliness among the children of the world; it is not a method of education, or health education, but it is a free spirit which quickens the life of the whole school in which it is organized.

Organization and administration. — The general organization of the Junior Red Cross is flexible enough to fit local situations of any character. Usually, though not necessarily, this organization operates in an entire system of city or county schools.

Adult committee. — A committee of adults, made up jointly of school people and citizens of the community who are familiar with and sympathetic with both educational aims and the ideals of the Red Cross, assumes the responsibility of the work. The work is frequently directed by a Junior Red Cross chairman, or executive secretary, who takes charge of the details, saving the time of school officials and teachers. The administration within the school is, of course, under the direct over-sight of the school officials concerned.

Junior Red Cross council. — Usually a Junior Red Cross council composed of student members is organized in each school. This council may be a sub-committee of the student council, an especially appointed, or an elective body composed of one or more representatives from each room. In a system of several schools, a city students' council in which there are representatives from all the enrolled schools of the city is frequently organized. In these council meetings the students pass upon suggestions made to them concerning services, carry back messages to their schools, bring reports of what has been done in other schools, and in other ways plan with the help and encouragement of the adult committee a constructive program of service.

Activities. — The Junior Red Cross organization offers fine opportunities for the utilization of school work and school activities for service purposes. There are opportunities for all grades, subjects, and interests. History, geography, nature study, civics, English, current events, modern foreign language, handwork, drawing and other subjects may be used to promote world understanding and friendship through the preparation of group letters and illustrative material interpreting our schools and country, to be sent to students of other lands. Correspondence from students of other lands, similarly interpreting their lives, supplements textbook material, and gives a sense of personal acquaintance and interest.

The *Junior Red Cross News* and *High School Service*, magazines issued to elementary and high schools respectively, publish material received through this system of international correspondence and from other sources, thus giving all enrolled schools the benefit of much more than they receive through their own correspondence alone. Reports of service activities among students of our country and other countries not only stimulate to new ideas for service, but give a sense of membership in a great world-wide organization. This and other material published is suitable for use in the classroom and is interesting for voluntary reading outside the class. There are similar publications for Junior Red Cross members in approximately twenty countries. These magazines and materials from them are also made available for modern language classes.

Typical projects in which all grades take part. — Entertainments prepared for assembly, for music, literary, or dramatic groups may be repeated as entertainments in hospitals, in old people's homes, or children's institutions.

Civic study is applied in service, through the participation in patriotic or community celebrations, help in " clean-up " campaigns, assistance with programs in foreign quarters, etc.

Thrift activities may be used to develop ideals of the service values of work and of money received for service. Money donated to the Service Fund maintained by Junior Red Cross auxiliaries must be earned through service or saved through sacrifice, as well as spent in service for the community, the nation, or the world.

First Aid, Life Saving, Home Hygiene, and Care of the Sick are studied in order to render service in times of need. Health activities are carried on in order to be more " fit for service." Health posters, health plays, newspapers, and other publicity are means of spreading the good news of health.

Each year thousands of boxes of Christmas gifts are packed for children of other countries who would not receive Christmas gifts. Christmas stockings are filled for disabled veterans throughout the United States.

Some opportunities for various grades. — In the primary grades cutting activities may be used for service ends. Chains, cut-outs, and transparencies may be sent as decorations or made into picture books or scrapbooks for entertainment in veterans' hospitals, old people's homes, and children's institutions.

In the intermediate grades, drawing, basketry, other handwork, and language study are utilized for service, through making tray decorations and favors or greetings cards for special days, calendars and blotters, joke books, woven mats, and other gifts for veterans' hospitals, old people's homes, children's homes, and individual shut-ins.

In the junior and senior high school, manual training, wood-work, shop, sewing, cooking, and other subjects are used for service in the making of writing boards, bedtables, lamp stands, magazine and book racks, laundry bags, neckties, candy, jelly, jam, and other comforts or treats for hospital patients. Layettes and rompers, and re-made garments are prepared for use in disasters of Europe where children are in need.

Service fund. — For the sake of broader usefulness, there is usually a Junior Red Cross Service Fund made up of contributions earned by members through the performance of service or by personal sacrifice. The funds may not be spent without the approval of the Red Cross Chapter, which acts upon the advice of the school committee. Officials in each school and the children themselves have an important voice in deciding how the funds shall be expended. Through the maintenance of such a service fund children in all enrolled schools are enabled to participate in national and international service enterprises.[1]

Boy Scouts

" The Boy Scout movement is a program of character building, of citizen development, leisure-time activities for boys. It is educational as well as recreational. It is vocationally purposeful. Its tasks are within a lad's reach and his progress at once challenges him though going at his own rate of speed. It is concerned with a lad's health and it prepares him to be resourceful in the out of doors. It trains the lad to accept responsibility not only for the assigned task but for the unexpected emergency. It brings the spirit of the Good Turn."

This quotation from " Community Boy Leadership " shows in brief the spirit and purpose of the Boy Scout movement. Although only a few years old this movement is now found in nearly

[1] Magazines, bulletins, and other material may be obtained from the American Red Cross, National Headquarters, Washington, D.C.

every country in the world. It was introduced into the United States only seventeen years ago, but now there are over 100,000 adult volunteer scout workers and well over half a million scouts enrolled in it.

Organization and administration. — The working unit of Scouting is the Troop, which is made up of not more than four Patrols each of which is composed of eight boys, including a Patrol Leader and an Assistant Patrol Leader.

The Scout Master is the leader of the troop. He is a man at least twenty-one years of age, chosen because of his good moral character and his interest and ability in boy's work. He is commissioned by the National Council upon recommendation of the Troop Committee. The Troop Committee is a small committee of men which supports the troop. This committee may be selected or appointed by the church, school, community house, or other organization responsible for the troop.

Where there are three or more troops scout work is controlled and supervised under the direction of the Local Council. This council represents the religious, educational, business, and civic interests of the community. The Local Council is responsible for the selection of the commissioned officers of scouting for the community. Scout Executives on full time and pay develop scouting in the city, country, or district, depending upon the type of organization. Commissioners or volunteer workers also assist in the development of scouting in the community. These officers represent what might be called the central or general office.

The United States is divided up into " Regional Districts " and over each district is a full-time Executive. At the top of the organization is the National Council made up of representatives from local councils and such others as are elected by the various agencies of boy workers. The President and ex-Presidents of the United States, governors, and other men of significance compose this council. The Chief Scout Executive, James

E. West, and his staff maintain national headquarters in New York City. Publications, bulletins, magazines, material of all sorts, charters, and commissions are handled through this office.

Method of scouting. — The scout method is "DO" rather than "READ ABOUT." The scout learns the principles by reading, listening to lectures, and by watching demonstrations; but he learns the activities themselves by actually practicing and doing them. A very carefully worked out plan of gradation and promotion, each phase with peculiar and suitable recognition by means of awards or honors, provides incentives for the boy to desire to make progress in the work. The activities are varied enough to appeal to all boys, and they are also so numerous that few boys would ever complete all of them.

Ranks of scouting. — There are three basic ranks in scouting — Tenderfoot, Second Class, and First Class, each of which has its appropriate work, activities, symbols, insignia, awards, and honors. When the scout has accomplished these ranks he may continue by winning Merit Badges and the winning of certain numbers and types of these badges entitles him to further rank and honor as Life, Star, and Eagle Scout.

Description. — *The Scout Oath.*

The Scout Oath: On My Honor I Will Do My Best
1. To do my duty to God and my country, and to obey the scout law
2. To help other people at all times
3. To keep myself physically strong, mentally awake, and morally straight.

The Scout Law:
1. A Scout is trustworthy
2. A Scout is loyal
3. A Scout is helpful
4. A Scout is friendly
5. A Scout is courteous
6. A Scout is kind
7. A Scout is obedient

8. A Scout is cheerful
9. A Scout is thrifty
10. A Scout is brave
11. A Scout is clean
12. A Scout is reverent

The Scout Motto: Be Prepared

The Scout Slogan: Do a Good Turn Daily

Merit badges.—After the boy has become a First Class Scout, he is eligible to qualify for all the various merit badges. These badges are given for projects and work with particular interests. The Scout, after passing an examination given by some one qualified to give it, is formally examined by a Court of Honor, or accepted by it as having passed the tests, and given the proper certificate and badge.

Scout policies. — The Boy Scout organization is non-sectarian, non-political, and non-commercial. The division into patrols and troops is for purpose of drill for developing unity, harmony, rhythm, and to instill such virtues as honor, obedience, loyalty, and patriotism. The uniform not only makes for uniformity, but is also most suitable for hiking and outdoor activities. All races and creeds are represented in scouting. The constitution and by-laws forbid involving scouts in any question of political character. No troop can be connected with business dealings, it can not solicit money, and no scout may work for pay while in uniform.

Scout program. — The scout program is educationally sound. In the first place, its activities appeal to the boy; in the second place, it capitalizes the " gang instinct " by its organization; in the third place, its activities are standardized with regular advancements and definite requirements for each rank; in the fourth place, its activities dove-tail with its ideals; and in the fifth place, the supervision is in the hands of male, adult, volunteer leaders.

Scouting and the public school. — *Reasons for relationship with public school.* — Scouting has become linked up with the public schools in a very definite relationship in many places in the United States. This is a reasonable development which promises much in the future. In the first place the scout program of activities provides for motivation and enrichment of the student and his work through the various badge awards (A merit badge in Scholarship is now awarded for work done in the school); the Scout Law is a sound basis for good citizenship as desired by the school; and the many occupations of scouting furnish both material and skill in the training for wise use of leisure.

In the second place, it seems logical that scouting should be fostered by the school because the school is the one organization to which all the boys of the community belong. They do not all belong to one or all of the churches, nor to the settlements, clubs, or other organizations which may offer opportunities for scouting connections. But they do all go to school and here then is fine opportunity for making available to them the educational and recreational possibilities of scouting.

In the third place, the school usually has good facilities for scouting activities. Churches and other places are frequently not equipped suitably for scouting meetings and activities. The school with its rooms, gymnasium, playground, auditorium, and swimming pool is much better equipped for this work.

In the fourth place, educated leadership is usually available in the school. The teachers may not all be scoutmasters but may serve on committees and councils and in other ways encourage and help to develop the program.

A Committee on Boy Scouts and Public Schools was organized at the Atlantic City Meeting, Department of Superintendence of the National Education Association, March 4, 1921. The purpose of this committee was " To study the Present and Future

Relationships of Boy Scouts and the Public Schools." In the *First Report* (1922), the committee stated:

That the committee is not alone in its belief that scouting is a very important asset to public schools is indicated by the practically unanimous approval o the superintendents who answered the questionnaire. Concerning the advisability of coöperation between the public school and the Boy Scouts there seems complete agreement.

There is enough material at hand to affirm that it is desirable for school officials, including boards of education, superintendents, principals, and teachers to share in scouting activities, not necessarily as executives, but on committees of the councils.

This committee sent out a questionnaire in 1922 concerning the relationship of scouting and the public school to 612 Scout executives and commissioners. Replies representing 325 different communities in forty-five states, the District of Columbia, and Hawaii were received. A few of the most significant findings as reported in the *Third Report* of the committee are as follows:

Use of school property. — In 72% of the communities the school building is used for regular meetings of scouts; in 80% for occasional meetings; in approximately 28% for storing paraphernalia; and in 7% the building is being used as a permanent headquarters. In 92% of the cases no charge is being made for this use of school property. The board of education of New York City recently voted $10,000 to be used to defray such expenses.

School coöperation in scouting. — About 80% of the replies stated that the schools actively encouraged membership in the Boy Scouts, and in about one third of the 325 communities there were troops made up entirely of school students.

Coöperation in personal service. — Further evidence of coöperation is shown by the fact that 90% of the communities responding are represented on the local council by teacher or principals of the public schools and in 77% of these communities the faculty is represented on Troop committees. In addition to these many other teachers, principals, and school authorities serve on courts of honor, in merit badge work, and other ways. In at least twelve of the communities members of the scouting staff are paid a part or all of their salary out of school funds; while twenty-three more are paid out of " public funds."

Educational coöperation. — In nearly all of the communities training courses for scout masters are maintained by the school system. School officials give volunteer service in about 45% of these instances. Scout work is recognized by school authorities definitely by credit awards, etc. in about 12% of the cases. For instance, Chippewa County (Michigan) High School, Hammond (Indiana), St. Joseph, and other schools allow one half credit for scouting. Mount Pleasant, Texas, gives one credit to an Eagle Scout; Beaumont, Texas; Beloit, Wisconsin; Birmingham, Alabama; Detroit and others allow credit given for merit badge work. Du Bois, Pennsylvania; San Diego, California; Johnstown, Pennsylvania; Okmulgee, Oklahoma, and others allow scouting activities to be given and taken during school hours. Correlation of scouting with school work in the form of field trips and dramatization in science, geography, in industrial, historical, and nature study is frequently made. Other means of coöperation include reading of notices, furnishing of equipment and printing of stationery for the scouts, while ushering, guiding, first aid, and other services are performed for the school by the scouts.

The purposes and values and methods of scouting are being increasingly recognized by school authorities. Scouting can be made a most important part of the life of the school. Its purposes and values are worthy and its methods are sound. However, the school must not formalize it and this is the danger in including it in the regular " curricular " schedule. Giving credit for scout work may demand more of formalization than is consistent with the general purposes, ideals, and methods of the organization.

The program has been called a "work program of organized play" and in order to retain the interests of the members it must remain such. But the wealth of personnel and material conveniences of the school may well be mobilized in the interests of this organization, and consequently in the interests of good citizenship.[1]

GIRL SCOUTS

Girl Scouts, an organization or movement in many respects similar to Boy Scouts, was originated and developed in England by Sir Robert Baden-Powell, the Father of Scouting, and Lady Powell. Mrs. Julie Tetlow, an American friend visiting the Baden-Powells, saw the wonderful possibilities of the movement, and with their help and coöperation founded the Girl Guides in America, enrolling the first patrols at Savannah, Georgia, in 1912. In 1915, National Headquarters were established at Washington, D. C., and the name was changed to Girl Scouts. The following year headquarters were moved to New York City. From the small beginning at Savannah, the movement has developed until in 1925 there were enrolled 120,000 Girl Scouts and 3500 Brownies (junior organization), supervised by 10,000 commissioned officers.

Purpose. — The purpose of Girl Scouts is to occupy the mind and time of the adolescent girl by teaching her through play the elements of home making, of building a strong body, and of becoming a good citizen.

Organization. — *The Patrol.* — The Patrol consists of eight girls. Each Patrol elects from its members a Patrol Leader who represents it and who has certain responsibilities in the work. The Corporal is an assistant Patrol Leader.

[1] The various material and supplies, handbooks and bulletins, as well as other interesting and suggestive literature, may be obtained from National Headquarters, Boy Scouts of America, 200 Fifth Avenue, New York City.

The troop. — From one to four patrols constitute a Troop, the administrative unit of the organization. Each Troop may own a flag and chooses from a list of flowers, trees, birds, etc., its crest and title. The leader of the Troop is the Captain, a woman at least twenty-one years of age, officially commissioned by National Headquarters. A Lieutenant and occasionally a Second Lieutenant are commissioned as assistants to the Captain. The Court of Honor, a committee of adults, backs the Troop and acts as its executive committee.

Council. — The Council is the local organization of interested public-spirited citizens who stand behind the Girl Scout program. In the larger cities Local Directors give full time to the promotion and supervision of Scouting activities.

National organization. — The Central and final governing body is the National Council which is made up of delegates elected from all local groups throughout the country. The National Executive Board maintains its headquarters in New York City, where the National Director has charge of the general work of the Field, Business, Publication, Education, Camping, Equipment, Registration, Research, and Accounting Departments.

Membership and ranks. — There are three ranks of Girl Scout membership: Tenderfoot, Second Class, and First Class. Before the girl is allowed to enroll as a Tenderfoot she must have attained her tenth birthday; have attended at least four meetings covering at least a month of time, and must understand the Pledge of Allegiance, Scout Promise, and Scout Laws.

Description. —

Motto:	Be prepared
Slogan:	Do a good turn daily
Pledge:	I pledge allegiance to the flag of the United States of America and to the Republic for which it stands; one nation indivisible, with liberty and justice for all.

Promise: On my honor I will try:
> To do my duty to God and my country
> To help other people at all times
> To obey the Scout Laws

Scout Laws:

1. A Girl Scout's honor is to be trusted
2. A Girl Scout is loyal
3. A Girl Scout's duty is to be useful and to help others
4. A Girl Scout is a friend to all and a sister to every other girl scout
5. A Girl Scout is courteous
6. A Girl Scout is a friend to animals
7. A Girl Scout obeys orders
8. A Girl Scout is cheerful
9. A Girl Scout is thrifty
10. A Girl Scout is clean in thought, word, and deed

Merit badges. — After the girl has attained the rank of Second Class Scout she is eligible to work for Merit Badges. About sixty of these badges are now available. The tests of proficiency are given by members of the Court of Honor, qualified teachers, or other individuals. The badges are awarded by the Court of Honor. Group badges are given for Scout Neighbor, Scout Aide, Woodcraft Scout, Scout Naturalist, and Land Scout, for winning certain badges under each of these headings. The " Golden Eaglet," a gold eaglet pin or pendant, is awarded to girls who have won twenty-one proficiency badges of which fifteen are specified. It is the highest award offered by Girl Scouts. To December, 1925, only 770 girls in the United States had won it.

During 1925 Girl Scouts earned 73,786 badges. Of these 26548 related to home making; 15,258 to health and the care of young children; 8862 to nature study, camping, and outdoor life; 6122 to games, sports, and other physical activities; 4949 to languages, journalism, and clerical and practical skills; 4898 to the various arts; 3641 to scholarship (high standing in school); and 3508 to civic activities.

Girl scouts and the public schools. — In the previous section on Boy Scouts, it was suggested that the school is a most logical place for a community relationship with scouting because of the relationship of the child with the school and also because of the personnel and facilities available. This also holds true for Girl Scouts, and the fact that in many communities there is a close relationship between scouting and the school proves not only that this connection is possible, but that it is successful. Girl Scout councils reported on this relationship for the first time in 1924 when this topic was included in the new annual report form. The following table shows the figures from the returns of 63% of the active councils for 1924. These figures do not include the smaller communities which have no councils. The figures are urban but informal reports suggest that scouting may be even more popular in the smaller communities in which there are usually fewer competing interests and fewer similar organizations.

TABLE V

THE TOTAL NUMBER OF PUBLIC SCHOOLS REPORTED BY 157 GIRL SCOUT COUN-
CILS IN THEIR TERRITORIES AND THE NUMBER ACTIVELY COÖPERATING
WITH GIRL SCOUTS

	TOTAL NUMBER OF SCHOOLS REPRESENTED	NUMBER ACTIVELY COÖPERATING	PERCENTAGES
Elementary . .	3894	727	18.7
Junior High . .	265	134	50.6
Senior High . .	371	128	34.5
Vocational . . .	131	25	19.1
Total	4661	1014	21.7

One hundred and fifteen councils reported on the details of coöperation. These specific acts of coöperation or encouragement may be classified under several headings.

1. *Promotion and Publicity:* Scouting as a school club activity; special periods for Scout work; school credit; use of bulletin board; publications; assemblies, and library space.

2. *Use of School Buildings:* Use of auditoriums, gymnasiums, and pools.

3. *Teacher Participation:* Usually leaders of troops or examiners for merit badges. Occasionally excused from other duties to perform these.

4. *Curriculum Recognition:* Information given to students concerning "scholarship badge" awarded for school standing; lists compiled of merit badge subjects covered in school classes.

5. *Privileges Accorded Girl Scouts:* Taking care of assemblies; excused early for public gatherings; allowed to go on important Scout duty during school hours.

6. *Financial Assistance:* Help in conducting financial campaigns; donations and loans of camp material and equipment, office equipment and supplies; printing, occasionally office provided or part of salary of director paid.

In conclusion it may be pointed out that while the most obvious relations between the Girl Scouts and the schools are along the lines of subject matter and the badge for school scholarship, and while school interest frequently begins with the providing of teachers as examiners for merit badges, the developments are in the direction of a fuller recognition of the part played by Girl Scouts and similar programs in the growth of the girl from childhood to womanhood and the educational value of such happy and creative use of her leisure time.[1]

Camp Fire Girls

Another great " character building program of fun " is that of the Camp Fire Girls. The work and ideals of the Camp Fire Girls had its direct origin in the home and later in " Wohelo," the private camp of Dr. and Mrs. Luther H. Gulick on Lake Sebago, Maine. Here for a number of years Dr. and Mrs. Gulick,

[1] Material for Girl Scout work may be obtained from National Headquarters, 670 Lexington Avenue, New York City.

with the desire to meet the needs of their daughters and their daughters' friends, worked out the beginning of what was later, with some modifications, accepted as the ritual and form of the Camp Fire Girls. The "birthday" of this organization was March 17, 1912. As in the case of Girl Scouts and Boy Scouts, Camp Fire is a movement, a program of activities for adolescents, and not an organization. It, too, has had a rapid growth and its popularity as an extracurricular activity is evidenced by the large number of Camp Fires found in public, private, and parochial schools.

Purpose. — The purpose of a Camp Fire is " To find romance, beauty, and adventure in the everyday things of life."

Method. — The method of Camp Fire is similar to that of the other two great organizations discussed in this chapter — that of *doing*. Its basis is in learning, but its method is one which emphasizes habit building through action. The three ranks of Camp Fire, the use of few required and many elective " honors," the awarding of beads for work well done, the use of a variety of activities, its symbolism, and the fact that it is a national organization — all help to make it attractive to the adolescent girl.

Symbolism gives the color and design to Camp Fire. It is founded on Indian symbolism but this has been expanded and beautified. Each girl finds a name for herself which expresses her ideal or ambition. She chooses and designs a symbol which she works into her headband. She weaves her deeds, desires, and dreams into more symbols on her ceremonial gown. In short, she tries to express herself in and through the activities of Camp Fire. To think that Camp Fire is an organization which teaches the girl to " play Indian " is as absurd as to suppose that Masons do nothing but build walls, or that Knights of Columbus spend their time in discovering new worlds.

Organization. — The basic organization is the Camp Fire or local unit composed of from 6 to 20 girls over eleven years of age, supervised by the Guardian, a woman at least eighteen years of age. This unit holds a charter from National Headquarters and has a direct relationship to it. In the larger cities where there are a number of Camp Fires a local Executive is appointed to supervise the work of the city. There are now fifty-two of these executives in the United States.

Basis. — The foundation of the Camp Fire is the home. Fire, the symbol of the home and hearth, appears in the name of the organization, in the symbols of the three ranks, and is the center about which the meetings of the group are held. Camp Fire dignifies and makes interesting the work of the home. More than 700 " honors " are listed in the Camp Fire Girl's *Manual* and all of these pertain to the activities in or about the home.

Description. — *Slogan.* — The slogan of the organization is " Give Service."

Law. — The law of the Camp Fire is

1. Seek Beauty
2. Give Service
3. Pursue Knowledge
4. Be Trustworthy
5. Hold on to Health
6. Glorify Work
7. Be Happy

Desires. — In each rank is to be found an expression of the ideals of the organization, a " Desire." The " Desire " of the first rank, woodgatherer, is as follows :

" As fagots are brought from the forest firmly held by the sinews which bind them, I will cleave to my Camp Fire sisters wherever, whenever, I find them. I will strive to grow strong like the pine tree, to be pure in my deepest desire ; to be true to the truth that is in me, and follow the law of the Fire."

Watch word. — The Watch Word is " Wohelo " made from the first two letters of the words, " work," " health," and " love."

Hand sign. — The hand sign of fire is made by crossing the fingers in front of the body (indicating crossed logs) at about the waist line. From this position the right hand is quickly raised, directly upward and following the course of an imaginary flame. As the hand rises the three fingers drop into an easy position against the thumb leaving the index finger pointing upward.

Ranks. — The three ranks of Camp Fire are " Woodgatherer," " Fire Maker," and " Torch Bearer." Rank is won by the winning of " Honors." Appropriate insignia go with each rank.

Meetings. — Regular meetings are held to help the girls formulate their daily work, and to teach new activities towards the winning of honors, and to keep up to date and illustrate the *Count Book* (record book). Often these meetings are held in conjunction with a hike or other trip. Ceremonial meetings are held monthly. At these meetings a ritual is used, the Count is read, Honors are awarded, ranks are conferred, and new members are received.

Honors. — The main activities of the Camp Fire center around the winning of Honors. These Honors are tasks grouped under seven Crafts. An Honor Bead is awarded for each Honor won, a different color for each Craft. Purple beads are awarded for the required Honors of each rank. The Crafts and beads are as follows :

Home Craft	orange	(flame)
Health Craft	red	(blood)
Camp Craft	brown	(woods)
Hand Craft	green	(nature)
Nature Craft	blue	(sky)
Business Craft	yellow	(gold)
Patriotism ⎫ Citizenship ⎭	red, white, and blue	

"Big Honors " are large beads awarded for the winning of from 8 to 15 of the smaller Honors. " Local Honors " may be awarded for special work of value and importance locally. "National Honors" are awarded for significant contributions of songs, stunts, plays, poems, photography, etc.

Camp Fire and the schools. — The possibilities of close tie-up between Camp Fire activities and the regular work of the school may easily be seen. The music teacher, the teacher of physical education, the domestic science and domestic art teachers, those in charge of dramatics, nature study, and others will find in the activities of a typical program an extra motivation for school work, and a correlation between those things which the girl learns in school as part of the school routine and the things which she does outside of school for the fun of it. This relationship is another way of saying " applied education."

In order to suggest what is actually being done in relating Camp Fire work to the school, the following data are presented. These data refer only to Camp Fire groups within the school and not to those outside it. Only enough will be presented to indicate practices. Much more could be presented.

Seattle: Camp Fire groups are organized in twenty-nine elementary and in eight high schools. These groups enroll 1250 members. Each Parent Teacher Association group has a Camp Fire Chairman who finds Guardians and works to interest women in becoming Guardians. Many of the schools have a Camp Fire room used every day of the week for Camp Fire meetings. Camp Fire and Boy Scouts were the only organizations permitted to go into the schools to organize.

Grand Rapids: Camp Fire groups are to be found in thirty-six elementary and six junior-senior high schools. Nearly nine hundred students are members and thirty-two teachers participate in these activities.

Minneapolis: Thirteen groups, five each in the elementary and junior high schools, and three in the senior high schools are organized in the public schools. All groups meet in school buildings, receiving regular permits from the Board for these meetings.

Greely: In the counties of Adams, Boulder, Larimer, Morgan, Weld, Washington, and Logan, Camp Fire groups are to be found in twelve elementary schools, twenty-one junior high and eighteen senior high schools.

These fifty-one groups have a membership of 681 girls.   Forty Guardians and fourteen Assistant Guardians are teachers in these schools.

Oakland: Camp Fire groups are organized in twenty eight of the schools. In many instances this work is counted towards the "Big Letter" earned in student affairs.   The girls assist on the playground, school affairs, act as messengers, usher, help to beautify school grounds, etc.

Kansas City: In thirty-eight schools are to be found fifty groups with a total membership of 700 students.   Thirty-nine of these groups are under teacher Guardians.   Most groups meet at the school, those in the junior high schools having regular activity periods for their meetings.

Atlanta: Twenty-three schools have Camp Fire groups.

Sacramento: In several schools the Camp Fire groups take charge of the assembly program during "Birthday Week."   At Stanford junior high school an activity period of forty minutes is given over each week to Boy Scouts, Girl Scouts, and Camp Fire Girls.   Each semester the Camp Fire Girls give a luncheon for the teachers, afterwards holding a ceremonial. They have charge of flowers for the entire school.   They hold an assembly each semester.   A special "Stanford Honor" is given for very good work.

The following quotation from a letter from an executive concerning the attitude taken by the public school authorities at Kansas City is typical :

The School Board is ready to help Camp Fire in any way possible by giving us the use of the buildings, auditoriums, and gymnasiums, and school equipment any time we want them, if it does not interfere with the Principal's plans or school activities.   By giving us permission with the coöperation of the principals to talk to assemblies each fall and present our program ; by giving the groups a room in which to hold their weekly meetings.   To my knowledge we have never been turned down yet by the School Board for anything we have asked, and we use the schools in some way nearly every day.

Another way to judge the popularity of the Camp Fire movement with educators is to consider the number of teacher-training institutions giving courses for the training of Guardians.   During 1925 such courses were in more than thirty-five universities, colleges, and normal schools, including seven state universities. For instance, the Colorado State Teachers College at Greely,

Colorado, has as a regular part of its curriculum five elementary and four advanced training classes for Camp Fire Leaders, the average yearly membership of which for the past eight years has been between 350 and 400 teachers. College credit towards graduation is given for successful completion of each course, and Training Course Certificates are issued by the National Headquarters of Camp Fire. These courses are elective.[1]

SUMMARY

Supplementary organizations of national scope may be utilized in the school to bring additional contacts and emphasis of value to the student, school, and community. The schools are recognizing these organizations more and more and making increased provision for them. There is a danger that this recognition will result in a formalization which will kill the interest of the student. The final authority and responsibility for the student groups of these organizations must rest with the school authorities.

[1] Material concerning Camp Fire may be obtained from Camp Fire Girls, Incorporated, 31 East 17th Street, New York City.

CHAPTER XXVI

MISCELLANEOUS ACTIVITIES

Not all of the activities of the modern high school can be adequately treated in one book. Nor can those which are discussed be treated as extensively as the author could wish. Consequently, it is necessary to limit and such limitation will mean that some activities be only mentioned. Those barely mentioned will be those which in the mind of the author are of the least relative importance. This judgment of relative importance of activities is based upon significance in the school and whether or not these activities belong in some other field of school life.

HEALTH

Although " health " should hardly be classified as an "extracurricular" topic, there are a number of activities in connection with it which may be easily introduced into the extracurricular program. The program suggested below is perhaps more suitable to elementary and junior high schools than to the senior high school, but some of the suggestions could be suitably followed in the senior school :

1. Visit from Cho-Cho, the Health Clown.[1]
2. Homeroom, assembly, and classroom discussion of such topics as:

Clothing	Common diseases	Food inspection
Food, cooking	Home sanitation	Prevention *vs.* cure
Ventilation	Community health	Eyes, ears, nose, and throat
Sleep	Flies, mosquitoes,	Health heroes
Water	and vermin	
Colds	Child Labor laws	

[1] Arrangements can be made through the American Child Health Association.

3. Record cards. Some schools report on matters of health as regularly as on matters of academic excellence. Such reports or inspections might include personal appearance, health, cleanliness, tidiness, suitability of clothing, completeness of attire, posture, rouge and makeup, and smoking.

4. Campaigns. Use of newspaper and other publicity; posters, tags, competitions, programs, dramatics, and pageants.

5. Development of sets of health slogans, rules, mottoes, and quotations.

6. Inspections by students and teacher. Under direction of sanitation squad, inspecting hands, teeth, nails, hair, and posture.

7. Contests. Poster; health poetry; health songs; scenarios.

8. Health questionnaire. May be used by both students and parents.

9. Birthday examination campaign. Student thoroughly examined on his birthday.

Material for health purposes may be obtained from the following sources:

American Child Health Association New York City
American Health Association, New York City
American Red Cross, Washington, D. C.
Government Printing Office, Washington, D. C.
Metropolitan Life Insurance Company, New York City
National Child Welfare, New York City
National Health Council, New York City
National Tubercular Association, New York City
United States Bureau of Education, Washington, D. C.
United States Department of Agriculture, Washington, D. C.
United States Department of Labor, Washington, D. C.

MOTION PICTURES

Motion pictures are coming to play a more and more important part in the school, in both curricular and extracurricular activities. There are three ways in which they are used. In the first place, the school may provide films for the students at noon, recess, or at other times during the day for more or less purely recreational purposes. If there is a long noon recess, and dancing or other recreation is not provided during bad weather, films may be shown in the auditorium. Or the school may show a good picture about once a month, usually on a Friday afternoon. A small fee of ten cents is charged to help cover expense, and the performance is then repeated at night for parents or patrons at higher prices. The third use for pictures is in connection with a campaign, drive, or other special occasion. Many films suitable for safety, vocational, food, and other campaigns are now available.

The school will have little success in competing with the local theaters, and should not attempt it as a regular policy. The pictures shown should be of a high class and more of an educational and less of a sentimental type than those usually shown in the theater. The theater, because of larger patronage, better equipment, and accessibility to " first runs " can be more successful with the picture than the high school. Consequently, the school will have more success running the more or less educational films, dramatizations of famous literature, scientific and industrial processes, historical events or episodes and travel films, rather than those on sentimental themes.

Material and information may be obtained from the following sources :

A Guide of the Study, Sources and Materials of Educational Motion Pictures, National Child Welfare Association, Inc., 70 Fifth Ave., New York City.

Bureau of Education, Department of the Interior, Washington, D. C.

Daypho-Bray Library of Films, Bray Productions, Inc., 130 W. 46th St., New York City.

Department of Agriculture, Washington, D. C.

Keystone View Company, Meadville, Pa.

Lectures and Sermons, Underwood and Underwood, 517 Fifth Ave., New York City.

List of Films, Educational Screen, Chicago.

List of Health Films, National Health Council, 370 Seventh Ave., New York City.

Loose-leaf Current Motion Picture Bulletins, National Motion Picture League, 1819 Broadway, New York City.

Motion Picture Bureau, International Committee Y.M.C.A., New York City.

Motion Pictures for Community Needs, Boliman, Holt, & Company.

Motion Pictures in Education, Ellis and Thornborough. Thos. Y. Crowell Company, 393 Fourth Ave., New York City.

National Board of Review, 70 Fifth Ave., New York City.

School Garden Association of America, 501 Fifth Ave., New York City.

Selected Pictures, National Board of Review, 70 Fifth Ave., New York City.

BIG SISTER AND BIG BROTHER

The new student at the school is lost in a maze of new activities, rooms, students, teachers, and regulations. Little wonder that many of the students drop out of school as soon as they have attained the proper age. The brutal hazing by high school students helps to hasten this day. School administrators are beginning to realize that they are responsible for a part of the drop outs during or immediately following the freshman year and are beginning to provide for means which will help to assimilate the new student. The handbook has been suggested as an important, impersonal means of hastening healthful adjustment. A big sister or big brother movement, now very popular in the college, is another way of helping the new student get acquainted; helping him adjust himself; promoting friendliness; stimulating interest in activities and school; and providing for each new student a guardian to whom he or she can go for advice, help, or information.

Such work should be in the hands of a special committee appointed by the council, or two such committees, one for the boys and one for the girls. These committees should develop substantial plans for this important work. Such a letter as the following might be used to mobilize the thought of the school toward this worthy activity:

Pittsburgh, Pa.

Dear Miss Brown,

Do you remember when you were a Freshman? Were you completely at sea when you first came to high school? Were you bewildered and "scared"?   Help your Little Sister overcome this!   Be her really and truly Big Sister!

Be a Big Sister for the sake of your Alma Mater!   Our School is depending on *you* to express its spirit.   Do you want this spirit to be warm and friendly or cold and formal?   Our cordiality may be expressed to the new girls through

S   tay with your Little Sister through registration.
E   scort her to the Freshman Reception and other functions.
R   ender all help possible to her.
V   isit her if possible, or write to her.
I   nterest her in activities.
C   are for her as a real sister.
E   manate school spirit, service, and friendliness; it will be contagious!

If you are willing to be a Big Sister (I'm sure you are) send me your name and address by return mail, and I will send you the name of your Little Sister.

Sincerely,

Chairman, Big Sister Committee.

Special activities of the year might well include banquets, receptions, hikes, parties, picnics, teas, and socials.   Such an organization would do much to make the school a more interesting place for the new students, thereby probably reducing the percentage of failures and certainly reducing the amount of painful "lostness" which the average new student feels.[1]

CLASS ORGANIZATION

Much has been said for and against the organization of school classes.   The main arguments against organization are (1) that the classes are so large that an efficient organization cannot be made, (2) that the class will be controlled by a small group, and (3) that such an organization sets up cliques and groups within the school whose interests are frequently at variance.   On

[1] THORNE, C. W., "The Development of the Senior Guide Plan in the High School," *Educational Review* 66: 13–14, June, 1923.

the other hand, it is stated (1) that such an organization helps the student to feel placed, (2) that many matters of strictly class nature cannot be handled in any other way, (3) that the practice of exercising the powers of membership in the class or smaller unit helps to educate the student in his duties as a member of a larger unit, (4) that certain duties or services about the school can be turned over to the classes, thereby giving opportunities for service, and (5) that good use can be made of class competition. In nearly all schools at least the two upper classes are organized. Frequently the freshman and sophomore classes are not allowed to organize formally. Personally, the author can see no valid reason for not allowing the freshman and sophomore classes to organize.

In general, two types of class meetings may be held. The first is the large meeting in which all the members of the class attend and transact any business which may come up. The second is that in which a cabinet of representatives from the various class-rooms meet. These representatives discuss the matter of business and then return to their classrooms to discuss it there. Voting is done in these rooms, and the cabinet members report results to the cabinet meeting. There is something to be said for this type of meeting. More pupils will have opportunity to discuss the matter, there will be less time lost in useless discussion, and there is a smaller chance of "stampede." On the other hand, there is a danger because of the looseness of the meeting. Then, too, the spirit engendered when a large group gets together is lost in the sectioned meeting.

Class organization will mean that activities of the groups will be organized better and the work better done than if no system existed. The work will concern such matters as business, dues, funds, pins, rings, socials, parties, receptions, picnics, contests between various classes in athletics, dramatics, academic work, assembly programs, debate, music, literary and publicity matters.

In some schools certain duties are assigned or taken over by the various classes; the freshmen class, for instance, may be responsible for general " housekeeping " of buildings and grounds; the seniors with " service and ushering," etc.

STATE CONTESTS

Statewide contests in athletics, music, academic subjects, debating, speaking, agricultural, and caring for school grounds, are increasing in popularity. Some of these activities have been discussed under appropriate headings elsewhere in this book. Louisiana, Oklahoma, and several other states make great capital out of this type of contest, issuing a sizable bulletin each year containing the names of the winners, records, and the like, in addition to the rules and regulations of the various events. Such contests are usually conducted at the state university. Such a contest not only brings together schools from the various parts of the state in wholesome competition and emphasizes school activities other than athletics, but also brings the contestant into direct contact with the university. Many of the contestants have never been away from home; many of them have never seen the university and this contact at such a time may exert an extremely significant influence on them. Consequently it is not only good for the pupil but also good advertising for the university. In a similar manner larger cities are withdrawing themselves more and more and having fewer and fewer dealings with the outside schools. A part of such policy is due, of course, to the pride of the city school and its desire not to be beaten by some smaller town school. A part of it is due to a desire on the part of the city officials to produce a complete program within the system. Such a program is handled by one head or one small group and thus complications with outside schools are avoided. On the other hand, it is probably true that the city school could learn much from the smaller town school. Size of school is no criterion of excellence in academic, athletic, music, debate, or other activities.

ACADEMIC CONTESTS

One of the fast developing extracurricular activities is the academic contest held by a number of colleges and universities throughout the country each year. In some instances these contests are part of a great state field day at the university. In others they are a contest complete in themselves. The contest held at the University of Pittsburgh each year is typical of this type of activity. In 1926 examinations were held in the following subjects:

American History	German
Chemistry	Latin (three contests)
Biology	Mathematics (two contests)
English	Physics
French (two contests)	Problems of Democracy
General Information	Spanish
General Science	

Two sets of tests are used, a preliminary and a final. The preliminary tests are held during the day at stated hours and are open only to contestants. The three pupils who rank highest in the preliminary tests compete publicly, at night. Thirty minutes is allowed for each subject in the preliminary tests. The final tests, usually held in only a selected few of the fields, last twelve minutes. The so-called "new" type of examinations, completion, matching, and multiple choice, are used. No true-false or essay type of questions is used. Mimeographed sheets are used in the preliminary contests and blackboards for the finals. Because the student has less than an hour for a test and in order to get a distribution in a group of a hundred or more pupils taking the particular test, many questions must be used.

Medals and ribbons are awarded winners and a cup to the

school making the best general showing. The danger with such a contest is the same as with athletics, that winning becomes the chief end and aim. In order to prevent pupils from cramming for these tests the announcements and eligibility blanks are not sent out until a late date and no sets of questions are provided any school. Some colleges include spelling, arithmetic, typewriting, and many other subjects in this program.

Such a contest does four things for the student concerned. It gives the non-athlete an opportunity to compete publicly in things of interest to him and in which he excels; it helps to motivate and emphasize academic work; it gives the pupil an opportunity to " fight " for his school; and affords him an opportunity to make a contact with the university. Needless to say, it is of value to the university in making contacts with the secondary schools and their coming graduates.

CAMPS AND CAMPING

Many schools now make provision for camping activities. This is a supplementation of the fine work being done by such organizations as the Girl Scouts, Camp Fire Girls, and Boy Scouts. In the larger cities where there are several high schools, a certain allotment of spaces is allowed each high school on the basis of its enrolment, and if these spaces are not contracted for by a certain time, they are made available to any school. Frequently the members of the faculty act as councilors, chaperons, and directors. A two weeks period is the usual time provided.

Camping should not be looked upon merely as a time for recreation but also as a time in which the pupil seriously studies nature. It is first-hand experience with nature and, in addition to a good program of games, sports, hikes, and tournaments, a good program designed to widen his acquaintance with and interest in nature should be followed. In addition to this it is a time for the boy or girl to become really acquainted with his neighbors, and also himself. He is away from the hustle and hurry of the city and has time to sit and think. Impressive camp fire talks are valuable educational aids.

A camper's club organized in the school is one method of arousing necessary enthusiasm for the camp and providing training and education in camp activities. Its program will concern camp life, discussion of last year's camp and plans, and preparations for the camps of the coming summer. Such a club has something really definite to look forward to, and this interest can be capitalized in helpful and educative ways. A great deal of material is available along this line, probably that published by Boy Scouts, Girl Scouts, and Camp Fire Girls, being the most valuable for campers of high school age.

Insignia

School insignia or monograms have always been awarded in connection with athletics and until recently rarely in any other activity. At the present time there is a growing demand that the student who gives to his school in other ways than in athletics be honored by being awarded some type of school monogram. Such an award will raise the standard of any activity in which it is made. There are two main bases of awarding insignia. The first is an awarding of different types of monograms for different activities. For instance, the football letter may be an eight inch block; the basketball, a four inch block; the track, a four inch " old English "; music club, four inch within a lyre; debating, encircled letter, etc. Many schools are tending toward small emblems of jewelry rather than the large monograms formerly given. The second general type is that in which a point system is utilized as the basis, the achievement of a certain number of points in restricted fields entitling the student to a certain type of emblem. The winning of additional points entitles him to a higher or more valuable emblem, thus providing for progressive awards. Usually about as many of these emblems are used as there are classes in the school. Bronze, silver, and gold emblems are frequently used. The awards are made by the central body which also has the right to revoke.

Such winning should be looked upon as the winning of an honor and not as the winning of medals or emblems intrinsically valuable. We are probably not yet at the place where the pupil will accept gracefully an emblem of no more intrinsic value than that which another student receives for a less honorable award, but the sooner that day comes the better it will be for contests and competition in general.

KITE TOURNAMENT

An interesting type of competition for elementary school and junior high school boys is the kite tournament. Such a tournament also makes a good show between the halves of a football game. Among the stunts for such a tournament are the following:

1. 100-yard dash. Kites to be started on signal, run on to the end of 100-yard cord, and wound back to the hand of the flyer.

2. Altitude Contests. Kites started with even lengths of cord. Flyer works up kite as high as possible, in five minutes, and returns to starting line, where altitude is measured or estimated.

3. Messenger race. "Messengers," pieces of cardboard, pulley and sail, eyelet, etc., are started up the string towards the kite. The first messenger to reach the kite wins.

4. Pulling Contests. Kites are run out to end of measured length of cords and scales used to determine pull of kites. Three or five pulls should be taken and averaged for the final score.

5. Novelty Competition. Unusual types or arrangements of kites, accessories, and flying material.

6. Stunt Flying. The kites by manipulation and by construction or bridling are stunted by the flyers. The one which performs the most unusual manœuvers wins. Kites must stay in the air.

7. Artistic Competition.   Kites are flown and judged for beauty, which will include color, shape, decorations, etc.   Kites will be examined both in the air and on the ground.

8. Kite Battle.   Kites are flown with equal measured cord.   The flyer attempts to down his opponent by sawing cord, colliding, or stabbing his opponent's kite.   The flyer must not interfere physically with opposing flyers on the ground.   All flyers keep within designated and marked space. The kite which stays up the longest wins.

BIRD HOUSE CONTEST

An activity of growing importance and value is the bird house contest.   In many cities the contest is sponsored by either the schools or an outside agency, usually a newspaper.   For instance, in Pittsburgh the *Chronicle Telegraph* holds such a contest each year for boys and girls from 10 to 16 years of age.   Four groups are designated, one each 10–13 and 14–16 years, both outside and inside the city.   The first five winners in each division are given a five-day trip to Washington.   Fountain pens, sweaters, electric lanterns, and cash prizes are other awards.   Nearly nine hundred such prizes are awarded to boys and girls each year.   The boys build bird houses, feeding stations, and bird baths of several types and kinds and the girls compete in making a laundry bag and a gingham frock.[1]

SUB-FRESHMAN DAY

A good project for the Council to promote in the interest of encouraging eighth graders to come to high school is to conduct a sub-freshman day.   The plan is developed and explained to the students of the high school and the students of the various schools which act as feeders to the high school.

A simple card or letter sent to the eighth grader will help break

[1] Material on such contests may be obtained from the Audubon Society, and the Department of Agriculture.   Many state departments of public instruction issue suggestions and directions in connection with the observance of bird day celebration.

FIGURE XVIII. — SOME OF THE 18,964 ENTRIES IN THE 1927 *PITTSBURGH CHRONICLE TELEGRAPH* BIRD HOUSE CONTEST

the ice and make him feel more at home. Such a letter might read as follows:

CONGRATULATIONS   EIGHTH GRADER

Dear Mr. (Miss) _____

Mr. (Miss) _____

a senior at Wampum High School will call for you at 8.15 A. M. Thursday, May 14, to take you for a day's visit to the high school. He will show you anything about the school you wish to see. You will be our guest, and you will be served your dinner at the school.

                     Chairman, Committee

A high school student, preferably an upper classman, brings the eighth grader to school and has him as his guest for the entire day. He brings him in the morning; takes him to classes; introduces him to the teacher, and attempts to interest him in the school and its life to such an extent that he will look forward with pleasure to coming next year. A suitable assembly program, posters, tags, and refreshments all help to make the visitor feel that he has had a good time and to increase his interest in high school.

COLLEGE DAY

The student council can find another good project in college day. The main purpose of this day is to show the pupils of the high school some of the interesting things about college. The day is not for the seniors alone, but for all of the students of the school. There are many college students available for such a day and these would be glad to help the cause especially if they were local graduates. The material for such a day may include such things as the following: slides and pictures depicting college life, games, college songs by the high school or the college musical clubs, pictures of colleges, pennants and banners, debates about colleges, short talks or posters on requirements, expenses, etc., display of college bulletins. Home-room discussion should center about this topic.

Good Will Day

One of the newcomers among " special days " demanding celebration is " Good Will Day." May 18 of each year was set aside by the World Conference on Education which met at San Francisco, June and July, 1925, for the purpose of emphasizing friendship and good will. Observance may vary in many ways. Assemblies, opening drills, pageants, dramatics, speaking, characterizations of great men, songs, discussion of contributions of various countries, current events, misery of children of other lands, and modern geography make suitable material.[1]

Girls' and Boys' Leagues

Many schools organize the girls into a league or club and the boys into a similar organization. The purpose of these organizations is to articulate and plan better for boys' and girls' activities. Because the members of each sex are organized into groups they can interest themselves more in appropriate activities valuable to the entire group. These organizations do not conflict with or in any way affect the regular clubs of the school. There may be divisions of these leagues for special interests or work, but they do not substitute for the usual club. Such a league holds parties and receptions, especially to new girls and boys; social hours; tea dances; special assemblies; drives for no powder, no paint, no smoking, no smut, suitable dress, courtesy, and in other ways boosts the general good of the groups. Such groups are valuable

---

[1] Additional suggestions and helps can be obtained from the National Council for the Prevention of War, 532 Seventh Street, N. W. Washington, D. C. or from the National Child Welfare Association, 70 Fifth Avenue, New York City.

in developing school spirit. Healthy competition between girls and boys may also be capitalized for the good of the school.[1]

School Advertisers

A group, club, or committee of " School Advertisers " may be found helpful in connection with the relation of the school to the community which supports it. Such a group has for its purpose the business of making the community better acquainted with, and more appreciative of, its school. Its work follows such lines as suitable newspaper publicity; bulletins and other reports; posters; service to parents' leagues or associations; explanations; entertainments of parents and citizen groups, and visitors; plays and campaigns for equipment or facilities. The danger with such a group is that in its enthusiasm and lack of definite connection with the school it may over-emphasize or misrepresent school activities. However, under careful direction it can do much to correct twisted reports and rumors which exist in every community concerning school activities. Its members take oath to " uphold the school and its interests and to present in a true, fair, and accurate manner the school to its community."

Home Projects

The home project is another activity which may, or may not, be properly classified as an extracurricular activity. Agricultural schools and small town schools have long used home projects: poultry and pig raising; cow testing; gardening; raising of wheat, oats, corn; canning; cooking; sewing; and such business projects as managing a shop, a news stand, or a newspaper route. To these music, drama, and outside reading have been added. Naturally only sound and substantial work of a limited

[1] Lewis, G. T. "An Every Girl Supper," *School Review* 32 : 134–41, February, 1924.

Wilson, E. E. "The Girls' League as an Agency in the Education of High School Girls," *School Review* 33 : 208–220, March, 1925.

kind should be accepted. Because this field is more strictly curricular than extracurricular, its administration and evaluation should not be in the hands of the students, but in the hands of the faculty and principal, although students may help to inspect and to handle exhibitions.

Parent-Teacher Association

The Parent-Teacher Association may be valuable or detrimental to a school, largely depending upon the personalities of the principal or other administrative officer of the school, on the one hand, and that of the president or chairman of the association on the other. If this president happens to be a former teacher, or if the association attempts to suggest or dictate policy or in other ways attempts to deal in affairs which require expert advice and attention, there probably will be trouble. On the other hand, if the association busies itself with aiding and assisting in matters within its field it may be of great value to the school and its life. Such an association may chaperon parties; furnish equipment; provide conveniences for dramatics; hold receptions; develop loan funds for student aid; and in other ways help the school to develop activities which are worth while.

References

Cubberly, E. P. *The Principal and His School*, Chapter XXVII. The Houghton Mifflin Company.

Mead, A. R. "Functions of Parent Teacher Associations," *Educational Administration and Supervision* 8 : 503–6, November, 1922.

Shuler, M. "The Parent Teacher Movement," *The American Review of Reviews* 66 : 65–67, July, 1922.

Handbook of Information about Parent-Teacher Associations and Mothers Circles, Secretary, National Congress of Parents and Teachers, National Education Association Building, Washington, D. C.

CHAPTER XXVII

SCHOOL BANKS AND BANKING

The banks of the country have had a phenomenal growth during the past half century. The main reason for this has been the rapid development of big business and the consequent prosperity. People have had more money than was necessary for immediate needs and consequently much of this surplus went into banks or was handled through them. Not a small influence in the development of banking has been the continuous educational campaign concerning savings, investments, and insurance carried on by financial institutions.

School banks and banking are a comparatively recent development and have also had a phenomenal growth. School banks originated in Europe about 1825, and were introduced into America about 1875, one being established at Beloit, Wisconsin, and one at Carlisle, Pennsylvania, about this time. One was established at Long Island City in 1885. However, such systems did not develop rapidly until after about 1915, when the American Bankers Association began an active campaign for savings banks in schools, and for thrift teaching. The emphasis placed upon savings during the War Savings campaigns gave a great impetus to school savings. The savings bank division of the American Bankers Association reported that for the year ending June 30, 1926, more than 11,000 schools had systems of banking; nearly 4,500,000 students were enrolled in these systems; nearly 3,500,000 students participated during 1926; the deposits for the year were $20,000,000; and the bank balances were approximately $32,000,000.

The statement that adults should be thrifty is a trite remark. If the adult should exercise thrift then he should be taught thrift as a child. No one is thrifty by instinct alone. Thrift is a habit like any other habit and as such must be developed by practice. The child must have money to save, invest, spend, and give, for all are concerned in thrift. The theory that when we open an account for a child in which deposits are made by fond parents and friends on Christmas day and on birthdays, we are teaching the child thrift is just as ridiculous as to think that mother's piano, on which she alone plays, will somehow make Mary a musician. The child must have a place in which he can deposit his savings regularly, and must be allowed freedom in judging and choosing, if thrift is to be taught him. School banking is not for the purpose of having the student accumulate money, but to help him acquire the habits of thrift. If the business of the school is to teach the student to do better the desirable things he is going to do anyway, then certainly it can well afford to give considerable time and attention to encouraging him to save systematically and to give, spend, and invest wisely.

Values of School Banking

1. It teaches the student to save systematically. — System and regularity must be taught. The amount of money the student saves is relatively small and should be a second consideration.

2. It teaches the student to spend wisely. — Saving does not mean miserly hoarding. It involves wise spending for wise spending is saving. A poor or unwise expenditure is always a waste. The student cannot be taught to buy all or many of the things which he will buy later in life. But he can be taught some of the general principles of buying, of using care and caution, of not being easily influenced by the salesman, and of studying advertisements.

Figure XIX. — The Classroom Bank at Business High School, Pittsburgh

3. It teaches the student to invest. — The student should be shown that depositing money in the bank may not always constitute real saving. That is, he should be taught that as he gets older and earns more money and has more money available for saving, that the ordinary savings account at the bank, while good and safe and possessing the merit of availability, may actually be losing money for him because his money is not bringing in as much income as it might if it were invested. He must be taught not to worship the bankbook nor to look upon stocks, bonds, and other investments as schemes devised to get his money. He should be taught that one person to whom he, as an inexperienced individual, can and should go for advice concerning investment is his banker.

4. It teaches the student to give. — All adults give more or less. Some give wisely and some give foolishly. Many undeserving causes are aided each year by " easy givers," thus encouraging the continuation of such causes. Giving involves gifts to charity, churches, colleges, distressed communities, and worthy enterprises. The student should be taught that giving wisely and systematically is a part of his financial life. It is a part of his saving.

5. Other values. — Student tellers, bookkeepers, directors, and other officers may receive valuable education incident to carrying on school bank work. Usually such work is done under close supervision.

CHOOSING A BANKING SYSTEM

Essentials of a good school banking system. — A number of different types of school banking are available. Some are better than others. A few suggestions on choosing a system should help to clarify thinking on the matter. The first consideration should always be the need of the student. A system is not designed for the naturally saving child of thrifty parents, but for the average child of improvident parents. The most important principles underlying a good system are as follows:

1. *It should be convenient.* — It will be hard enough for the student to carry his money past the Scylla and Charybdis of candy shop and toy store without going off the beaten track to strange lands where the bank is situated.

2. *It should provide for regularity.* — It must have a regular day each week for deposit, not only to harmonize with the school schedule, but for the greater effect in causing the student to save regularly.

3. *It should be elastic.* — It must be broad enough to treat all children alike so that no distinction will be made between the student with the dollar and the one with the penny. It should be easily adapted to local school and banking conditions.

4. *It should interest the students.* — It must be attractive enough in form to catch the attention of the individual child and the imagination of the group in order to overcome the temptation of the child to spend his money freely. Depositing when bank day comes around must be made " the thing to do."

5. *It should give some banking experience.* — It should give the student some experience in actually depositing and withdrawing money.

6. *It should provide opportunity for withdrawal.* — It should be possible, but not too easy, for the child to withdraw part or all of his money at any reasonable time. If he has to run the gauntlet of older people before withdrawing his money he will stop long enough to consider the justifiability of his action. On the other hand, however, if he cannot withdraw his money he will hesitate to deposit it.

7. *No opportunity for temptation to dishonesty or theft should be provided.* — No money or security should remain in the school, either in machines or in the teacher's desk, to tempt the adven-

turous. It is a sad result when a child is tempted to crime by the very means intended to teach him thrift.

8. *The time of the teacher should be safeguarded.* — Nothing can be taught successfully in the school unless it has the willing and enthusiastic support of the teacher.   Therefore the time required for banking procedure should be as limited as is consistent with good principles.   No bookkeeping should be required, and no clerical error should force a teacher to search for hours for the pennies which will not balance.

9. *The teacher should be free from any financial responsibility.* — Teachers are honest, but they are not trained in banking methods, and have no facilities for handling money.   If the teacher feels that in addition to the extra burden of the work she will have to make up any deficiencies that occur from the banking transaction she will have less joy in the task.

10. *The teacher should never be subjected to any reflection on her honesty.* — Dishonest or weak children, to cover up the disappearance of mother's penny given for deposit, should never be able to arouse suspicion of the teacher's integrity in the mind of even the most ignorant and prejudiced parent.   Nothing rankles more in the heart of a conscientious person than a suspicion of dishonesty, no matter how unfounded, and situations might arise of extreme consequence to some inexperienced teacher through a defect in the safeguards of the system.

11. *The teacher should be assisted in her work by some intelligent follow-up.* — At present there are no simple textbooks on thrift and the burden of thinking up new ideas, examples, and applications falls rather heavily upon the individual teacher.   The squirrel, ant, bee, and Benjamin Franklin are apt to pall if served too often.   Outside help should be enlisted from the professional and business men of the community to keep the attention of the children intelligently aroused.

Types of School Banking Systems

The various types of school banking systems fall into three general classifications which may be called the Stamp Card, the Pass Book, and the School Bank. There might be added a fourth, the type in which the student goes to the commercial bank and transacts his business. All of these systems are widely used. The term " Pass Book " may not be entirely accurate as a designation for the second type because pass books are used in the third and fourth types, but for our purpose here such a classification is sufficient.

1. Stamp card system. — In this system the bank issues stamps or certificates in small denominations from one cent up, and the child purchases these stamps in the school either from the teacher or from some form of automatic machine. These stamps are pasted on a card, or in a folder or book, and are redeemable at the bank. When a certain sum has accumulated, one, two, or five dollars, the bank will open a regular account with the student. One variation of the system is that in which a card with figures is punched to represent the amount deposited. Another variation is that in which the stamp is not pasted on, but stamped on by the teacher or machine.

Advantages. — The main advantages of this system are that it provides continuous opportunity for saving; in the case of the machine it relieves the teacher of any participation and responsibility; and it saves the bank from the bother of keeping small accounts.

Disadvantages. — In this type of savings system many of the children are not having regular relations with the bank or with banking procedure. The process is more akin to the slot-machine (one of the instruments commonly opposed), or to the purchase of postage stamps or Christmas seals. In fact, in one town last year many children pasted tuberculosis stamps on their cards, and could not understand why the bank failed to honor them.

Further, when a child can save only a few cents each month, it takes a year or more for him to reach the point where he can open an account, which is the end we are striving for. As a result, although a principal may believe, with a certain basis of truth, that a large proportion of children in his school are participating from the fact that every child will at some time or other buy a stamp, yet experience shows that a comparatively small percentage of the enrolment ever attain to the actual possession of a book.

Another bad feature of this system is that frequently, when a student has slowly and conscientiously accumulated fifty or sixty cents worth of stamps, he loses his card. He knows the bank has his money, and that the teacher knows that the bank has his money, and yet he cannot get it. This disgusts him with the whole affair, and it may leave a bitterness toward both the bank and teacher.

It might also be said that this system is hardly good banking ethics, and probably only the small amount involved permits the bank to consider it. For the bank to issue a demand obligation with no effective check on the identity of the purchaser is not good business, and as some of these securities are bound to be lost the bank will always have outstanding obligations which will have to be carried on its books for years.

2. Pass book system. — In this type of system, the pass book is issued to each depositor in the school. The student's account is opened directly in the school and a local bank (or several banks) acts as depository for the joint fund in the name of the school. On reaching the specified amount, the student's money is transferred to an ordinary savings account. A brief description, taken from the material issued by the largest of such systems, Educational Thrift Service Inc., Woolworth Building, New York City, will explain this type of school banking.

I. The System

1. **EXPERIENCE.** — The system has nine years behind it. A few details for the year 1925–1926 are as follows: —

Number of cities using system	404
Number of school buildings	6,303
Number of school teachers	59,305
Number of school enrollments	1,980,370
Number of pupils operating accounts	1,692,423
Number of deposits during 1925–26 school year	32,104,400
Average number of deposits each week	802,610
Amount deposited during 1925–26 school year	$14,665,774.05
Average weekly deposit	$366,664.35

2. **TECHNIQUE.** — Each child has his own pass book. Tuesday morning of each week is bank-day in each school room. Entry is made in book by student or teacher, and carbon copy coupon bearing printed account number is torn out. Pass book is returned to student and taken home; coupons and cash are placed in envelope and sent to principal, who places envelopes in a bag, locks it, and sends it to the bank. That is all; the school is then finished with banking until the following week, when the same process is repeated. The balance sheet is segregated into units of 200 accounts each, which automatically confines errors to limited areas and provides maximum speed and accuracy. At the bank the accounts are kept on the coupons by a substitution-posting system. Nothing is left to chance.

3. **FLEXIBILITY.** — It will operate in one bank, or two or three banks, or all banks, depending on local conditions and desires. Deposits may be any amount from one cent up; it is equally adaptable to the child of poor parents who is struggling to form a valuable habit with a penny a week, and to the more fortunate or ambitious one who is depositing ten and twenty dollar bills.

4. **NO DISCRIMINATION.** — The student who deposits a penny does so in exactly the same kind of pass book as the one who deposits $50.00.

5. **SIMPLICITY.** — This system requires but ten minutes each week of the teacher's time, and requires no bookkeeping knowledge or ability from her. She keeps no records of any kind.

The results of a survey in eighteen cities show that to handle a given number of transactions in the Educational Thrift Service system requires 17% of the working force needed to handle the same number of transactions in the ordinary manner.

6. ACCURACY. — At the bank an automatic double-check operates on each teacher's envelope and each coupon.

7. SAFETY. — No money or other article of value (such as stamps) is ever kept in the school over night, nor for a longer period.

8. SOUNDNESS. — The psychology of the weekly entry in the pass book is sound.

II. THE INSTALLATION

1. IN SCHOOLS. — Members of our trained staff, under the close supervision of our Director of Installation, visit each school room and thoroughly explain the system and leave the necessary supplies.

2. IN BANKS. — Our expert accountants handle all work at the bank the first day, and see that the system is functioning with smoothness and satisfaction.

III. THE SERVICE

This is our chief distinction. While the system itself is the brain of our unprecedented success, the service is its heart. It begins on the first day and never ceases.

BUTTONS. — A membership button in the School Bank Club of America is given to each student in a room when that room has enrolled all its students as depositors. This is announced on the back of the large BANK DAY TOMORROW card which is furnished each room.

RETURN VISITS. — Members of our service staff make return visits to each school room each year, to maintain the interest of the teachers and students.

BANNERS. — A handsome school savings banner is furnished to each school to aid in stimulating the percentage of depositors.

WEEKLY SUMMARY. — This is a report mailed to each principal each week, of the relative standing of the various schools, based on percentage of enrollment depositing.

CONTESTS. — Each year cash prizes are offered by us to the schools maintaining the highest percentage in school savings throughout a given period of weeks or months.

BULLETINS. — We provide the schools periodically with bulletins, varied in size and appeal, to be posted in rooms or halls or the principal's office.

TEACHERS' LETTERS. — We send letters to teacher, both regarding thrift generally, and regarding special questions and problems in school banking.

THE HOMES. — On installation, we hand an announcement to each student, to be taken home to the parents. Thereafter we continue at different times to send leaflets, pamphlets, and letters to the parents through the children.

THE GAZETTE. — Our monthly thrift magazine is called the Educational Thrift Gazette, and each month copies are furnished free for distribution in all schools.

Various other items of service are used when they seem necessary or advisable. Sometimes teachers' guessing contests are conducted; photographs are taken of teachers and students in 100% rooms or buildings; prizes are offered to teachers for suggestions; etc.

From time to time our accountants visit the banks to explain any short cut that may have been discovered or invented, and to straighten out any minor difficulties that may have arisen.

The American Bankers Association, New York City, also issues bulletins, sample blanks, and other material of use and value to the school teacher or administrator interested in school banking. In some cities the banks themselves send men to care for the deposits of the pupils, thus relieving the teacher of this work.

Advantages of this system. — These systems are valuable in that they are easily installed; they demand regular saving; and they give the student familiarity with banking methods.

Disadvantages of this system. — The chief objection to them is that they impose more work upon the teacher. However, this work is small, and the older students can be trained to do it under the supervision of the teacher as acceptably as she can do it herself.

3. School bank. — The third type of school savings system is that in which an actual bank is organized, housed, and conducted in the school. The following description of the bank in the New Kensington High School, Pennsylvania, by Mr. L. W. Korona, Head of the Commercial Department, illustrates this type of banking organization:

The Students Savings Bank of New Kensington High School was organized several years ago. Its present purpose is two-fold; first, to encourage thrift among the students, and second, to take care of the accounts of the high school. All accounts of the high school, excepting personal ones, are controlled by the Board of Activities — a board composed of the high school principal, members of the faculty, representatives from each class and from the Athletic Association. This Board of Activities is separate from the Students Savings Bank, but closely associated with it in that it authorizes the cashier of the bank to pay by check all bills contracted for by each class or organized club in the school that has an account in the Students Savings Bank.

EQUIPMENT. — The bank is located in a room made especially for that purpose. It has three windows, similar to regular bank windows with small bars in them. The bank has as its equipment a metal cash box, a filing cabinet, a supply closet, a Monroe calculator, and a Burroughs calculator. All money wrappers, pass books, counter checks, deposit slips, record cards, check books, etc., are either furnished by the local banks, or paid for from the General Sinking Fund. This fund is a surplus accumulated from the money left by each graduating class and also from the interest on the savings accounts in the local banks.

REGULATIONS. — The bank is operated by the Commercial Department, and is governed by the following regulations:

Board of Directors

President — Superintendent of Schools
Vice President — High School Principal
Secretary — Secretary of School Board
Members — Two members of the Faculty

Officers of the Bank

Cashier — Head of the Commercial Department
Assistant Cashiers — Two assistant cashiers are appointed by the cashier, one from the senior class and one from the junior class.

Rules

The Students Savings Bank will be open for business daily from 12 : 30 P.M. to 1 : 00 P.M.

The Cashier must keep on file daily, weekly, and monthly balance sheets and statements. The Cashier must prepare a monthly report for the Superintendent of Schools showing deposits, withdrawals, and balances of all accounts.

All money of the Students Savings Bank shall be deposited with the three local banks. The following accounts shall be carried:

1. Checking Account. This account must represent at least 40% of all resources (excepting loans) available to the Students Savings Bank.

2. Savings Account. This account may include 60% of all resources (excepting loans) of the Students Savings Bank.

3. Interest Account. This account includes all money received as interest by the Students Savings Bank from loans and deposits. This account may be expended only by vote of the Board of Directors.

There shall be a branch of the Students Savings Bank in the grade school building of the district, where a representative of the bank shall report to receive deposits and to make payments to the depositors.

Three auditors shall be appointed by the Superintendent of Schools to audit all accounts.

The manner in which business is carried on in the Students Savings Bank is the same as it is carried on in a commercial bank. When the pupil makes a deposit for the first time, he makes out a deposit slip. He receives a pass book which he presents upon making further deposits. If he wishes to withdraw money he fills out a counter check, and the cashier pays him the amount after ascertaining that he has sufficient funds deposited to cover the check.

The accounts are divided into two kinds — personal and impersonal. The Junior bookkeeper keeps the personal accounts and the Senior bookkeeper keeps the impersonal ones. There are three separate files for the personal accounts — one for the high school and one each for the grade schools. Each account is kept on a 5 × 7 card. This is a printed card and provides space for name, building, number of account, date, deposit column, withdrawal column, and balance column. The impersonal accounts are kept in a loose leaf ledger. These accounts are not as numerous as the personal ones but their transactions involve more money. Among the impersonal accounts are the Athletic Association, Cafeteria, Kentonian (school paper), and an account for each class.

When a bill is to be paid, it must first pass the Board of Activities. Upon finding the bill to be correct, the Secretary fills out a printed form giving the account to be charged with it. This authorizes the cashier to draw on the particular account for the amount. The cashier writes the check and gives it to the Secretary who sends it to the firm owed.

Conclusion. — No one can say which type of banking is the best. A bank in the school most nearly represents the actual banking procedure, and consequently has considerable merit in its favor. On the other hand it is probably true that in this type of banking, there is neither the systematic drive for savings nor the regular teaching of thrift which comes through the pass-book system which the teacher administers weekly. In any case there is far more merit in these latter two types of banking than in the stamp card type.

Teaching Thrift

Principles. — The main purposes of the school bank are not accomplished when the system or instrument has been selected and installed. Thrift is a habit, or group of habits, and habits come only by continued practice and application. The two fundamental principles which underlie all savings are (1) regularity of saving, and (2) consideration before spending.

Activities. — The banking or thrift committee or club of the school can use a variety of activities in teaching and learning thrift. Probably for the first six grades all that can be done is to encourage the students to save regularly. The older of these students might be taught to keep accounts of their expenditures. For the students in the grades above the sixth the following activities may be suggested:

Making a budget. — The student makes a budget for his own guidance. He recalls his expenditures of the past month and makes up a budget on this basis. During the next month he tries to live on this budget. He may also make a budget for his home. Even for shorter periods of a week or two, this procedure is not only educative, but interesting to the students.

Keeping a record of expenditures. — The committee may encourage the keeping of records of expenditures or expense accounts, first for a trial period of a week or two, and then for

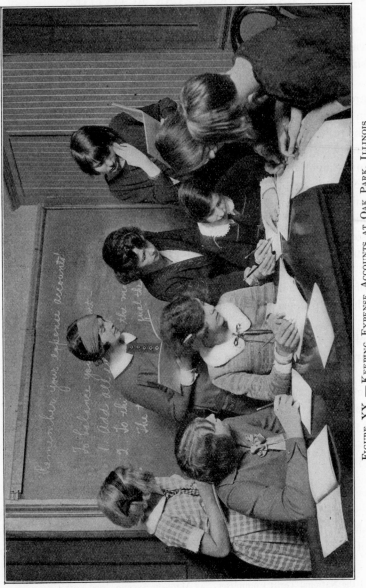

FIGURE XX. — KEEPING EXPENSE ACCOUNTS AT OAK PARK, ILLINOIS

longer periods. It will be educative to the student to add the various items at the end of the periods, and to note the relative size of his expenditures.

Studying investment. — A number of activities may center around investment, although probably none of them should result in actual investment of the student's money. Brief talks about the principles of good investment; the purposes and values; how and where to buy; warning against false schemes; a study of investment advertising; and teaching the student to appreciate good arguments for investments may be used. Such topics might cover such items as life insurance, accident and health insurance, investment in building and loan associations, and in some of the local commercial and industrial projects, and a discussion of mortgages, stocks, and bonds.

Making a will. — The students might be taught the importance of making a will, and might even make wills disposing of hypothetical property themselves.

Giving systematically. — Such topics as investigation of cause; pity as an emotion versus pity as a motive; how much to give; and variety in giving are suitable for discussion.

Other activities. — Other activities might have to do with letters for the parents; reports; publicity; assembly and classroom talks, discussions, and dramatization; visits to banks (300,000 New York City students visited the banks during the school year 1922–23); essay, poster, and similar contests; special day celebrations; drives and campaigns.[1]

SUMMARY

Thrift is an important element in the life of the citizen and should be developed in the school. Thrift is composed of a group of habits relating to saving, spending, investing, and giving.

[1] Good material for drives and campaigns may be obtained from the Secretary of the National Thrift Committee, 347 Madison Avenue, New York City.

These specific habits must be taught. The main principles of teaching thrift are regularity of saving and consideration before spending, investing, or giving. The three main types of school banking systems are the stamp card, the pass book, and the school bank. A number of interesting thrift activities can be taught through a central committee or club.

REFERENCES

ATWOOD, A. W. *How to Get Ahead.* Bobbs-Merrill Company.

BOWMAN, M. E. "School Savings Banks," *School and Society* 16 : 309–316. September 16, 1922.

CHAMBERLAIN, A. H. and J. F. *Thrift and Conservation — How to Teach It,* The Lippincott Company.

DAVIS, F. G. "A School Bank," *School and Society* 12 : 232–236, September 18, 1920.

DONHAM, S. A. *Spending the Family Income.* Little, Brown and Company.

ELDRED, A. "Conservation of Resources, School Savings Banks and Thrift Education." *Proceedings* of the National Education Association 56 : 645–649.

GOODELL, J. A. "Ben Franklin in Your School," *Journal* of the National Education Association 13 : 24–25, January, 1924.

JACKSON, B. B. and Others, *Thrift and Success.* The Century Company.

KIRKPATRICK, E. A. *Use of Money.* Bobbs-Merrill Company.

LARRISON, E. R. *Training in Thrift.* Abingdon Press.

OBERHOLTZER, S. *School Banks,* United States Bulletin, Number 46, 1914.

PALMER, H. H. "Thrift in the High School," *Education* 35 : 422–426, March, 1915.

SABLE, F. "A Bank Project," *Journal of Educational Method,* V, IV, number 2, 77–81, October, 1924.

School Savings Banking. Published by the Savings Bank Division of the American Bankers Association.

SONNENBERG, H. J. "A Model School Savings Bank," *Education* 39 : 240–243, December, 1918.

UPTON, C. B. "The Secret of Thrift," *Teacher's College Record* 19 : 431–460, November, 1918.

—— *The Secret of Thrift,* American Bankers Association, Savings Bank division, 5 Nassau St., New York.

WILLIAMS, B. G. "How One School Banks," *Journal* of the National Education Association 12 : 381–382, November, 1923.

WOODWORTH, L. D. "New Data on School Savings," *Journal* of National Education Association 12 : 234–235, June, 1923.

ZOOK, G. F. "Teaching of Thrift in Schools," *School and Society* 10 : 581, November 15, 1919.

CHAPTER XXVIII

FINANCIAL ADMINISTRATION OF EXTRA-CURRICULAR ACTIVITIES

A program of extracurricular activities necessarily includes the raising and spending of money. The rapid growth and development of the public high school has been paralleled by the increase in number and complexity of extracurricular opportunities, organizations, and activities. In the past, and in fact in many schools now, these activities have not been sufficiently officially recognized and school administration has made little or no provision for conducting them along reasonable and business-like lines. They just " grow up " and " exist," some better, and some worse, and few of them as well as they might with sound sympathetic guidance. If the activities themselves " just exist," certainly little more can be said of the financial administration of them. The present demand for efficiency in educational affairs, together with the necessity for a closer and more effective organization of extracurricular activities (especially since many schools require of all students a certain amount of credit in these activities) has brought with it a most sensible demand that these activities and their finances be handled in accordance with sound business principles.

VALUES

Many values of sound financial organization of the extra-curricular activities might be mentioned. Most of them are so obvious that little discussion is needed.

1. *Good business organization teaches the student to use good methods in his own financial matters.* — All of the students in the

school will handle funds of their own.   Moreover, many of them will go into positions of trust and confidence in which they will handle funds of employers or of the public.   The very best methods of handling money are the least we should expect our students to participate in or to witness.

2. *It helps to develop the extracurricular program.* — The second main value of a sound business organization is its effect upon school life and activities.   In many schools each organization handles its finances in any way it chooses.   Scattered accounts, books, records, and duplication of function and work are the result.   Because there are numerous accounts to be audited, audits are not frequently made.   There is no correlation of finance or of activities.   Desirable results in the financing of extracurricular activities are possible only where the system guarantees a uniformity in the handling of funds.   By being in the hands of a central committee which is interested in the school at large and not in specific activities only, over-emphasis and too generous support on the one hand and under-emphasis and lack of support on the other will be avoided.   The activities will then be articulated.

In schools which have no centralized control of extracurricular finances, it frequently happens that various organizations of the school have money left in the treasury at the end of the year. Frequently, too, such organizations make hasty and foolish expenditures of this money.   Little wonder that many schools are bitterly assailed by citizens of the community for these orgies of spending "what's left."   The students will justify it on the basis of "we raised it and we can spend it as we please," but rarely see the weakness of such argument.   The accounting system should be permanent so that it will not be affected in the least by changes in personnel of organizations or faculty.   The values of extracurricular activities depend, in part at least, upon their continuity and permanence.   Continuity depends upon organization and support and a large part of organization and support is based directly upon financial matters.

The principal is the head of the school and responsible for all that goes on in the school. Among his other duties is that of keeping in touch with the activities and their finances. His time is too valuable to be spent in scrutinizing and trying to read reports that are not uniform and that have to be explained to him. Moreover, a guiding of the purse can be made to carry a satisfactory supervision of the activities concerned.

In short, the business system should afford reasonable protection to all concerned, organizations, school officials, or others interested. Each party concerned in the handling of funds should have a check upon every other party in order that all may have mutual guarantees and protection. This is the basis of business. The healthy growth of extracurricular activities depends upon sound financial methods.

Current practices in raising funds for extracurricular activities. — The funds by which extracurricular activities are supported come from a variety of sources. Among the most important are the following:

Athletics
Dramatics
Musical programs, and concerts
Fairs, circuses, and bazaars
Picture shows, lyceums, and lectures
Fees, dues, and assessments
Sales of candy, pennants, books, and supplies
Activity tickets
Profits on various activities, publications, etc.
Subscriptions, donations, and collections
Fines: book and violation
Interest on funds

Tag days
Profits from the cafeteria
Sale of junk, scrap iron, papers, and rags
Locker fees
Grants from the board of education

Athletics. — More money is involved in the high school athletic program each year than in all of the other activities combined.

Traveling expenses, equipment, officials, guarantees, and the like are heavy. These expenses must be met. It was pointed out in the chapter on athletics that therein lies the most dangerous part of interscholastic athletics. In order to meet the heavy expenses of an athletic season, good-sized crowds must be assured and good-sized crowds usually do not attend games of losing teams.

Furthermore, if there is a central school fund into which all moneys are deposited and from which they are disbursed to the various activities as needed irrespective of their share in directly producing them, the success of the team and its consequent financial success is all the more important. The relationship is very close. Small income means small support for programs of extracurricular activities, while large income means large support for them. It will be a great day for interscholastic relations, as well as for secondary education in general, when school boards subsidize athletics and charge a nominal fee (or none at all) for admission to these contests. This will remove the main demand for a winning team. Teams will still win and lose, but finances will no longer dominate the picture.

Dramatics, musical programs, and fairs. — These activities are good money-makers. Their expenses are usually small while their incomes are usually large. Care must be taken, however, not to over-emphasize finances, especially of dramatics and music. The main purpose of either of them is not the raising of money.

Their purpose is largely educational. Fairs and bazaars are somewhat different in this respect.

Picture shows, lyceum courses, and lectures. — Many schools make extensive use of the lecture course to make money. Most of them also have in mind the worthy ideal of bringing before the public worthwhile entertainers, musicians and lecturers. The usual procedure is for the students to sell the tickets. Such a method of raising money has its merits. It is somewhat dangerous because of the size of contract usually assumed.

Fees, dues, and assessments. — Clubs and organizations may have dues and fees, provided they are nominal. Initiation fees and irregular assessments are impracticable. It happens sometimes that exclusiveness becomes an ideal of a club and a good way to make it exclusive is to have large fees or dues. This should not be tolerated in a public school.

Sales of candy, pennants, books, and supplies. — In many schools the " G. O." or " General Organization " conducts a store where candy and supplies are sold and any profit resulting is turned into the general fund. The purely service end of this arrangement is commendable. In some instances pressure has been brought to bear by town business men to have this store closed, because it hurt " legitimate " business. This sort of logic is queer. In some schools only a candy table is found. Serious questions of dietetics are raised by this activity.

Activity tickets. — Many high schools are now imitating colleges in charging each student a fee as he enrolls. This fee entitles him to a ticket which admits him to all of the activities of the year. A slight variation of this is where a student is sold a ticket which entitles him to admittance to these activities. This plan has its advantages and disadvantages. Its main weakness, as far as financial obligations are concerned, is that the price of such a ticket is usually rather large, and this tends to discourage buying, even though this sum would be much smaller than the total price of the activities attended. True, the student could pay for it in installments, but this entails an enormous amount of bookkeeping trouble in checking up on and " stopping " unpaid tickets, etc. It is sound business procedure in one way, however, for it allows a more accurate estimate of the budget for the year.

Profits. — Profits on yearbooks, newspapers, or other activities are frequently used to increase the size of the general fund. However, these activities should not be made or looked upon as profit-making propositions. They should not be deficit producers either, at least, to any great extent. Their purpose is not financial. If substantial profits are made these should be turned back into the form of more or better publications and activities.

Subscriptions, donations, and collections. — Having the students make subscriptions to the fund is much more dignified and businesslike than taking collections or holding tag days. It is, however, merely a makeshift. Difference of ability to subscribe and zeal of workers and subscribers tend to make it of doubtful value. Voluntary subscriptions are inadequate.

Fines. — Some schools turn all book fines into the general fund. Such a procedure is hardly proper. The proper place for the fine to go is into replacement; that is the purpose of the fines. Anyway, fines and penalties for the violation of books, rules, and traditions, are usually small and irregular.

Interest. — Interest on funds is usually so small that substantial help may not be expected from it. The chief value of interest is to be found in its educative influence upon the student. The principal who wants a big fund in the bank, helps to develop in the student a similar obsession for finances and finances become the chief end of the extracurricular activities. Better a small fund and many activities than a large fund and few. This does not apply, of course, to good business methods of having a surplus or emergency fund; nor does it apply to the raising of funds for large special purposes. It applies only to " interest bearing funds."

Tag days. — This is the least discriminate method of supporting anything. It is only glorified begging. It cheapens not only the activity for which it is conducted, but its financial return is always low in comparison with what it might have been, had more dignified and worthy means been employed. Progressive cities have abolished tag days of all sorts and have established community chests, supported by taxation, and administered by a representative committee, out of which funds are allocated to worthy causes on the basis of a budget previously made up. Tag days are organized begging, and the sooner school affairs are looked upon as essentials and not as the recipients of charity, the better it will be for the school and its community. About the only thing which is good that can be said about tag days is that they do advertise. But they are unsound and undignified.

Cafeteria. — In some schools, the cafeteria turns over its profit, whatever it may be, to the general fund. In some schools, even conducting the cafeteria is considered and classified as an extracurricular activity. Unless it is being used for instructional or motivational purposes, it is no more an extracurricular activity than the shoveling of coal into the furnace. Shoveling coal feeds the furnace; running the cafeteria feeds the students. If one is extracurricular, so is the other.

The practice of using the profits of the cafeteria to support the extracurricular activities cannot be justified. By the same token the treasury of the extracurricular activities should not meet any deficit the cafeteria might happen to incur. Further, good cafeteria management demands that the cafeteria be self-supporting (usually) but that it need not be a maker of profit. That is not its purpose and any profit accruing should be returned in the shape of increased service to the student patrons.

Sales of junk, old iron, rags, and papers. — Occasionally a school will have a "clean up" week and receipts from all junk sold will be turned over to the general fund. Such a method of raising money is hardly dignified. It tends to cheapen not only the students who do it, but the activities which they are trying to support. The sale of unclaimed "lost and found" articles is slightly different. However, the affair is usually more of a "stunt" than a sale, and small income is realized.

Locker fees. — Lockers are not maintained for money-making purposes. If fees are charged they should be used for repairs or replacements. This does not apply to key deposits but to actual rentals of lockers. The student has as much right to receive a locker without charge as he has to receive his desk.

Grants from the board of education. — Selling soup, peanuts, and gum, taking up collections, holding tag days, and the like probably do more to belittle extracurricular activities than any other one thing. If these activities are of value they are worth spending taxes for. School boards are doing this more and more, by giving them places in the schedule; by allowing teachers' time for the handling of them; by appointing directors of them; and by buying equipment for them. The next step will be the subsidizing of them by the board so that all the uncertain and unbusinesslike methods of trying to support them may be abolished. Such a procedure will do at least two things; first, it will add to the dignity and importance of such activities, and second, because school money is being put into them it will mean that more definite and tangible results will be demanded. Small fees might still be charged but the main bill would not be paid by a collection of small moneys raised in all sorts of ways and from all sorts of sources.

FINANCIAL ACCOUNTING OF EXTRACURRICULAR ACTIVITIES

A study embracing over four hundred high schools of the methods of accounting used in connection with the extracurricular activities was recently made.[1] The most important of the data obtained are shown below. Some schools are, of course, represented in some items and not in others. The total number of schools represented in the various items in the tables below is usually about 275–300. The enrolment of these schools varies from 30–4700 students. Thirty-six per cent of these schools enroll fewer than 500 students; twenty-eight per cent enroll from 500–1000; and thirty-six per cent enroll more than 1000 students. In other words, each classification contains about one third of the cases.

Per student cost of extracurricular activities. — Figures on per student extracurricular activities costs are not accurate. The following figures do, however, give a general idea of this cost.

TABLE VI

SHOWING APPROXIMATE PER STUDENT COST OF
EXTRACURRICULAR ACTIVITIES IN 268 HIGH SCHOOLS

Per Student Cost	Number of Schools	Per Cent of Schools
Less than $1.00	5	1.9
$1.01– 2.00	28	10.4
2.01– 3.00	20	7.4
3.01– 4.00	29	10.7
4.01– 5.00	19	7.1
5.01– 6.00	19	7.1
6.01– 7.00	31	11.6
7.01– 8.00	21	7.6
8.01– 9.00	9	3.3
9.01–10.00	17	6.3
10.01–11.00	11	4.0
11.01–12.00	8	3.6
Over $12.00	51	19.0
	Total 268	100.0

[1] Much of the following data is taken from the unpublished thesis for the M. A. degree of Mr. Myers B. Horner in the library of the University of Pittsburgh.

The amounts of money handled through the extracurricular organizations as scheduled by the 268 schools ranged from $300 to $125,000, the median amount being about $4000.

From the figures it will be seen that the median cost per student of extracurricular activities in these schools is between six and seven dollars. Dement in her study of ten schools found the per student cost to be slightly higher.[1]

Data on organization as revealed by this survey.—In order to get data on the general organization for financial control, a number of questions were asked. The following data show this material.

1. Is the active treasurer teacher or student?
   Principal, teacher, or secretary, 237 . . . . Student, 25; Both, 20
2. Is the treasurer bonded? . . . . Yes, 42; no, 240
3. If so, how much? . . . . Range $1,000–$15,000
   Median $5,000
4. Do you have a school bank? . . . . . . Yes, 47; no, 245
5. If so, is it operated by the same organization that handles the extracurricular funds . . Yes, 15; no, 32
6. Do you have a central treasurer? . . . . Yes, 169; no, 103
7. Is all money deposited in one fund? . . . Yes, 140; no, 138
8. If so, are the depositors (such as organizations and activities) allowed to withdraw as much as they deposit? . . . . Yes, 116; no, 46
9. Or may they withdraw as much as needed irrespective of amounts of deposit? . . . As much as needed, 56
10. Do you include finances of cafeteria in extracurricular accounts? . . . . Yes, 29; no, 222
11. Do you include supplies, book sales, etc. in extracurricular accounts? . . . . Yes, 25; no, 258
12. Do you include locker fees in extracurricular accounts? . . . . Yes, 21; no, 230
13. Are deficits paid by the board of education? Yes,[2] 38; no, 222

[1] "Values in Extracurricular Organizations in the High School," *School Review*, January, 1924.

[2] Four other schools reported that deficits in "athletics," only, are paid by the Board.

14. If not, how are deficits paid?	Carried over. From general fund, entertainments, etc.
15. Is the central office of your financial organization in the principal's or superintendent's office?	Yes, 218; no, 49
16. Is the financing of extracurricular activities and the accounting therefore in charge of the commercial department?	Yes,[1] 78; no, 188
17. Does a committee, board of finance, or the like pass on requisitions or requests for money?	Yes, 132; no, 115

Types of financial organization and accounting systems. —
In general there are two types of financial organization of extracurricular activities on the basis of control. These are decentralized and centralized organizations.

Decentralized. — In this type of financial organization each club or activity handles its funds as it chooses. Of course, there may be limitations in the matter of bookkeeping, auditing, reports, use of surplus, etc., but in general each organization can raise and spend its money as it desires. Because this system, or lack of it, can hardly be recommended, no time shall be taken to discuss it. It may work, and probably does work in many schools, but the final test of an activity or organization is neither whether or not it follows recognized procedure, nor even whether or not it merely gets results, but rather whether or not it gets as good results as are possible to be gotten.

Centralized. — The second type of control is that in which there is a central treasurer who handles all of the moneys coming in from all of the activities, and a central control which administers this central fund. In a general way there may be said to be

---

[1] Some of these schools do not have a commercial department. On several returns it was stated that this department would handle these finances if there were such a department in the school. Perhaps a good guess would be that about one half the schools having commercial departments handle the extracurricular finances through them.

two additional variations of this one type. These three types do not differ greatly in general principles. In the first type the principal or designated officer handles the funds, keeps the books, etc., and disburses on proper requisition. In the first variation this work is done by the commercial department of the school, and in the second variation by this same department through its laboratory — the school bank. It will be seen that the type of centralized control usually depends on the size of the school. The first would probably fit the small school, the second, the medium sized, and the third, the large school.

Finances handled by principal or central officer. — Procedure and forms. — The central treasurer (principal, secretary or similar officer) is the custodian of all school activity funds. He should be properly bonded and should have regular office hours, or be easily available. This central treasurer should not supplant the organization treasurers. These still function in the collection of organization fees, assessments, and funds. These funds are deposited with the central treasurer and disbursed upon an order issued by the proper disbursing officer of the organization depositing them. When the treasurer of any organization deposits with the central treasurer he should receive a duplicate carbon copy receipt. The form of this receipt might be as follows:

Wampun, S. E.........192..No.....

BARNARD SCHOOL

Office of the Treasurer

Received of....................................$...........
....Dollars
on account of..
which is to be credited to...........................account
....

Treasurer of Extracurricular Activities

Central Treasurer's Receipt

This receipt should be printed in two colors, the original and duplicate being different. The original is retained by the central treasurer and the duplicate becomes a part of the records of the organization making the deposit. The central treasurer keeps a complete file of his original receipts by organizations after he has made the necessary book entries. By this method there can never be any doubt as to the exact amount of money which an organization deposits. Both the organization depositing and the central treasurer have a check upon each other and at the end of any given period of time the organization by totaling its receipts and expenditures may know the amount of its balance. No money should be deposited without the issuance of a receipt.

Whenever the disbursing officer of an organization desires to pay a bill, he issues a " Pay Order " to the central treasurer.

Wampun, S. E...........192..Order no...

BARNARD SCHOOL

EXTRACURRICULAR ACTIVITIES

Pay to the order of.................................$......

....Dollars

For.......................................as per attached

invoice and charge same to...........................account

Approved.........................Sponsor

....

Disbursing Officer of

.....................Organization

PAY ORDER

This pay order should always be issued in duplicate (of different colors). The original should be delivered, together with the invoice to be paid, to the central treasurer, and the duplicate should remain with the records of the organization. Upon receipt of a " Pay Order " the Central Treasurer issues a voucher check for the amount of the invoice, retaining a record on the check stub.

No. 210   Wampum, S. C..............192....No. 210

..............192..   FIRST NATIONAL BANK

Account   Pay to the order..................$....

charged............

To.................   ....Dollars....

For................

     Order No.......   For....................................

Balance............

Deposit............   Barnard School

Total..............   .... Activities' Fund

This check.........

Balance............   ....

                                 Treasurer

TREASURER'S CHECK

In case this form of check were used for paying bills, it should be accompanied by a " Remittance Advice " so that the vendor would know the items covered by the check. Many schools are using a remittance check as shown below which removes the necessity for a Remittance Advice. The stub in the case of this check would be the same as shown above.

BARNARD SCHOOL   No......

                                 Date..............192..

Date...........................   Account to credit if other

                                than that of maker of check

Items included in remittance........

                                ....

Amount disbursed..................

                                ....

Net...............................

                                ....

Pay to the

order of....................................$...............

Wampum, S. E.   Barnard Activities Association

                          By........................

    First National Bank   Treasurer

TREASURER'S CHECK INCLUDING REMITTANCE ADVICE

The original bill or invoice is always on file and can be referred to easily. No bill should be paid by the central treasurer until he receives an original invoice from the seller.

When an organization desires to purchase goods it uses a requisition blank. This blank is made out in triplicate, and after approval one copy goes to the vendor, one to the organization disbursing officer, and one to the central treasurer. The following is an illustration of such an order.

BARNARD SCHOOL		No...

Date....................

M ....

Please furnish the following materials

To ....

Quantity	Articles	Price

Ordered by.......................................
Charged to.......................................

Barnard Activities Association
Per....................

REQUISITION BLANK

A report on the sale of tickets for a campaign or entertainment should be required. No tickets should be issued without a signed receipt for the number issued, and upon the close of the ticket sale a complete account of tickets and money should be furnished on some such form as this:

TICKET REPORT

BARNARD SCHOOL.................192....

Received.........Tickets or at $...... Total $.............
          Periodicals
to be sold for the...
Date of entertainment (or periodical)..................192......
I agree to turn in all receipts and unsold tickets (periodicals), not
later than.........hours after this event.
                   Signed..............................
Date....................192....
Received for......tickets sold $......
No. of tickets returned......Value $......
          Total $..............
          Signed...................
               Treasurer

TICKET REPORT

Summary accounts of athletic contests, dramatic or musical programs and other performances might be made on such a form as this:

EXTRACURRICULAR ACTIVITIES REPORT

BARNARD SCHOOL, WAMPUN, S. E.

                   ....192....
Entertainment......................................
Given...............192.... by........................
Ticket Sales................. $...........................
Royalty $................... ....
Costumes $.................. ....
Advertising $............... ....
Incidentals.................. ....
Total...................... ....
                      Net Proceeds............
                      Organization.............
                      Sponsor.................

EXTRACURRICULAR ACTIVITIES REPORT

Other blanks and records may be arranged and prepared according to the local needs of the high school. Some schools will use a great number of reports while others will use few. The size, number, and general organization of the activities will determine the number and type of blanks and reports that ought to be used.

Bookkeeping. — The system of bookkeeping employed should be accurate and as simple as is consistent with good principles. A standard columnar book which can be purchased at any supply store is sufficient. It should be looseleaf, preferably, although that is not absolutely necessary. The needs of the school will determine the size of sheet to be used. This plain looseleaf book may serve as a journal, ledger, cashbook, distribution ledger, or for any other accounting service.

a. General account. — The first pages of this book should be reserved for the daily or weekly entries of all transactions irrespective of organization or purpose. It would appear somewhat as follows:

DATE	ITEMS HANDLED	RECEIPTS	TOTAL RECEIPTS	CHECK NO.	DIS-BURSED	TOTAL DIS-BURSED	BANK BALANCE
Jan. 1	Balance Forward						$2,240.00
Jan. 5	Athletics (Basket Ball Game)	70.50					2,310.60
Jan. 5	Junior Class Pennants			621	80.10		2,230.50
Jan. 7	Athletics (Traveling expenses)			1	12.50	92.60	2,218.00
Jan. 8	Sale of Candy (Senior Class)	50.40	120.90				2,268.40
Jan. 8	Purchase of Candy (Senior Class)			2	40.10	132.70	2,228.30
Jan. 10	Ticket Sale (Dramatics)	370.25	491.15				2,598.55
Jan. 12	Royalty for Dramatics			3	25.00	157.70	2,573.55
Jan. 13	Purchase of books (Dramatics)			4	100.00	257.70	2,475.55

CENTRAL TREASURER'S GENERAL ACCOUNT

A sufficient number of sheets in the standard columnar book should be set aside in the first part of the book to operate the " General Account " for the entire year.

   b. Special accounts. — Following the General Account will be entered an account sheet for each organization or activity in the school. These should be arranged in alphabetical order. If the account book is a looseleaf binder, new accounts may be added in the alphabetical arrangement at any time during the year. If not looseleaf, the new accounts may be opened at the end of all other accounts operating. All accounts should be indexed for easy accessibility. Below is illustrated an account of one of the activities of the school.

DATE	ITEM	RECEIPTS	TOTAL RECEIPTS	CHECK NO.	DIS-BURSED	TOTAL DIS-BURSED	BANK BALANCE
Jan. 1	Balance in Treasury						1510.10
Jan. 5	Waubonsie B.B. Game	80.40					1590.50
Jan. 7	Traveling Expenses to Bunkum			622	40.50		1550.00
Jan. 15	Purchase of Supplies			7	40.20	80.70	1509.80
Jan. 15	Blue Grass B.B. Game	260.23	340.65				1770.05
Jan. 17	Purchase of equipment			623	210.20	290.90	1559.85
	Forwarded		340.65			290.90	1559.85

ILLUSTRATIVE ACCOUNT OF THE BARNARD ATHLETIC ASSOCIATION

A trial balance on the above account can always be struck by taking the sum of the receipts of all accounts and comparing it with the sum of the receipt column in the General Account. A similar total of all disbursements of all accounts should check with the total disbursements in the General Account. The sum of the bank balances of all accounts should always be the same as the final bank balance shown in the General Account. Monthly reports of all the funds in the school should be made to the principal.

Finances handled through commercial department. — In this variation of financial accounting for extracurricular activities, the necessary forms and books may not be essentially different from those previously described though actual ledgers, journals, cash book, and distribution ledger may be used in place of the single book described above.

The essential difference between this plan and the one previously discussed lies in that the actual clerical, bookkeeping, and financial work is being done by students of the commercial or business department under the supervision of their central treasurer, whereas in the first type all this work is done by the treasurer alone. A section of the business department becomes the banking headquarters of the school. Many of the student leaders of the extracurricular activities are not enrolled in the business department but all are under the control of the business department as far as the business relations of the respective organizations are concerned.

All letters dealing with extracurricular activities are dictated, typed, and mailed by the business department; all accounts are kept; and salesmanship classes receive practical experience in sales work, for all ticket sales and campaigns are put under their charge. Thus the centralization of accounting for student finances and the placing of this work in the department of business education gives valuable actual business experience to the students.

Finances handled through the school bank. — The most complete type of financial organization consists of the operation of a real school bank which handles both individual and organization accounts. This would be a wider extension of the type suggested above and would give practical banking and business experience to a great many more business department students.

Finance Committee. — The school should have the financial affairs of its extracurricular activities supervised by a Board of

Finance or Finance Committee. This body might be elective or appointive, preferably the latter. It should represent the general main interests of the school and not particular specialized activities. It should be composed of both faculty members and students.

One splendid arrangement where there is a council or other central representative body is to have a Finance Committee as a standing committee of this body. The chairman at least should be a member of the council. Other members may be chosen from the school at large, if desired. The head of the Commercial Department, or some other competent faculty member should act as adviser. This adviser should probably be the Central Treasurer. If not, the Treasurer should be a member of the Committee. The Committee does not legislate. It is an advisory Committee. It makes suggestions, prepares budgets, and receives applications for funds. It is a clearing house for all financial matters. It deliberates and then recommends to the council what action it thinks wise. The council may accept or reject its reports as it sees fit. This type of Committee is necessary in schools in which all of the moneys are placed in a common fund and used for the good of all activities irrespective of whether or not all activities helped to produce them.

The council, Finance Committee, or other competent body should make a budget for the year, this budget to include all recognized activities of the school. Each activity should prepare its own budget and the Committee should then make its budget on these smaller budgets. This general budget after adoption becomes the financial guide of the school for the year. This is in accordance with good business principles. Such a budget may vary all the way from a mere statement of a lump sum to be allocated to the various organizations to the intricate and carefully worked out scheme used at Tulsa, Oklahoma, in which each activity is assigned a certain percentage of the total income. In addition to budgetting, this Committee should be responsible for the proper auditing of all accounts at least once each semester. The complete financial statement of the school should be published in the school newspaper or magazine at least once each year. Holding a training course or school for treasurers or financial officers of clubs and organizations, in which these are taught the fundamentals of accounting and finance, is another job for this Committee.

There are many methods of accounting which are suitable for the extracurricular program. No system should be taken over bodily by any school. A serious consideration of the local situation, its conditions, possibilities, and limitations must precede any attempt to fit a system into it. Building a careful, accurate, business-like procedure takes time.

Summary

A program of extracurricular activities involves adequate financing. Funds used to support these activities now come from a variety of sources, many of which are " cheap," and these cheapen both the activities and the individuals connected with them. The extracurricular program should be financed by the board of education. A study of over two hundred high schools revealed the per student cost of extracurricular activities to be between six and seven dollars. This survey revealed other interesting data concerning methods of financing. The two general types of financial organization are " decentralized " and " centralized." In the centralized type the funds are handled through a central office and are usually supervised by a central board or committee. The blanks and forms required are central treasurer's receipt; pay order; treasurer's check and requisition blank. Other forms may be utilized as required. The bookkeeping system should provide for two accounts, the " general," which accounts for all money received or paid regardless of club or organization, and the " special," which accounts for each activity. The commercial department may handle the funds under the supervision of a central finance board or committee.

REFERENCES

BACON, F. L. "The Correlation of Extracurricular Activities with the Department of Business Education," *School Review* 30 : 671–678, November, 1922.

BARNHART, E. W. "Student Finances," *Proceedings* of the National Education Association, 1915, 908–910.

BROOKS, G. F. "Handling of Activity Funds," *The Scholastic Editor* 3 : 9–10, December, 1923.

BROWN, R. E. "Financing High School Organizations," *Educational Review* 59 : 153–159, February, 1920.

CARDEN, A. M. "The Control of Student Activities," *Education* 38 : 14–17, September, 1917.

DEMENT, A. L. "Values of Extracurricular Organizations in the High School," *School Review* 32 : 40–48, February, 1924.

ENGLEHART, N. L. and GRILL, G. W. "Internal Accounting for Extracurricular Activities in Public Schools," *Teachers College Record* 26 : 753–754, May, 1925.

FOWLER, B. P. "Social Organization of the High School," *School and Society* 12 : 386–399, October 30, 1920.

GRILL, G. W. "Internal School Accounting," *Proceedings* of the National Association of Public School Business Officials, May, 1922.

GROTE, C. "Regulation of Extracurricular Activities," *Journal* of the National Education Association, 1922, 752–758.

HARWOOD, H. M. "Extracurricular Activities in High Schools," *School Review* 26 : 273–281, April, 1918.

HOLCH, A. E. "Student Activities in High Schools," *Education* 45 : 606–618, June, 1925.

HORST, H. M. "Student Participation in High School Responsibilities." *School Review* 32 : 342–355, May, 1924.

JOLLY, L. F. "An Accounting System for High School Organizations," *School Review* 31 : 136–142, February, 1923.

JONES, G. "Systematizing the Financial Affairs of High School Student Organizations," *School and Society* 15 : 611–612, June, 1922.

JONES, G. "Internal Accounting in High Schools." *American School Board Journal*, April, 1923.

LEWIS, G. T. "Centralizing Student Activities in the High School," *School Review* 31 : 612–626, October, 1923.

McKOWN, H. C. and HORNER, M. B. "Financial Administration of Extracurricular Activities." *Twenty-fifth Yearbook* of the National Society for the Study of Education, Part II, Chapter X, 1925.

MEREDITH, F. G. "The Correlation of Extracurricular Activities with the High School Business Education," *Vocational Education Magazine*, pp. 282–284, December, 1923.

MYERS, J. S. "Student Social Life," *School and Society* 13 : 541–547, May 7, 1921.

PRINGLE, R. W. *Adolescence and High School Problems*, Chapter XVI. D. C. Heath and Company.

PRUNTY, M. "Sane and Systematic Direction of Extracurricular Activities," *Sixth Yearbook*, National Association of Secondary School Principals, pp. 1–8, 1922.

SCOTT, M. J. and HILL, C. W. "Financial Accounting in Student Activities," *School Review* 32 : 442–444, June, 1924.

WARD, R. W. "Financing Student Activities," *Seventh Year Book*, National Association of Secondary School Principals, pp. 57–61, 1923.

WILDS, E. H. *Extracurricular Activities*, Chapter X. The Century Company.

CHAPTER XXIX

ENCOURAGING AND LIMITING PARTICIPATION IN EXTRACURRICULAR ACTIVITIES

The means and methods of encouraging and limiting student participation in extracurricular activities are usually grouped together and classified more or less inaccurately as " point systems." Such systems or plans equate these activities and also make provision for the recording of the values on the basis of the students' participation therein.

PURPOSES OF A POINT SYSTEM

To distribute more evenly the opportunities for participation. — In any high school there are a few students who are interested in many activities, and on the other hand there are some students who are interested directly in few or no activities. The student who has shown that he can discharge responsibility is the one who is given added responsibility, while the one who has never done anything is the one to whom his fellows hesitate to charge responsibility.

Three classifications of activities may be made : (1) those on a voluntary membership basis — such as a club, (2) those on a selective or elective basis such as an editorship or managership, and (3) those in which the student " tries out." In other words the student may not participate because (1) he does not want to, (2) because he is not elected or, (3) because he does not have the requisite skill or technique. If he does not participate because he does not want to, the school can encourage him, if in no other way than by requiring him to participate. The school requires him to participate in his regular curricular work, and it can as easily justify requiring him to participate in the extracurricular work. Further, if fewer places are taken by the more experienced, and by those who naturally participate more easily, there will be more opportunity for other students to participate.

To prevent the student from overloading. — This purpose is closely allied to the first. The student who can do, does. If he is carrying a good load of curricular work and handling many activities in addition, he can easily attempt too much with one or more of several results — physical or mental harm, dissipation of energies, or failure to develop real high attainment in any field. It is wise for students to carry loads while at school, but this does not mean they should carry unreasonable loads in either curricular or extracurricular activities.

To develop and maintain a higher standard of attainment. — The student who takes an active part in many activities cannot be expected to develop all of them to their highest attainment, because of their number. If opportunities are distributed so that the student has only a very few active interests, there is more possibility that these will be done well. This is not necessarily true because the high grade student might do a job better in a short time with little attention than the average student with longer time and more attention. But it is probable that more time and attention on the part of the average student would be more effective than hastiness on the part of the better student.

To equate activities where credit for graduation is required. — It has been suggested that if extracurricular activities are valuable for one student they are probably valuable for all. But not all students will voluntarily participate in them. Requiring credit in them for graduation is perhaps the easiest way of requiring the student to participate. Such a requirement would also dignify these activities, and dignifying them would bring the demand that they be really effective in terms of results. This would add to the worth and attractiveness of the entire program.

TYPES OF SYSTEMS

In general, the types of organization for limiting and encouraging participation may be classified under the three heads (1) Point, (2) Major and Minor, and (3) Group Systems. Various combinations of these might add other classifications.

1. Point system. — In this type of organization the activities are evaluated on a basis of points. These points range from 1 to 5, 10, 20, or more. The basis of allotment is usually the amount of time required for the activity, or the estimated importance of the position. In the percentage plan the activities are evaluated on the scale of 1 to 100 per cent. A typical point scale system is that used in the high school at Fort Wayne, Indiana. The schedule of points is as follows:

	Points
Senior class president	8
Editor of the *Spotlight*	8
Editor of the *Caldron*	8
Business manager of the *Spotlight*	8
Business manager of the *Caldron*	8
Advertising manager of the *Spotlight*	8
Advertising manager of the *Caldron*	8
Student manager of athletics	8
News editor of the *Spotlight*	7
News editor of the *Caldron*	7
Part in senior play	7
President of any school organization	5
Circulation manager of the *Spotlight*	5
Circulation manager of the *Caldron*	5
Part in school play	5
Member of debating team	5
Member of athletic team	5
All offices not listed above	4

Points

Committee chairman of organization	4
Member of second school team	4
Member of the *Spotlight* staff	4
Membership in organization other than class	2

A student's participation is limited to fifteen points.

In order to suggest a little more in detail a plan by which points might be allowed, the following scale is presented. It may be a good plan, or a bad one, or both. It is suggested in order that the principal, teacher, or committee interested may have another set of material to consider in connection with the formulation and development of a point scale system. It must be adapted to local situations:

A Suggested Point Scale System

ATHLETICS

Points

Captain of Football and Basketball team	15
Captain of Track and Baseball Team	10
Captain of Class Team	5
Member of School Team	5
Member of School Squad	3
Cheer Leader	3

CLASS ORGANIZATION

President of Seniors and Juniors	8
Vice President, Secretary and Treasurer of Senior and Junior Class	5
President of Sophomores and Freshman Class	5
Vice President, Secretary and Treasurer of Sophomore and Freshman Class	3

STUDENT GOVERNMENT

President	15
Other Officers	10
Home Room Representatives	5

CLUBS

Points

Hi-Y, Girl Reserves, Friendship, Literary, Mathematics, Science, etc.

President	5
Secretary	4
Members	1–2

DRAMATICS AND ORATORICAL ACTIVITIES

Senior Class Play	3–5
Assembly Program	1–4
Debating Squad	5
Debating Team	7
Declamation and Oratorical Contests	3
Members of Dramatic Clubs	1
Major Parts in each play	2
Minor Parts in each play	1

NEWSPAPER AND YEARBOOK

Editor-in-chief of Newspaper	15
Assistant Editors	8
Business Manager	15
Business Assistants	10
Editor-in-chief of Yearbook	12
Assistant Editors	6
Business Manager	12
Business Assistants	8

MUSIC AND ART

Glee Club (student leader)	6
Members	3
Orchestra or Band (student leader)	8
Members	5

MISCELLANEOUS

Outside music or art
Committee work
Hobbies, jobs, or worthy projects
(Points to be determined)

MAXIMUM NUMBER OF POINTS TO BE CARRIED

Pupils with less than "C" average	10
Pupils with "C" average	15
Pupils with "B" average	20
Pupils with "A" average	25

The matter of relative importance of office holding and membership is taken care of usually by the difference in number of points allowed. In the Walla Walla High School, Washington, a point system is used by which the student is limited to sixteen points, which must be distributed as follows:

Official (office holding), six; and membership, ten; elective clubs (Senate, Seminar, etc.), seven; Technical (French, Classical, etc.), two; and Honorary, one to two points.

In some instances the credit allowed for membership in an organization depends upon the size of that organization, using as a base the smallest number of students who can participate at any one time. In other words the smaller the organization the larger the amount of credit allowed its members.

2. System of majors and minors. — In this type of organization the various activities of the school are compared and classified as majors and minors. The majors are the more important of the two; that is, they are those which under the point system would have the largest number of points attached. The number of majors and minors which the student is allowed to carry is limited. For instance, he might be allowed to carry two majors, or one major and two minors, or three minors.

The basic principles of organization of this type of plan is illustrated by the following schedule which is in use at Fifth Avenue High School, Pittsburgh, Pennsylvania. All activities are classified as majors or minors:

MAJOR	MINOR
Baseball	Camera Club
Basketball	Commercial Club
Football	Debating Club
Class play	German Club
Debating Teams	Journal Staff (minor officers)
Soccer	Literary Society
Society Play	Mathematics Club
Swimming Team	Penmanship Club
Track Team	Technical Club

A student whose scholarship, strength, and conduct permit may belong to one major and two minor activities or to three minors. No student may belong to two majors at the same time.

The following plan is a combination of the "Point" and "Major and Minor" systems. It is in use in the High School at Decatur, Illinois. The student may elect one of the following plans:

1. Membership in the two five-point organizations with the privilege of selecting other organizations to the extent of four points. (Total — 14 points.)
2. Membership in one five-point organization with the privilege of selecting other organizations to the extent of seven points. (Total — 12 points.)
3. Membership distributed among organizations which count one, two, or three points, provided he does not carry more than ten points:

The point values of activities follow:

5 points — Football, interscholastic and interclass basketball, track, editor-in-chief of publications, business managers, debating and public speaking.
4 points — Senior class president
3 points — Tennis, hockey, circulation manager of publications.
2 points — Societies, orchestra, glee club, band, Junior class president, learned orations, interpretive reading.
1 point — Class vice-presidents, class secretaries, class treasurers, heads of departments of publications.

3. Group system. — In this type of organization the activities of the school are classified under such heads as Sports, Academic, General, etc. The student is limited to membership in one organization under each group. The intention is, of course, to force the student to widen his interests and to prevent him from specializing in the activities of only one of these groups. In the Central High School, Grand Rapids, Michigan, all activities are classified into five groups: Academic, Arts, Athletic, Social, and General. No student is allowed to belong to more than one organization under the same group at the same time.

THE RELATION OF MARKS TO PARTICIPATION

Shall the student with low marks be allowed to keep up his extracurricular work? It should be recognized that in general the student's first duty is to his curricular work. On the other hand, low marks should probably decrease, but not prohibit participation. One plan is to allow participation on the basis of the quality of the academic work done. If the student makes barely passing marks, say 75%, he is allowed to carry only one major or a certain limited number of points. If his average is 80 he may add a minor, if it is 85 he may add a major, etc. In this way he will not be overburdened, and he will also have an additional motive for doing better work. Another plan is to have a group of " sub-minors " or small point memberships, which are unrestricted and which the student can carry irrespective of his marks. Such permission will not only be valuable to the student but may help to keep him in school. The student who feels that he is unsuccessful and shut out from his fellows is easily discouraged.

A sub-committee of the council or a specially appointed " Point Scale " Committee may be selected to develop an equitable plan; to make necessary adjustments; to hear complaints and allow excess credits. This committee should have a good representation of faculty members.

ENCOURAGING PARTICIPATION

As yet but few plans have been devised to encourage the student to participate in extracurricular activities. Nearly all the plans have been aimed at limitation of participation. There are, however, a few schools which encourage participation by offering suitable recognition, awards, medals, pins, and certificates. The following certificate used at the High School at Avalon, Pennsylvania, illustrates one type of recognition. It is awarded at commencement.

FIGURE XXI. — THE "ACTIVITIES CERTIFICATE" AWARDED BY THE HIGH SCHOOL AT AVALON, PENNSYLVANIA

RECORD CARDS

Record cards are necessary if any requirement is made in connection with extracurricular activities. They will be found useful in curing evils of over-working or under-working and in helping to determine a reasonable policy for extracurricular organization and administration. If a "Point Scale" Committee is established one of its important duties will be developing a set of suitable records.

Activity	192–		192–		192–		192–		Total
Assemblies									
Banking									
Baseball									
Basketball									
Class									
Clubs									
(1)									
(2)									
(3)									
(4)									
Council									
Debating									
Dramatics									
Football									
Publications									
(1)									
(2)									
(3)									
(4)									
Committees									
(1)									
(2)									
(3)									
Other Activities									
(1)									
(2)									
(3)									
(4)									

ACTIVITIES RECORD CARD

Name....................   Class....................

Total

Remarks

Three different records may be used; (1) the permanent record card; (2) the report of the sponsor to the clerk or main office; and (3) the report card to the parent. All three are not absolutely necessary. It would be possible, for instance, to get along with only the permanent record card. The size of the school and its organization and other aspects of the local situation will determine what records will be required.

1. Permanent record card. — This card, as its name implies, is the office card on which the permanent record of the student is kept. If the " regular " permanent record used for curricular activities is large enough, one side of it may be utilized for the student's activity record. If it is not large enough a special card may be used for the purpose. Such a card must provide for two variables (a) the different semesters, and (b) the different activities. If the student is marked in these activities his mark may be designated along the side of the number of credits entered. The card on page 579 illustrates a simple usable form of this blank.

2. Sponsor's report blank. — The purpose of this blank is to provide for the office or clerk the records of the individual students, showing the type of activity, number of hours, or period of time, character of the job, and the ratings by the student superior and the sponsor. Such reports may be made up individually, one for each student, or they may be made upon a sheet which includes all of the students interested. The blank at the top of the next page illustrates the latter type.

3. Student report card. — A report card to the parents may also be used. This card, however, is probably unnecessary. The parent should know what his child is doing, but this might be included on the regular report card. One or two items in spaces left for " Activities " might be satisfactory. Such an arrangement would not be as complete as a separate card, but there is danger of too much detail and duplication to say nothing of the additional work involved.

SPONSOR REPORT BLANK					
Activity			Sponsor		
Period Covered			Date		
Name of student	Activity	Nature of work, time spent, etc.	Student Superior rating	Sponsor rating	Points
Remarks					

It has been stated that " anything which exists, exists in quantity and therefore can be measured." We may not have all of the instruments or standards as yet for measuring everything, and a great deal of our measurement will for a long time be of the comparative type, or " greater," " smaller," " more " or " less," but the closer we can get to accurate measurement the more intelligent will be our educational efforts. The first step in the measurement of results in activities must necessarily be a measurement of participation in them. There is a danger of formalizing these activities and a consequent decreasing of their attractiveness, but at the same time if they are valuable enough to be recognized in the school they deserve the best we can do in organization and administration, and this suggests some method of equating and evaluating them.

Summary

The main purposes of a point system are (1) To distribute more evenly the opportunities for participation, (2) To prevent the student from overloading, (3) To develop and maintain a higher standard of attainment, and (4) To equate activities where credit is required for graduation. The three main types of systems are (1) Point system, which evaluates each activity or participation in terms of points, the number of points which the student may carry being limited, (2) Major and minor system, in which all activities or participations are classified under these heads and participation limited, (3) Group system, in which all activities or participations are classified into several groups and the student limited to participation in one of each group. Low marks should decrease participation but not prohibit it. If records are to be kept, blanks will be necessary, the essential ones being (1) Permanent record card and (2) Sponsor's report blank. A report to the parents may also be found useful. The use of a point system dignifies and systematizes these activities but may result in an undesirable formalization of them.

References

Dement, A. L. "Values in Extracurricular Activities in the High School," *School Review* 32 : 40–48, January, 1924.

Fretwell, E. K. *Philadelphia School Survey*, Book IV, p. 147.

Grote, C. "Regulation of Extracurricular Activities," *Journal* of the National Education Association 11 : 752–758, 1922.

Harwood, H. M. "Extracurricular Activities in High School," *School Review* 26 : 273–281, April, 1918.

Hobson, C. S. "An Experiment in Organization and Administration of High School Extracurricular Activities," *School Review* 31 : 116–124, February, 1923.

Koos, L. V. "Evaluating Extracurricular Activities." *Twenty-fifth Yearbook* of the National Society for the Study of Education, Part II.

Lewis, G. T. "Centralizing Student Activities in the High School," *School Review* 31 : 612–626, October, 1923.

LYMAN, R. L. "Guidance Program of the Holmes Junior High School," *School Review* 32 : 93–104, February, 1924.

MORNEWEK, C. D. "Control of Extracurricular Activities by the Point System, "*The High School Teacher* 11 : 169–170, May, 1926.

PRUNTY, M. "Sane and Systematic Direction of Extracurricular Activities," *Sixth Yearbook* of the National Association of Principals of Secondary Schools.

RYNEARSON, E. "Administration and Supervision of Student Activities in the School Program," *First Yearbook*, National Association of Secondary School Principals.

STEEPER, H. T. "Extracurriculum Activities of the High Schools," *Education* 39 : 367–373, February, 1919.

TERRY, P. W. *Extracurricular Activities in the Junior High School*, Chapter IV, Warwick and York.

VAUGHN, T. H. "Point System and Record Card for Extracurricular Activities," *School and Society* 16 : 745–747, December 20, 1922.

WINNER, H. E. "Place Value of Extracurricular Activities in the High School," *Journal* of the National Education Association, 1021–1023, 1923.

CHAPTER XXX

DIRECTOR OF ACTIVITIES, DEAN, SPONSOR, AND TEACHER

The increasing importance of extracurricular activities in the school, evidenced by the increasing amount of time and attention being given to them, demands that they function all the more effectively in the life of the student. As a direct result of this demand there is opening up an unexplored field in the guidance and direction of these activities. It is only reasonable that the more intelligent the leadership given to the organization and administration of these activities, the better will be the results from them. The rapidity of the development of the movement for deans, advisors, and directors shows the trend of attitude taken towards them by hard thinking practical school men. For instance, the National Association of Secondary School Principles adopted this resolution:

Whereas, the present development of socializing aims in education shows the increasing necessity for supervision and advisory contact with the students and the necessity of organizing the extracurricular activities of the school, and

Whereas, many high schools of the country have with benefit to the schools and the community recognized the work of Deans or Advisors by an allowance of time or of salary, or both.

Therefore, be it resolved, that this association express its belief that such work should be officially recognized in every high school in the country.[1]

As yet there is considerable inaccuracy in terminology and variation in the conception of the relationships and duties of the

[1] *Fifth Yearbook* of the National Association of Secondary School Principals, 1921, p. 69.

various offices. This is to be expected in pioneer work. The purpose of this chapter is to help clarify thinking on this important point.

Not all schools will have directors or deans, but all schools will have many of the activities suggested and all schools will have a more or less intelligent guidance of these activities. The suggestions for relationships and activities will apply to those who are responsible irrespective of their title.

DIRECTOR OF ACTIVITIES

The average high school principal carries a great load of work and responsibility. In a school of any size he cannot give personal attention to all activities of the school. This is especially true if he has more of an interest in one field than in another. His school may be well developed in one field and undeveloped in another because the average principal has neither an equivalence of interests nor the ability to do all things well. As a result of this situation many large schools now have a number of principals or assistant principals, one in charge of administration and routine, another in charge of supervision, and another in charge of activities. Each principal specializes in a particular field and develops that field. Of course proper articulation of all activities is made, but each department of the school is the better developed and supervised because it is managed by a person not only interested but also competent in this field. Such organization dignifies each field and secures added results if for no other reason than that the school authorities have a right to expect added results in return for the added investment in staff time.

Work of the director. — The work of such a director is, as the name suggests, the responsibility for the initiation, encouragement, and development of this phase of school life. He is an administrative officer responsible for all activities, and as such should have administrative control over them. His work will touch all of the students in the school. He will be concerned with plans for interesting every student in the school; encouraging and limiting participation; helping to provide material equipment and securing the proper articulation of the various activities. A part of his work will have to do with the discouraging of those activities which should be discouraged and of substituting others more valuable for them.

His program must be fair and properly proportioned. It is probably true that he will be more interested in some items than in others. However, he must see the program in the proper perspective and proportion and he must not be influenced by his own interests in particular phases. The most important activities will receive the most time, the most important concessions, and the largest amount of equipment. His relation to the sponsors must be based upon logical and careful consideration of values so that the teachers themselves will not feel that he is slighting some phases and over-emphasizing others.

It is not the function of the director to sponsor all of the activities of the school. That is as unreasonable as to suggest that the principal should teach all of the subjects in the curriculum. The director is an administrative and supervisory officer, and as such will perfect plans, and lead. As such a leader he will be seconded by the teachers and sponsors of the individual groups or activities. The individual teacher will still be the expert in his particular activity. The director will do much the same type of work that the principal does in providing the equipment for the teachers in their respective fields.

Relations with the principal. — A most important relationship of the director is that with the principal. The principal is the head of the school and as such is responsible for everything that goes on in the school. Naturally, he will have the final discretion in any matter which concerns it. He sees activities and opportunities in their perspective and in their relationships to each other, and often he may not have the same view of a particular interest that the enthusiast has. The director must recognize this office and must work hand in hand with the principal. His major plans and programs must be discussed with the principal.

The director does not assume the principalship, he merely develops one side of school life. The principal will not discourage nor veto meritorious plans without good reason. The principal must look upon the director as the expert in these activities, and the director must look upon the principal as his superior officer. What injures one injures both, what helps one helps both.

The principal must recognize that the task of the director is that of initiating and developing the extracurricular activities of the school. He must not be considered a keeper of books, a runner of errands, an answerer of the telephone, nor a general handy man. The position is a specialized one of great importance and high requirements. It is administrative and supervisory, not clerical. It is very easy for the principal to unload a part of his own duties upon this director, especially if he is not entirely in sympathy with the work. Possibly the principal may plan to have some one appointed to whom he could turn over detail. Such an attitude on his part will prevent any real development in the field of activities.

Relations with teachers. — The director must be an educator of rare ability, because he has teachers to educate and teachers are frequently hard to teach. In many instances the teacher has been at his work a long time, and habits and attitudes are firmly established. It is much harder to teach a teacher to change a procedure or habit which he has been following for a number of years than it is to teach him a formal subject. The director must not move too rapidly. Many of the directors now being appointed are younger and of more recent schooling than many of the teachers already employed. Frequently an antagonistic or hostile attitude is shown towards the newcomer.

Such an attitude complicates the work of the new young director. He has no easy task, but if he has ideas, enthusiasm and personality, it is far from impossible.

In any faculty there are three types of teachers. There are variations and combinations of these, but three basic types are easily distinguishable. The first is the teacher who looks upon the school as a house in which subjects are taught. He believes that the school exists only for passing on subject matter, and such terms as leadership, initiative, responsibility, and citizenship are not in his vocabulary. To him the school exists only for scholarship and the only leaders are scholars. He considers outside activity as intrusion upon school work and a waste of time. The director of activities would do well to spend his time and energy teaching those who are willing to learn, rather than to waste his time in trying to educate some one whose mind is closed to educational progress.

A second type of teacher with whom the director will have to deal is the one who already has brought his activity to a high state of development. He is in charge of assemblies or clubs, he has taken the work seriously and developed it to a high state of effectiveness. The director can probably do little with this teacher because he knows more about his duties as sponsor than the director himself. However, he can encourage the teacher to further development, and utilize the services of the latter in the encouragement of other sponsors. The teacher will be closer to the other members of the faculty than the director, and this contact can be capitalized to the general good of the school.

A third type of teacher is the one who is willing to learn and anxious to serve, but who lacks the knowledge, skill, and material with which to work. Most teachers will be found to be of this type. Nearly all teachers recognize the values of these activities and are willing to accept responsibility for a share in them, but many do not know what to do nor how to do it. In other words, they lack a program. This program is not to be handed to them already made by the director any more than the principal hands them plans already made for use in their classes. The director will gather material, make it available to the teachers, put these teachers in touch with similar activities elsewhere, and in other ways supply the material and principles with which to work.

The director will cultivate the teachers' friendship in a wholesome and dignified manner. Many of the people we do not like are the ones we do not know. Some teachers will resent any attempt on the part of the director, especially a new one, to " tell " them anything. The director must cultivate such persons. He must show by his manner that he knows activities are secondary interests of the teachers, and that the most important concern of the teacher is his classroom work. He will be sympathetic and patient in his dealings and will lead rather than drive.

Faculty committee on activities. — A general committee of the faculty will be of great assistance to the director. This committee with the direction of the chairman helps to determine the policy, suggests the program, and in other ways helps to shape the activity of the life of the school. Such a committee will be valuable not only because several heads are better than one, but also because it will have a most salutary effect upon the other members of the faculty, especially upon those members who are inclined to look upon the new officer as an intruding upstart. Consequently, this committee should be composed of those members who are highly respected by their colleagues, those who have an interest in activity life, and those who are educatable.

Relations with students. — Another important relationship of the director will be that with the students of the school. He will be a popular member of the faculty — probably the most popular — because his work has more to do with the things in which the average student is interested. Furthermore, he will rarely make assignments or set tasks; he will give no examinations; seldom will he punish the students; and he will be in much closer contact with the student than will the teacher, because of the difference between the informality of activity work and the formality of classroom work. It will be easy for the small-minded teacher with limited perspective to be jealous of his popularity and success. Probably it would not break the heart of such a teacher to see his program fail. The director must go forward with his work undiscouraged by petty jealousy and unfair criticism. He must remember that the only person who makes no enemies and of whom others are not jealous is the one who accomplishes nothing. The greater the man the greater the jealousy and criticism directed against him. It is for the director to ignore littleness of spirit and remain fair-minded and agreeable towards the faculty.

The director will be popular with the students but popularity must not mean lower standards of work nor undue informality. He must take his work as seriously as if he were a regular classroom teacher and he must not be affected by praise or censure of student groups. He will make enemies of some students on account of appointments or plans. His job will be done better when he preserves his equanimity and proper relationship to all concerned. He will welcome criticism and constructive suggestions at all times. In this connection it should be stated that the director must not pass judgment upon a teacher before a student or a student committee. If there is a criticism of an adviser, he should talk it over privately with that individual who is responsible for the activity and through whom it is to be carried on.

Qualifications of the director. — A consideration of the work of the director will show that the requirements for such an office are of a high order. He must be a leader. As a leader he must be a teacher, an administrator, a counselor, and a friend. He should have the best educational and professional preparation as well as good experience in teaching. These requirements are necessary in order that the other members of the faculty have proper respect for him. Nothing breaks down morale more quickly than the knowledge that the leader is not as well prepared to lead as the follower. A pleasing personality, sympathy, unbounded enthusiasm, and a sound educational philosophy, in addition to the more technical requirements, are the requirements for this office.

The majority of schools are probably too small to have a full-time director of activities. In such cases, a part of the time of a suitable teacher may be given to the organization and administration of these activities. Many schools will never be able to give even this much time to the activities which will remain where they are now, in the hands of the principal. In any case, all of the basic principles suggested above will apply whether the outside activities be directed by a full-time or part-time director or by the principal.

THE DEAN OF GIRLS

The office of " Dean " or " Adviser " of girls is another of the many high school imitations of the college. However, it is unlike some of them, in that it is a most commendable one. The rapidly growing recognition given to the field of outside activities is evidenced by the increasing number of deanships, the organization of deans' associations, the time devoted on educational programs to a discussion of their work, and the general good will of communities toward this office. The duties of the first deans of women in colleges were largely disciplinary in nature. To be seen coming from their office was all that was necessary to start a scandal. It is true that much of their early duty did concern discipline. When the deans themselves saw the possibilities of the office they gradually changed it from an office of discipline to an office of educational assistance. Of course discipline is frequently handled through this office, but the real dean is the one who sees beyond such affairs. She is an educational constructionist.

Title. — A number of terms are being used to designate this office of the school. Among the most commonly used are " preceptress," " adviser," " teacher adviser," " mother," " lady principal," " counselor," " welfare worker," and " dean." The term " dean " is preferable to any other. It is dignified and unsuggestive of anything unpleasant. " Preceptress " is a cold, formal term; " adviser " suggests the unpleasant; " mother " is sentimental; " lady principal " is stilted; " counselor " applies more accurately to vocational work; and "welfare worker " has already a recognized connotation. "Dean of girls " is more appropriate in the high school and "Dean of women," in the college and university.

Work of the dean. — In the large school the business of the dean is to develop students in those ways in which they are not developed by regular classroom work. The dean is responsible for the development of the social, civic, and personal attitudes and emotions rarely provided for in a formal classroom life. The possibilities of this office are extensive. They range all the way from merely handling disciplinary cases to directing and supervising the entire extracurricular program of the school.

Miss Sturtevant of Teachers College says of the office of dean :

Her task is not merely a salamangundi of pick-up jobs, of managing details of parties, of serving on committees, of chaperoning dances ; deans are not primarily patterns of social decorum, assistant clerks to principals and presidents, nor yet the confidential advisers of high school and colleges to speak to girls on subjects taboo to men.

She then quotes from Miss Richmond's Book, *What Is Social Case Work*, as follows :

The field of the dean is the development of personality through conscious and comprehensive adjustment of social relationships, and within that field the dean is not more occupied with the characteristics of the individual than of the environment, is not more able to neglect the one than the other.

The work of the dean of girls has been described briefly by Miss Eula W. Deaton, Dean of the Austin High School, Chicago, and classified into five tasks.[1]

1. Keep the children in school
2. Connect them with what is best in city and community
3. Teach proper use of leisure
4. Satisfy love of organization and need for self-expression
5. Teach students how to live harmoniously with other people

It would not be possible to propose a program for a dean of girls because of the new situations continually arising and also because of the differences in local conditions, and school organization. It is possible, however, to suggest some of the work of this office as handled in various schools. This will show the general type of activities which have been and are being handled through this office. Naturally, not all of the activities would be found in any one school and many of them may be handled more profitably by other offices, but at least they are suggestive of the general work of this office. No significance should be attached to the order in which the activities are listed.

Scholastic Relations:

Guidance of freshman, details of enrolment, advising
Receptions for new students
Handling absence, tardiness, excuses, dismissals
Handling failures, investigating causes
Establishment of good emotional attitudes towards school
Encouragement of better scholarship
Keeping the students in school
Unusual cases of discipline

[1] See bibliography for this reference. A very fine chapter on "The Dean of Girls" will be found in the *Community and Its High School*, by P. E. Belting, published by D. C. Heath and Company.

Health and Hygiene of Students:

Program of discussions on sleep, diet, exercise, bathing, recreation, functions

Advice in personal matters

Care in emergencies, sickness, accidents

Physical education, corrective measures

Provision for rest and hospital facilities in the school

Establishment of proper relations with physician and nurse

Provision for supervision of cloak rooms and toilets

Education in improvement of home conditions

Social Relations:

Formulation of social calendar providing for all recognized activities of the school

Regulation of parties, dances, receptions

Permission in unusual cases or requests

Supplying chaperonage and patronage

Supplying material and information for social use

Encouragement and discouragement where needed

Supervision of organization and administration of the extracurricular program of the school

Providing for chaperonage for girl's teams, clubs, hikes

Morals, Manners, Courtesy:

Provision for teaching of manners and courtesy

Supervision of activities in which boys and girls meet

Character and personality ratings

Counselling in love affairs

Remedial work with seriously unsocial cases

Programs of constructive citizenship

Social conduct in classroom and out

Good taste in dress, makeup, smoking, and other personal matters

Publicity and campaigns by use of posters, newspaper, home, room, assembly, tags

Curricular Guidance:

Discussion of curricular of school

Information on courses, teachers, books, marks, tests

Schedule making and readjustments

Information on colleges and universities, entrance requirements, standards, social and athletic life, expense

Information on trade schools, location, requirements

Vocational Guidance:

Vocational Information, books, literature, charts, graphs, guides, posters bulletins

Student analysis charts, blanks, records, and work

"Choose your vocation" campaigns

"Stay in school" campaigns

Employment and placement work

Working permits and certificates

Follow up work

Coöperation with employment bureaus and managers

Establishment of these outside relationships

Information about continuation schools, trade schools

Service to Students:

Survey of the needs of the students

Student aid, shoes, books, carfare, clothes, food

Information on boarding and room

Establishment and supervision of student loan fund

Administration of scholarships

Welcoming of new students and helping them to get started

Financial assistance

Service to sick student, flowers, fruit, books

Care of absentee's belongings

Help for the student who has been absent for some time

Provision for supplying of special coaching

Distribution of Christmas baskets, gifts

Parties for eighth graders, poor children of the community

Office Work and Relationships:

Supervision of reports, records, supplies

Regular office hours

Special "at home" days to encourage office visits

Private and personal conferences

Provision for rest rooms, first aid equipment

Records of work accomplished, plans, recommendations, items to be worked upon

Relationships with Teachers:

Establishment of coöperation between faculty and dean

Education of faculty in its share of responsibility

Education of the faculty to see the dean as a helper and not as a hearer-of-tales, a snooper, trouble hunter, or general disciplinarian

Non-interference with regular work of the teachers

Home Visitation:

Visiting home of drop outs

Talking with parents about the students doing poor work, those in school, or other difficulty

Encouraging the home to set conditions for effective school work, home study, sleep, food, quiet, few social or work distractions

Visitation of sick or injured students

Development of better understanding between home and school

Outside Relationships:

Meetings with Mother's Clubs, church groups, women's clubs

Publicity through newspapers and other channels

Contacts with industrial and commercial firms

Seeking coöperation with places of amusement

"Mother's and Daughter," "Big Sisters" banquets

"Visit the school" campaign or day

Coöperation with charity and service institutions

Qualifications of the dean. — It is needless to state that the requirements of a dean of girls are very high. Miss Elsie Smithies of the University High School, Chicago, asked a great many high school boys and girls, college men and women, mothers and professional men, the question as to the qualifications requisite in a dean of girls. Certain traits were included in all of the replies. The general summary was as follows: "She must have a broad understanding, well developed sensitiveness to youthful emotions, impulses, whims, temptations, and weaknesses. Her ideals and morals must be exemplary. She must have scholarship, a sense of humor, a magnetic and optimistic personality. She must be youthful, if not in years at least in spirit. She must have sound common sense, and sane balanced judgment. She should have good health, no nerves, pep, and good sportsmanship." Many thought that she should be married and have a few daughters of her own. Such a requirement is certainly of a high order. It may be discouraging to those who contemplate entering the field but at the same time such a set of opinions indicates the high regard held for the deanship. This is very encouraging.

Any teacher entering upon this work should make a serious study of her duties. Good intentions, sympathy, and personality are useless without the knowledge and technique. There are now available regular courses in this field and a teacher should no more consider herself competent to fill such a position without special training than she should consider herself competent to teach her subject without special training. She needs ideas and contacts with schools other than her own. Teachers College, Columbia University, offers a substantial course in this field and rare opportunities for direct contact with the many deans in and around New York City.

Dangers. — The two chief dangers connected with the creation of an office of dean of girls in the high school are (1) that too much will be expected of the office or attempted by it, and (2) that the office will be looked upon as an " unloading " place for some of the principal's tasks.

Few schools will have both a director of activities and a dean of girls. The dean is more commonly found than the director. In this case she is responsible for the work of the director as discussed in the previous section. If there are both a dean and a director, then she will handle the more intimate relationships of the work with the girls and will coöperate with the director in the general social program as it relates to the girls of the school.

THE SPONSOR

The sponsor is the teacher who is responsible for a particular phase of the extracurricular life of the school. He acts as adviser or counselor to a club, a publication, or an assembly committee. In a general way his work will not be very different from that of the director or dean. He will be responsible for the organization and administration of the club, its program of activities, and its plans. His chief contributions to the organization will be judgment, experience, and enthusiasm. Naturally he must be interested in his club, and he must work with it as seriously as he works with his regular classes. If his club fails he will look upon such failure as his own failure. He must remain an adviser and a counselor. Any attempt to dominate will only antagonize the group and prevent or delay good results. He will recognize his superior in extracurricular, as in curricular affairs.

The Teacher

Extracurricular activities exist in all schools, and they have to be handled by the regular staff of the school. Consequently a part of the teacher's regular load should be a share in the administration and supervision of these activities. The teacher who looks upon these activities as a " let down " in control should learn to appreciate their importance. He must be openminded enough to look upon education as a developing story and not as a closed book in which everything worth while has been written.

Summary

Increasing provisions are being made for handling the extracurricular program. Many schools now employ a full-time or part-time director whose duties center around the organization and administration of these affairs. This director must coöperate with his superiors, colleagues, and students, for his work concerns them all. A faculty committee on activities will be found helpful. The dean of girls is a new office in the high school, and one which promises great development in the future. The work of the dean centers around the activities, life, and interests of the girls. There is danger that both the director and dean will be overloaded with detail and routine work, and that the more important duties of these offices will be neglected. What the director is to the program as a whole, the sponsor is to the individual club, organization, or activity. These activities exist in every school and each teacher should take a reasonable attitude towards them. Each teacher should have a share in handling them.

REFERENCES

AGERTER, R. F. "The Duties of a Student Adviser," *School Review* 30 : 37–44, January, 1922.

ALLTUCKER, M. M. "Counseling Plan for Bridging the Gap between the Junior and Senior High Schools," *School Review* 32 : 60–66, January, 1924.

BELTING, P. E. *The Community and Its High School*, Chapter IV. D. C. Heath and Company.

BIRGE, E. A. "What a President may Expect from a Dean of Women," *Proceedings* of the National Education Association, 1923, 399–402.

DEATON, E. W. "The Work of a Dean of Girls and Its Relation to that of a Dean of Women," *Proceedings* of the National Education Association, 1919, 420–425.

DICK, G. S. "What a President may Rightly Expect from a Dean of Women," *Proceedings* of the National Education Association, 1918, 395–396.

FRETWELL, E. K. "The Adviser of Girls and the Extracurricular Activities of the High School," *Educational Administration and Supervision* 10 : 71–78, February, 1924.

GAYLOR, W. G. "Dean of Girls in High School," *Educational Administration and Supervision* 3 : 496–498, October, 1917.

GETHMAN, C. W. "To the High School Principal," *Seventh Yearbook*, National Association of Secondary School Principals, 1923, 11–115.

HEFFERAN, W. S. "How the Needs of the High School Girl are being Met by the Parent," *Proceedings* of the National Education Association, 1924, 525–528.

JONES, G. "Survey of Extracurriculum Activities in the High School," *School Review* 34 : 734–744, December, 1926.

KEELY, M. "The Significance of the Dean of the High School Girl," *Seventh Yearbook*, National Association of Secondary School Principals, 1923, 115–121.

LESTER, L. A. "A New Title: an Old Task," *Journal* of the National Education Association 13 : 326, December, 1924.

McDONALD, J. "Problems for the Dean of Women," *Proceedings* of the National Education Association 62 : 520–525, 1924.

POWER, C. "The Social Program for the Unsocial Girl," *School Review* 32 : 773–778, December, 1924.

PURDUE, J. M. "Deaning in the Public High School," *Proceedings* of the National Education Association, 1918, 404–406.

RADBOURN, S. M. W. "The Personal Advisory System in the Fresno High School," *School Review* 34 : 772–776, December, 1926.

RICHARDS, F. L. "What a Dean may Rightly Expect from the President," *Proceedings* of the National Education Association, 1918, 399–402.

ROWELL, E. "The Girl Problem in High School," *Proceedings* of the National Education Association, 1917, 258–262.

SMITH, H. M. "What a Dean may Rightly Expect from the President," *Proceedings* of the National Education Association, 1918, 397–399.

SMITHIES, E. M. "Qualities Essential to a Dean of Girls," *School Review* 32 : 203–208, March, 1924.

STEVENS, R. "Adviser of Girls in High School," *Teachers College Record* 20 : 301–323, September, 1919.

STURTEVANT, S. M. "The Relation of the Work of a Real Dean of Girls to the High School Girls," *Seventh Yearbook* of the National Association of Secondary School Principals, 1923, 121–125.

TERRY, P. W. "Coöperation of Teacher Advisers," *Twenty-fifth Yearbook* of the National Society for the Study of Education, Part II, Chapter IX.

—— *Extracurricular Activities in the Junior High School*, Chapter VI, Warwick and York.

WARREN, L. Y. "The Program of a Dean of High School Girls," *School and Society* 17 : 693–694, June 23, 1923.

WILDS, E. H. *Extracurricular Activities*, Chapters VI, VII. The Century Company.

WILSON, A. "The Need of Standardizing the Qualifications of Deans for High Schools," *Proceedings* of the National Education Association 58 : 215–217, 1920.

WOOLEY, M. W. "Some Ideals for Deans," *Proceedings* of the National Education Association 56 : 411–413, 1918.

CHAPTER XXXI

CONCLUSION

There has been no attempt at completeness in the discussions of this book. A complete discussion would take several volumes. Not all of the activities of the school have been covered, and those which have been included have not been covered so completely as desirable. Within a decade a dozen good books on this general topic will appear, each emphasizing or discussing in its own way this important phase of school work. And when the dozen are published, the tale will not have been told.

The author of this book has attempted to present in brief form the purposes, principles, and values of extracurricular activities, and to suggest many possible programs. The average teacher needs a list of practical plans of procedure. He has little time for theories; he must organize and get results promptly. He must have a solid background of educational theory, but many of his educational courses have been theoretical, and they leave him to devise his own plans of application. It is hoped that this book may serve as a manual, and if the teacher is benefited by its suggestions as to organization and administration, the purpose of the author will have been achieved.

DANGERS OF EXTRACURRICULAR ACTIVITIES

A wave of interest in extracurricular activities is sweeping the country. This wave of interest will have very salutary effects upon the organization and administration of this part of school life. Experimentation, research, and study will be enhanced.

On the other hand, there are dangers involved. The person who is swept along on a wave of enthusiasm and interest has not much time in which to think seriously and plan wisely, especially if he has had little or no experience. As a result, he may find himself in all sorts of difficulties. Probably the three most important dangers in connection with extracurricular activities are (1) overemphasis, (2) formalization, and (3) lack of community support.

1. Overemphasis. — A school principal recently stated, " My side show is eating up my main tent!" At least three explanations of this situation might be made. His " main tent " was not particularly strong or important; or his " side shows " were getting beyond his control; or perhaps a combination of the two conditions existed. The teacher or administrator who looks upon the school as a place in which subjects are taught, and who looks upon the subjects as something sacred, is very easily made jealous and suspicious of anything which threatens in any degree the integrity of the traditional school organization or program. The teacher of the new day, the one who is more interested in teaching students than in teaching subjects, and the one to whom the student is the most important and sacred thing about the school, will welcome any suggestion whereby he may teach the student the better. True, not all of the suggestions may be of value to him, but he will be alert to all that comes, and he will endeavor to experiment, measure, weigh, evaluate, and adapt. He has no fear of " side shows " nor has he any petty jealousies concerning subjects, or traditional school organization. To him education is a progressive science.

On the other hand, this teacher will not allow the extracurricular side of school life to dominate the entire program. In some schools, athletics appear to dominate everything. The school authorities should observe relative values and preserve a reasonable ratio between curricular and extracurricular work. They should plan as wisely and intelligently for one as for the other, and the community should be taught to recognize and demand an adequate and well-balanced program.

2. Formalization. — A second danger is that of excessive formalization of these activities — making them tasks which the student is required to perform, reducing them to the level of other school tasks, robbing them of their attractiveness, and crushing student spontaneity and interest. While there is danger of excessive formalization, it is true that, at the present time, almost any degree of formalization would add to their effectiveness in most schools. Systematic regulation of these activities by their official recognition as a legitimate part of the work of the school, by setting aside schedule and teachers' time for them, by providing equipment, by recording participation, by limiting and encouraging participation, and by teaching teachers to be " leaders," would help to place them on a more substantial basis and guarantee more educative results from them.

3. Lack of community support. — The school administrator and teacher have two educational tasks. The first is the education of the students, the second is the education of the patrons of the school. Many administrators neglect the latter. Many bond issues are refused each year, and many progressive educational programs are delayed or defeated because the administrator has failed to educate his community. The citizen may know that the system needs equipment or new buildings, but this does not mean that he has the active conviction that will impel him to vote for these improvements. The citizen demands progress in the material spheres of life, but he is proverbially slow to recognize or sanction progress in education. The way he was taught when he went to school is to him the best way. The community, then, must be constantly stimulated to desire progress in education as it demands it in business and commerce and in the professions.

Research in Extracurricular Activities

Measurement. — Measurement in education has developed very rapidly during the past few years. But we have expressed our measurements in terms of regular curricular work only. We have assumed that, if the student attains a certain degree of success in arithmetic, history, English, or Latin, a corresponding degree of success in life is assured him. We have made few attempts to measure the contributions of the school to the life of the citizen. In the future, measurement will not be so concerned with that mark which the student receives in his arithmetic class in school, as with that mark which the individual makes in life as a result of his study of arithmetic.

While a beginning has been made in the measurement of curricular work, little or nothing has been attempted in measuring results in the extracurricular field. As time goes on, as the extracurricular activities are more seriously studied, as more intelligent provision is made for their administration and organization, and as the influence of tradition and emotion becomes less and less, a more definite measurement of their results will be demanded.

This demand for a definite measure will then result in a study of the comparative values of different organizations and activities, and such studies will lead ultimately to the conclusion that certain activities are more desirable than others and therefore should be those recognized and encouraged. This weeding out process may eliminate many of the activities we have to-day, while others which we do not now have may appear in their places.

Further, any plan of measurement will not only show relative values among activities but it will also show relative values within the activities. It will help to evaluate methods of control, finance, and reward.

Experimentation. — Measurement and evaluation will be assisted by experimentation. A great deal has been attempted in extracurricular activities, but probably little controlled experimentation has been done. Experimentation has for the most part been of a "we-tried-this-and-it-did-not-work-so-we-tried-something-else" type. Not much more than a passing glance has been given to ascertain why it did not work or to what extent it did not work; or to determine whether or not it would have worked better under other conditions. School administrators must look upon their schools as laboratories for such experimentation, in the same way that they look upon them as laboratories for experimentation in methods of teaching, classification, or other curricular adjustment.

Measurement, experimentation, and research will help to articulate the so-called extracurricular activities of the school with the so-called curricular activities. They will cause to be recognized more effectively the fact that the main work of the school is to make good citizens, and that no part of school work has any monopoly on procedure in developing citizenship. As this is done, the terms extracurricular and curricular will disappear, and sharp lines between their activities will no longer be drawn by either the educator or the patron of the school. The work of the school will then be looked upon as " citizenship-producing activity."

Measurement, experimentation, and research may reveal a great field lying just beyond — the field of usefulness of the so-called extracurricular activities as selective agencies. It may be that more can be learned about the student through his participation in these affairs than can be learned about him through the more or less repressive activities of the classroom. The whole program of guidance and adaptation may be aided materially by the discoveries in this new field.

Job analysis in this connection will be carried much farther than it has been carried. A more complete and detailed analysis of both student and activity will be the first step in fitting the school more clearly to the student. The sponsor and her duties and their relation to the school and its life are other phases which will be analyzed and scientifically studied. The results of such analysis will be the foundation upon which the school of the new day will be built.

In conclusion, let us remember that these activities always have existed, and probably always will exist in one form or another. Then if our philosophy of education is sound — if the purpose of the school is to teach the student to do better those desirable things which he is going to do anyway, to reveal higher types of activities, and to make them both desired and possible — the educator dare not allow a program of extracurricular activities to " just grow up." He must use as much intelligence and educational sense in building a program of these activities as he uses in dealing with the regular work of the school. And the extent of his failure to live up to all of his possibilities will determine the amount of his failure in the biggest job in the world — training for citizenship in a democracy.

INDEX

Academic contest, 519–520

Accounting, financial, 554–567

Activity report blank, 562

Adolescence, 13

Advertising, in school newspaper, 318; a necessity, 351; selling space, 351–353; price of ads, 354; writing the ads, 355; in yearbook, 403–404; in handbook, 429–430

Adviser, teacher, 9, 60

Advisor of girls. *See* Dean of girls.

Advisory council, of Hi-Y, 487

Airplane club, 101

Alumni, in yearbook, 398; at parties, 289

American Bankers Association, 529, 539

American Dancing Masters Association, 287

American Ideals, home-room program, 32

American Torch Society. *See* National Honor Society.

Amusement, afforded by parties, 280

Annual, see Yearbook.

Approbation, love of, 18

Arbor Day celebration, 86

Arista Society, 434

Armistice Day celebration, 83

Art, home-room program on, 31

Art Crafts Guild, 406

Assembly, origin and development, 69; values of, 69; organization for, 70; committee on, 48, 70; material for, 71–75; typical programs, 75–89; schedule for the year, 89–91; singing, 91

Assessment, for yearbook, 404

Athletics, history of, 237; development of interscholastic athletics, 237–238; values of, 238–243; objections to, 244–249; suggestions for improving, 249–262; local athletic association, 262–264; interscholastic athletic association, 264; National Athletic Scholarship Society, 264; aristocracy, 247; committee, 49, 259–260; in newspaper, 312, 346; in yearbook, 394–396

Attendance committee, home room, 27; commencement program, 467–468

Autographs, in yearbook, 392

Avalon High School, Pennsylvania, activities certificate, 578

Awards in citizenship, 211

BADEN-POWELL, SIR ROBERT, founder of Girl Scouts, 501

Balance, in newspaper, 336

Balloting, in citizenship contest, 203

Banks and banking, school, history of, 529; values of, 530–531; choosing a system, 532–534; types of, 535–542; teaching thrift, 542–544; deposits in school banks, 529

Beats, newspaper, 310

Beloit, Wisconsin, school bank in, 529

Ben Blewett High School, St. Louis, honor society, 439

Benjamin Franklin Junior High School, New Castle, Pennsylvania, music in, 141

Big Sister and Big Brother movement, 515–516

Bird Day celebration, 88

Bird house contest, 523

Birmingham, Alabama, citizenship contest, 212; sportsmanship program, 242

Board of education, athletic committee, 261; should subsidize athletics, 262

Board of publications, for handbook, 430